Medicine & Society
In America

Medicine & Society
In America

Advisory Editor

Charles E. Rosenberg
Professor of History
University of Pennsylvania

AUTOBIOGRAPHY

OF

SAMUEL D. GROSS, M.D.

WITH

SKETCHES OF HIS CONTEMPORARIES

EDITED BY HIS SONS

IN TWO VOLUMES

VOL. I

*A*RNO *P*RESS & *T*HE *N*EW *Y*ORK *T*IMES

New York 1972

921 924
G 878
V. 1

Reprint Edition 1972 by Arno Press Inc.

LC# 71-180576
ISBN for Vol. I: 0-405-03980-8
ISBN for Vol. II: 0-405-03981-6
ISBN for set: 0-405-03953-0

Medicine and Society in America
ISBN for complete set: 0-405-03930-1
See last pages of this volume for titles.

Manufactured in the United States of America

AUTOBIOGRAPHY

OF

SAMUEL D. GROSS, M.D.

IN TWO VOLUMES.

VOL. I.

AUTOBIOGRAPHY

OF

SAMUEL D. GROSS, M.D.,

D. C. L. OXON., LL. D. CANTAB., EDIN., JEFF. COLL., UNIV. PA.,
EMERITUS PROFESSOR OF SURGERY IN THE JEFFERSON MEDICAL COLLEGE
OF PHILADELPHIA.

WITH

SKETCHES OF HIS CONTEMPORARIES.

EDITED BY HIS SONS.

IN TWO VOLUMES.

Vol. I.

PHILADELPHIA:
GEORGE BARRIE, PUBLISHER.
1887.

PRINTING-OFFICE OF THE PUBLISHER

PREFACE.

IN submitting to the public the AUTOBIOGRAPHY OF DR. SAMUEL D. GROSS, the Editors deem it due to the memory of their Father to state that death alone prevented him from giving to the work that careful revision which is so noteworthy a feature of his previous productions.

A large part of the preliminary Memoir of Dr. GROSS was read by the late Professor AUSTIN FLINT before the American Medical Association at its meeting held in Washington in May, 1885.

The Editors tender their hearty thanks to JOHN W. HUFF, Esq., an old friend of Dr. GROSS, for valuable assistance kindly rendered by him during the passage of the work through the press; to GEORGE BARRIE, Esq., the Publisher, who has spared neither expense nor trouble to make the mechanical features of the book attractive to the reader; and to JAMES BEATTY, Esq., for zealous services contributed by him.

SAMUEL W. GROSS,
A. HALLER GROSS.

PHILADELPHIA, April, 1887.

CONTENTS OF VOL. I.

CHAPTER VII.

CHAPTER VIII.

CHAPTER IX.

CHAPTER X.

CHAPTER XI.

CHAPTER XII.

CHAPTER XIII.

CHAPTER XIV.

MEMOIR.

MEMOIR

OF

SAMUEL D. GROSS, M.D.

SAMUEL D. GROSS, the son of Philip and Juliana Gross, was born near Easton, Pennsylvania, July 8th, 1805. Like Newton, Burns, Cobden, and Whittier, he communed at an early age with Nature and Nature's God. His childhood was passed on his father's farm; and to the salutary open-air life led by him over the hills and valleys of this picturesque portion of Pennsylvania, combined with a sound constitution inherited from his parents, he attributed in great measure that vigorous health, that immunity from disease which enabled him to perform a vast amount of intellectual labor, and to achieve a conspicuous reputation wherever Surgery is cultivated as a science, or wherever the works of its great masters are cherished by its votaries. A strong love of nature remained throughout his life one of the sources of his keenest enjoyment. There were few forest trees, few flowers with the names of which he did not become familiar, few birds with whose notes he was unacquainted. Probably Thoreau did not more enjoy the varied beauties of Nature; nor could the youthful Audubon, with all the enthusiasm of even his Southern temperament, have been much more sensitive to her voices and teachings. The simple plants which he cultivated with love and tenderness on his father's farm gave place during his residence in Louisville to rare and beautiful flowers, among which he loved to work and to live. No visitor at his office during his latter years could fail to observe a vase of these sweet-smelling emblems of refinement and purity upon the table where he wrote surrounded by the books he loved so well; and when the days were gradually shortening and the end of his life was near, these "dear tokens of the earth" greeted him with their fragrance and were loved by him to the last.

We are told that at the age of seven years Warren Hastings, lying on the bank of a rivulet near the old manor which had once belonged to his ancestors, determined that one day he would become the owner of the estate; and that through all the changes of his remarkable career the resolution made at that time so ruled him that finally, when affluent and powerful, he became the purchaser of Daylesford.

A similar, though more noble, ambition early took possession of young Gross. Before the age of six years—a period of life when nearly all of those who subsequently occupy a commanding position in the eye of the world are noted only for empty prattle and light-hearted amusements—he had conceived the idea of becoming a Physician. This purpose, from which he never swerved, became so essential a part of his being that he could no more have been untrue to it than could the needle deflect from the pole.

Through the struggles and trials of his life this idea dominated him. His wish was gratified. He lived to see himself honored and beloved as one of the high priests of a profession which he regarded as the most sacred of all callings—for which even on his death-bed he was found still laboring. Only a few days before he died, when, greatly prostrated by physical weakness, he had begun to realize that his end was not far off, he corrected the proof-sheets of two elaborate papers written with all the fire and vigor of a mind still fresh and unimpaired.

Even some of the games of his youthful days assisted him in that branch of the profession to which he devoted himself. He attributed much of the accuracy of his eye and the dexterity of his hand to the practice of pitching quoits and pennies—games in which he was an adept. Agassiz, it is said, owed much of his dexterity in manipulation to the training which his eye and hand had acquired in some of the plays of his childhood. It is related of him that when a little fellow he could make well-fitting shoes for his sisters' dolls, that he was not a bad tailor, and that he could make a miniature water-tight barrel.

His burning ambition to be a Physician impelled young Gross when only seventeen years of age to enter the office of a country practitioner, where, finding that the education which had been obtained in country schools was inadequate to the demands which might be made upon it, he determined as far as possible to remedy his defects by a course of study at the Wilkesbarre Academy and at the Lawrenceville High School. When nineteen years old he entered upon the study of medicine in the office of Dr. Joseph K. Swift, of Easton; and afterwards he became a matriculate of the Jefferson Medical College and a private student of Dr. George McClellan, the Professor of Surgery in that institution. Few youths studied more persistently, more systematically, or with greater self-reliance.

"One day, while a student in Swift's office," says he, "I came across the following passage in Dorsey's Surgery, in the chapter on Aneurism—a passage which had no little influence upon my future professional life. 'On the 15th of August, 1811, I was consulted,' says Dorsey, 'by Alexander Patton on account of a tumor in his right groin. . . . It occasionally gave him severe pain, and incapacitated him from all labor. In June last he applied to Dr. Irwin, of Easton, the place of his residence, who instantly apprised him of the nature and importance of his complaint, and advised him to go to Philadelphia.' In pondering on this passage, I asked myself the question, Why was this man sent to Philadelphia, and not treated at Easton? The answer was not long in coming. Because Irwin felt incompetent or afraid to undertake the operation necessary for his relief. From that moment I determined so to study my profession as to be able to meet every emergency, however difficult or unexpected, and, consequently, never to send any patient away, unless he was in a hopeless condition.''

In 1828 young Gross received his medical degree; and in less than a year, having in the mean time opened an office in Philadelphia, he had translated Bayle and Hollard's General Anatomy, Hildenbrand on Typhus Fever, Hatin's Manual of Obstetrics, and Tavernier's Operative Surgery; and in 1830 he published a treatise on the Anatomy, Physiology, and Diseases of the Bones and Joints.

Practice came slowly; and in eighteen months, believing that he could succeed better in his old home than in Philadelphia, he returned to Easton. There he took the brave young wife who had consented to share his privations and his struggles, and who, during their long and singularly happy wedded life, rejoiced with him in the successes which from time to time crowned his efforts.

In some of his writings he deferred much to her judgment; and though he could not say of her—as John Stuart Mill said of his wife—''all my published writings were as much her work as mine,'' still Dr. Gross was often heard to declare that he was indebted to her for many valuable suggestions after, as it was his custom to do, he had submitted to her the manuscript of an address or valedictory discourse. His devotion to this cultivated and noble woman was one of the most beautiful features of his life. Though her death in 1876 left him during the rest of his pilgrimage naught but a blessed memory, to that memory he was ever constant. He could not share with another the love which he had given to her; and when the final summons came, he was still true to the one who had filled his heart with sunshine and happiness.

Whilst practising his profession at Easton, Dr. Gross spent several hours a day in dissecting. He made observations on the temperature of the blood; and a series of experiments on rabbits for the purpose of throwing light on manual strangulation. He found time also to compose a work on descriptive anatomy, which, however, was never published.

In 1833 he went to Cincinnati as the Demonstrator of Anatomy in the Medical College of Ohio. This position he retained till 1835, when he accepted the chair of Pathological Anatomy in the Medical Department of Cincinnati College.

The hard study and the unremitting labor given to the subject of the chair, combined with constant dissections, enabled Dr. Gross in 1839 to publish his Elements of Pathological Anatomy, the first work on this subject in the English language, which passed through three editions, and which brought him fame and a large practice. "His Elements of Pathological Anatomy, issued in 1839, in two octavo volumes of more than five hundred pages each, did more," says Dr. Da Costa,* "to attract attention to the subject than anything that had ever been done in this country. The book, illustrated profusely with wood-cuts and with several colored engravings, reached three editions. It is a mine of learning, and its extended references make it valuable to this day. Its merits have been fully recognized abroad; and on no occasion more flatteringly than when the great pathologist, Virchow, at a dinner given to Dr. Gross at Berlin in 1868, complimented him publicly on being the author, and, pointing to the volume, which he laid upon the table, gracefully

---

* Biographical Sketch of Professor Samuel D. Gross by J. M. Da Costa, M.D., LL.D., 1884.

acknowledged the pleasure and instruction which he had often gained from it. As another acknowledgment of its merits, we find that soon after the publication of the second edition the Imperial Royal Society of Vienna made Dr. Gross an honorary member."

In 1840 Dr. Gross accepted the chair of Surgery in the University of Louisville. There he resided for sixteen years, with the exception of the winter of 1850–'51, which he spent in New York, as the successor of Valentine Mott, in the chair of Surgery in the University of that city.

A series of experiments which he made on dogs resulted in the publication by him of his next work, An Experimental and Critical Inquiry into the Nature and Treatment of Wounds of the Intestines.

His treatise on Diseases of the Urinary Organs was published in 1851; and his treatise on Foreign Bodies in the Air-Passages in 1854. The latter was a pioneer work, and has received the highest praise. "From it," says Dr. Da Costa, "all subsequent authors have largely copied their facts, and of it the distinguished laryngologist, Morell Mackenzie, has declared that it is doubtful whether it ever will be improved upon."

Besides the works mentioned Dr. Gross was a liberal contributor to the periodical press during his residence in the West, publishing reports of important cases, and elaborate biographies of such men as Daniel Drake and Ephraim McDowell.

The years which he passed in Louisville were among the happiest of his life. Though immersed in a large and constantly increasing practice, performing an amount of literary and professional work that seems astounding, he found time to cultivate close relations with the people among whom he lived. Probably no physician was more beloved or more trusted by his patients; certainly few men were more popular. Not only was his beautiful residence the abode of that bounteous hospitality for which Kentucky is famous, but artists, scientists, and distinguished men and women of America and from foreign climes found within its walls a hearty welcome at reunions, in which the strains of music mingled with flashes of wit and humor.

When in 1856 Dr. Gross had been elected Professor of Surgery in the Jefferson Medical College, he feelingly refers, in his introductory lecture to the students of that college, to his regret at leaving Kentucky:

"It was pleasant to dwell in the land of Boone, of Clay, and of Crittenden; to behold its fertile fields, its majestic forests, and its beautiful streams; and to associate with its refined, cultivated, generous-hearted, and chivalric people. It was there that I had hoped to spend the remainder of my days upon objects calculated to promote the honor and welfare of its noble profession, and finally to mingle my dust with the dust and ashes of the sons and daughters of Kentucky. But destiny has decreed otherwise. A change has come over my life. I stand this evening in the presence of a new people, a stranger in a strange place, and a candidate for new favors."

During the meeting of the American Medical Association in Louisville in 1875 the citizens vied one with another in doing Dr. Gross honor. As the train in which he was travelling neared the city and stopped at different stations, some of the passengers would look at the handsome imposing figure seated in the car, and would greet in an affectionate manner him who many years before had been their "beloved physician;" and soon after his arrival his old friends, patients, and former servants testified most feelingly that the lapse of nearly a quarter of a century had not dimmed their recollection of his never-failing kindness to them in the days that were dead and gone.

When in 1879 Dr. Gross delivered in Danville the memorial address at the dedication of the monument to Ephraim McDowell, Dr. Cowling presented on behalf of the Kentucky State Medical Society the door-knocker of

Dr. McDowell to Dr. Gross, and thus touchingly referred
to the estimate in which he was held by the people of
Kentucky:

"It belongs by right to you, Dr. Gross. This household genius passes most fittingly from the dearest of Kentucky's dead surgeons to the most beloved of her living
sons in medicine. She will ever claim you as her son,
and will look with jealous eye upon those who would
wean you from her dear affection.

"And as this emblem which now is given to you hangs
no longer in a Kentucky doorway, by this token you shall
know that all Kentucky doorways are open at your approach. By the relief your skill has wrought; by the
griefs your great heart has healed; by the sunshine you
have thrown across her thresholds; by the honor your
fame has brought her; by the fountains of your wisdom
at which your loving children within her borders have
drunk, the people of Kentucky shall ever open to you
their hearts and homes."

And when the noble mind was forever hushed in death,
Kentucky was still constant. One of her sons, a former
pupil, Dr. D. W. Yandell, wrote in his honor the beautiful
classic tribute with which this Memoir closes.

Though filled with regret at leaving his home in the
West, Dr. Gross at once received a hearty welcome at the
hands of the medical profession and of the citizens of
Philadelphia. It was a matter of pride with him to lecture in the institution in which twenty-eight years before
he had been a student. New friendships were formed,
new ties were made, new tendrils were put forth, and he
soon became as popular in the profession and out of it as
he had been in Louisville.

All his leisure not devoted to his college duties, to the
cares of a large office and consultation practice, to the
editorship, with Dr. Richardson, of the North American
Medico-Chirurgical Review—the successor of the Louis-

ville Medical Review—and to the preparation with Dr. Da Costa of the third edition of the Pathological Anatomy, was now given to the composition of his System of Surgery. The first edition of this work appeared in 1859; and the sixth in 1882, in which year he severed his connection with the Jefferson Medical College. His successors were his son, Dr. Samuel W. Gross, and Dr. John H. Brinton.

In 1861 appeared his Manual of Military Surgery; and in the same year he published The Lives of Eminent American Physicians and Surgeons of the Nineteenth Century, for which he prepared the memoirs of Ephraim McDowell, Daniel Drake, and John Syng Dorsey. The enumeration, however, of his contributions to medical and surgical literature, before and after he left Kentucky, would greatly exceed the limits appropriate to the present sketch. Suffice it to say that he was never idle. At the Complimentary Commemoration Dinner given to him in 1879, he said, "My conviction has always been that it is far better for a man to wear out than to rust out."

And so Dr. Gross grew in honor, crowned with the highest professional triumphs, devoting himself to his office practice, to writing, and to the pleasures of literature, cheered and solaced by the love of his devoted children and grandchildren.

Early in the winter of 1883–'84 his constitution began to fail, and his family became seriously alarmed at his symptoms. In addition to dyspepsia there was every indication of a fatty heart. But Dr. Gross did not despond, nor did his work cease. He thought he had still much to do for the good of his profession; and though he frequently expressed to the members of his family the belief that he had not many months to live, he went, accompanied by one of his daughters, on March 31st, 1884, to Atlantic City, cherishing the hope that his health might be sufficiently restored to enable him to take part at the meeting of the American Surgical Association and of the American Medi-

cal Association in Washington in May. This hope was
never realized. In a few days he returned to Philadelphia completely worn out, and suffering with nausea. His
son, Dr. Samuel W. Gross, and his friend, Dr. Da Costa, did
all that skill and affection could suggest. Knowing the
intimate relations which existed between Dr. Gross and
myself, they and the members of his family thought that,
even though I might not be able to render much assistance during an illness which day by day seemed to increase, my presence might cheer and comfort him. And
so it was that I paid several visits to my old friend as the
shadows began to deepen around him. His resolute mind
knew no such thing as fear. His only regret was that
of leaving forever the family which he loved so dearly,
and which idolized him, and of leaving undone much
professional work.

Each visit paid by me found him weaker than the previous visit; and finally on the 5th day of May, 1884, as I
stood at the bedside of the one who, above all his brethren,
was held in honor and esteem by the medical profession of
America, it was but too apparent that the labors of Samuel
D. Gross had ended, and that he was near the close of his
earthly life. I left his bedside to be present, on the following day, at the annual meeting of the American Medical
Association in Washington. The President of the Association in his opening address referred to the absence of
Professor Gross, who, in a letter which was one of the last,
if not the very last, written before his decease, requested
that an invitation be given by the American Medical Association to the International Medical Congress to hold its
meeting in this country in 1887. The announcement of
his serious illness called forth a quick and warm response
from the members of the Association. It was a remarkable
coincidence that at the very hour the Association was engaged in a discussion as to the manner in which heartfelt
sympathy should be expressed and conveyed to Professor

Gross—shortly before one o'clock P. M. on May 6th, 1884—
he was in the article of death. The telegram which carried
the resolutions adopted by the Association reached its destination but a short time after he had breathed his last.

On the announcement to the Association of the death
of Professor Gross, a committee was appointed to "take
such action as it might deem proper." * As the chairman
of this committee, with the approval of my fellow-mem-
bers, I submitted to the Association some reflections on a
life memorable for services in behalf of medicine and the
medical profession; on a life precious as an example; and
on a character which inspired esteem and affection.

I do not propose to write a biography of Professor Gross.
This has been done by able hands.† Nor would I have my
reflections regarded purely in the light of a eulogy. My
desire is to contemplate his life and character from the
vantage-ground of a long and intimate personal friendship.
Disclaiming any attempt at rhetorical efforts in the way of
panegyric, I will survey his life and character with reference
to his long and preëminently successful professional career,
and to the qualities which distinguished him as a man.

My friendship with Professor Gross commenced when
we were colleagues in the Medical Department of the
University of Louisville in 1852. Friendship ripened
quickly into close intimacy, which continued without for
an instant a shadow of a difference up to his death. We
were more than friends. Esteem and affection are terms
which, although superlatively qualified, express inade-
quately my attachment to him. I loved him. The sentiment of love, that divine attribute of humanity, was I

---

* The members of the committee were as follows: Drs. Austin Flint, T. G.
Richardson, L. A. Sayre, John H. Packard, F. H. Hamilton, Moses Gunn,
W. T. Briggs, and I. M. Hays.

† A Memoir by I. M. Hays, M.D., American Journal of the Medical Sciences,
July, 1884. A Biographical Sketch by J. M. Da Costa, M.D., LL.D., December
19th, 1884. A Sketch by J. Ewing Mears, M.D., 1885.

believe reciprocal. I can, therefore, as I think, without presumption, view his life and character with an insight embracing the feelings, aims, and motives underlying external appearance and actions.

The life of Professor Gross, from the beginning to the end of his long professional career, was a life of work— work as a student, as a writer, as a teacher, and as a practitioner. From first to last he was a diligent student. If in his advancing and advanced years he held tenaciously to opinions previously formed, it was not from lack of knowledge covering recent views, but because they failed to subvert his belief. To hold fast to his belief after due deliberation was a strong mental characteristic. His was not a mind to be carried away by every wind of doctrine. He may have been open to the charge of undue tenacity of convictions. If so, it was not from a pride of personal opinions, but from a reluctance to relinquish aught which he had been led to believe was true. Conservatism entered largely into his mental constitution. His mind rebelled against immature innovations. Yet no one at heart was more desirous than he for progress in medical knowledge and improvements in its practical applications.

A few months before his death I was present with him at a consultation in a case which involved certain surgical questions. He entered fully into a discussion of these and of kindred topics which the case suggested. Associated in the consultation was a comparatively young surgeon who was a skilful operator, and eminent for his knowledge of the literature of surgery. He afterward expressed his admiration at the familiarity of Professor Gross with the latest contributions to surgical knowledge not only in our own language but in that of Germany and of France. The last edition of his great work on Surgery, published but seventeen months before his death, is remarkable as showing a thorough acquaintance with contemporaneous publications, bibliographical and periodical, relating to the Surgical Department of Medicine. His life-work exemplified the motto, "once a medical student always a medical student"—a motto which all who aspire to true success in the profession of medicine will do well to adopt.

Professor Gross, as already seen, commenced the practice of literary composition at the beginning of his professional life. He was a voluminous writer. His vacations were infrequent and generally of brief duration. He was always engaged either in writing or in making preparations to write one of his various contributions to medical literature. The six editions of his System of Surgery represent an immensity of labor.

From his life may be learned the importance of early practice to those who aspire to authorship. How many who cherish such an aspiration in the dim future remain content with present inaction! Continued procrastination is equivalent to indefinite postponement, and the latter to inability. The art of composition, in addition to ambition and capacity, requires practice, and practice comes from love of that kind of work. Authors in medicine do not spring like Minerva in full armor from the head of Jove.

Another lesson which his life teaches is that great literary labors may be performed in conjunction with other occupations which are irregular, time-consuming, and claiming precedence. Under how different circumstances are these labors performed by the medical practitioner and teacher as compared with those who make literature a profession! The practice of medicine often leaves but few hours of leisure. They can rarely be counted upon, and to systematize them is seldom possible. Moreover, medical practice engrosses not only the time, but the thoughts and feelings of the practitioner. How was Professor Gross able to perform so vast an amount of literary work? By the use of whatever hours could be appropriated without the neglect of professional, social, or domestic duties, and by utilizing moments which would otherwise be lost. During the evenings or the portions of evenings which would be appropriated for study or writing he was at home only to his intimate friends, and they were considerate enough to disturb him but seldom. A large part of his writings, as he assured me, was composed in his carriage while driving to see his patients. And his children relate that during his residence in Louisville he always took one of them with him in his carriage when visiting patients several miles from the city, and that on these occasions they were often surprised to hear him talk aloud for fifteen minutes at a time. "What are you doing, father?" "Oh, nothing but lecturing to my students, or writing a page of a book," he replied with a smile. The thoughts thus given utterance to, if intended for a book, were reduced to writing the evening of his return to the city. The results of this system of daily industry would seem incredible to one not prepared to form an estimate by observation or personal experience.

Professor Gross resolved at the outset of his professional life to become a Medical Teacher. Is not this true of most of those who have been eminently successful in acquiring the art of teaching? Observation shows that few who begin late in life attain to much success. In many respects Professor Gross was a model teacher. As a speaker he was fluent, deliberate, clear, and emphatic. His hearers could not but feel that his object was to instruct, not to excite admiration for his own attainments and skill. He had the faculty of appreciating the kind of information to be communicated to medical students by oral teaching, and of knowing how to communicate it. Herein lie the secret and the popularity of the successful teacher. The personal appearance of Professor Gross in the lecture-room was most prepossessing. His tall commanding figure, his clear voice, his features beaming with intelligence and animation, his zealous manner—all contributed to render his teachings effective. He had that magnetism which is a gift invaluable to a speaker.   Apart from these advantages, his preëminent success was an outcome of his love of the labor and of a deep sense of the responsibility which the duties of a teacher involve.   As an evidence of the latter I quote the words with which he concluded his inaugural address on entering upon the duties of Professor of Surgery in the Jefferson Medical College: "Whatever of life, and of health, and of strength remains to me, I hereby, in the presence of Almighty God and of this large assemblage, dedicate to the cause of my Alma Mater, to the interests of Medical Science, and to the good of my fellow-creatures." *

As a practitioner, the characteristics of Professor Gross, irrespective of his ability and skill in medicine and surgery, were attentiveness and a deep interest in his cases, conjoined with geniality and kindliness.   These characteristics were in harmony with self-respect.   He neither belonged to the bullying nor to the cajoling class of practitioners.   His face and manner brought into the sick-room beatitude.   In this aspect his professional life might well be held up as a model for imitation.

Turning from the life-picture of Professor Gross in its professional aspects, the contemplation of his character as a man awakens higher sentiments than admiration.   As a student, author, teacher, and practitioner he was grand. But in him there was not that incongruity so often painfully conspicuous between the outward and the inner man. We are constrained to admire the achievements of his intellect, but the excellence of his heart inspired affection and love.

Sensitiveness and tenderness he had in a marked degree. In the performance of his professional duties these were held in complete control by the force of his will; but there were occasions when his feelings could not be kept

---

* Quoted from the Biographical Sketch by J. M. Da Costa, M. D., LL. D.

in restraint, even in the presence of other than his intimate friends.

The death of Daniel Drake took place during a winter session of the College at Louisville. Dr. Drake and he had been associated as colleagues, and they were warmly attached friends. Dr. Gross attempted to announce to the class the death of his friend who had been recently connected with the College. He had scarcely commenced when his feelings overcame him; his utterance was prevented by audible sobbing; and he was obliged to leave the lecture-room.

His kindness toward every one with whom he was brought into contact was a noticeable trait of his character. There was no appearance of pseudo-dignity, nor of the cold reserve of self-conceit. That he was gratified by the approbation of others, and pleased by the honors which were showered upon him, he made no effort to conceal. He was, however, as desirous of honorable estimation for his friends as for himself. He was ever alive to opportunities to promote the welfare and reputation of those to whom he stood in friendly relations. He was prompt to encourage worthy efforts, in the way of contributions to medical knowledge, by those with whom he was personally unacquainted. Many a writer, a stranger to him, has been surprised by a note from him expressing his gratification and kind wishes. Professor Gross was a constant attendant upon the meetings of the American Medical Association, and how many can recall with pleasure his benignant smile and his cordial salutations! All who have known him will remember the quiet playful humor associated with his kindly disposition. His badinage was of a nature to enliven, but never to offend or to cause pain. Sarcasm and ridicule had no place in his discourse; nor was his conversation profane or unclean.

His home was open to all who had any claim upon his attentions. He was considerate and generous alike to the guest who was renowned in letters at home and abroad, and to the young physician and the medical student. As has been said by Froude, "Nowhere is a man known better than in his own family. No disguise is possible there; and he whom father and mother, brother and sister love, we may be sure has deserved to be loved." No father was ever kinder, no husband more affectionate. They who are privileged to enter this circle are blessed with sweet remembrances which must now take the place of those social pleasures that death has interrupted.

The character of Professor Gross was full and round. It had no glaring defects. It was not angular or distorted. He had quick, strong impulses; but they were generally right, and he was not led astray by them if their tendency was otherwise. He was fond of amusements and rational conviviality; but his life affords no sanction of immoderate devotion to pleasure. He was temperate in all things without asceticism or fanaticism. He had a frank nature and was open-handed, but not improvident. He was generous as regards his professional services whenever circumstances called for the exercise of generosity.

Probably no more correct estimate of Dr. Gross could be given than that which is taken from the Memoir by Dr. I. M. Hays in the American Journal of the Medical Sciences: "Dr. Gross's majestic form and dignified presence, his broad brow and intelligent eye, his deep, mellow voice, and benignant smile, his genial manner and cordial greeting, remain indelibly impressed upon the memory of all who knew him. He was a man of deep mind and broad views, and he was a model of industry and untiring zeal. He always had some literary work in hand, and he was in the habit of rising early in the morning, generally at six o'clock, and accomplishing considerable writing before breakfast. His style was vigorous and pure, and the amount of work he accomplished was simply immense. It is safe to say that no previous medical teacher or author on this continent exercised such a widespread and commanding influence as did Professor Gross. His writings have been most learned and voluminous, and his classes among the largest that have ever been collected in this country. As a citizen he was public-spirited and influential, and he always most jealously guarded the *esprit de corps* of his own profession. In every project to advance its interests or to protect or honor any of its deserving members he was foremost. On account of the universally recognized eminence of his authority as a surgeon he was frequently called into court as an expert to testify in malpractice suits, and he was ever ready cheerfully to give his time, knowledge, and influence in maintaining the right; and he never thought any trouble too great to aid an unfortunate professional brother. He took a deep interest, too, in the struggles and success of young men, born perhaps of his own experience, and he was always ready to assist them by his counsel and advice.''

It was my privilege to see him repeatedly during the last days of his life. Feeble as he was, his cheerfulness, his inclination to humor, and his hospitable attentions did not leave him. He talked with interest of the meeting of the American Medical Association, which was near at hand, and of the International Medical Congress which was to meet at Copenhagen in a few weeks. He expressed regret that he could not be present at these meetings. In answer to a question of his friend and former colleague, Professor Richardson, "What message do you wish to send to the members of the American Medical Association?" he said, "Give them my love." He manifested pleasure in the announcement, shortly before his death, that the University of Edinburgh and the University of Pennsylvania had conferred on him the degree of Doctor of Laws. He declared that he had no desire to outlive capability for work and usefulness. He died without much suffering, and with all the devoted members of his family around his bed.

The post-mortem examination, which was conducted by Dr. Da Costa, showed that Dr. Gross had labored under marked gastric catarrh. There were irregular thickening of the mucous membrane of the stomach, and fatty heart. The right kidney contained a large cyst. The brain weighed forty-eight ounces. In accordance with the instructions contained in his will, the body of Dr. Gross, after a strictly private funeral service on May 7th, was taken to Washington, Pennsylvania, and cremated. On Sunday, May 11th, the ashes were deposited in Woodlands Cemetery next to the coffin of his wife.

The property of Dr. Gross save a few legacies was divided equally among his four children. His wet preparations, diagrams, and museum were bequeathed to the Jefferson Medical College. He left his medical library, numbering over five thousand volumes, to the Philadelphia Academy of Surgery. To this institution he also bequeathed the sum of five thousand dollars, the interest of which is to be paid every five years to the author of the best essay on a subject connected with Surgical Pathology. The marble bust of Dr. Gross now graces the hall of the College of Physicians.

Rarely has the loss of a medical man been so keenly felt by the community in which he lived or throughout the country. Telegrams and letters of condolence and resolutions of sympathy transmitted by various medical and surgical organizations in different States testified to the love and respect with which the memory of Dr. Gross was cherished.

So passed away, having nearly reached the age of fourscore years, one whom all delighted to honor. His physical strength was not greatly impaired until up to a short time before his death, and his mental faculties were maintained to the last. We shall see him no more in this world. But his life-work and his character death cannot destroy. These remain a priceless legacy to the profession which he loved, and which will ever hold his memory in grateful remembrance.

"IN MEMORIAM.

WITHIN THIS URN LIE THE ASHES OF

SAMUEL D. GROSS,

A MASTER IN SURGERY.

His life, which neared the extreme limits of the Psalmist, was one unbroken process of laborious years.

He filled chairs in four Medical Colleges in as many States of the Union and added lustre to them all.

He recast Surgical Science, as taught in North America, formulated anew its Principles, enlarged its domain, added to its art, and imparted fresh impetus to its study.

He composed many Books, and among them

A SYSTEM OF SURGERY,

Which is read in different tongues, wherever the Healing Art is practised.

With a great intellect, carefully trained and balanced, he aimed with undivided zeal at the noble end of lessening human suffering and lengthening human life, and so rose to the highest position yet attained in Science by any of his countrymen.

Resolute in truth, he had no fear; yet he was both tolerant and charitable.

Living in enlightened fellowship with all laborers in the world of Science, he was greatly honored by the learned in foreign lands, and deeply loved at home.

BEHIND THE VEIL OF THIS LIFE THERE IS A MYSTERY WHICH HE
PENETRATED ON THE

SIXTH DAY OF MAY, 1884.

HIS MEMORY

Shall exhort and his Example shall encourage and persuade those who come after him to emulate deeds which, great in themselves, were all crowned by the milk-white flower of

A STAINLESS LIFE.*"*

xxxii

AUTOBIOGRAPHY.

AUTOBIOGRAPHY

OF

SAMUEL D. GROSS, M. D.

CHAPTER I.

OBJECT OF THE WORK—BIRTH AND CHILDHOOD—SCHOOL-DAYS—AMUSEMENTS—
EARLY DESIRE TO BE A PHYSICIAN—ENTER UPON THE STUDY OF MEDI-
CINE—TURNING-POINT IN LIFE—RETURN TO SCHOOL—ACADEMY AT WILKES-
BARRE—STUDY GREEK THROUGH THE MEDIUM OF LATIN—DISLIKE OF
MATHEMATICS—FOND OF LANGUAGES—JUDGE JONES'S FAMILY—NARROW
ESCAPE FROM DROWNING—ACADEMY IN NEW YORK—LAWRENCEVILLE HIGH-
SCHOOL—LAFAYETTE.

IT is my wish to write a sketch of my life for the gratification of my children and grandchildren, and for the benefit
of such members of my profession as may feel an interest
in me from my long connection with it. Possibly some
good may grow out of such a labor, by stimulating the
ambition of those who may come after me to work for the
advancement of science and the amelioration of human
suffering. The devotion which I have shown to my profession may, perhaps, exert a salutary influence upon the
conduct of young physicians, and thus serve to inspire
them with a desire to excel in good deeds.

According to the family record, I was born on the 8th of
July, 1805, within two miles of Easton, Pennsylvania. My
parents were natives of the neighborhood, and were of

German descent, their grandparents having emigrated, as early as the seventeenth century, from the Lower Palatinate. Many of the Pennsylvania Germans who had come from that region at about the same period settled in Lancaster, Chester, Montgomery, Bucks, and Northampton counties. My father, Philip Gross, was highly distinguished for his integrity, for the elegance of his farm, and for the beauty of his horses, which were amongst the finest in the country. The farm embraced two hundred acres of the best land, in a high state of cultivation, with an excellent orchard, famed for its good fruit. My father was a tall, handsome man, with light-blue eyes, a well-shaped mouth, a neatly-shaved face, and a high bald head. He was of a kind, generous disposition. His moral character was cast in the finest mould ; he was popular with his neighbors, by whom he was much respected as an upright citizen. During the war of the Revolution, which occurred in the maturity of his manhood, he spent his time and money freely in the service of the Government, in connection with the Quartermaster's Department, at Valley Forge and other points in Eastern Pennsylvania. Of his religious convictions, if he had any, I am ignorant. All that I remember is that he was brought up, as his parents had been, in the Lutheran Church. He died in November, 1813, at the age of fifty-six, when I was in my ninth year. He had long been an invalid, and was finally seized with apoplexy, which proved fatal in a few days. He was buried at Salem Church, two miles from his residence.

My mother, whose maiden name was Brown, survived my father many years, dying in March, 1853, at the advanced age of eighty-six. She was nearly all her life a victim of asthma. She was a woman of a noble, tender, and loving heart, a most excellent wife and mother. She was a devoted member of the Lutheran Church, and spent most of her later years in the perusal of her Bible and other religious works. In truth, she was a most pure and exemplary Christian, full of faith in the promises of the Redeemer. To her good training I am indebted, under Providence, for the moral part of my character. Her early advice and admonition, prompted by a heart that never knew any guile or deceit, served to guide me through the thorny paths of boyhood and youth free from the vices which so easily beset us at those tender periods of our existence. It was she who taught me to revere religion, to love my neighbor, and to respect the laws. No one who has not experienced it can fully appreciate the influence which a mother's precepts and example exert upon the character of a child. It is incomparably greater than that of the father ; it has something in it so pure and holy that it associates her in his mind with all that is good and lovely in our nature. The child looks upon her as a guardian angel, who watches by day and by night every step that he takes, every word he utters, every action he performs, and who is ever ready to applaud or to chide him, according to the conduct he exhibits. So true is all this that it may be assumed, as an axiom in morals, that a boy who has had a good and devoted mother can never be a bad man. His conscience would not permit it, despite the worst cerebral and mental organization. It is ever present to recall the image of the fond mother. It constitutes a shield and a buckler, which protect him from the bad influences by which he is surrounded, and which are so peculiarly trying to the young and inexperienced.

I had two sisters and three brothers. My brother, the Rev. Joseph B. Gross, was for many years a clergyman of the Lutheran Church, a man of varied learning, unusual intelligence, and of very respectable talents. He has written a number of works, the great aim of which has been to set forth the origin and progressive development of religious ideas and worship among mankind ; to point out the fallacies as well as the evil tendencies of numerous so-called orthodox articles of faith ; to vindicate and enforce the true teachings and unadulterated principles of the Gospel ; to suggest and inculcate various social and political reforms ; and to introduce to the notice of the public various interesting and important historical and scientific facts for the greater enlightenment of the people.

Reared as I was in the country, my childhood was exempt from all the vices and allurements which so constantly beset the life of a boy brought up in a city. My only companions were a few lads in the immediate vicinity of my father's residence, who, like myself, were brought up in "the fear and admonition of the Lord," and whose chief amusements were of a perfectly innocent character. I had naturally a great horror of everything that was vicious or immoral. My "conscientiousness," as the phrenologists term it, was highly developed. My timidity was remarkable, and followed me, often most cruelly, late into life. In my boyish days, and even after I had become a student of medicine, I rarely spoke to any one older than myself without blushing. My early habits no doubt greatly contributed to bring about and keep up this painful feeling. My father, although he died comparatively young, was free from vice and gave me a good constitution—one which, combined with prudence as respects my mode of living, has enabled me to do an enormous amount of work as a practitioner, a writer, and a lecturer, and which has carried me, thus far safely, into my seventy-first year. I thank God that during my early days I enjoyed the advantages of pure country air and of a pure country life!

My parents had a perfect appreciation of the importance of mental training, and accordingly embraced every opportunity to send me to school. I was not seven years of age when I entered upon this task—a task which no boy ever detested more than I did. My recollection of my early school-days is very vivid. The schoolhouse—a log cabin—

was nearly one mile from our house, and the road which led to it was far from pleasant. In bad weather the walking was disagreeable, and my brother and myself often sat, despite the care of our parents, the greater part of the day in damp shoes and stockings. Notwithstanding this we were quite healthy. The schoolhouse stood in the midst of a beautiful grove of maple and oak trees, which served at the same time as our playground. Ball was the common amusement before the opening of the morning exercises, and also during the midday recess. It was a sport of which I was always very fond, and I therefore often left home at an early hour in the morning to indulge in it before the ringing of the bell. My companions were the children of the neighborhood, mostly considerably older than myself, with none of whom I was very intimate. I had not been long in the spelling-book before the Old Testament, in which every member of the class was expected to read a verse, was placed in my hands. When my turn came I was always in a state of trepidation, for I rarely knew my part, being much more intent upon sport than upon study. I had balked and stammered over my lessons for several weeks, when all at once, much to the surprise of the teacher and my classmates, my mind seemed to be unlocked, and I read with the greatest ease, pronouncing the proper jaw-breaking names with wonderful accuracy for one so young and so shy. From that time I began to take more interest in my studies, and to think less about play.

The methods of punishment in vogue in this school and in similar contemporaneous establishments in the surrounding country, although they have been long obsolete, are worthy of mention here, as serving to show one of the peculiarities of that period. They were three in number, and I shall never forget the horror which at least two of them inspired in my mind. One was a pair of large leather spectacles; the second a red cap suspended from the ceiling;

and the third a veritable rod, composed of hazelwood. The last was nothing in comparison with the other two. To whisper to one's next neighbor was an offence ; to talk aloud or laugh was a crime, sure to be visited with a message from the leather spectacles. It was not often that I received this missive, but on several occasions it was, much to my horror, perched upon my nose. The red cap was suspended over my head but once, and, as I have often since been told by my brother, two years and a half my senior, it made me cut a most sorry figure, with a sad, downcast countenance, indicative of profound shame and mortification. My brother's own feelings were deeply wounded. The cause of my punishment was the utterance of a "naughty word," the import of which I did not, at the time, at all comprehend. Of the rod I had no personal taste. After the red cap affair my conduct greatly improved, and I was never afterwards summoned to the teacher's desk. The name of this worthy, whom I occasionally met after my entrance into the medical profession, was Seiple, naturally a very amiable man, but a rigid disciplinarian.

I cannot say whether it is still the custom, as it was in my early days, for children, as they trudge along to school, to take off their hats and to make their obeisance whenever they meet a grown person. In the winter, snow-balling was a universal practice, both among boys and girls, and it was not uncommon for boys not connected with the school, as they passed along, to be severely pelted, half a dozen urchins perhaps setting upon them at one time.

In two instances two young fellows, who were in love with the same girl, engaged for a long time in a hand-to-hand fight almost every evening after the school was dismissed. As these rencounters occurred on the highway, the teacher was powerless ; it is true, he took them to task about it, and threatened dismissal. Things went on in this way until one evening one of the young scamps threw a handful of ashes into the other's eyes; this was followed the next morning by the peremptory expulsion of both. The young girl, a pretty little blonde, the bone of this contention, seemed to enjoy the fun amazingly. What ultimately became of her I never learned.

The morning exercises were generally opened with the singing of a short hymn, or with a brief prayer. In some of the schools the children recited in common, producing thus a jarring, buzzing noise, which fell harshly upon the ear, and was in every way objectionable, as tending to cause confusion and to assist in concealing ignorance.

After the death of my father the old homestead was sold, and my mother moved into a small rented house a few miles off—a maternal uncle, who had taken a fancy to me, taking charge of me. He was a good-natured man, not distinguished for any special quality, without children, and always very kind to me. During my sojourn with him my chief occupations were to go to school in the winter, to snare rabbits in the autumn, to shoot birds with a bow-gun in the spring, to pitch quoits and play ball, and to play cards in the long winter nights with him and with his neighbors. As he lived several miles from the nearest church, it did not often fall to my lot to attend divine worship; and yet, strange to say, notwithstanding many temptations, I never consciously did a mean thing. I had naturally a high moral sense, and an utter detestation of misconduct and crime. I was known throughout the neighborhood as an honest, steady boy, so sober, thoughtful, and quiet as to have earned, at a very early age, the sobriquet of "Judge." At play I was always uncommonly active, and there were few lads of my years who excelled me in manly exercises. Of quoits I was extremely fond, and if I had engaged in that kind of amusement as a means of livelihood, I am sure I should have made money at it. I was, in fact, an expert in it. Pitching pennies was another occupation to which I was much devoted, and in which no youth of my age in the neighborhood excelled me. Pitching for "keeps" was always very exciting, and never failed to be attended with advantage. Even now, at the distance of half a century, I can most vividly recall many of the very spots which served as the arenas of this agreeable pastime. One hundred and fifty to two hundred pennies were not unfrequently clustered around the "meg" at a time, and formed too great a bulk to be removed in one handful. To pick up the "heads" was most exciting sport, not unlike that which a lucky sportsman experiences in bagging his game.

One of the earliest acts of kindness shown me by my uncle was a present of a "bow-gun," in the exercise of which I became an adept, both in target-shooting and in the killing of birds. Holidays were more or less given up to this kind of amusement, generally in company with some of the boys in the vicinity. Many a bird fell a victim to my deadly aim, the thrush in particular, as he hopped about among the briers by the fence side; sometimes a woodpecker, and now and then a robin, a jay, or a catbird.

These various exercises were not without benefit to me in after life in the practice of my profession, inasmuch as they served to impart precision to the eye and hand, compelling them to move in concert with each other, so necessary in handling a knife in performing operations. Pitching quoits is particularly useful in this respect, and should be diligently cultivated by young men destined for a profession in which manual dexterity and great accuracy of eye are essential elements.

As I grew older I laid aside my bow-gun for the shotgun, and "gunning," as it is called, was for many years a favorite sport with me. Davy Crockett, it has been said, could bring down any squirrel from the highest tree ; my accomplishments never extended so far, though my shot often performed its mission with unerring effect. I never killed a deer or a fox, and I was never engaged in that very animating sport known as bear-hunting.

In the autumn a regular part of my occupation was rabbit-snaring, an art of which I was passionately fond, and in which I usually did a good business, considering that rabbits were not particularly numerous in the neighborhood. The season generally began about the middle of October, when the foliage was pretty well off the trees, and terminated about the close of November. An adjoining wood thickly studded with underbrush always served as the field of my operations. After the snares were set the visits were invariably made early the next morning, so that I could return in time for breakfast. It was seldom that I brought home more than two or three rabbits, and sometimes I came back without any. On rare occasions the animal would be found alive, his hind leg instead of the neck having been caught in the noose, a circumstance which always greatly enhanced the excitement. In the winter, when the ground was covered with snow, I sometimes "treed" a rabbit, and smoked him out of his lodgings. The labor required to accomplish this feat was often very considerable, and was generally the more exciting, as it was nearly always performed by several boys, who vied one with another for the possession of the prize.

I do not know whether rabbit-snaring is still practised or not. To me it was a most delightful and healthful occupation. The process is a simple one. The whole apparatus consists of a stick of live underwood, a piece of twine two feet and a half long, a cylinder of wood with a part of an apple fastened on the end, and half a dozen short, slender twigs placed circularly in the ground to keep the noose extended. The rabbit, attracted by the fragrance of the apple, is strung up the moment he touches it, being thus speedily and unceremoniously strangled by the rebound of the stick which holds the cord.

During my early boyhood one of my favorite amusements was hunting birds' nests in my father's orchard, which, although not very extensive, embraced many fine trees. These nests were always appropriated by the first finder, who carefully watched them, and afforded the birds every possible protection during the hatching season. Sometimes disputes arose between my brothers and myself respecting the ownership, but these were generally amicably adjusted, the rights of the original discoverer being always scrupulously respected. The occupants of the orchard were the dove, bluebird, robin, wren, woodpecker, and Baltimore oriole, whose nest hung literally in the air. Of course, no one could approach. No gun was ever heard in the orchard, and the consequence was that all the birds were unusually tame.

I visited this orchard fifty years after I had left it as a boy. All its beauty had disappeared. Only eleven apple trees remained to tell the sad story, and they were gray and hoary with the frosts of many winters, full of dead branches, and without a sign of fruit. They had passed the period of bearing, and were in the sear and yellow leaf of autumn, the dilapidated survivors of a former generation, sad emblems of the frailty and decay of human life! The very house in which I was born had disappeared; the grand barn and all the outhouses were gone, and one small stable alone stood to mark the spot, near which was our daily playground. Even the avenue leading from the main road to the old house, lined on each side in my early boyhood with cherry and Lombardy poplar trees, was no longer visible. The little wood which served as my garden was utterly effaced. What rendered the visit more sad and impressive was that, on the day on which it was made, early in October, not a human being was on the premises, the residents being in attendance upon a funeral in the neighborhood.

Fighting humble-bees, wasps, hornets, and yellow-jackets is a favorite pursuit with all boys on farms, and of this kind of work I did my share in my childish days, receiving many a sting as the reward of my temerity and cruelty. A swollen lip, cheek, or eyelid was of common occurrence. Of all these insects, none sting more ferociously than the hornet and yellow-jacket, especially during the procreating season. The honey of the humble-bee was a poor compensation for the suffering thus endured. Hornets' nests were usually assailed with stones; the others with sticks and clubs. It seems to me as if I could still hear their angry buzzing, whining sounds, as they sailed in straight lines to revenge themselves upon their assailants. These were cruel sports, certainly, and yet they were perhaps, in view of the rapid multiplication of these insects, not without their value.

Of fishing I was excessively fond as a boy, although I never had much luck; and after I grew up I rarely indulged in it, believing that the definition of the great lexicographer is not without its significance—"A bait and a hook at one end and a fool at the other." On two occasions I spent a whole night in "gigging," as it is called, in company with some neighboring boys, and succeeded in carrying off a goodly number of the finny tribe, dazed by our torchlights, constructed of the bark of the birch tree. It was fine sport, carried on in a hot summer's night, standing often up to the waist in the water, and excited to the highest pitch by surrounding events, the merry laugh, and the recital of a good story.

Among the books which formed my uncle's library, those in which I took the greatest interest were the Bible, Æsop's Fables, almanacs, and some volumes of geography, history, and romance. Of these books, my favorites were the Bible, especially the Old Testament, and Æsop's Fables. The latter was an illustrated edition, and served to beguile many a lonely hour. Among my father's books was one on the Witches of the Hartz Mountains, with a very curious wood-cut, representing these poor creatures, always in women's attire, as riding on pitchforks and broomsticks. The work, a good-sized duodecimo, was adorned with red margins, now so fashionable, and was printed near the middle of the last century. The stories in the Old Testament interested me very much, and before I was fifteen years of age I had read the entire Bible, with what understanding I will not pretend to say. Of almanacs I was always very fond, and even now I am often entertained by this kind of reading. The fact is, good almanacs generally furnish a great deal of valuable information, and it is not surprising that old ones should often command a high price at public sales. The elegant almanacs which during the last ten years have been annually published by Mr. George W. Childs, proprietor of the Philadelphia Public Ledger, will be regarded as great literary treasures a hundred years hence. What would a man not now give for a copy of Poor Richard's Almanac, the product of the brain, pen, and printing-press of Benjamin Franklin?

During my stay with my uncle I led, in the main, a very easy kind of life. In the winter my time was regularly spent at school; and, although I was a careless boy, more devoted to amusement than to study, I nevertheless picked up a considerable amount of valuable knowledge. The schoolhouse was a log cabin, very simply furnished, but well warmed and sufficiently comfortable, affording accommodations for upwards of thirty boys and girls, from the ages of eight or nine to nearly twenty. Among them was a beautiful maiden, with blue eyes and flaxen hair, with whom I fell desperately in love, without, however, disclosing my passion, which my great diffidence prevented me from doing. She was by several years my senior, and, finding that I had a rival, I wisely remained silent. An altercation afterwards took place between him and another suitor, eventuating in a serious hand-to-hand fight, followed by black eyes and no little scandal throughout the school. There never was a greater truism uttered than that

"Every lassie has her laddie." Falling in love is a natural consequence of our nature. Long before I was seven years of age I was desperately smitten; indeed, to such a degree that I was rendered miserable. I shall never forget little Phœbe Van B., a girl somewhat younger than myself, with pale features, light eyes and hair, and a sweet, gentle voice, who was the early object of my adoration. Her image is still fresh in my memory, although of the original I lost sight before I was fourteen years old. Our attachment was strong and mutual, and for many months we were inseparable companions, happy only in each other's society. I have seen so many instances of this "falling in love" among very young children that I long ago came to the conclusion that it is one of the physiological conditions of our organization. The occurrence is not unfrequently attended with an amount of gallantry that would put to blush older lovers.

In my early childhood I was passionately fond of flowers, and before I was seven years old had a little garden in a secluded dell, lined by rocks and fringed by small forest trees, in which I cultivated the columbine, the poppy, the anemone, and other wild flowers. It was a sort of fairy spot, in which, in the early spring and summer, many of my happiest hours were spent. Rasselas, prince of Abyssinia, in his wildest fancies, was never more happy in the valley of Amhara than I was in this secluded spot, to which, even now, my mind often reverts with pleasurable emotions. My childhood was indeed a most joyous one.

The chief holidays at that period were Christmas, New Year, and Easter. These seemed to be much farther apart then than now, and their arrival was always anticipated with a kind of joyous anxiety. Kriss Kringle always brought gifts, of which cakes formed an important part. Children's books had not then so independent an existence as they have now. Like angels' visits, they were "few and far between." The colored Easter-egg came regularly with every revolving year, concealed in the grass in the family garden, as the gift of the rabbits—a pretty idea, imported originally from Germany, and of late years so much neglected that there is danger of the custom becoming obsolete. The New Year was always ushered in by the firing of guns and pistols, commencing punctually immediately after the clock struck twelve, the party consisting of old and young men, assembled from the vicinity, and growing steadily by accretion as they passed from house to house, extending happy greetings to their friends, followed by the simultaneous discharge of their guns. On such occasions it was not uncommon for the younger members of the party to make sentimental addresses to their sweethearts. Coffee, cake, and sausages were always served after the greetings were over, and the merriment was often enhanced by the circulation of "the intoxicating bowl." These New Year greetings, which were peculiar to the German settlements, were often continued until a late hour in the morning, and were seldom attended by any mishaps, social or physical.

In my childhood I was a firm believer in ghosts, witches, hobgoblins, devils, evil spirits, and, in short, everything that was weird or supernatural. I believed that the very air was filled with these creatures, that they were on the constant lookout for bad people, and that they were particularly wicked and dangerous at night. During one winter I lived near a church, the graveyard of which I never passed without whistling or a sense of horripilation; whistling to keep the ghosts away and to tell the family where I might be found in case of an attack. After I became a student of medicine I could have slept comfortably, certainly without fear, amid a hundred corpses. This feeling was not peculiar to me; it was shared by all the younger members of the family and by all the children in the neighborhood. It made me for a long time a great coward, afraid to go out at night, or to sleep alone in the dark. I was more than twelve years of age before I was able to

shake off these terrible impressions of my childhood, the result, not of superstition on the part of my parents, who
knew better, but of an education designed to make me
good by inducing me to believe that all my acts were
watched, and that these acts would be rewarded or pun-
ished according as they were good or bad.

Children are emphatically the creatures of circumstances.
The prejudices in which they are reared are sure to influence them, if not during their whole lives, at any rate for
a long time, or until they are counteracted by other sur-
roundings or by riper reasoning powers. There is hardly a
child that is not impressed with the conviction that Santa
Claus is a reality, a sort of mystic personage, living in a
cave or some secluded valley, and coming down the chim-
ney on Christmas nights to dispense his favors. This belief, handed down from generation to generation, from
parents to their offspring, is a delightful delusion which
seldom leaves the mind before the sixth or eighth year of
childhood.

One of my uncle's amusements, as I have mentioned,
was playing cards, in which I myself soon became quite
a proficient. Whenever a hand was needed I was ready
to fill the gap. My favorite games were euchre and
seven-up. I never learned Boaston or poker, not having
had the advantage of General Schenck's instruction. In
time I became very fond of cards; we often sat at the table
until a late hour of the night, and after I retired I was sure
to dream of them, the cards often floating, as it were, bodily
before my eyes. I found that this would not do; the fascination was growing upon me, and I therefore determined
to break it up. This I did before I had reached my fourteenth year. I made a vow that I would not play again
for twenty years, and this vow I scrupulously observed
during all that period. To conquer one's self requires resolution, often great courage; but the effort, if persistent
and earnest, seldom fails of its purpose. No man should

allow himself to become a slave to habit or to anything whatever. It is better, as Rip Van Winkle says, to swear off, and to assert his independence.

I must not forget to mention that during the cherry season I occasionally killed a woodpecker in a novel and curious manner. A thin, slender pole was inserted in the ground close to the trunk of the tree, with the other end protruding at the top. When the bird had obtained his cherry he would perch upon the side of the top of the pole to eat it at his leisure. The moment he was fairly seated in his fancied security the pole was struck below with an axe, causing thus a violent vibration, which, sent through the legs of the poor bird to the spinal cord and brain, generally occasioned instantaneous death by concussion of the nervous centres. In my work on Surgery I have referred to this operation as an apt illustration of the mode of production of concussion of the brain and spinal cord from falls on the feet and nates.

Leaving my uncle in my fifteenth year, I went back to my mother, and bethought me of some useful occupation during the rest of my life. Various suggestions were made to me, but none were sufficiently enticing to induce me to adopt them. I had had from my earliest childhood the strongest desire to be a "doctor." How that feeling was engendered I have never been able to explain. Perhaps it was from seeing occasionally a physician at my father's house in times of sickness. However this may have been, this desire had seized me before I was six years of age, and continued to haunt me more or less until I was able to gratify it. There are natural-born poets; and, if there ever was a natural-born doctor, I was that one. The impulse was too strong to be resisted. My views of life now became somewhat settled; and, as my education was still very defective, I at once began to remedy it. I had made considerable progress in the study of the German language; I had read quite a number of books, and was able to write German with some ability. My English had been neglected, and I therefore determined to take up the language systematically. I also, in due time, commenced the study of the Latin language. My progress, however, was not rapid in either. I had been brought up in a German settlement, and therefore knew practically little of English. This was a serious impediment, and it cost me much labor and trouble to surmount it. Then, again, my early teachers were themselves indifferent English scholars; and my progress would have been still less if I had not by this time become thoroughly impressed with the necessity of self-reliance and hard work. I labored diligently at my books, and made considerable progress in reading, composition, and arithmetic. Latin dragged heavily along, and as yet I had not attempted Greek. Indeed, there was no one in the neighborhood who had much acquaintance with the classics.

At the age of seventeen I considered myself competent to commence the study of medicine, and I accordingly entered the office of a country physician; but he afforded me no aid, and I therefore soon quit him and tried another, with no better luck. They had none but old, if not obsolete, books; they were constantly from home, never examined me, or gave me any encouragement. With the aid of Fyfe's Anatomy and a skeleton, I learned some osteology; but even this was up-hill business, and I at length gave up in despair. I found that my Latin was inadequate, and that I could not understand the technicalities of medicine without some knowledge of Greek. With some degree of hesitancy, lest I should give offence, I disclosed my feelings to my preceptor, and, much to his honor, he at once released me from any obligations to serve out my term of study. *This was the turning-point in my life.* I had pondered the matter with much care; it had worried and fretted me for days and nights; and, as I was naturally very diffident, it required all the courage I could summon to make

1—3

known my wishes. The promptness with which they were seconded gave me such relief that I once more drew a long and comfortable breath. I had made a great discovery—a knowledge of my ignorance ; and with it came a solemn determination to remedy it.

The school which I selected was the Academy at Wilkesbarre, famous in its day for the large number of its pupils, and at the time under the charge of Mr., afterwards Judge, Joel Jones, a graduate of Yale College, a gentleman of great kindness of heart, a good linguist and an excellent teacher. He was assisted by a brother, Mr. Samuel Jones, who was afterwards for many years the principal of a celebrated classical school in Philadelphia. I lost no time in beginning my studies. Latin, English grammar, mathematics, and Greek formed my daily occupation, and no youth ever worked harder than I to acquire knowledge. I generally slept with a book under my pillow, especially if I had anything to commit to memory. My progress was commendable. Still I had a fearful task before me in Buttmann's Greek Grammar, as it was entirely too large and difficult for a beginner. However, I succeeded in mastering a good portion of it, and was able to apply a considerable number of its rules. This grammar had just been introduced to the American student, through a translation by the late Edward Everett, made soon after his return from Europe, while tutor at Harvard University. My Latin grammar was that of Adam, rector of the High School at Edinburgh ; it was too voluminous a book for a beginner, but, nevertheless, a most excellent one, which held its position for a long time in the affections of the European and American student. My English grammar was an abridgment of Lindley Murray's, for a long time the only grammar used in this country. Within the last forty years great changes have taken place in school-books, not perhaps always for the best, although in many instances the gain, by simplifying the

process of teaching, has been vast. The only Greek lexicon in my school-days was Schrevelius's, which, as the
definitions were all in Latin, few pupils could master.
The labor thoroughly disgusted me, and the consequence
was that I never had any love for the Greek language. To
understand Latin was hard enough, but to study Greek
through such a medium was positively absurd; nay, more,
an insult to common-sense and an outrage upon human
nature. Ross's Greek Grammar, used in some of the
schools and colleges in the country, was constructed upon
the same principle, and yet it maintained its place as a
text-book for many years. To study Greek with such
agencies was as severe a task as for an ox to tread out
corn. I never think of it without a shudder, and wonder
that teachers could ever have been so foolish! I had become a graduate in medicine when I saw for the first time,
upon the counter of a New York bookseller, a copy of
Groves's Greek and English Lexicon, then recently published. This was in the autumn of 1828. I welcomed the
book as the harbinger of a new era in educational progress;
the reign of Ross and Schrevelius was soon over, and the
study of the Greek language became a comparatively easy
task.

When Oliver Goldsmith went to Holland it occurred to
him that he might replenish his exhausted purse by teaching the Dutch a knowledge of the English language; but
he soon found that to do this it was necessary that he
himself should understand Dutch, and so, like a sensible
man, he abandoned the enterprise. What a pity Ross and
Schrevelius had not heard this anecdote before they wrote
their books!

Studying Greek through the medium of the Latin language was very much such a task as the law student had
before him when he attempted to obtain a knowledge of
his profession by reading such jargon as met his eye in
Coke upon Littleton. Blackstone lifted a heavy load off

his brain by the publication of his immortal Commentaries; and what Blackstone did for the English student Kent did for the American.

Mathematics I detested. I never understood the most simple rule in algebra. As to Euclid, I would rather have worked in the mines of Siberia than have attempted to solve one of his problems. If opportunity had offered, I should have made a good linguist; I was fond of the study of languages; and, if I had been a teacher, I should have gone over the ground philosophically. The German was my native tongue, the English an acquired one; and as to the French, although I could not speak it, I translated it with facility. The Italian I read at one time sufficiently well to enable me to understand some works in surgery, which I was obliged to consult in the composition of a paper on the Results of Surgical Operations in the Treatment of Malignant Diseases, prepared by me many years ago for the American Medical Association, in the Transactions of which it was published.

I must not forget to say a few words here of the Jones family, of which Joel was a member. It was, in many respects, a remarkable one. It emigrated from Connecticut. The mother was a Huntington, a woman of great refinement, and of a strong, vigorous mind. Of the four sons Joel became the most eminent. Quitting teaching he studied law, and settled at Easton. After the election of Hon. George Wolf as Governor of Pennsylvania, he was appointed one of the commissioners to revise the code of Pennsylvania, and afterwards he became a judge of the District Court of Philadelphia, an office which he held for several years. He was subsequently elected president of Girard College and mayor of the city. He held these offices, however, only for a short time, and then returned to the bar, at which he ended his life. He was too honest and too sensitive for the times in which he lived—utterly unfitted by nature for the contentions and strife of active life ; otherwise he might have become a very distinguished man. He shrank from contact with the world. He was a close student, a capital linguist, and an excellent Biblical scholar. His library was extensive, and abounded in rare works on law and general literature. He left behind him a work in manuscript on theology, which was published after his death, and which was highly esteemed for its learning and piety. He was essentially a "book-worm."

The Rev. Dr. Joseph H. Jones, who was for many years pastor of the Spruce Street Presbyterian Church of this city, was a man of great piety, of refined and cultivated mind, and of great activity in useful and charitable work. He was for many years president of the Society for the Relief of Superannuated Clergymen.

Samuel Jones, a younger brother, was, as already stated, the principal of a classical school in this city, which he superintended for many years, and which turned out some of the best educated men in different pursuits in Philadelphia. As a classical teacher he was very popular. Late in life he engaged in coal speculations, and finally died of an incurable malady. Matthew Hale Jones, the youngest male member of the family, was a successful lawyer at Easton. There were four daughters, all highly respectable women, two of whom died in early life.

The academy at Wilkesbarre was a celebrated institution in its day. It was open both to boys and girls. After Mr. Jones left it, however, it lost caste, and was finally abandoned. My connection with it lasted only one year. I would have remained longer, but the difficulty of inducing my guardians to advance me the necessary means embarrassed me, and at length compelled me, much against my wishes, to leave it.

The janitor of this academy was a "character," known by the sobriquet of "Old Speck." A German by birth, he represented himself as one of Bonaparte's soldiers. One of his stories, afterwards often repeated to his annoyance, was that, during the retreat of the grand army from Russia, when the soldiers were hard pressed for food, he stole a dead child, concealed it in his knapsack, and finally devoured it. The word "speck" had reference to this exploit, and it was never uttered without making him very angry. Of the young men who were pupils at the academy during my connection with it few attained distinction.

An incident occurred during my residence at Wilkesbarre which came very near proving fatal to me. My brother, several years my senior, a young man named Haynes, to whom I was much attached, and I went out bathing one day in the Susquehanna. It was late in the afternoon, after school hours. Haynes and I went in together; my brother probably fifty yards off. I suddenly heard a cry and saw a struggle in the water. My brother had disappeared. Naturally enough with great rapidity I ran to his aid. He at once seized me and we went down together. Fortunately this lasted only a few seconds. As good luck would have it we got upon a ledge of rocks, and were thus saved, after having been under the water several times. I shall never forget the horror of the occasion, the thousand things that flashed, like lightning, through my mind, and the great relief I felt when I was assured of a safe foothold. Neither of us could swim.

Apropos of Judge Jones : I had the pleasure of dining with him in 1845, and in the course of conversation he mentioned to me, in the presence of his excellent wife, the great awe which he felt about the learning and accomplishments of Philadelphia lawyers on his elevation to the bench. He often, he told me, sat up till a late hour in the morning preparing his decisions, until he found, in a short time, that he had nothing to fear, as the learning and ability of the bar had been vastly exaggerated. Distance had evidently lent "enchantment to the view." The Philadelphia bar is still a great one, but, like every other bar in America, it has lost its eloquence. Any attempt of this kind is now regarded as useless; arguments and facts having taken its place as better adapted to secure the ends of justice. The only exception, perhaps, to this rule is in trials for murder, in which a display of forensic eloquence is still occasionally witnessed. Uneducated and unprincipled lawyers—"pettifoggers" as they are termed—have done much to lower and degrade the legal profession, just as similar characters in our profession have defiled our ranks. I wish we could say that the clergy were free from these impure creatures!

After completing the year at Wilkesbarre I went the following winter to New York, where I attended a classical school in the Bowery, under the care of Mr. Shea, an Irish patriot. But as my progress here did not satisfy me, I returned at the end of six months to Easton, where I found my former teacher, Mr. Joel Jones, who was now a candidate for practice at the bar, and who kindly consented to give me private instruction in Latin and Greek.

After six months I became restless, and hearing of the High School at Lawrenceville, New Jersey, I spent the next six months in that institution, thus completing my course of studies. This school was then, as it is now, a celebrated institution, attracting pupils from different and even remote States. The principal was the Rev. Dr. Isaac Brown, a Presbyterian clergyman, a graduate of Princeton College, and a kind-hearted, excellent, pious gentleman, who had made teaching the business of his life. He was assisted by several ushers. While under his supervision I studied Greek and Latin, geography and mathematics, and devoted much time to miscellaneous reading. Among the works that interested me very much were Marshall's Life of Washington and Hannah More's writings. The number of pupils was upwards of fifty, more than one-half of whom were boarders in the house. Mrs. Brown was a noble woman, who kept a close watch upon the welfare of the inmates. Grace was said at every meal; and, although there was occasionally a little disorderly conduct, the establishment was, in the main, conducted with the greatest propriety and decorum. On the Sabbath every boy was expected to attend church, and Dr. Brown's prayers and sermons were often fatiguingly long and uninteresting.

It was towards the close of the session—if I mistake not, on the 24th of September, 1824—that General Lafayette, the nation's guest, passed through Trenton on his way from New York to Philadelphia. The whole country, far and near, was in a state of ferment to behold the illustrious patriot, the companion of Washington, and the friend of America, and an immense concourse of people assembled on the hill back of Trenton to bid him welcome. The crowd had waited from early morning until late in the afternoon, when, at length, the "conquering hero" came, seated in a carriage drawn by four white horses, "the observed of all observers." The welkin rang with shouts and huzzas, handkerchiefs were waved, hats were thrown into the air, cannons boomed, and bands discoursed sweet music of welcome. The veteran bowed in every direction, evidently delighted with what was passing around him, as indeed he might well have been. On alighting from his carriage, he was conducted into the State House, where, after an address of welcome by—if I mistake not—the Governor of New Jersey, he had a public reception, followed by a magnificent ball in the evening. The next day, being Sunday, he attended divine service, and on Monday morning left for Philadelphia. Lafayette was dressed in plain citizen's clothes, and had a very ruddy face, with a remarkably prominent nose.

Lawrenceville is situated nearly midway between Trenton and Princeton, at what was formerly known as Maidenhead, the scene of a rough skirmish between a portion of the British and American forces during the war of the

Revolution. During my attendance at its High School there were but few houses, with a church and a graveyard, and no tavern or blacksmith shop, those important requisites of a country village! There were some good dwellings in the neighborhood, among others a very large one occupied by a Mr. Green, whose son, Henry Woodhull Green, afterwards became Chief Justice and finally Chancellor of the State of New Jersey. I revisited Lawrenceville for the first and only time since my school-days immediately before the war, as an invited guest at the semicentennial celebration of its High School, then, as since, under the charge of the brothers Hamill. My old teacher was present, but he had retired from the school, and was living near Trenton, where, about eighteen months later, he was gathered to his fathers. Dr. Brown was of Huguenot descent, a sincere Christian and a good man, a little too fond of the birch; for he would occasionally flog some of the younger boys most unmercifully, especially one of his nephews, who, excepting that he was somewhat mischievous, seemed to me to be quite as good and well-behaved as any of his fellow-students.

It will thus be perceived that my education was a desultory one, and yet I certainly acquired much valuable knowledge for future service. The manner in which I pursued my education was not a matter of choice with me. It grew out of the circumstances in which I was placed. My guardians did all they could to thwart my efforts, and often failed to supply me with money to pay my board and tuition, thus subjecting me not only to great chagrin, but to the loss of valuable time and unjust expense. I should have fared much better—infinitely better in every respect—if, as was my wish, I could have pursued my studies uninterruptedly at one institution, as, for example, the grand old academy at Wilkesbarre. My patrimony was ample, and would have lasted longer if it had been properly applied.

1—4

CHAPTER II.

THE choice of a profession is one of the greatest per-
plexities of a young man's life. No one, perhaps, ever
experienced this in a greater degree than Nathaniel
Hawthorne. Originally inclined to lead a seafaring life,
he wrote to his mother that he did not want to be a
doctor, and live by men's diseases; or a minister, or a
lawyer; and he concluded that there was nothing left for
him but to be an author. No such difficulty presented
itself to me. If I was not born a doctor, I was determined
from my earliest boyhood to study medicine; and, although
I have sometimes thought that I had mistaken my calling,
I am not sure that I have not done well in being a doctor,
and living by men's diseases. The author of The
Scarlet Letter, the Twice-Told Tales, and The House
of the Seven Gables did far more for his own reputation
and for the glory of America as an author than he ever
could have done as a sea-captain, a position which he so
much coveted in his youth. It is said of Physick that,
in his early professional life, he constantly expressed his
regret that he had not adopted his father's occupation—
that of a jeweller. Sir Astley Cooper, the great London

surgeon, was induced to take up the profession by seeing Mr. Donne, of the Norfolk and Norwich Hospital,
perform an operation—probably lithotomy—in a "mas-
terly manner;" and Nathan Smith, one of America's
great physicians and surgeons, had his mind first directed
to the study of medicine by witnessing an operation in
the hands of Dr. Goodhue, who became afterwards his
preceptor.

I was nineteen years of age when I commenced in
earnest the study of medicine. My preceptor was Dr.
Joseph K. Swift, of Easton, a graduate of the University
of Pennsylvania, and a practitioner of some note, with
considerable pretension to scientific knowledge, and a
deadly hatred of quackery. The understanding was that
I was to remain under his tuition for three years, inclusive of two lecture terms, and that he was to receive,
as an office fee, two hundred dollars, for which he
was to furnish me with the use of certain books, and to
examine me once a week on such branches as I might be
studying. His library was small, and its contents of little
value. He had no apparatus of any kind, plates or diagrams, no specimens in materia medica, or anatomical preparations; nothing, in short, but a skeleton, and this, with
the aid of Wistar's Anatomy, was the first thing I set about
to master. In less than two months I had accomplished
my object; I knew pretty well every foramen, prominence,
and suture, and was complimented upon my progress. I
then went to the ligaments and muscles, and at length to
the viscera, and of course learned but little. From anatomy I went to surgery, then to materia medica, and finally
to midwifery and the practice of medicine. The works on
these subjects that were put into my hands were Dorsey's
Elements of Surgery, Chapman's Materia Medica and
Therapeutics, Burns's Midwifery, edited by James, and
Thomas's Practice, edited by Hosack. Chemistry I did
not study, being told that it could not be learned out of the

lecture-room without the aid of experiments, and no assertion, I am sure, is more true. I was generally examined on
Saturday, and it is due to preceptor and pupil to say that
they were always punctually at their post. From an hour
to an hour and a half was usually consumed in this way;
the book which I was engaged in reading being always
spread out on the table before my "master." I need not
say that this was a dry and unprofitable mode of studying
medicine; it was acquiring knowledge under difficulties;
it was a waste of precious time; and I was therefore glad
when the period arrived for attending lectures. I was
eager for a new field, where I might obtain some substantial information, and some remuneration for my pains. I
had all along felt that, like Sisyphus, I was engaged
in rolling stones up hill, and doing myself no good beyond the slight reputation I gained as a devoted student.
Besides, I had seen no practice; my preceptor was not
popular, and few of his patients could be visited by an
"unfledged doctor." Swift, I am sure, took an interest in
me; but it soon became apparent to me that such instruction as I was receiving from him had little value, and fell
far short of what a student had a right to expect from his
preceptor. Perhaps, however, this was not his fault, but
the fault of the vicious system of office pupilage, still prevalent in nearly all sections of this country, a system which
cannot be too pointedly condemned, and concerning which
I shall have more to say.

Knowing how important it was for a physician, ambitious
to excel in his profession, to have some knowledge of the
French language, I took private lessons from an English
lady, then a resident of Easton, and in a few months had
made such progress as to enable me to read pretty fluently
any ordinary work. The time thus spent was not allowed
to interfere with my medical studies. This was an agreeable
pursuit, which, while it served to strengthen my memory,
assisted me in laying up valuable information for future

use. Wanostrocht's Grammar, Boyer's Dictionary, a phrase book, and the Life of Charles XII. of Sweden by Voltaire, constituted my chief armamentarium for this kind of work. I made attempts to speak the language, but I never could get my tongue to take kindly to it. For the sake of its admirable medical literature, I would strongly advise all medical students to study French.

During my pupilage at Easton I became interested in the study of mineralogy, having imbibed a taste for it from Dr. Swift, who had a choice collection of minerals, to which he was constantly adding by way of exchanges. He had had the first gatherings at Wolf's quarry, as it was called, two miles above Easton, on the west bank of the Delaware, one of the finest localities of the serpentine minerals in the country, and one of the few where crystals of serpentine have been found. At this quarry and in its vicinity many of my happiest hours were spent. My custom was, during the summer months, after getting through with my medical studies, to spend a few hours in the afternoon at least once, and often twice, a week, in search of specimens, and when I left Easton I had accumulated a beautiful collection, enriched by domestic and foreign exchanges, amounting to upwards of two thousand specimens. Among those with whom I corresponded at this period for improving my collection were Professor Silliman, of New Haven, Major Delafield, of West Point, and Dr. Darlington, of West Chester, Pennsylvania.

I had studied medicine nearly one year when my health broke down. I became very weak, my appetite gave way, and my nervous system was thoroughly wrecked. Sleep forsook my pillow, and I was harassed by horrid dreams. I kept a light burning all night in my room lest I should die in the dark. On one occasion I dreamed that my grave was being dug ; I saw people at work throwing up the earth and getting ready to deposit all that was mortal of me. I awoke suddenly, jumped up hastily, raised the nearly exhausted wick of my lamp, and, in a deep perspiration, gradually regained my self-possession. It was a fearful moment, one which I shall never forget. Any unexpected news greatly alarmed me. The ringing of the town bell for a funeral was most fearful to me. As to studying, that was impossible. Every effort of the kind only served to worry and to distress me. There was then no chloral, no bromide of potassium to assuage my suffering. Fortunately I was the owner of an excellent saddle-horse, and as soon as spring fairly opened I started for Niagara, in company with a brother, a distance of three hundred and fifty miles. We made, on an average, from twenty-five to thirty miles a day, resting occasionally a day or so, as was found necessary for comfort. Much of the country through which we passed was in a wild, uncultivated state. Rochester, as I well recollect, was bristling with the stumps of recently felled trees; the roads were indifferent, and few travellers were to be seen anywhere. The most fashionable hotels in the larger towns through which we passed were known as the Eagle Hotels, generally provided with excellent accommodations at reasonable charges. At Buffalo, which was then already a city of great importance, we saw some of Red Jacket's men, magnificent specimens of Indians—tall, handsome, and straight as arrows. Some of them were idling or lounging about; others were engaged in drawing up logs from the shore of Lake Erie. We did not visit the chief's reservation. During our stay I made the acquaintance of a pleasant gentleman, Dr. Stagg, a rising physician, who had a fine collection of dog-tooth spar and other specimens of the famous Lockport minerals, and who, on taking leave of us, kindly gave me a letter of introduction to his old preceptor, the celebrated Dr. Samuel Latham Mitchill, of New York.

We reached the Falls of Niagara in about sixteen days, saw all the objects of interest in a state of virgin purity, not, as now, defiled by art and bad taste, and then turned our faces homeward. Ten miles from the Falls we stopped at a village inhabited by the remnant of dirty, squalid Tuscarora Indians, now almost extinct. Here we saw no men at all comparable to those we had met with at Buffalo. They belonged entirely to a different set of beings. The women were decidedly ugly, and the children dull and heavy-looking. Much of the road along which we travelled was skirted by the Erie Canal, alive with boats, freighted with the produce of the rich country through which, like a snake, it meandered. The Mohawk Valley, so beautiful and fertile, and even then so highly cultivated, interested us very much. At Albany, after a rest of a few days, we sent our jaded horses on flats down the Hudson, while we ourselves took passage on one of the New York steamers. Altogether I was absent six weeks ; all my nervous symptoms had disappeared, my digestive organs were in excellent condition, my sleep was never better, and my brain was again in working order ; in a word, my health, previously so undermined, was completely restored. I had simply been overworked and overdrugged, and the horseback exercise, with the exhilarating influence of change of air, food, and scene, did the work of restoration. I regard exercise on horseback as the most salutary exercise an invalid can take. Exercise in an open carriage is also very good, while riding in a railway car is worrying and fatiguing, only fit for robust people.

Thomas Sydenham, that great observer of nature—the English Hippocrates, as he is often called—was fully aware of the beneficial effects of horseback exercise. Having charge of a patient whom nobody had been able to cure, he told him one day that there was a physician, a Dr. Roberts, at Inverness, Scotland, who was famous for his treatment of dyspeptic and nervous disorders, and strongly advised his patient to visit him. The distance was considerable, but that need not discourage him, as all he required was a good horse. As he rode along his health rapidly improved ; but on reaching Inverness, and inquiring for Dr. Roberts, he was greatly mortified to find that there was no such man in the town. Determined to seek redress, he rode back as he came, and called Sydenham to account for what he had considered a great insult. "How is your health?" inquired the great man. "My health is excellent," was the answer ; "but you told me an untruth, and I want an explanation." "I knew," was the reply, "that there was no such physician as Dr. Roberts at Inverness, but I also knew that, buoyed up with hope, the journey at this genial season of the year would cure you of your maladies."

Swift was anxious that I should attend lectures in the University of Pennsylvania, his Alma Mater, and accordingly gave me letters to Professors Dewees and Horner, the former of whom was a relative by marriage of Mrs. Swift. I had, however, heard so much of the brilliant achievements of Dr. George McClellan, Professor of Surgery in the Jefferson Medical College, then recently founded, that I made up my mind to disregard his wishes and to matriculate in the "new school," as it was called. I therefore did not deliver Swift's letters. I became at the same time a private pupil of McClellan, and never re-entered Swift's office, although I had paid him his full fee when I left Easton. This, I believe, gave offence.

I arrived in Philadelphia in October, 1826, several weeks before the commencement of the session, and at once entered the dissecting-rooms, spending most of my time in the study of practical anatomy. Revolting as the sight and odor were to me during the first few days, I soon became passionately fond of dissections, and henceforth made practical anatomy a special study. I seldom retired during the first half of the session of the college before late at night. In the autumn I spent a month upon this study during the day, before the opening of the regular lectures, and in the spring I did the same, after the session had terminated.   I thus became a fair practical anatomist.   I was particularly fond of surgical and visceral anatomy.   I shall never forget the deep interest I felt in the structure of the brain and in the origin and distribution of the nerves, especially the great sympathetic, phrenic, and pneumogastric.   The discoveries by Magendie and Sir Charles Bell of the functions of the nerves of motion and sensation at that time profoundly interested professional men, and enlisted the attention alike of teacher and pupil.   McClellan was an enthusiast, and I was not long in sharing his feelings.

The Faculty of the school consisted of McClellan, Professor of Surgery ; N. R. Smith, Anatomy ; John Eberle, Practice of Medicine ; William P. C. Barton, Materia Medica ; Jacob Green, Chemistry ; John Barnes, Obstetrics, and Benjamin Rush Rhees, Institutes of Medicine and Medical Jurisprudence.   Before the opening of my second course Smith was called to the chair of Anatomy in the University of Maryland, Baltimore, in which he continued for about two years.   He then succeeded Dr. Davidge in the chair of Surgery, which he occupied until 1869, having in the meantime earned a world-wide reputation as a surgeon and teacher, and enjoyed an immense practice.   In the following spring Barnes was replaced by Eberle, who now taught both medicine and midwifery ; and McClellan lectured both on anatomy and surgery.   The Faculty consequently consisted of five members only during my second term. McClellan was the master genius of the establishment, a fluent and popular lecturer, full of energy and enthusiasm, but utterly without system.   Every student was warmly attached to him, and "Mac" was the name by which he was generally designated.   As an operator, he was showy, and at times brilliant, yet he lacked the important requisites of a great surgeon—judgment and

1—5

patience. He frequently jumped at conclusions, and was therefore often at fault in his diagnosis. He was the founder of the college, and for a number of years its great pillar. A native of Norwich, Connecticut, and a graduate of Yale College, he came to Philadelphia in 1817, was a pupil of Dr. John Syng Dorsey up to the time of that gentleman's death, and took his degree in 1819 in the University of Pennsylvania. He soon acquired practice, married an amiable and accomplished lady in 1821, and in 1824 obtained a charter from the Legislature of Pennsylvania for the Jefferson Medical College. He died in 1847, in the fifty-first year of his age, after a brief illness, of perforation of the bowel. At the time of his death the Collins Printing House had in hand a portion of the manuscript of a work entitled The Principles and Practice of Surgery, a small volume, issued as a posthumous production under the supervision of his son, the late Dr. John H. B. McClellan. The work proved to be a failure, both in a commercial and professional point of view. The best things in it are its cases, most of which are portrayed by the hand of a master. Early in life he wrote some good reviews, particularly one of Baron Larrey's Surgical Memoirs of Napoleon's Campaigns.

Next to McClellan the most prominent man in the school was Dr. John Eberle, the Professor of Medicine, a short, dark-visaged man, of German descent, a native of Lancaster County, Pennsylvania. He was a bookworm, but an indifferent lecturer. Still he was a good writer, and well versed in medical lore. His lectures were written out in full, and read with little animation or variation of tone. He was an instructive teacher. His great fault was his citation of authorities, and his want of confidence in the statement of his own views. A teacher should be bold and decided in his opinions ; not too positive, but sufficiently so to be authoritative. The student cannot judge for himself. The knowledge that is placed before him must be, so to speak, well digested for him, otherwise it will stagger and bewilder, not instruct him. Eberle was a good writer. His work on Materia Medica and his Practice of Medicine, published before he was forty-five years of age, were able productions, which passed through a number of editions, were widely used as text-books, and gave him an extensive reputation. The Materia Medica received the compliment of a German translation at Weimar. Later in life he published an excellent work on the Diseases and Physical Education of Children. In 1831 he was enticed away from Philadelphia to the Medical College of Ohio, at Cincinnati, where for several years he occupied the chair of Medicine. He finally removed to Lexington, Kentucky, and became professor of that branch in the medical department of Transylvania University. He had made a false step in leaving Philadelphia, where he had some friends and some practice; and, although he received a guarantee in Kentucky of three thousand dollars a year, he did not improve his pecuniary condition materially by the change. He had experienced numerous disappointments, had but little practice, and was pretty well exhausted physically and mentally by the long-continued use of opium, tobacco, and porter. His career at Lexington was brief. He had hardly entered upon his professional duties when he was seized with the illness which in a few weeks destroyed his life, leaving his family helpless, and, in a great degree, destitute. He died February, 1838, in the fifty-first year of his age.

Eberle edited for a number of years the American Medical Recorder. He afterwards became editor of the American Medical Review, a journal issued jointly at first by himself and by George McClellan, and subsequently by Eberle, McClellan, Nathan Smith, of New Haven, and N. R. Smith, of Philadelphia. He contributed liberally to the periodical press, and was one of the most able and caustic medical reviewers the country has ever produced.

His faults as a physician and a man were timidity and indecision. He was an indifferent practitioner except in chronic diseases, with the nature and treatment of which he seemed to me to be well acquainted. The American Medical Review was begun in 1824, and was suspended in 1826, at the close of the third volume, probably for the want of patronage.

Our chemist was an old bachelor, a simple-minded man, not deeply versed in the science which he professed, but an agreeable and instructive lecturer, with a good deal of sophomoric flourish, and a mild, gentlemanly address. Altogether a worse man than "Old Jacky Green," as he was familiarly called by the students, might have occupied his chair.

Barnes, the obstetrician, held his position only one session. Having been weighed in the balance and found wanting, he was placed on the retired list. He was the dullest lecturer that it was my lot ever to hear, destitute of all the attributes of a successful teacher.

William P. C. Barton was a surgeon in the navy, and one of the best botanists of his day in this country. He distinguished himself in early life by his beautiful work, in two volumes, on the Medical Botany of the United States. He was withal a good lecturer, of the conversational order, and an instructive teacher, thoroughly familiar with his subject. In his dress he was very particular, and in his temper a bitter man. During his lectures he often indulged in caustic criticism at the expense of a member of his class, who failed to answer his questions. Zooks, a middle-aged man from Western Pennsylvania, was the special object of the shafts of his sarcasm, much, I am sorry to add, to the merriment of Zooks's fellow-students. Notwithstanding his oddities, I was fond of Barton, and during the latter years of his life a very pleasant correspondence passed between us. He was for several years Chief of the Bureau of Medicine and Surgery of the Navy, and was a man of marked ability. His dislike for Chapman was invincible. He never let an occasion slip without giving him a dig under the fifth rib. One of his estimable daughters became the wife of ex-Judge F. Carroll Brewster, the distinguished jurist.

Benjamin Rush Rhees was a "dapper little fellow," with an amiable disposition and a good deal of pomposity about him. He always read his lectures, but, as he had a good voice and an enthusiastic manner, he was an acceptable though not an instructive teacher. He died young, and left behind him no works to perpetuate his name. His whole life had been a series of struggles. He was a graduate of the University of Pennsylvania, and took an active part in the establishment of the Jefferson Medical College, in which he was the first Professor of the Institutes of Medicine and Medical Jurisprudence. He was a superficial man, with few original ideas and no adequate conception of the importance of the two branches which it was his business to teach. As a man he was popular and highly respected. His lectures were largely copied from Bostock's Physiology and from Fonblanque's and Beck's Medical Jurisprudence.

The school at this time was very unpopular, and many predictions were afloat that its existence would be of short duration. But it went on despite the opposition of its enemies; its friends gradually increased in number and influence, and before it had attained its silver wedding it was one of the most flourishing institutions of medicine in America. I have recently, through the kindness of Professor J. H. Brinton, read an address delivered on the 8th of March, 1825, by Professor Rhees, in which, in eloquent terms, he sets forth the objects of the college, the reasons which prompted its founding, and the determination of its trustees and faculty to build up a school which should be an honor alike to its founders, to the profession, and to the country. The meeting at which this address was delivered was opened with prayer by the venerable president of the college.

Such were the men from whom I imbibed my medical knowledge during the two courses of lectures which I attended. They were perhaps, in the main, as competent instructors as any similar number of teachers in the schools of this country at that period; for, after all, everything depends upon the student himself, his industry, his habits of attention, his culture, and his natural capacity. His knowledge must come chiefly through his own personal exertion. Lectures, however able or erudite, are only aids. They never can make a good physician or a great man out of a dunce.

I studied hard during the sessions of the college as well as during the recesses; I was always punctually in my seat, and never missed a lecture, except during the second winter, when I was confined for two days to my room by an attack of pleurodynia. I worked early and late, and lost no occasion to profit by the opportunities that were afforded me. I was determined to qualify myself well, especially in the practical branches. I was very fond of anatomy and surgery, and therefore made them objects of particular inquiry. During the eighteen months of my connection with McClellan I had witnessed many important operations, and had seen a good deal of medical practice. My mind, too, was well disciplined; I had not only industry, but ambition; my morals and habits were good, and I was a stranger to all amusements. Medicine was the goddess of my idolatry. When, therefore, the time for my examination arrived I had no misgivings in regard to the result. I had planted carefully, and believed that I should ultimately receive the reward of my industry. The thirty-five minutes which I spent in the "Green Room" of my Alma Mater were amongst the happiest of my life, and I could not help giving expression to my feelings in the presence of my assembled teachers. Such, indeed, was my hilarity that McClellan, my private preceptor, who knew me intimately, was induced to ask me afterwards "whether I had not been drinking?"—although he was well aware that I was one of the most temperate of youths, and as sober as a judge on the occasion in question. My examination, I had reason to believe, gave entire satisfaction. The commencement day came; McClellan delivered the address to the graduates, and I was one of twenty-seven who received, at the end of the third session of the college, the honors of the doctorate. My thesis, to the composition of which I had devoted unusual care and labor, was on the Nature and Treatment of Cataract. I had seen many cases of this disorder during my Philadelphia pupilage. It is a subject which, during my prolonged professional life, has deeply interested me.

McClellan, on this as on many other occasions, was not on time. He kept the audience waiting for at least ten minutes, much to the annoyance of President Green, an old man; and when, at length, he made his appearance, he could hardly read his manuscript, so badly was it written. In fact, as I afterwards learned, he had been engaged upon the composition of his address up to the very moment of leaving his house for the college.

After a short visit to my mother at Easton I returned to Philadelphia, which I determined to make my future residence. I accordingly took an office at the corner of Library and Fifth Streets, immediately opposite Independence Square, and announced myself as a candidate for business.

To spend my leisure to the best advantage, I at once began the translation of a work on General Anatomy, hoping by its publication not only to acquire a little reputation, but to obtain means of support, which, ere this, had been quite exhausted. Indeed, I took my office with feelings of great doubt and misgiving, not knowing whether it would be in my power to pay my rent or board. I knew that business in a city like Philadelphia, crowded with professional men of great talent, influence, and experience, must be slow of acquisition, and that I should be most fortunate if I could, for the first three or four years, keep my head above water.

I had determined, long before I finished my course of studies in Jefferson Medical College, to undertake the translation of some French work as soon as I should receive my degree. The one that I had selected was Edwards's Manual of Surgical Anatomy, which I had procured some time previously, and which I had read with great care. A few days before I thought of setting about my task, I found, much to my disappointment, at Carey & Lea's store, a copy of an English edition of the work from the pen of Mr. Coulson, of London. This was soon after republished in Philadelphia with notes by Dr. James Webster, afterwards Professor of Anatomy at Geneva, New York. Thus was my first hope blighted. While I was in doubt what to do next, Dr. Dobson—"Old Judah" as he was styled—placed in my hands a book on General Anatomy, by Bayle and Hollard, of Paris, just fresh from the press. It was well arranged, concise, and apparently adapted to the wants of the profession in this country. Setting vigorously to work, I finished my translation in two months, which, in view of my imperfect knowledge of the French language, my want of intimate knowledge of the subject—for general anatomy was not then systematically taught in any of our schools—and the fact that I had to travel over nearly four hundred pages, was, to say the least, not slow progress. An incident happened near the completion of this, my first, literary effort which deserves brief mention. Messrs. Carey & Lea, at that time the principal publishing house in the city, had agreed to publish my translation, and to pay me two hundred dollars for it. When the work had sufficiently progressed to be put to press I placed some of the sheets in their hands, and during the conversation which ensued incidentally remarked that I should inscribe the translation to my preceptor, Dr. George McClellan. This was enough. In a week the manuscript was returned to me with a note declining the publication. The real cause of its rejection was the fact that the firm was friendly to the University of Pennsylvania, whose Faculty were hostile to Dr. McClellan, the founder of the Jefferson Medical College. Upon stating the circumstance to him, McClellan consulted Mr. John Grigg, since distinguished as a successful and enterprising publisher, who immediately committed the book to the press, on the terms previously offered me by Carey & Lea. The work formed an octavo volume of about three hundred pages, and was well received by the profession, having been adopted as a text-book by several of the schools. I need not say that the translation was a faithful, though not perhaps an elegant one. The edition numbered two thousand copies. A new one was never called for, owing to the fact that the subject had not then attracted much attention, notwithstanding that the great work of Bichat had been translated a number of years previously by Dr. Hayward, of Boston.

The work which I next translated was Hatin's Manual of Obstetrics, a small practical treatise, which I finished in three weeks, and which was also issued by Mr. Grigg, my compensation being seventy-five dollars. An appendix, containing Magendie's celebrated paper on the cephalospinal fluid, translated by my friend Dr. Gardner, a fellow-graduate, was added to secure its sale, which, it was feared, would be seriously injured by the simultaneous appearance of a translation of the same work by a physician of New York. I sent a copy of this little book immediately after its publication with a polite note to the late Dr. Dewees, Professor of Midwifery in the University of Pennsylvania, who, however, took no notice of either. Meeting, soon after, the wife of my first preceptor, Mrs. Swift, Dr. Dewees referred to the subject, and he observed that I might be a clever and promising young man, but that the Faculty of the University could take no notice of anything that emanated from the Jefferson School. I mention this fact simply to show the state of feeling that existed at that time between the two institutions.

My third translation was Hildenbrand on Typhus Fever, a German work of much celebrity in its day. The translation was published by Mr. Bliss, of New York, in the winter of 1829. It was completed in two months, and cost me more hard labor than both the other works. My remuneration was one hundred and seventy-five dollars. I never learned how the book sold, but I fear that it had a limited circulation, owing to the want of interest in the subject on the part of the profession.

Tavernier's Operative Surgery was my next effort. This work was comprised in two octavo volumes of nearly five hundred pages each, and I rendered it into English in less than three months. My rule was always to translate at least from twenty to twenty-five pages a day, whatever might be my other engagements, and it was thus I accomplished so much in so short a time. Mr. Grigg issued the book, and it formed a handsome volume of four hundred closely printed pages. This was the first treatise on operative surgery ever published in the United States. It had an extensive circulation. The work, although wholly a compilation, was well arranged, and is still one of the best books on the subject. Mr. Grigg paid me four hundred dollars for my labors.

Having disposed of these translations, the first and last of the kind I ever attempted, I forthwith commenced the composition of an original work, which was issued by Mr. Grigg in the autumn of 1830 under the title of The Anatomy, Physiology, and Diseases of the Bones and Joints. This work formed an octavo volume of nearly four hundred pages, and was written in the space of little more than three months. The title was unfortunate ; it should have been A Practical Treatise on Fractures and Dislocations, with an Account of the Diseases of the Bones and Joints, which the profession, especially the younger members of it, would have better understood. The work was well received, and two thousand copies were exhausted in less than four years. Notwithstanding this, no other edition was ever issued ; first, because I had no time to bestow upon it the requisite attention, and, secondly, because I had not the experience which was necessary to make the work what it should be. I need hardly add that, young as I was when the book was issued, I had to depend for the facts mainly upon the labors of others, though in the composition of it I used my own language. I have often thought that this work, if entirely rewritten and brought to a level with the existing state of the science, might be rendered useful to the younger members of the profession, to whom the subjects of which it treats are a stumbling-block, and who are so often prosecuted for malpractice in consequence of the mismanagement of cases of fractures and dislocations. For this book I never received a cent of remuneration!

All these works were published in about eighteen months after I took my degree. The different translations and the book on the Bones and Joints formed nearly fifteen hundred pages octavo. In addition to this, I assisted the late Dr. Godman in translating the Duke of Saxe-Weimar's Travels in the United States, published soon afterwards by Carey & Lea. This work was written in German, and I completed about two hundred pages of it in less, I think, than a fortnight.

My practice during this period was, of course, limited ; I went little into society and took hardly any recreation. Depriving myself of pleasure and amusement, I devoted my time to my task, thus literally verifying the saying of the Roman, *Nulla dies sine linea.* I labored day and night under the stimulus both of ambition and of poverty.

The house in which I had my office was kept by a Mrs. Eaton, and was the resort of many well-bred men. Among the boarders were Mrs. Sparhawk, a venerable lady, and her daughter, Miss Eliza, who subsequently married Judge Joel Jones, my former private tutor. In the list of gentlemen was a Mr. Chester, a high-toned man, a lawyer by profession, long since dead ; the Rev. Mr. Brewer, an old retired clergyman, the head of a young ladies' seminary ; "Johnny Vaughan," as he was called, a kind-hearted man, a broken-down merchant, an Englishman by birth, and, at the time referred to, librarian of the American Philosophical Society ; the Spanish consul, whose name I no longer remember ; and Sears Cook Walker, a young man of my own age. Dr. Brown, brother of our minister at the court of France, and the first Professor of Medicine in Transylvania University, at Lexington, Kentucky, was for a short time a boarder in the house ; and, learning that I was engaged in translating a French work on Anatomy, he was kind enough to entertain me occasionally with an account of the more prominent physicians of Paris.

I do not know that I have ever seen a more beautiful type of a man than Dr. Brown. He had a large head and a magnificent physique, and in his manners and address was a thorough gentleman. With a mind well stored with knowledge, added to wealth and leisure, he still failed to achieve reputation as a teacher, writer, or practitioner. Mr. Vaughan was a great talker, and possessed a large fund of interesting information. One of his habits was to pick up an acquaintance whenever he could and bring him to dinner. It was on one of these occasions that he brought in Dr. John D. Godman, the anatomist, naturalist, and author, whom I was happy to find seated next to myself at table. I had heard much of Godman, but, until now, had never seen him. My feelings were at once deeply interested. I saw before me a thin, frail, sickly-looking man, about the medium height, with a pallid face, black hair and eyes, long lashes, heavy brow, and a clear, sonorous voice, interrupted at intervals by a hacking cough, only too surely denotive of the existence of the relentless disease which, ere long, consigned him to an early grave. His countenance wore an expression of deep melancholy, which it was distressing to behold. In his conversation there was nothing unusual either in manner or matter ; it was commonplace. I noticed particularly his dress : his coat, once black, was much worn, and torn at the elbow ; his hat was decidedly shabby ; and his shoes had evidently not been brushed that morning. Altogether the picture was a sad one, so sad as to make an impression upon my mind which has never been effaced. Godman was poor all his life. At the age of two years he lost his mother, and, as we are informed by one of his biographers, he soon after became fatherless, friendless, homeless. Poverty literally pursued him from the cradle to the grave. "I have," he once exclaimed to a friend, "eaten the bread of sorrow and drunk the cup of misery." Gifted beyond most of his professional contemporaries, he failed in almost everything in which he was engaged. With great powers as an anatomical teacher, he attracted large but unremunerative classes, and the two medical schools with which he was for a time connected yielded him no substantial emoluments. As an operator he was a failure. At Cincinnati, in the Medical College of Ohio, in which he held for a short time the chair of Surgery, he lithotomized a man, but was unable to extract the stone. The poor fellow, it is said, walked afterwards all the way to Philadelphia, where he was relieved of his burden by Professor Gibson, of the University of Pennsylvania. At New York, in Rutgers Medical College, in which he occupied the chair of Anatomy, his health soon broke down, and he was obliged to seek recreation and renewed life in the West Indies some weeks before the close of the first session. The school, in which he had for his colleagues such men as Hosack, Mott, Francis, and Macneven, was not remunerative, and, what was worse, its doors were soon permanently closed by the courts of New York on account of some illegality in its charter. On his return from the West Indies, Godman took up his residence at Germantown, and henceforth devoted himself exclusively to literary pursuits, which, however, afforded him and his family but a scanty subsistence. For eighteen months he performed daily an astonishing amount of work, breathing, as he did, all this time with but one lung, the other having been destroyed by tubercles. When at length the hour of his departure arrived he was nothing but a skeleton. Such a life was a life of true heroism, of sublime self-sacrifice. It was during these latter days that I became more intimately acquainted with him, calling occasionally at his residence and dining with him several times in town. Among his last labors was a translation of Levasseur's Account of Lafayette's Tour through the United States, and of the Travels of the Duke of Saxe-Weimar. The latter was a German work, in which, as I have before said, I rendered him important assistance. He died in April, 1830, in the thirty-seventh year of his age.

Godman wrote well and constantly. He was a prolific contributor to the medical press, was for a while editor of the Philadelphia Journal of the Medical Sciences, and prepared the articles on Zoology for the Encyclopædia Americana. His work on American Natural History is well known ; and his Rambles of a Naturalist has had many admirers on account of the beauty and fascination of its style. Notwithstanding the deficiencies of his early education, he was an excellent linguist, a good scholar, and a polished writer. Annapolis is entitled to the honor of his nativity.

Of Mr. Sears C. Walker I saw a great deal while in the society of these people. He was within a few months of my own age, somewhat above the middle height, with light hair, eyes, and complexion. He was timid and reticent, eschewing ladies' society, and keeping aloof from nearly all in the house. He would, now and then, enter my office, but his visits were always brief, and he rarely seemed to be at his ease. He was connected with a classical seminary, and spent all his leisure in the study of mathematics, for which he had great fondness. To a common observer he presented all the characteristics of an abstractionist—of a man who lived within himself and for himself only. The social world afforded him no enjoyment; he felt like one who had no time to throw away upon ordinary mortals. As he grew older, as his mind became more expanded, he became dissatisfied with the routine of a teacher in a classical school, and panted for a wider field. The study of astronomy had long been a passion with him, and to this he now devoted most of his time. His first scientific labor was the construction of a set of parallactic tables, in 1834, adapted to the latitude of Philadelphia. Soon after, he published in the Memoirs of the American Philosophical Society an elaborate series of original observations on occultations. In 1837 he prepared a plan for the organization of the observatory of the Philadelphia High School; and eight years later he took charge, at the instance of Mr. Bancroft, then Secretary of the Navy, of the observatory at Washington. From this time on his career was a series of triumphs in astronomical observations, in coast surveys, and in researches to determine the differences of longitude by telegraph and other means. That a brain so arduously and incessantly engaged in scientific investigations requiring the highest order of intellect should wear out prematurely is not surprising. In 1851 he had a slight paralytic seizure, evidently due to softening of the brain. As he strenuously persisted in his labors, this was soon followed by mental alienation, which continued up to the time of his death, in 1853. Thus perished, at the early age of forty-eight, one of the brightest intellects of the age, an ardent devotee of science, and a great mathematician and astronomer. Walker was a native of Wilmington, a small town in Sussex County, Massachusetts. He was born in 1805. From my early knowledge of him, of his remarkable diffidence and reticence, and of his retired habits, almost amounting to solitude, I had no idea that he would live to become so shining a light in the world of science. He was never married; he had no fancy for the society of women. He would much rather contemplate Venus in the heavens than Venus in petticoats.

The income from my practice during the first year did not exceed three hundred dollars, if, indeed, it reached that sum. My patrimony was exhausted, and I had, unfortunately, to pay heavy board and office rent. Under these circumstances I had no business to marry, and yet, the following winter, I did marry. Left a widow at the age of twenty with one child, my wife was quite as poor as myself. We were greatly in love with each other, and as we could not brook separation any longer we consummated an engagement which had existed upwards of a year. Of course we were foolish, very foolish; but how could we help it? Poor people had often married before, and they had contrived to live and to thrive, and why should not we? We economized as much as we could, but it was up-hill work; and, after a vain struggle of eighteen months, we left the city, with sad hearts and tearful eyes, for Easton, where I soon acquired a respectable share of practice, the income from which enabled me to keep my head above water, although, for a while, not without difficulty. Gradually, however, I got into good business, and when I left, two years and a half afterwards, in October, 1833, for Cincinnati, I was generally regarded as a scientific practitioner. I soon made myself known as a hard-working, industrious student.

I spent all my leisure among my books, and attended with great assiduity alike the poor and the rich. To keep up and extend my knowledge of practical anatomy, I erected at the foot of my garden, directly in front of a hotel, a little building as a dissecting-room, and obtained a subject from Philadelphia, going there myself in a buggy for the purpose. I dissected generally several hours a day as long as my material lasted, doing the work with great care and neatness, and performing at the same time the more important operations unmolested. I obtained in this way a great deal of information, and, as I was anxious to impress my knowledge thoroughly upon my mind, it was my habit every evening to write out an account of my daily examinations. All my leisure during the summer months was spent upon the composition of a work on Descriptive Anatomy, which, however, I never entirely completed. I have still in my possession the manuscript of it. A few months more would have enabled me to finish it, but other business prevented, and I have not been sorry that it was never published. I am aware of no prior effort in the English language to change the nomenclature of anatomy from Latin into English, a plan which, at my suggestion, was adopted by my pupil, Dr. T. G. Richardson, now Professor of Surgery in the University of Louisiana, New Orleans, in his work on Anatomy, and subsequently by Professor Leidy, of the University of Pennsylvania, in his text-book on Anatomy. Among the French and German writers this peculiarity of nomenclature has been in use for at least two centuries.

I had an ardent desire in my professional youth to become an experimentalist, both with a view of throwing light upon certain obscure points in physiology, and of earning some reputation. My earliest inquiries were directed to the investigation of the temperature and coagulation of the blood, topics which, although they had received considerable attention, were in need of further

examination. Hewson and Thackara, of England, had
both written upon the subject; I had read their works,
and noticed their defects. A large field was spread out
before me; and if I had not been obliged to earn my
bread by my daily labor, which necessarily distracted my
attention, I might have earned substantial reputation
in this branch of study. As it was, I worked hard,
with little benefit. The coagulation of the blood interested me very much, and I frequently visited the slaughter-
houses in Philadelphia to examine this process in the ox,
sheep, and hog. Venesection was then a very fashionable practice, and I lost no opportunity of making experiments upon the temperature and coagulation of the
blood of the human subject in health and in disease.
These investigations extended through several years, and
resulted in some satisfactory conclusions, which, I now
regret, were never published. I not only verified the
observations of Hewson and Thackara, but I struck out
into untrodden paths. After I left Philadelphia I made
a series of observations upon the temperature of venous
blood—altogether fifty in number—mostly of healthy persons, and found it, on an average, to be 96° of Fahrenheit,
the maximum being 104°, and the minimum 92°. In
books on physiology the average temperature of the blood
is usually stated at 98°, which, I am sure, is entirely too
high. The results of these observations were published at
Cincinnati, in 1835, in the second volume of the Western
Medical Gazette.

I noticed in these observations a singular phenomenon,
then, if not still, unknown, that, if the arm be tied firmly
for five or six minutes before opening the vein, the temperature of the blood which flows during the first half
minute or so will be several degrees lower than the temperature of that which issues subsequently. In this experiment the blood necessarily remains stationary in the
superficial veins, and its diminished temperature is, no

doubt, owing to the want of the friction which it experiences in its circulation, as well, perhaps, as to the partial interruption of the nervous fluid caused by the pressure of the fillet.

My next experiments were made upon excretion to ascertain the rapid transit of certain articles, when taken into the stomach, through the blood by the kidneys. For this purpose I selected rabbits, to which, after having tied both renal arteries, I administered protoxide of iron. The animals were generally killed within fifteen to thirty minutes, and in every instance, upon applying to the urine in the bladder, ureters, and kidneys, a solution of cyanide of potassium—a most delicate test—well-marked traces of iron were found in that fluid. My confrères, who remember the doctrine of solidism, so dominant in the schools in our younger days, will see that these investigations were not without their significance. Taken in connection with experiments made with other articles, they went to show how readily substances introduced into the stomach find their way into the circulation, to be afterwards eliminated by the kidneys and other emunctories. Solidism, long since exploded, assumed that all impressions upon the human system in health and disease were made through the organs and tissues, and that the blood was, so to speak, a mere passive fluid, designed, to be sure, to nourish the body, but incapable of receiving or conveying the germs of disease.

Another experiment, which interested me very much, was one which had been performed some time previously by Gendrin, an eminent French pathologist, who, in 1826, published a great work, in two volumes, on inflammation. This experiment was nothing more nor less than the inoculation of a cat with the virus of smallpox, taken from a young man whom I was then treating for a severe attack of this disgusting disease. The object was to ascertain whether, as the French writer had asserted, variola could be produced in this manner in an inferior animal. I performed this experiment, not without some misgivings, in my office, soon after my marriage, and as the cat was not the most pliant of subjects, but disposed to protect its rights, I had no little difficulty in accomplishing my purpose. However, after a good deal of exertion, and some scratches imprinted upon my fingers, I succeeded in inserting a considerable quantity of fresh virus in its neck. The animal was now replaced in the box and carefully watched. Apart from some suppuration, such as so often follows upon wounds, simple and complicated, no effects resulted; and in a few days, apparently without any constitutional disturbance, my feline patient was set at liberty. I did not repeat the experiment.

My experiments upon wounds of the intestines occupied me more than two years, and involved the sacrifice of upwards of seventy dogs. An account of them will be found in the Western Journal of Medicine and Surgery for 1842–'43. It was afterwards published in book form. Nearly the whole edition of the work was lost in a fire which destroyed the printing-office. The book was favorably spoken of in the medical journals, especially in the British and Foreign Medical Review, edited by Dr. John Forbes, of London, which contained an elaborate and critical notice of it.

During my residence at Easton, in 1833, I served several times as an expert in important trials, and, on one occasion, as the chief medical witness. The case was that of Goetter, a man who had killed, by manual strangulation in the eighth month of her pregnancy, a woman whom he had seduced. I made the post-mortem examination, but neglected to open the skull, and on this account I was subjected to a good deal of annoyance during the trial, as the defence partly rested upon the ground that the woman had died of apoplexy. It was evident, however, from the marks upon her neck and the condition of the face and lungs that she had died from asphyxia, and I gave my testimony ac-

cordingly. The man was convicted solely upon circum-
stantial evidence; but the day before his execution he confessed that he had choked the woman to death with his
hand. To throw light upon this mode of death, I performed
twelve experiments upon inferior animals, principally rabbits, and carefully noted the results, which were afterwards
published in the Western Journal of Medicine, edited by
Dr. Daniel Drake, under the title of Observations on
Manual Strangulation. An outline of these experiments
and of the Goetter case will be found in a note in Beck's
Medical Jurisprudence.

The Goetter trial constituted, I have always thought,
the most important event of my professional life at Easton.
It attracted great attention, not only on account of the
atrocity of the murder, but of the ability of the counsel
engaged in conducting the defence, the master spirit being
the late James Madison Porter, a shrewd and accomplished
lawyer, celebrated for his dexterity as an examiner of witnesses, which, combined with a certain amount of impudence, caused him to be greatly feared. Besides all this,
he was an able advocate. My examination lasted the
best part of a day, and, as I had thoroughly prepared myself at every point, my testimony was received with much
respect by the court and jury. An attempt to invalidate
some of my conclusions by bringing in several physicians
as experts failed to make any adverse impression.

Mr. Porter at the time adverted to was in the prime and
vigor of life, and in the enjoyment of a better practice than
any other member of the Easton bar. It was several years
before this event that he founded Lafayette College, originally a manual labor institution, with the late Rev. George
Junkin at its head. The college building, a rented farm-
house, was situated in South Easton, and was provided
with shops and machinery for the benefit of the students,
most of whom literally supported themselves by the sweat
of their brow; board and lodging being furnished them at

a low price. The establishment made slow progress, and no one who then watched it would have supposed that out of its loins would spring the flourishing institution now widely known as Lafayette College. Dr. Junkin was an unpopular officer, a Presbyterian preacher of the "Old School," and a man who, as he walked along, never took his eyes off the ground, being evidently lost in deep thought, and, consequently, in no condition to notice any one—student, friend, or citizen. Of native kindness he had an abundance ; he was a good disciplinarian, and was regarded by many as a strong man in the pulpit for his argumentative powers and the depth of his reasoning. His sermons, however, were always very long, and therefore unpopular, especially with young persons.

Soon after the organization of the college I was surprised one day to receive a notice of my election to the chair of Chemistry. Upon inquiry as to what my duties would be, I was informed that they would for the present be merely nominal. I therefore considered myself as perfectly safe in accepting the position, which I should probably not have done had the reverse been the case, as I had never made chemistry a special study. This chair, since the reorganization of the college, has been very creditably filled by Dr. Traill Green, a native of Easton, who, like myself, was a private pupil of the late Dr. Joseph K. Swift of that town. Mr. Porter, the president of the college, was a man of great enterprise, and deeply interested in the prosperity and development of Easton and its vicinity. He took an active part in the building of the Delaware Division of the Pennsylvania Canal and subsequently in that of the Delaware and Morris Canal in New Jersey. When Mr. Tyler became President, he was offered a seat in his cabinet as Secretary of War, but he was not confirmed by the Senate. Late in life he was struck down by apoplexy, under the effects of which he finally succumbed. Some time after the first attack, which left him with partial hemiplegia and somewhat impaired mental powers, he wrote me a long letter, begging me to use any influence I might have in procuring him the chair of Medical Jurisprudence in the Jefferson Medical College; but as there was no provision for such an office the matter of course fell through. I learned subsequently that he was in straitened circumstances, and this was probably the reason of his desire to be made a professor.

Andrew Reeder, one of my most intimate and valued friends, was one of the rising members of the Easton bar at the time of my departure to the West. We had known each other for many years, and had been classmates at the Lawrenceville High School, New Jersey. His education was respectable; and he possessed more than ordinary talents and legal acumen, united with great industry and ambition, and a high sense of honor. He was a warm, active Democrat, and was for some time Governor of Kansas, an appointment bestowed upon him by President Pierce. I was then a resident of Kentucky, and upon hearing of his good luck lost no time in sending him a letter of congratulation. Strange things happen. While Governor of Kansas his path was crossed by Dr. William A. Hammond, of the United States Army, afterwards for some time Surgeon-General in the war of the Rebellion. When Hammond got into difficulty with Secretary Stanton —a difficulty which finally led to his dismissal—Andrew Reeder was employed to collect testimony in this city by the examination of witnesses against the late Surgeon-General, and I never saw a man who entered more eagerly upon the discharge of the duties of his office. His object was to revenge himself upon his Kansas enemy, and how he acquitted himself the result only too clearly showed. I was anxious, as the friend of both, that he should be merciful, and even throw up the appointment, but to this he lent a deaf car.

The fate of Andrew Reeder, as Governor of Kansas, is

well known. Unwilling to sacrifice his self-respect at the
demands of the border ruffians, and in constant conflict
with the legislature of the State, which moved about
from one place to another, and whose illegal acts he was
compelled to veto, he was succeeded by Wilson Shannon,
ex-Governor of Ohio. My friend's life was finally imper-
illed, and he was compelled to seek safety in flight in the
disguise of a common laborer. Reeder was born near
Trenton, New Jersey, and died in 1864, leaving behind
him the reputation of an honest citizen and a good man.

The most illustrious member the Easton bar has ever
had was the Hon. Samuel Sitgreaves, a gentleman of high
social and professional standing, and for some years minister under John Adams's administration at the Court of
St. James. He was a man of fine literary taste, of great
intelligence and refinement, an extensive reader, a great
lawyer, and the possessor of a large library. He was not
popular with the people among whom he lived, as he was
too great an aristocrat to be estimated by them at his real
worth. He died at an advanced age. He was a tall, ele-
gant-looking man, with a noble presence, such as would
have attracted attention anywhere.

The medical profession of Easton at the period in question was in a decidedly mediocre condition, without science,
without learning, without progress, and apparently without ambition. Every man seemed to live in and for
himself. Hardly any two could be found willing to meet
each other in consultation. Jealousy and ill-feeling were
the order of the day. Each physician had of course his
little clique or faction. This poor fellow had this fault,
and that one that. But upon one thing all were agreed:
they all bled, all gave emetics, all purged, all starved
their patients. They were all real Sangrados, mowing
down alike the infant, the youth, the adult, and the
old man. Tartrate of antimony and potassium was the
favorite emetic, calomel and jalap the accepted cathartic,

and water-gruel or panada the common fever diet. Very few of them ever read a medical book; and, as to social intercourse, that was of course wholly out of the question under the circumstances. The remuneration for professional services was contemptible in the extreme. For a visit in town the ordinary charge was fifty cents, and double that sum for a ride into the country. Bleeding and extraction of teeth, at that time very common operations, generally commanded twelve and a half cents each! Every physician put up his own prescriptions. Swift, my first preceptor, was unpopular in his manners, and possessed, as he imagined, of a preëmption right to the best practice in the place; but the truth is, his practice was limited, and he made but little headway, even in his best days, in securing the confidence of the public. His early life was unproductive, and the last twenty years or more were spent in suffering, caused by epithelial cancer of the face, from the effects of which he finally died. During nearly all this time he was confined to his house, unable to attend to practice, and the consequence was that poverty was superadded to ill health. I can imagine no fate, no destiny, more sad than this. With all his faults— perhaps I should rather say defects—Swift had many excellent qualities; he was undoubtedly a man of brains, with a clear intellect, and a lofty sense of the dignity of his profession. As previously mentioned he had a choice collection of minerals, now in the possession of Lafayette College; but he never cultivated mineralogy or geology as a science. Mrs. Swift, who wrote some pretty poetry, and was a contributor to some of the magazines of the day, survived her husband several years. They were both great readers of light literature; and early in life their little house was the resort of most of the prominent strangers who visited Easton on business or pleasure.

In the summer of 1832 the Asiatic cholera appeared, for the first time on the American continent, in Canada, and then in New York. Early in July it broke out with great violence in New York City, producing much consternation among its inhabitants, as well as everywhere else in the Atlantic States. Easton, only eighty miles off, participated in the alarm, and at a meeting of the town council, held on the 19th of July, 1832, I was appointed to visit New York for the purpose of investigating the disease and conferring with the medical gentlemen of that city upon the most approved mode of treating it; and I was requested to report such other matters connected with the subject as might be of benefit to the citizens of Easton in averting the epidemic, or which might have a tendency to lessen its malignity, should it unfortunately appear in that town.

In compliance with this injunction, I soon after visited New York, arriving there just in time to witness the disease in all its horrors. In fact, it had just attained its height; for, upon the day of my arrival, the 29th of the month, it had destroyed not fewer than three hundred and eighty-five persons—an enormous mortality, considering the comparatively small size of the population, and the fact that great numbers of people had fled the city to escape the pestilence. During my sojourn, which lasted nearly a week, I visited all the cholera hospitals and witnessed the treatment pursued in them by the professional attendants. I also conversed with some of the most distinguished physicians of the city respecting the nature and treatment of the disease and the best mode of averting it. Little, however, was learned in this manner. No one seemed to have definite notions upon any of these points. Empiricism reigned with unlimited sway. Every hospital had its peculiar formulæ; every physician his peculiar views. At the Greenwich Street Hospital, one of the largest and best-ordered establishments of the kind in the city, the attendants, Drs. Roe and Lee, relied mainly upon emunctions of mercurial and capsicum ointment, with calomel, camphor, and capsicum internally. The whole body of the patient was incased in a thick layer of this ointment, and numerous persons whose duty it was to apply it were at hand. From all I could learn this mode of treatment was more successful than any other at the time in vogue. Dr. Roe was an oddity. He appeared to have an idea that the best preventive of the disease was the maintenance of a copious perspiration, and he accordingly constantly wore, buttoned up to the chin, a thick drab-colored overcoat, although the thermometer at the time stood generally at from 94° to 98° in the shade. He seemed, however, to flourish under this load of clothing, for he never had an attack of the disease. I was told that he was a most worthy and intelligent man. He afterwards enjoyed a large private practice, and died very suddenly only a few years ago of disease of the heart. His colleague, Dr. Charles Lee, survived him, and was well known as an able writer and distinguished lecturer, being connected at one time with at least four medical schools. I need not add that most of the patients who recovered under this mercurial treatment were horribly salivated.

What struck me as remarkable in cholera patients at this time, and what I never witnessed afterwards in this disease to the same extent, was the extraordinary spasmodic twitching of the voluntary muscles after death, by which the body was frequently thrown into violent contortions. The features were not so much disturbed as the limbs, especially the legs, which were in numerous instances thrown about in different directions, literally kicking the air and everything else coming within their reach.

After having spent nearly a week in this city of charnel-houses, in constant attendance upon my duties, I left for my home, and in a few days after published a report of my investigations. The paper, which occupied several columns of the Easton Argus, presented a plain unvarnished statement of what I had seen and done, without any attempt to unravel the nature and causes of the epidemic, or to indicate the best means, except a proper observance of the laws of hygiene, of preventing its dissemination. Of the medical treatment, of which I had learned nothing that was at all satisfactory, very little was said. The town council paid me one hundred dollars for my services; a considerable portion of which I spent in the necessary expenses of the journey.

CHAPTER III.

In the spring of 1833 I wrote to Dr. Eberle, one of my
old college preceptors, then a professor in the Medical College of Ohio, at Cincinnati, saying that I should be happy
to obtain the place of Demonstrator of Anatomy in that
institution, adding that I was anxious to qualify myself as a teacher of anatomy, and that I was only waiting for an opportunity to enter upon my labors.   The
mail soon brought me a letter from the good man, who
said that he would lay the matter before his colleagues,
and expressed the belief that he could be instrumental in
serving me.   The result was that I was soon appointed
to the position in question, and in October, 1833, I
accordingly removed to the Queen of the West, as Cincinnati was then called.   My family at this time consisted of four members, including two little children, my
stepson and one of my own sons having died some time
previously of scarlet fever.   The journey, which was
tedious, and was performed partly by stage, partly by
canal, and partly by steamboat, occupied a little up-

wards of thirteen days. The evening before my departure I counted my money, and found in my purse the enormous sum of two hundred and thirty-seven dollars! Of this, more than one hundred dollars were left on the wayside. With the remainder I commenced life in Cincinnati, "a stranger in a strange land;" for Eberle, and Mitchell the dean of the college, were my only acquaintances. I took three letters of introduction to men of influence in Cincinnati. Of these I delivered two; but, as they received no attention, I never delivered the other, addressed to a gentleman who afterwards attained eminence in the world as an astronomer, and who became a general in the Union army—Professor Ormsby M. Mitchel. After this I never, except on one occasion, accepted a letter of introduction to any one, having independence enough to rely upon my own resources and address for advancement in my profession. I, however, soon carved my own way; I was popular in my new office of demonstrator; went to housekeeping early in the following spring, and rapidly acquired practice—the proceeds by the end of the first year amounting nearly to fifteen hundred dollars, which sum, added to my college receipts, was quite sufficient for my support, and satisfied me that I had done wisely in making the West my home.

A little incident occurred soon after my arrival at Cincinnati which, at the time, caused me considerable annoyance. I had hardly entered upon the discharge of my official duties, when, early one morning, Dr. Mitchell called at my lodgings and asked me whether I had seen a certain article in reference to myself in the Cincinnati Gazette, adding that the Professor of Anatomy had taken umbrage at it, and that, in consultation with some of his colleagues, they had come to the conclusion that it would be best, at all events for the present winter, that I should not lecture in the amphitheatre, as had been agreed upon when I accepted the office of Demonstrator of Anatomy.

Upon inquiring what the offensive article was, for I had
neither seen it nor heard of it, he informed me that it was
a complimentary notice of myself, in which the writer con-
gratulated the Medical College of Ohio upon its acquisition
of so able an anatomist—a kind of puff, intended, as the
Professor of Anatomy, naturally a very jealous man, supposed, to be a reflection upon his own ability as a teacher.
It required no consideration as to what I should do on the
occasion. I therefore at once said, "If the Faculty debar
me from lecturing in connection with practical anatomy,
as had been stipulated, my only course is to withdraw
from the school and get along as best I may. My object
in emigrating to the West," I continued, "was to qualify
myself for teaching anatomy, and if this privilege be
denied me I shall be sadly disappointed." Mitchell there-
upon went away, but returned the same afternoon, saying
that the Faculty had decided to fit up for me a lecture-
room in the attic of the college, close to the dissecting-
room. This was accordingly done, and I now began
in earnest to organize the department, which, up to
that time, had been shamefully neglected; for upon my
arrival at Cincinnati I found everything in the department of practical anatomy in the college in the most miserable condition. There was not a table, not a water-
tank, not a bench, not a wash-basin in the room; in short,
nothing that denoted that any dissections had ever been
carried on within its walls. Some students had already
assembled, and the session was to open in a few days. No
time was to be lost. Everything was to be done, and
done promptly. Carpenters were at once procured, and
in less than a week my room had quite a furnished
appearance. Out of about eighty-six students, my class
numbered nearly sixty. I gave regularly three lectures
a week, chiefly on surgical and visceral anatomy, kept
the rooms well supplied with subjects, and thus laid the
foundation of the study of practical anatomy, up to that

time a nominal matter in the Western States. In the spring and autumn I delivered private courses to small classes, earning little money, but heaping up valuable knowledge, and acquiring some reputation as a zealous anatomist and as a respectable lecturer.

I may here remark that in one of these private courses my class numbered five students and a half. I say half, because one of the young gentlemen, under some pretence or other, although very desirous of attending my course, could not, he said, be always present, and I therefore admitted him at half price, my ticket being ten dollars.

The summer after my removal to Cincinnati I became joint editor, with Dr. Eberle, Dr. Alban G. Smith, and Dr. Gamaliel Bailey, of the Western Medical Gazette, an arrangement which continued in force until my retirement from the school in the summer of 1835. During my connection with this journal I furnished an elaborate paper on Intra-Uterine Respiration in its Relation to Infanticide, an account of several surgical cases, and several reviews, among others one of Dr. William Beaumont's treatise on the Functions of Digestion. These were the first papers which I ever prepared for any medical journal. They were well received.

I remained in the Medical College of Ohio only two sessions. I did not like my situation. The Faculty was especially a weak one, composed, for the most part, of selfish, narrow-minded men, with moderate scientific attainments, and little ability as teachers. I could not forget the illiberal conduct which had sent me to the garret instead of affording me free access to the amphitheatre. The writer who had fired the squib in the Gazette knew his man; and, although I had reason to believe that he had no wish to annoy me, he unwittingly did me a positive injury.

In 1835 the Medical Department of the Cincinnati College was organized, with a chair of Pathological Anatomy, to which I was unanimously appointed by the trustees. My colleagues were Drs. Daniel Drake, the founder of the school, Joseph Nash McDowell, Landon C. Rives, John P. Harrison, Horatio G. Jameson, and James B. Rogers, nearly all men of brains, energy, and laudable ambition, with a full appreciation of their positions as professors in a new and rival institution. Jameson and Rogers were brought from Baltimore under a guarantee each of fifteen hundred dollars. At the end of the first session Jameson, having failed to give satisfaction, returned to Baltimore, and Dr. Willard Parker succeeded him in the chair of Surgery.

The school continued in operation until 1839, when it was disbanded, Parker having accepted the chair of Surgery in the College of Physicians and Surgeons of New York, and Drake that of Pathological Anatomy and Clinical Medicine in the Louisville Medical Institute, better known afterwards as the University of Louisville. The class during the last session of the college numbered, if I mistake not, one hundred and fourteen, and the school was destined, if its career had not thus been unexpectedly arrested, soon to outstrip the Medical College of Ohio, as it had a far abler Faculty. The event did not disappoint me, for, notwithstanding we had a respectable class, and had made fair progress, the enterprise barely paid, and as we had lost two of our best men it would have been difficult to carry on the institution.

The downfall of the Cincinnati College was, as I now view it, a fortunate circumstance for me. It left me, in 1839, free to devote myself to my practice, which had already become large and lucrative. The retirement of Dr. Drake caused angry remarks on the part of certain members of the Faculty, chief of whom was McDowell, his brother-in-law. Drake knew how difficult it would be to build up a great school in the existing state of affairs, and the offer received from Louisville, with the promise of rapid reward, was too tempting to be resisted. He was poor, had had numerous reverses, and needed assistance. Besides, he had lost nearly all his practice, and was not likely to regain it if he should remain in Cincinnati. The retirement of Parker could not be immediately remedied.

Some errors were committed in the original organization of the college. It was without funds, even without a suitable edifice; and there was not a member of the Faculty who had a hundred dollars lying idle in bank. Upon five of us devolved all the expenses of the outfit for a successful course of lectures, besides the guarantee of the two professors above named. The whole scheme looked like an attempt to roll logs up a steep hill. One great mistake was the appointment of Dr. Jameson to so important a chair as Surgery. He had been a signal failure as a teacher of surgery in the Washington Medical College at Baltimore, and was superannuated when he was invited to Cincinnati. Any fire he ever might have had had long been extinguished. He was too unsympathetic to please the student; too old to acquire practice. He felt the loneliness of his situation, and was glad, on the offer of a thousand dollars, to return to Baltimore. In his earlier days he was not without some merit; he was a bold surgeon, and performed some creditable operations. As a teacher he was a sad failure, and he should have had sense enough never to venture into a Western lecture-room in the presence of such a man as Daniel Drake and some of his colleagues. Jameson was the founder of the Maryland Medical Recorder, and he wielded a caustic pen as a reviewer, although he could lay no claim to the character of an elegant writer. His journal perished before he set out for Cincinnati. After his retirement from his chair, he spent the remainder of his days in indigence and obscurity.

James B. Rogers, our other imported colleague, was unlike his fellow-townsman; indeed, the very opposite, for he was a brilliant teacher, and decidedly the most excellent lecturer on chemistry I have ever listened to. I do not except from this eulogy, so justly merited, even his brother, Robert E. Rogers, so well known for a third of a century as an eloquent expounder of the same branch of science, and for a number of years my honored colleague in the Jefferson Medical College. Rogers belonged to an extraordinary family of scientists. The father, a Scotch-Irish gentleman, came to this country near the close of the last century, graduated in medicine, in 1802, in the University of Pennsylvania, and was Professor of Natural Philosophy and Chemistry in William and Mary College, at Williamsburg, Virginia, from 1819 until his death in 1828. Had he lived a third of a century longer, he would have had cause to be proud of his four sons, every one of whom made his mark in the study of the natural sciences, especially chemistry and geology.

After he left Cincinnati James removed to Philadelphia, where he engaged as a private teacher of chemistry, besides lecturing for a number of years on that branch in Chapman's Medical Institute, and assisting his brother, Professor Henry D. Rogers, in his geological surveys of Pennsylvania and Virginia. He also occupied, for a short time, the chair of Chemistry in the Franklin College of this city; but the crowning glory of his life was the chair of Chemistry conferred upon him, in 1847, on the retirement of the great Professor Hare, in the University of Pennsylvania. He had hitherto met with nothing but crosses and rebuffs, a victim of the *res angusta domi.* A bright future seemed to be dawning on him. This, however, was destined to be of short duration. The deleterious gases of the laboratory, preying upon a constitution naturally delicate, had long been undermining his health, and were now gradually sapping the foundations of life. After a connection of five years with this great school he closed his mortal career in 1852. He left no legacy for his family except an honored name.

Henry D. Rogers, after having earned a great reputation as a scientist, spent the evening of his life in Glasgow as Regius Professor of Natural History in the University of that city. His geological and palæontological researches and his various writings made him widely known in both hemispheres, and his death, in 1866, was everywhere much regretted.

Professor William B. Rogers, after having occupied several scientific positions in Maryland and Virginia, removed to Boston in 1853, where he assisted in founding the Massachusetts Institute of Technology, of which he was the first President. He was the author of a number of scientific treatises, and President, in 1875, of the American Association for the Advancement of Science. His death took place suddenly, while he was in the act of distributing the prizes on commencement day to the students of the Institute of Technology.

Professor Robert E. Rogers, the sole survivor of this remarkable family, is still actively engaged in the discharge of the duties of his chair in my Alma Mater. The only family that presents any parallel to this in this country was that of the Becks, mentioned elsewhere.

A circumstance of a personal nature connected with my early colleague I must not omit to refer to here, inasmuch as it serves to show the importance of preserving letters, too often destroyed almost the moment they are received. I have already stated that Rogers came to us under a guarantee for three years, pledged to him by five members of the Faculty. When the school was disbanded, my share amounted to three hundred dollars, which I liquidated by check drawn on Philadelphia in 1841, soon after my removal to Louisville. Six years after this, what was my surprise when, one day, I received a letter from him kindly reminding me of my supposed indebtedness. Assured that the obligation, principal and interest, had been discharged long ago, I promptly consulted my well-filled bag of letters in the attic of my house, and there, after an elaborate and fatiguing search, found the desired voucher in the handwriting of my excellent friend, whose memory had for once proved treacherous. A more honest man, and, I may add, a more amiable one, than James B. Rogers never breathed.

Dr. John P. Harrison was, if I mistake not, a native of Kentucky. He had made all his arrangements to move to Philadelphia when, as he was on his way to that city, he was offered the chair of Materia Medica and Therapeutics in our infant school. He had culture, with enthusiasm and earnestness in the lecture-room, and was popular with the students; but he was essentially a weak man, an imitator, as a writer and lecturer, of the inelegant styles of Caldwell and Chapman, and, like them, a hide-bound solidist—men who did not think it possible for the blood to be endowed with the slightest vitality. It is difficult now to conceive that there existed physicians so recently who could have believed in such absurdity. After the dissolution of our school he accepted the corresponding chair in the Medical College of Ohio, and wrote a work on Materia Medica and Therapeutics, which fell, as he might have supposed it would, stillborn from the press.

Our Professor of Midwifery was Landon C. Rives, a gentleman of education and refinement, a native of Virginia, and the brother of William C. Rives, at one time minister at the court of France. He discharged well the duties of his chair, was popular, and commanded general respect by the gentleness and urbanity of his manners. He had but one fault; he lacked industry, a gift so valuable in a teacher. He disliked writing, and never made an attempt at authorship. The Medical College of Ohio was glad to secure his services as Professor of Obstetrics after the downfall of our bantling. I was warmly attached to

Rives, and we remained devoted friends up to the time of his death. Of Drake and Parker mention will be made in due time in connection with various labors.

McDowell was an eloquent and enthusiastic teacher of anatomy; he had a remarkable gift of speech, and could entertain and amuse his class in a wonderful degree. He never hesitated to go out of his way to abuse a professor in another school, or to talk disparagingly of a colleague; and borrowing money from students was not regarded by him as a crime. His conduct in St. Louis, where he settled after the breaking up of our school, was that of a madman rather than that of a sane person. During the late war he embraced the Southern cause, fled to Europe, and finally, with the reputation of an erratic genius, he died in a state of utter bankruptcy. Jealousy was one of his consuming vices, and no man ever wagged a fouler tongue. With proper training and proper self-restraint he might have become a great and shining light in medicine, instead of being a byword on the part of the public and of his professional brethren. Such was Joseph Nash McDowell!

Our hospital, so necessary an adjunct to a well-organized medical school, was generally deficient in inmates, and we had, consequently, to do the best we could under the circumstances. Our nurse was an Irishman, named John, and our enemies amused themselves by saying that, when we were short of patients, John served as a substitute by imitating all sorts of accidents and diseases. Great rivalry existed between the two schools, and our opponents used every possible effort to keep our students out of the Commercial Hospital, at that time the only institution of the kind in Cincinnati.

The Cincinnati College had, as contemporaneous organizations, a literary and a law department. It was the intention of its founders, especially of Dr. Drake, to establish eventually a great university. Its President was the Rev. Dr. W. H. McGuffey, at one time President of the Miami

University, a man of culture and great force of character, who afterwards occupied a chair in the University of Virginia, and acquired distinction as a writer of school-books. Conjoined with his duties was the office of lecturer on Mental Philosophy, and he was one of the ablest and most eloquent speakers I have ever listened to. In the literary department the principal professors were Ormsby M. Mitchel; Mr. Harding, a young man of some cleverness; and Alexander H. McGuffey, a brother of the president and a son-in-law of Dr. Drake. In the law department were Edward Mansfield and Judge Timothy Walker, author of An Introduction to American Law, a work of merit. I am not certain that Benjamin Drake, a brother of my colleague, did not also, for a time, occupy a chair in it.

After the downfall of the College I devoted myself, heart and soul, to the practice of medicine and surgery. My business rapidly increased, and when I left Cincinnati in the autumn of 1840 my books for the preceding twelve months showed an income of a little upwards of nine thousand dollars. I had for several years a large consultation practice, and patients began to pour in upon me in considerable numbers from a distance. The names of more than one hundred of the most respectable and influential families of the city were upon my ledger, including many warm personal friends. My knowledge of the German language was of great use to me during my residence at Cincinnati, especially the early part of it, as much of my practice, before I became generally known, was among the German emigrants and persons of German descent, natives of the country.

After my appointment to the chair of Pathological Anatomy in the Cincinnati College, I commenced at once a course of study to aid me in the discharge of my official duties. Indeed, I may say, I abandoned myself almost wholly for the first few years to the illustration of my department. I bought all the books upon the subject that

I could find, and my medical friends did all they could to throw post-mortem examinations into my hands. A large field was thus afforded me for the study of morbid structure, which I most gladly and thoroughly worked up. It was my custom to make the dissections as complete as possible, spending often upwards of two hours upon each case, and carrying away with me the more interesting specimens for future and more minute inspection. After a careful and sometimes protracted examination, of which full notes were always taken, the specimens were thoroughly macerated, and then preserved in alcohol. In this way I laid the foundation of a museum of pathological anatomy, which, when the college was broken up, contained a large number of valuable preparations.

It was from these dissections, from an elaborate course of reading, and from numerous visits to the pork and slaughter houses of Cincinnati, that I derived the knowledge upon which I founded my work on Pathological Anatomy, issued in 1839, in two octavo volumes of more than five hundred pages each. The work was illustrated by numerous wood-cuts and several colored engravings. Dr. William E. Horner, Professor of Anatomy in the University of Pennsylvania, had, it is true, previously published a small book on Pathological Anatomy; but it was made up mainly of extracts from Broussais and other writers, interspersed with cases and dissections occurring in his own practice, private and hospital. As far as I know, mine was the first attempt ever made in this country, or, indeed, in the English language, to systematize the subject and to place it in a connected form before the profession. The book was well received. A second edition, greatly enlarged and thoroughly revised, much of it having been rewritten, was issued in 1845 by Barrington & Haswell, of Philadelphia, in one large octavo volume of eight hundred and twenty-two pages, illus-

trated by colored engravings and two hundred and fifty
wood-cuts. It was full of marginal references, which
greatly enhanced its value. A third edition—the last
one—modified and carefully revised, and illustrated
by three hundred and forty-two engravings on wood,
appeared in 1857 from the press of Blanchard & Lea.
It formed an octavo volume of seven hundred and
seventy-one pages. It was, in some degree, an abridgment
of the second edition, and yet it comprised a very good
outline of the existing state of the science. I was assisted
in its preparation, especially the microscopical portion, by
Dr. J. M. Da Costa, now my distinguished colleague, who
was well informed on the subject. The labor of re-
writing and dovetailing of course devolved upon me. I
never liked this edition. It always seemed to me as if
the work had been emasculated, inasmuch as I left out all
marginal references and all that related to diagnosis.

The work, in its original form, cost me much labor and
anxiety. It was written when I was a young man, without
any one to advise or guide me, in my leisure hours, often
snatched from sleep, and under the exhaustion of fatigue,
when one is ill-qualified for healthful mental exertion. A
solitary lamp was generally my only companion, in a basement office, and it was often past the hour of midnight
before my head pressed its pillow. Upwards of three years
were spent upon its composition. When the manuscript
was completed I offered it to different publishers in
Philadelphia and New York, but no one was willing to
undertake its publication, and it was only after a good deal
of hard work that I finally succeeded in inducing Marsh,
Capen, Lyon & Webb, of Boston, to bring it out. After
much delay it at length appeared, under the title of Elements of Pathological Anatomy. For this edition I received
no remuneration. The Boston house failed soon after its
publication, and did not even pay the proof-reader, the late
Dr. Jeffries Wyman, who had kindly agreed to perform

this office for me. The second edition yielded twelve hundred dollars, and the last edition one thousand dollars. The work was dedicated to my friend and colleague, Dr. Daniel Drake.

There is one feature of this book which is worthy of special notice. I refer to the fact that the description of the morbid anatomy of every organ in the body was preceded by an account of its healthy color, weight, size, and consistence, founded upon original observation, a plan until then unknown in such works. The labor bestowed upon these investigations involved much trouble and painstaking. It was an important advance in the study of pathological structure.

While this work was in progress I contributed a considerable number of papers, original and in the form of reviews, some of them quite elaborate, to the Western Journal of the Medical and Physical Sciences, edited by Dr. Drake; instructed a number of office students; attended to a large and onerous practice; and never missed a lecture. In 1839, soon after the collapse of the Cincinnati College, I was unanimously appointed Professor of Medicine in the University of Virginia, a compliment so much the more honorable because it was entirely unsolicited on my part. In fact, I knew nothing of it until I received my official notification. The offer was promptly declined. The chair was soon afterwards given to Dr. Howard, of Baltimore. I had also during my residence at Cincinnati the offer of the chair of Anatomy in the University of Louisiana, at New Orleans, founded by the late Dr. Charles A. Luzenberg, who was a graduate of the Jefferson Medical College, and for a number of years a warm personal friend.

Among those who were most prominent at this time as practitioners were "Charley" Woodward, as he was familiarly called, a man of great mental and physical activity, whom I frequently met in consultation, and who never saw me without telling me how many patients

he had already visited during the morning, and how much
he had "booked" the day before; Dr. Richards, a refined
and an excellent gentleman, who enjoyed for a long
time the most select practice in the Queen City; Vincent
Marshall, who was distinguished mainly as the husband
of a noted belle in her day—for his anecdotes of Mott
and Strong, whose pupil he had been—and for button-
holing his friends on the street; John Morehead, Professor of Midwifery in the Medical College of Ohio, an
Irishman who, although he lived nearly half a century in
this country, never became a naturalized citizen, and late
in life returned to Ireland to inherit a large estate; William Wood, a man of some talent, but of an ill-grained,
crooked disposition; Israel Dodge, the prying doctor, as
he was called, who knew everybody's business better
than his own; Dr. Simmons, who afterwards settled in St.
Louis, where he married his second wife's daughter, and
was driven from the town; John Shotwell, a man of ability, who took special delight in persecuting his old friend,
Dr. Drake; and Dr. Silas Reed, who became engaged in
a "difficulty" with Dr. Jedediah Cobb, which, through the
happy interposition of the police, did not terminate in a
duel.   Mason and Whitman, the one a fussy man, and the
other a dull, heavy one, buried themselves under their dignity, and had but a small share of practice.   Professor Reuben D. Mussey enjoyed a commanding surgical business,
and Dr. Noah Worcester, his partner, a shrewd Yankee,
made a specialty of skin diseases, on which, I think, he
wrote the first treatise ever published in this country.
There was an oculist in the city, of great pretensions, of
the name of Waldo, whose habit was invariably to pray
with and for his patients before he operated upon them.
Cobb never enjoyed a commanding practice, and Eberle
was too much of a bookworm to secure the favor of the
people.

I must not forget to mention, in this place, the name

of a physician who, although young and obscure during my residence in Cincinnati, loomed up afterwards as a practitioner and a politician. Dr. John L. Vattier was a graduate of the Medical College of Ohio, and in his early days was a druggist. Being gradually drawn aside from his profession, he became a State senator, was postmaster at Cincinnati under Pierce and Buchanan, and served in various positions of trust and honor until his death in 1881. He was a man of fine physique, and the idol of his friends. He was the survivor of the Last Man Society, of Cincinnati, founded in that city during the invasion of the Asiatic cholera in 1832, and composed originally of seven members. A bottle of wine was sacredly preserved in a casket, to be opened by the survivor, and for many years he sat down alone at the table, with six empty plates and chairs, sad reminders of the past, and drank to the memory of his departed friends. After his death a touching sketch of his life was published in the Cincinnati Lancet from the pen of Dr. J. H. Buckner.

The society of Cincinnati was at that time very good. It contained many cultivated men and women, and there was, for a long time, a club which met at one another's houses to read essays and discuss literary matters. The entertainments were usually very simple and unostentatious, consisting of coffee, tea, lemonade, cake, and ices. Dr. Drake sometimes treated his guests to doughnuts, and to lemonade dipped out of a buckeye bowl, which acquired an American celebrity. He thus entertained one evening a large party given to General Winfield Scott. The occasion excited a good deal of merriment at the expense of the host. The hero of Lundy's Lane had no doubt expected a more substantial repast.

Among the men whom I also frequently saw were Judge Jacob Burnet; General William Lytle, and his son; Dr. Lyman Beecher; Charles Hammond, editor of the Cincinnati Gazette; Rev. Dr. Calvin Ellis Stowe, the husband of Mrs. Harriet Beecher Stowe, and Professor in the Walnut Hill Theological Seminary; Salmon P. Chase, afterwards Chief Justice of the United States; Archbishop Purcell; Judge Wright, an astute lawyer and politician, the successor of Charles Hammond in the Gazette; Bishop McIlvaine; Rev. Dr. Brooke, an eloquent preacher of the Episcopal Church; the Rev. Dr. Aydelotte; Judge David K. Este; George Schoenberger, and Wright Smith, a whole-souled man, of whom I have many pleasant recollections. "Billy" Greene, as he was familiarly called, was a pretentious lawyer, but a pleasant, sociable, and intelligent gentleman from Rhode Island.

One of the eccentric men, of whom Cincinnati at one time had several, was Mr. Nicholas Longworth, originally from Newark, New Jersey. He had settled in the West many years previously, and had, by judicious investments, acquired great wealth. He was a man of small stature, and was noted for his oddities, a marked one of which consisted in walking along the thoroughfares of the city, whittling pine sticks with a small knife, and lost, apparently, to all surrounding objects. Of course, everybody knew him. In his later years he exerted himself in introducing grape culture in the neighborhood of Cincinnati, and he was one of the first in this country to manufacture champagne, of which he had at one time a large supply in his cellar, built expressly for that purpose.

In the autumn of 1837, late in October, if my memory is not at fault, General Andrew Jackson, on his way to the Hermitage, stopped at Cincinnati as the guest of General William Lytle. The evening after his arrival a grand reception was given him, which was attended by all the prominent citizens of the place. The crowd was immense, the grounds were brilliantly lighted, and the whole scene was one to be remembered by those who witnessed it. My wife and myself were of the party, and thus an excellent opportunity was afforded us of obtaining a view of a man

who, during his political career, had perhaps more friends
and more enemies than any other American ever had. On
this occasion, in looking at this great man—for so the
world must regard him—I was forcibly impressed by his
venerable appearance, the dignity of his demeanor, and the
suavity and grace of his manners. He had the elegance
and polish of a courtier. His hair, nearly white, was
brushed back, as in his earlier days, and his countenance
shone with peculiar benignity. No one who then stood in
his presence would have supposed that he could ever have
stamped his foot in a rage and uttered the memorable
words, " By the Eternal, I'll hang you on Capitol Hill if
you do not stop these treasonable acts !" He was the lion
only when excited—the lamb in his ordinary life. He
could roar, but there was also music in his voice, as sweet
and gentle as that of the most delicate and refined woman.
I had long felt a desire to see this extraordinary personage ;
and I left the house of General Lytle with the conviction
that I had looked upon an honest man without the aid of
the lantern of Diogenes. General Jackson was accompanied by Mr. and Mrs. Polk.

Lyman Beecher was a man of rare character, of great
powers of mind, and of indomitable energy. Early in
life he worked, it is said, in a blacksmith shop ; but
becoming disgusted with his occupation he entered Yale
College and afterwards studied divinity, in which, as is
well known, he gradually rose to great and well-merited
eminence. By rare industry he surmounted the obstacles
which his poverty and early deficiencies had placed in
his path, and long before he attained middle age he had
acquired the reputation of being a learned man. As a
preacher, he was eccentric, argumentative, and dogmatical, and withal tedious, his sermons being always long
and decidedly dry. Although in my judgment he was not
a very eloquent speaker, he commanded good houses on
account of the orthodox character of his discourses. His

pronunciation of certain words was peculiar. For example, he always said "natur" for nature, and "critter" for creature—sounds which, coming from a great preacher, grated harshly upon one's ears. In private conversation he was exceedingly agreeable and communicative, and he had the happy faculty of making every one feel at ease in his presence. He was for nearly twenty years President of Lane Seminary at Cincinnati, took an active interest in the temperance cause, and was the author of a number of works much esteemed in their day. Lyman Beecher affords a significant illustration of what may be accomplished by persistent effort, guided by a vigorous intellect.

One of the most brilliant men in Cincinnati at the time here referred to was Robert Lytle, generally known by the sobriquet of "Bob." He was a man of brilliant intellect, eloquent, impulsive, handsome, fascinating in his manners, and distinguished for his ability in controlling the masses. Like his father, one of the early settlers of Ohio, and a gentleman at one time of great wealth, Robert was a strong Democrat; he was a capital stump orator, and represented the Cincinnati district for a time in Congress. His popularity was his ruin. I attended him during his last illness. Death, the immediate cause of which was phthisis, overtook him at New Orleans, whither, despite my remonstrance, he went to eke out his brief existence.

Salmon P. Chase, whom I knew well as a young man, was tall and handsome, erect as a pole, ambitious, highly cultured, and very agreeable in his manners. A teacher of a classical school in his younger days, he studied law in the office of Chief Justice Cranch, of Washington City, and by industry, talent, and genius gradually rose to be Governor of Ohio, Secretary of the Treasury under Mr. Lincoln, and Chief Justice of the Supreme Court of the United States. Such an amount of success betokens great natural ability, and an amount of labor such as few men, even of iron constitution, can endure.

One regrets, in looking at Mr. Chase's pure and patriotic life, that he failed to attain the goal of his ambition—the Presidency of the United States, an office which he was so well qualified to fill with credit and dignity. As a financier during the critical period of our history, when our currency was tottering to and fro, his labors were of inestimable service.

Timothy Walker, a contemporary of Chase, was the impersonation of a *bon vivant*. He had a large head, a ruddy complexion, and a stout, masculine frame, which looked as if it might last a hundred years; and yet, under the influence of fast living, with three and often four heavy meals a day, washed down with generous wine, he broke down at a comparatively early age. Apoplexy did the work. Although Mr. Walker occupied a high position at the bar, and was successively a judge, a lecturer in a law school, and a writer on law of some note, he was inferior to Mr. Chase in great intellectual qualities, and in those attributes of character which place a man head and shoulder above his contemporaries.

Of Bishop, now Archbishop, Purcell my recollections are very pleasant. He is one of the most affable and genial of men, a delightful talker, full of anecdote, rich in knowledge, a finished scholar, and a popular as well as a great preacher. The Catholic Church is indebted to him for much of the influence and elevated position which it enjoys in the Western States. I had personally lost sight of the good Archbishop for nearly a third of a century, when, in June, 1875, I had the pleasure of meeting with him at the Cathedral, on Logan Square, at the conferring of the pallium upon Bishop Wood, a ceremony by which that good prelate was made an archbishop. He had the same bland countenance and the same cordial shake of the hand as at our last interview in Cincinnati.

The Cincinnati Gazette was for a long time the principal political newspaper, not only of Cincinnati, but of all the States east of Kentucky. Its editor at the period in question was the well-known Charles Hammond, under the influence of whose trenchant pen the Gazette obtained a wide circulation. He was one of the most caustic of writers, and one of the most bitter of men. Many of his articles were of a withering character; and he never hesitated to slaughter an enemy when it suited his spleen or his interest. I am not certain of his nativity, but my impression has always been that he came from South Carolina.

Of the men with whom I was personally acquainted in Cincinnati, none gave me heartier welcome when I arrived than Dr. Gamaliel Bailey. We had been students together in the Jefferson Medical College of Philadelphia for two winters, and had taken our degree at the same time, parting on commencement day with regret, lest we should not meet again. I was therefore agreeably surprised when I found that my old friend was a resident of the Queen City. He had preceded me by several years, and had already made many friends and had done some good work, although as a practitioner he had made little headway. He had been for some time connected with the Cincinnati Medical Gazette, had assisted Dr. Eberle in the composition of his work on the Diseases of Children, and had contributed numerous articles to the daily press. He soon afterwards founded the Herald, the first antislavery newspaper published in Cincinnati; and in 1836, in conjunction with Mr. J. G. Birney, he established the Cincinnati Philanthropist, an abolition journal, which, notwithstanding his press and other material were destroyed by a mob, he continued to issue until 1847. In that year he went to Washington City, where he immediately founded the National Era, which at one time had a wide circulation. It was in this paper that Mrs. Harriet Beecher Stowe's "Uncle Tom's Cabin" first appeared. Bailey was by nature a self-willed man, bold, stubborn, de-

termined, and not to be pushed aside from any undertaking in which he had once fairly embarked, or which
involved the defence of what he regarded as important
principles. To these qualities, which as often destroy as
make men, and which are always sure to hatch a numerous
brood of enemies, he added no inconsiderable amount of
fanaticism, which often betrayed him into difficulties. His
wife, a clever little woman, of more than ordinary culture, was in unison with his antislavery movements, and
was herself a frequent contributor to the Era. Many of
her articles were spirited and well written. Life with
Bailey was a constant struggle; he was poor when he left
Cincinnati, and my impression is that he never enjoyed
pecuniary prosperity. In stature he was about the middle
height, well proportioned, with black eyes, and a handsome face, expressive of benevolence. He was a native
of Mount Holly, New Jersey, where he was born in December, 1807. His death occurred at Washington City,
in June, 1859, in the fifty-second year of his age. Bailey
was never designed by nature for a practitioner of medicine; his manners were cold, and he was too retired in his
habits to be popular with the masses. As a philanthropist
he was sincere in his convictions and honest in his acts;
and his name will always be associated by the colored
race with the names of Garrison, Lundy, Knapp, Beecher,
and others.

Bishop Charles P. McIlvaine was a magnificent man,
tall, erect, well formed, with the mien and bearing
of a prince, just such a man as would anywhere, in a
crowd, in the street, or in the social circle, attract
general attention. His features were fine; his eyes were
brown, his forehead and nose well shaped, and his mouth
and teeth perfect. It has been said that he strongly
resembled Washington; and in looking at Stewart's celebrated portrait of the "Father of his Country" I have
often been struck with the comparison. He belonged

emphatically to that old school of gentlemen who at one time abounded in this country, but of whom few are to be seen in our day. Bishop McIlvaine had all the graces and accomplishments of the Christian gentleman. Affable, kind, courteous, he touched the hearts of all with whom chance or business brought him in contact. If, in early life, as was said of him, there was a certain hauteur in his manner, he certainly had nothing of the kind in his riper years. Young men, and young women too, often assume airs; and it is quite possible that the young and handsome divine might occasionally have indulged in such a freak. Men who are much courted and caressed, or who are great favorites with the ladies, are very liable to be spoiled and sometimes even ruined. Petted and feted, he never for a moment lost sight of the dignity of his office or of his self-respect. As he was a prince of a man, so he was a prince of a bishop. Few men ever wore their clerical robes with more grace and dignity. As he stood up in the pulpit, earnestly expounding the doctrines of the Bible, or controverting some heretical notions, there was a majesty about him, a sort of divine presence, which at once riveted the attention of his hearers and carried with it the force of conviction. His voice was not only sweet, but strong and well modulated, his manner earnest and impressive, his gestures graceful. His sermons, which were often, if not generally, argumentative and learned, abounded in strong sense, and rarely, if ever, offended by their length ; their style was uniformly polished, scholarly, and free from cant or affectation. Of his numerous works, the ablest, perhaps, is his Evidences of Christianity, which, written when he was comparatively a young man, has passed through numerous editions, and has made his name widely known at home and abroad. Some of his writings were of a controversial character, and were severely criticised by his opponents. Of this character was his Oxford

Divinity, which brought him into collision with the Oxford Tractarians, but in favor with the authorities of that famous university, which, in token of its appreciation of his distinguished merits, conferred upon him, in 1853, the degree of D. C. L. He occupied many positions of trust and honor, and was bishop of the diocese of Ohio for upwards of forty years, or from 1832 up to the time of his death, in 1873.

My acquaintance with this good prelate extended over a third of a century. During the latter years of my residence in Louisville he was for nearly a week an inmate of my house, having been called thither by business connected with the church. It was during this visit, made in midwinter, that an occurrence took place which came very near proving fatal to a large number of persons, including the Bishop. He had said good-bye to my family and was on his way to the other side of the Ohio River to take the train for Cincinnati. As the river was full of ice, the ferryboat soon became uncontrollable, and was by the merest accident prevented from being swept over the falls. As no very secure landing could be effected, it was not without great difficulty that the passengers, including men, women, and children, were at length put on shore. While this was going on every entreaty failed to induce the Bishop to leave the vessel, and it was not until after every one was safely landed that he quit it. Had it not been for his courage and great presence of mind it is impossible to say what might have happened during the great alarm and confusion which had seized all on board.

I saw Bishop McIlvaine for the last time in July, 1872. He was then sojourning with his daughters in St. John's Wood, near London; and, having learned that Mrs. Gross, my son, and myself were in lodgings on Princes Street, he was kind enough to visit us. During the hour which he spent with us he talked with his accustomed vigor and animation, dwelling with peculiar gratification upon his interviews with the Prince of Wales and his family, and telling us some interesting anecdotes about the children. It was not, however, without deep concern that I witnessed the change which had taken place in his appearance since we had parted with him a few years before in Philadelphia. He had become thin and pale, and there was a sinister stoop in his shoulders denotive of debility. The day was uncommonly hot, and I would fain have ordered a carriage for him had he not resolutely declined the offer. As he walked away from the door my eye followed him, and I observed to my wife and son, "We have seen the last of the good, dear Bishop." My prophecy proved to be only too true. In the autumn he left London for Florence, where he expired on the 12th of March, 1873, at the age of seventy-five years. He was a native of Burlington, New Jersey.

It was in the summer of 1837 that Mr. Webster stopped at Cincinnati during his western tour, and that I had an opportunity of being introduced to him. This office was kindly performed for me by my friend and colleague, the late Dr. Daniel Drake, who had made Mr. Webster's acquaintance many years before at Boston, when the great statesman paid him more than ordinary attention. Mr. Webster was accompanied by Mrs. Webster and a daughter, and was staying at the Pear Street House, then the most fashionable hotel of Cincinnati, as the guest of the city. It was nearly three o'clock in the afternoon when we called, and as it had been announced in the morning that Mr. Webster would address the people a great crowd had already assembled around the hotel. We made our way into the parlor, where we found him seated on a sofa listening to the conversation of some political friends, in which he apparently took but little interest. He received us very courteously, made a few commonplace remarks, and then relapsed into silence, from which it was impossible to rouse him. He seemed to be dull and heavy, as a

lion or tiger may be supposed to be after having gorged
himself with a heavy meal.   I would not have it inferred
from this remark that Mr. Webster was actually in this
condition; but the impression left upon my mind was that
and nothing else.   After sitting perhaps ten minutes we
rose and took our leave.   I subsequently learned that Mr.
Webster had occasional fits of lethargy and abstraction.
An hour later he appeared upon the balcony of the hotel,
accompanied by General Harrison, who introduced him to
the populace.   Thanking the crowd for their cordial reception of him, he commenced in slow and measured tones
to discuss some of the great political questions which were
then agitating the country, but he never rose during the
hour he thus occupied to that enthusiasm which was so
common a characteristic of western stump orators.   As a
speaker, he did not favorably impress me.   He was ponderous and monotonous, and as to his gestures, nothing
could have been more awkward or more ungraceful.   His
forearms, flexed at nearly a right angle with the arms,
moved up and down like sledge-hammers.   Although there
was occasionally some cheering, the address failed to touch
the hearts of the audience.   If Mr. Webster had been an
invalid, one could readily have accounted for his want of
animation and enthusiasm; but this was not the case.
Fatigued he might have been, and probably was; but he
was robust, and in the full vigor of life; and although he
lost some of his stiffness, if I may so call it, as he proceeded with his address, most of the crowd went away disappointed.   I certainly was so myself, and I heard many
others express themselves in a similar manner.   Mr. Webster was a solid rather than a sprightly man, and it is said
that he never made so great an effort as when he was fortified by a pint of brandy and a big beefsteak.

During my residence at Cincinnati I often met with
General William Henry Harrison, the "Hero of Tippecanoe."   At that time he lived at North Bend, on the Ohio

River, sixteen miles below the city; but he often visited it, either on business or pleasure. He was a tall, slender man, and, notwithstanding his advanced age, had an unmistakable soldierly air and bearing. He had long been a victim of facial neuralgia, which, with occasional attacks of dyspepsia, gave him a "lean and hungry look," in striking contrast to the fat and sleek appearance of some of his friends. Personally he was very popular, and the record which he made as a brave soldier during the war of 1812–14 rendered him a conspicuous citizen. His private character was without reproach. With such a history, it is not surprising that the Whig party, in 1840, should have put him in nomination for the Presidency, with John Tyler on the ticket as his lieutenant. "Tippecanoe and Tyler too" became the watchword of the party, and was sung day and night throughout the Union, at the glee clubs, and in every political procession, almost invariably accompanied by one or more "log-cabins," as offsets against the many emblems of the Democratic party, headed by Martin Van Buren, of New York. As the canvass advanced, Harrison became more and more confident of his success; and late in October, on the evening prior to my departure for Louisville, my future home, in taking leave of me at the house of a common friend, he accompanied me to the door, and, pressing my hand, he said, "My dear doctor, before we meet again you will find that I am President of the United States. I feel sure of my election." His words proved prophetic. I never saw him again. His brief career at the White House is well known. Naturally and by long habit an early riser, he forgot, in his familiar walks and visits to the market, that he lived on the pestiferous banks of the Potomac, where with every breath he inhaled malaria, which in a few weeks consigned him to an untimely grave, as it subsequently did President Taylor.

General Harrison was a great talker and an agreeable

companion, very fond of ladies' society. He had a large fund of anecdotes at his command. At our last interview, above referred to, with much glee and a twinkle in his brown eyes, he told an anecdote, which caused much merriment among our friends. A young Pennsylvania German farmer, a personal acquaintance of mine, was exceedingly anxious to see the general, now the Presidential nominee of the Whig party; and knowing that I resided at Cincinnati he called upon me to give him a letter of introduction. He reached North Bend late in the evening, and after a good night's rest and a hearty breakfast the general pointed out the objects of greatest interest on his farm, among others his horses and cattle. My friend admired everything, but nothing struck his fancy half so much as a three-months'-old calf browsing on the lawn. Boiling over with enthusiasm, he exclaimed, "Cheneral, mein Gott, dat is a mighty fine calf; Cheneral, a mighty fine calf; sure a man vat can raise such a calf is wordy to be Bresident, and I'll wode for him." The general had a great deal of *bonhomie*, with a keen perception of the ludicrous, and was, when in his best humor, to use an English expression, a "jolly man," enjoying a hearty laugh and a good story.

CHAPTER IV.

DURING the spring of 1840 the chair of Surgery in the
Louisville Medical Institute, afterwards the University of
Louisville, became vacant by the forced resignation of Dr.
Joshua B. Flint, who had failed to receive the approval of
his colleagues and pupils as an efficient teacher. Soon after
this event the dean of the Faculty, the late Dr. Charles
W. Short, visited me, in his official capacity, with an offer
of the vacant place, and a guarantee of three thousand
dollars. Before I accepted it I visited Louisville to in-
form myself more fully of the condition and prospects
of the school. Satisfying myself that it was destined,
under proper management, to take a high rank, I removed to Kentucky late in the following October. The
Faculty was, with one or two exceptions, a very able
one. The most distinguished members at that time were
Charles Caldwell, Daniel Drake, and John Esten Cooke,
who had long been teachers, and had earned an extensive reputation as writers. Cooke was the author of a
work on Therapeutics, and was well known on account
of his peculiar doctrines in regard to the nature and
treatment of diseases. Jedediah Cobb was well-known

as an excellent lecturer on anatomy, and as a neat, beautiful dissector. Short enjoyed a wide reputation, both at home and abroad, as a botanist. Yandell, who had long taught chemistry, was a capital talker and an able, pungent writer. Miller was a rising man, although a dull lecturer; he has since earned an enviable reputation as an author and as a practitioner in female diseases. I was the youngest member of the Faculty; or, if not absolutely the youngest, there was a difference of only a few days between Yandell's age and my own. I had never taught surgery, although I had long studied it, and was thoroughly acquainted with its principles and practice. I therefore felt no misgivings in entering upon the discharge of the duties of my chair. Although I stood by the side of able men, among the foremost in their particular branches in their day, I felt certain that I should succeed. My acceptance of the chair had been a conditional one. If, at the close of the session, I did not fancy my prospects, or failed to give satisfaction, I could return to Cincinnati, where my friends were ready to extend to me a cordial welcome. I determined, however, to remain and to identify myself with the destinies of the school. The class during the first winter of my connection with it numbered two hundred and four. It was subsequently increased to four hundred and six, the largest it ever had. As we had no rent to pay, the net proceeds of each chair amounted for quite a number of years to nearly five thousand dollars annually.

My reception by the medical profession of Louisville was anything but cordial. The medical school had many enemies. The recent ejection of Dr. Flint had raised an active opposition, through which, as I had become his successor, I largely suffered, although I was personally a stranger to them, and had never said or done anything against any of them. As soon as it became known that I had signified my determination to remain in the school, as I did about six weeks before the close of the session, they opened their battery upon me in one of the public journals of the city, fabricating all kinds of stories, with a view of disgusting me with my colleagues, and driving me from the place. Of all this abuse I never took the slightest notice, scarcely even in private, and the consequence was that they gradually ceased their opposition, the only effect of which was to place me in the light of a persecuted man, and to raise up friends for me. I had the respect and confidence of the citizens, the good-will of all my colleagues, and the affection and esteem of my pupils. My ability as a teacher of surgery and as an operator was conceded long before the end of the first session; the school flourished despite the malice and detraction of its foes; and my success as a practitioner was a foregone conclusion. I felt, like Luther, that, although every tile upon every doctor's house was a devil, no one could arrest my progress or do me any serious injury. I was, it is true, placed in a false position with many good citizens, persons who were unacquainted with me, and who therefore formed a wrong estimate of my character. This, however, did not last long. My efforts were gradually appreciated, and I soon triumphed over those designing men, not a few of whom became afterwards my warm personal friends, deploring the part they had taken against me.

The University of Louisville was, and perhaps still is, governed by a self-appointing board of trustees. The city of Louisville gave it one hundred and fifty thousand dollars, including a large lot, and a most commodious edifice, library, chemical apparatus, and anatomical museum. All that the professors had to do was to deliver a certain number of lectures during every session, and to pocket the proceeds of their tickets. Their only expenses were janitor's hire and coal and gas bills. In 1849 an attempt was made by the city of Louisville, through the Supreme Court of Kentucky, to wrest the government of the school from the hands of the men who had managed its affairs so well, and to make the board elective by the people. It was at this particular crisis that I received the offer of the chair of Surgery in the University of the city of New York; and, in doubt as to how the suit might terminate, I was induced to accept the offer with a guarantee of four thousand dollars. Accordingly I passed the winter of 1850-'51 with my wife and three of my children in New York. The winter was decidedly the most charming I have ever spent. My labors were comparatively light. I gave four didactic lectures and held two clinics a week; and, as I had but little private practice, I gave myself up to sight-seeing, the theatre and the opera, private parties, and visits to the hospitals. I also attended a course of lectures on the microscope by Mr. Goadby, an English gentleman, and spent much of my leisure upon the composition of my work on the Urinary Organs, commenced several years previously, and completed a short time before the close of the lectures.

My colleagues in the New York University were Granville Sharp Pattison, John W. Draper, Gunning S. Bedford, Martyn Paine, and Elisha Bartlett, all men of distinction and of more or less ability. Pattison had earned a world-wide reputation as a brilliant teacher of anatomy; Draper was well-known as an accomplished chemist and physiologist, and he afterwards achieved immortal fame by his work on The Intellectual Development of Europe. Bedford, although an unpopular man, was a successful teacher and writer; Paine was celebrated for his great learning, his dulness as a lecturer, his peculiar doctrines, and his diffuse style as an author; and Bartlett enjoyed a national reputation as a lecturer and a graceful writer. Mott had resigned the previous spring, and I succeeded to his chair. I was then forty-five years of age, full of ambition, and determined to do justice to my posi-

tion.   Although the class numbered upwards of three
hundred and fifty, and my ticket was twenty dollars, my
colleagues, to meet my guarantee, were obliged to make up
for me nearly two thousand dollars.   The school, moreover, was unpopular with the New York profession; the
college edifice was ill adapted to its object, living and rents
were exorbitantly high, and, in short, the prospects of the
institution were not such as, in my opinion, to render it
desirable to continue my connection with it.   Long before
the session terminated I was solicited by my late colleagues
at Louisville to resume my chair in its University.   Dr.
Paul F. Eve, who had succeeded me, had offered to resign in my favor if I wished to return.   The suit, which
had been pending when I left, had in the mean time been
decided in favor of the board of trustees; and, as an additional inducement, my house had remained unsold.   There
was, therefore, no obstacle to my return.   Having delivered the valedictory at the Commencement, soon after the
close of the session I left New York on my return to
Louisville, and in less than a fortnight tendered my resignation.   Had I remained in New York I have no doubt I
should have soon obtained a large practice, but, as I had
left a better school, and had a more commanding surgical
practice than any man in the Southwest, I deemed it
prudent to retrace my steps, although I have sometimes
regretted that I did not remain there.   Dr. Alfred C. Post
succeeded me; and, after the death of Pattison, a few
years later, Mott reëntered the school as ex-President of
the Faculty and lecturer on Operative Surgery.

On my way from New York to Louisville I left with
Blanchard & Lea of Philadelphia the manuscript of a
work entitled A Practical Treatise on the Diseases, Injuries and Malformations of the Urinary Bladder, the Prostate Gland, and the Urethra, which was published by
that firm in 1851.   Such a work had long been needed,
and it was at once accepted as an authority upon the sub-

jects of which it treated. The only monographs on these affections, of any importance, in the English language, were those of Sir Benjamin C. Brodie and Mr. William Coulson, two comparatively meagre productions, deficient in completeness and unsatisfactory, although valuable, especially the first. The object of my work, as expressed in the preface, was to present, in a systematic and connected form, a full and comprehensive account of the diseases and injuries of the organs in question. The materials had been long accumulating upon my hands, and not less than three years were finally spent in arranging them for publication. The original design was to issue a separate volume of plates, of the size of nature, as a companion to the book; but it was soon discovered that this would so much enhance the expense as to place the work beyond the reach of many of those for whose benefit it was more particularly prepared. It was illustrated by upwards of one hundred engravings on wood, of which nearly one-half were expressly made for it. A second edition, greatly enlarged and improved, was issued in 1855. It formed a closely-printed octavo volume of nine hundred and twenty-five pages, illustrated by one hundred and eighty-four woodcuts, and comprised, along with my personal experience, a digest of the existing state of the science. In an appendix of twenty-nine closely-printed pages is the first and only attempt ever made by any writer, as far as I am aware, to furnish a complete account of the prevalence of stone in the bladder and of calculous disorders in the United States, Canada, Nova Scotia, Europe, and other countries. The preparation involved an immense amount of labor in the way of correspondence, extending through a period of several years, and yet up to the present time I have never seen it referred to by any writer, either American or European. Such is reputation! Such the reward which one obtains for one's labors! A new edition of this work has just been—September, 1876—issued under the able editor-

ship of my son, Dr. S. W. Gross. He has rewritten much
of the work, has introduced much new matter, and has
thus produced a valuable treatise, fully up to the existing
state of the science.

My work, A Practical Treatise on Foreign Bodies in
the Air-Passages, was issued from the press of Blanchard
& Lea in 1854, in an octavo volume of four hundred and
sixty-eight pages, illustrated by fifty-nine engravings on
wood. Its composition occupied me upwards of two years.
It was the first attempt to systematize our knowledge upon
the subject, and the work is therefore, strictly speaking, a
pioneer work. My original intention was not to write a
book, but to compose a short monograph for some medical
journal. I had not, however, proceeded far before I discovered that I had formed a very imperfect idea of the
enterprise, and that, in order to do it justice, much time
and study would be required. "If," says the preface, "in
the providence of God, the work shall be instrumental in
saving the life of one human being, or even in ameliorating
the sufferings of a single individual, I shall feel myself
amply remunerated for the time I have bestowed upon its
composition. If there be any situation better calculated
than another to awaken our sympathy, it is when we see
before us a fellow-creature who is threatened every instant
with destruction, in consequence of the lodgment of a foreign body in the air-passages, without the ability to expel
it or the power to inflate the lungs. It was this reflection
which first induced me, many years ago, to turn my attention to the subject, and which has finally impelled me to
write this treatise." This work has now been long out of
print. A new edition, much abridged, might be made the
basis of a complete treatise on the surgical affections of the
air-passages.*

---

* Dr. Morell Mackenzie, the highest authority on the subject in Europe, in
speaking of this work nearly thirty years after its publication, makes the following remarks: "This invaluable essay gives full reports of two hundred cases, and

Soon after I had gone to Louisville I instituted a series of experiments upon dogs, with a view of determining more accurately than had hitherto been done the nature and treatment of wounds of the intestines. The investigations were commenced in the spring of 1841, and were continued, with various intermissions, for more than two years. The object was, in the first place, to inquire into the process employed in repairing such injuries; and secondly, and more particularly, to test the value of the more important methods of treatment recommended by surgeons from the time of Ransdohr, a practitioner of the early part of the last century, down to our own. The experiments, upwards of seventy in number, were performed exclusively upon dogs, as the most eligible animals that could be procured for the purpose. The results, originally published in a series of papers in the Western Journal of Medicine and Surgery, were finally embodied in an octavo volume of two hundred and twenty pages, illustrated by wood-cuts and colored engravings. The work was exhaustive, and comprised an account of my own researches and a sketch of the literature of the subject. It was favorably noticed in a long review by the British and Foreign Medico-Chirurgical Journal, edited by Dr. Forbes, and was quoted approvingly by Mr. Guthrie in his work on Military Surgery. I have never seen any allusion to it in any of our own journals, or by any of our own writers.

The labor spent upon these experiments was very great, and the expense itself was not inconsiderable, as I was obliged to pay for nearly all the dogs, and to hire a man to watch and feed them. My colleagues were kind enough

---

is so complete that it is doubtful whether it will ever be improved upon; indeed, the excellent articles of Bourdillat and Kühn, subsequently published, the former based on three hundred, and the latter on three hundred and seventy-four cases, only confirm the conclusions previously arrived at by Gross."—Diseases of the Throat and Nose, vol. i. p. 540. Philadelphia, 1880. It may be added that Kühn plagiarized much of the material of this work.—EDITORS.

to give me the basement rooms in the college for the accommodation of the poor creatures. The experiments, besides, involved a great sacrifice of feeling on my part. I am naturally fond of dogs, and my sympathies were often wrought to the highest pitch, especially when I happened to get hold of an unusually clever specimen. Anæsthetics had not yet been discovered, and I was therefore obliged to inflict severe pain. The animal while under torture would often look into my eye, as if to say, "Is it possible you will torment me in this way? What have I done to deserve all this? Have I done you any harm?" I have sacrificed for this purpose nearly one hundred dogs, and if I were not thoroughly satisfied that the objects had been most laudable, I should consider myself a most cruel, heartless man, deserving of the severest condemnation. The experiments of Jones on hemorrhage, of Smith and Travers on wounds of the intestines, of Magendie and Sir Charles Bell on the functions of the nerves, and of hundreds of physicians upon the action of medicines upon the human frame have shed an immense flood of light upon the healing art, putting to flight the ill-timed sentimentality of the societies for the prevention of cruelty to animals, which have made so much ado about this matter.

My dogs were no inconsiderable source of annoyance to several of my colleagues. The rooms in which they were lodged became infested with fleas, which, when the air became heated in autumn by the stoves in the college, skipped about in every direction. My friend, the Professor of Chemistry, was especially molested by them, being obliged to appear before his class with his boots over. his trousers, to prevent them from effecting an entrance to his body. I do not know whether, like Sir Humphry Davy, he ever boiled any to determine their affinity with the lobster, but no doubt he often felt the effects of their probosces. When the experiments were terminated the worthy dean, a venerable gentleman in spectacles, formally burnt the fleas at the stake—another evidence of the unfeeling character of medical men!

During my residence at Louisville I was a liberal contributor to the Western Journal of Medicine and Surgery, conducted by Drake and Yandell, assisted, for a time, by Dr. Thomas W. Colescott, one of my former private pupils. Among my earliest papers was an account of a case of axillary aneurism, for which I had tied the subclavian artery. It was accompanied by a statistical notice of all that had been done in regard to the surgery of this vessel up to that period. My case was almost unique, only one similar case having occurred previously. Another elaborate paper was published in 1852 on the diseases and operations on the jaws. I also wrote occasional reviews, chiefly of an analytical character, sometimes critical and even caustic. As already stated, my experiments on wounds of the intestines were published in this journal; and one of the latest of my contributions to its pages was A Discourse upon the Life and Character of the late Dr. Drake, embracing nearly one hundred pages.

In 1851 I prepared a report on Kentucky Surgery for the Kentucky State Medical Society, afterwards published in its Transactions, the meeting having been held at Louisville. It embraced nearly two hundred pages, and cost me a great deal of labor, augmented by the large correspondence which it involved with the physicians of different parts of the State, and even out of the State. It was a complete history of Kentucky surgery. It contained a full biography of Ephraim McDowell, of Danville, with a vindication of his claims as the originator of Ovariotomy—claims now universally acknowledged. McDowell performed his first operation in 1809. In this report is also contained a brief account of a girl, named Amanda McGuire, of Mississippi, who was born blind, and whom, at the age of eighteen, I restored to sight by an operation for cataract.

In 1852 I sent to the Philadelphia Medical Examiner, edited by Dr. Francis Gurney Smith and Dr. John B. Biddle, a short account of the use of adhesive plaster in the treatment of fractures, in which I proved that I had been the first to describe the method in my work on the Diseases of the Bones and Joints issued at Philadelphia in 1830. The method had been claimed by a number of physicians, none of whom were entitled to it. It was first practised by Dr. Joseph K. Swift, of Easton, my early preceptor, in a case of compound fracture of the leg in an Irishman, whom I saw several times during his protracted confinement. I was so much pleased with the plan that I briefly described it in my work. Swift himself never published any account of it.

In 1853 I sent to the American Medical Association, at its meeting in Richmond, Virginia, a comprehensive report on the Results of Surgical Operations in Malignant Diseases. It comprised one hundred and thirty-seven pages of its volume of Transactions, and embodied the experience of the principal surgeons of all ages and countries. It was a painstaking production. The report attracted wide attention among medical men.

In 1856, at the meeting of the American Medical Association at Detroit, I read a report on the Causes which Retard the Progress of American Medical Literature, covering upwards of twenty pages of the Transactions. This report elicited a good deal of discussion at the time, and was afterwards variously criticised by the medical press of the country. It took strong grounds against the editing of foreign works by American writers, and animadverted in severe terms upon our medical journals for their indiscriminate praise of European reprints. These two circumstances, especially the latter, made the paper unpopular. Its effects, however, were excellent. Since then few

English works have been reprinted in the United States
under the auspices of American editors; and the American
periodical press has indulged much less than formerly in
toadyism, at one time such a prominent feature in its
conduct.

In the winter of 1856, Dr. T. G. Richardson and I
founded the Louisville Medical Review, a bi-monthly
journal of medicine and surgery, the first number of
which was issued on the 1st of May following. I had
no fancy for this kind of work, as I was too busily engaged
in practice to attend to its drudgery; and it was not until
after repeated solicitations and interviews with Dr. Richardson, who had been a favorite pupil of mine, and not
until after I had been assured that I should be relieved
of all such labor, that I finally consented to have my
name placed on the title-page as senior editor. The first
number appeared with a very respectable list of Western
and Southwestern collaborators, and with a fair prospect
of success, inasmuch as the Western Journal of Medicine
and Surgery had for some time been discontinued, on account of the decline of its subscription list. It opened
with an excellent review by Professor Yandell of Mansfield's Life of Dr. Drake, accompanied by an admirable
engraving of that physician. The second article was from
my own pen, entitled August Gottlieb Richter: his Works
and his Cotemporaries—a retrospective review, in which
I introduced an account of Desault, Benjamin Bell and An-
tonio Scarpa, all great men in their day, whose lives and
services marked an important epoch in the professional
history of their respective countries. The article caused
me much labor and research, although it occupies only
thirty-five pages of the journal. I believe it to be one
of the best things I have ever written, if "best" be at all
applicable to anything I have done in this way.

The July number contained the report of a case—one of
the most remarkable on record—of hypertrophy of the

gums, in a lad ten years of age, whom I relieved by a surgical operation, and whose history was widely disseminated by the medical press, as well as embodied in the current works on surgery and on dental science.

Only six numbers of the Louisville Medical Review were published; for, by a strange coincidence, soon after the appearance of the first number, both editors received and accepted appointments in Philadelphia: Dr. Richardson the chair of Anatomy in the Pennsylvania College, and I that of Surgery in my Alma Mater as the successor of the late Dr. Thomas D. Mütter.

During my residence in Kentucky I contributed several papers to the American Journal of the Medical Sciences, edited by Dr. Isaac Hays. One of these was the report of a case, full of interest, of gunshot wound of the neck, involving the spinal cord and subclavian artery, and causing death by convulsions.

During the first winter of my connection with the University of Louisville I boarded with my family at the Louisville Hotel, uncertain whether I should continue in the school or return at the close of the session to Cincinnati. After that question was finally disposed of I took a house, and in the month of April removed to my new field of labor, opening at once an office and becoming a candidate for business. The proceeds during the first year of my practice fell somewhat short of two thousand dollars; but as my family was small and inexpensive, this sum, together with my college proceeds, was more than sufficient for my immediate wants. My practice rapidly increased; patients with all kinds of diseases flocked to me from different parts of the valley of the Mississippi; I was often sent for to go a considerable distance from home; I performed numerous surgical operations, and did a large consultation business. I had also at this time constantly about me private pupils; and Dr. Cobb and I delivered regularly, for a number of years, spring courses of lectures on surgical

anatomy and operative surgery.   My income thus became
quite large, and, as a consequence, I determined to build for
myself a large and commodious dwelling in a pleasant part
of the city.   My house was a double one, fifty feet front, with
two offices, a fine garden, and a small conservatory, which
furnished my family with flowers from one year's end to
the other.   The garden was a source of constant happiness
to me.   Although I employed a gardener, I spent much
of my leisure—not much at any time—in embellishing it,
often transplanting flowers and weeding the beds with my
own hands.   It was delightful to watch the flowers, to
individualize, and even, so to speak, to pet them.   These
were indeed happy, thrice happy, moments, full of innocence and bliss, thoroughly shared by my dear wife and
most of my children, who were equally fond of flowers.
One of the greatest sources of our distress on leaving Kentucky was that we could not carry with us our garden and
conservatory.   The summer before we left a Lamarcque
rose had literally spread over the entire conservatory, and
had borne upwards of twelve hundred blossoms.   The
house was elegantly furnished, and was one of the most
beautiful residences in Louisville.   My office door opened
upon nearly an entire square of shrubbery and trees on the
opposite side of the street, so that I lived, as it were,
in a forest, redolent in summer of the fragrance of
flowers and musical with the song of birds.   Was this a
foretaste of Paradise, or was it only an illusion?   When
I left Louisville, in 1856, I parted with this property for
four thousand dollars less than it had cost me.   Our house
was for many years the abode of an enlarged and generous
hospitality.   Distinguished strangers, professional and non-
professional, were welcome guests at our table.

I remained at Louisville for sixteen years—from October, 1840, to September, 1856—and became thus closely
identified with the people and the interests and prosperity
of the city, as well as the pride and glory of the State of

Kentucky. I had, with my seven years' residence at Cincinnati, become, in fact, a Southwestern man, in feeling and in habit.

General regret was expressed, both by the medical profession and the citizens of Louisville, when it was understood that I had determined to remove to Philadelphia, and this feeling finally culminated in a ball, given to my family and myself at the Galt House, the evening before our departure. I received numerous letters from medical men in various parts of the Southwest remonstrating against my removal, on the ground that, as I had earned my reputation in the Southwest, that section had a claim on me which no light considerations should ignore. I had, however, made up my mind to go, and no argument could have induced me to remain. The university was in a declining condition; it had lost some of its very best and most distinguished men; some of the men that remained were weak and vacillating in their conduct; and the men that were elected to the vacant chairs were distasteful to me. In short, I saw nothing but vexation and annoyance in the future; and when the position of Professor of Surgery in my Alma Mater was unanimously tendered to me, both by the Board of Trustees and Faculty, I did not feel at liberty to decline it, although it was a sore trial both to me and to my family to break up our pleasant relations and attachments in Kentucky. The sad events that followed during the war, arraying families against families and friends against friends, dividing the medical profession, and introducing the spirit of discord into all ranks and conditions of society, proved that I had made a wise decision. The sixteen years which I passed in Kentucky were, in the main, among the happiest of my life, notwithstanding the hostility which I had to encounter at the beginning—an opposition alike unjust and, for a time, extremely annoying to me and to my family.

It may not be out of place at this point to make a brief

record of my impressions of some of the distinguished men whom I met during my residence in Kentucky. Notices of others will be found in my diary and elsewhere.

In February, 1838, occurred one of the most famous duels of modern times, and one which gave rise to the most intense excitement throughout the country on account of its political character. The circumstances were the more surprising, because it was clearly shown, even after the exchange of shots by the combatants, that no difficulty or personal animosity had ever existed between the parties—William J. Graves and Jonathan Cilley, both members of Congress, the one from Kentucky, and the other from Maine. The immediate cause of the duel was a letter addressed by J. Watson Webb, editor of the New York Courier and Inquirer, at that time one of the most prominent and influential papers in the United States, to Mr. Cilley, on account of words uttered during debate, reflecting upon the character of Mr. Webb in reference to matters relating to the United States Bank. This letter, the delivery of which was intrusted to Mr. Graves, Mr. Cilley declined to receive, on the ground that he did not wish to be drawn into any controversy with a public journalist. Under these circumstances Mr. Graves considered it his duty to challenge Mr. Cilley. The parties met at three o'clock, on the 24th of February, near Washington City, close to the boundary line of Maryland and the District of Columbia, accompanied by their seconds and their surgeons, Henry A. Wise, of Virginia, and Dr. Foltz, U. S. N., acting for Mr. Graves, and General George W. Jones, of Wisconsin, and Dr. Duncan, of Ohio, for Mr. Cilley. Upon the field were John J. Crittenden and Mr. Menefee, of Kentucky, as the friends of Mr. Graves, and Mr. Bynum, of North Carolina, and Captain James W. Schaumburg, U. S. A., as the friends of Mr. Cilley. The weapons were rifles. The distance was ninety-two yards. The choice of position fell to the lot of Mr. Wise, while Mr. Jones had the giving of the word. Three shots were exchanged, at the last of which Cilley fell mortally wounded, and in a few minutes expired. It is due to the parties concerned in this transaction, now all deceased, to state that ineffectual efforts were made after the first and second shots to arrest further firing. Mr. Cilley, after what he had pointedly said to Mr. Webb and Mr. Graves in his early correspondence with these gentlemen, could not recede from the stand taken by him. As I have said, he declined to receive Mr. Graves's letter because of his desire to avoid any controversy with Mr. Webb, and in making this statement he neither affirmed nor denied anything respecting that gentleman's character, nor intended to show any disrespect for Mr. Graves. The attempts to adjust the duel during its progress hinged solely upon these latter points, the second of Mr. Graves insisting that the fight should proceed, unless Mr. Cilley should enter a direct disclaimer of any personal exceptions to Mr. Webb as a gentleman and a man of honor, or an indirect one by placing the refusal to receive the note of Mr. Graves upon the ground of privilege. This Mr. Cilley had twice refused to do, and had twice exposed himself to the fire of his antagonist. The result of the third shot has already been stated.

The history of duelling does not show a sadder blot upon its bloody escutcheon than this transaction. Here were two men in the prime of life, of generous natures and noble bearing, members of the national councils, between whom no unkindly feeling had ever at any time existed, fighting for a principle, to satisfy what has been called the "code of honor"—a combat in which one is mortally wounded.

When this duel took place I knew nothing personally of Mr. Graves, but within a few years after, during my residence in Louisville, I made his acquaintance, became his family physician, was for a time a near neighbor of his, and attended him during his last terrible illness. It affords me great pleasure to bear testimony to his private character. A more devoted husband or a kinder father never existed. He was a very handsome man : tall, erect, with a clear brown eye and a manly countenance, with an enthusiastic nature, and a chivalrous disposition ; a warm friend, and a true, patriotic citizen. Bred to the law, he early abandoned the bar for politics, in which he rendered most important service to the Whig party, of which he was for a number of years one of the acknowledged leaders in Kentucky. In the Presidential canvass in 1844 he took a most active part, often driving in his sulky from fifty to seventy miles in the twenty-four hours to meet engagements in different sections of his State. Such labor, combined with the excitement incident to a great campaign, and with stump-speaking, of which he was an admirable representative, ever ready, full of enthusiasm, and full of his subject, could not fail to tell fearfully upon a constitution already seriously undermined, and it is therefore not surprising that he eventually succumbed under its effects. His last illness was protracted. I have, in the course of a long professional life, witnessed much suffering, but never, in any individual, such a frightful concentration of it. His disease was epithelioma, or cancer, of the bladder, which compelled him to keep his bed for three months, during which he daily used large quantities of morphia and chloroform to mitigate his torture. Indeed, during the last few weeks of his life he was kept almost continually in a state of partial insensibility from the effects of the latter medicine. Notwithstanding his frightful sufferings, no groan or murmur of complaint ever escaped his lips. He was emaciated to a skeleton. His death was a great loss to his family, his friends, and his party.

Within a few years after the death of Mr. Graves a statement went the rounds of the public prints that during his

last illness he had labored, in addition to his other sufferings, under remorse of conscience on account of his duel
with Cilley. The assertion, I need hardly say, was without
the shadow of truth. Living within two doors of him, I
saw him frequently three, four, five, and even six times in
the twenty-four hours, and never, on any occasion, either
when his mind was perfectly clear, or clouded from the
effects of suffering, or the stupefying influence of morphia
and chloroform, did he ever refer, directly or indirectly,
to the occurrence. He had long ago made up his mind
that the combat was one of necessity, and that he could
not, as the "code" was then interpreted, have avoided it
without a sacrifice of honor, which, to a man of his gal-
lant nature, is always more precious than life itself. I
took an early opportunity to contradict this statement,
believing it was my duty to do it as the physician and
personal friend of Mr. Graves and his excellent family.

Among the many noteworthy families of Kentucky
during my residence in that State there was none more
remarkable than that which produced the three Breck-
inridges—Robert J., John, and William C., all men of
force of character, and eminent preachers, in charge of
refined and cultured congregations. Robert J., the eldest,
was long known as the fighting parson, from his bitter
controversies and aggressive disposition; but he was undoubtedly the most able and talented of the three. All
were good speakers, all preached long sermons, and all
were strongly wedded to the Presbyterian faith, in which
their mother, a woman of uncommon intellect, had reared
them. Robert long held the supreme power in the Presbyterian Church, not only in Kentucky, but in the great West,
and broke many a lance with the strong men of other denominations. In his personal appearance he had few of
the prominent characteristics of the staid and dignified
clergyman. When I last saw him, in 1853, at the Agricultural Fair at Lexington, he had on nankeen trousers, a

white vest, and a spotted necktie, and I was told that this was his ordinary summer wear. It was certainly a very sensible dress, but it was so unclerical as to attract general attention, and became therefore a subject of unfavorable comment.

Dr. John Breckinridge was directly the opposite of Robert in disposition and habits. He was an amiable man, with a deep sense of modesty, and it is questionable whether he ever had an enemy. He enjoyed a high reputation as a preacher, and the love and admiration of all who knew him. He died comparatively young, the victim of pulmonary phthisis, for which, during his latter days, I attended him for a short time in consultation. His first wife was a daughter of Dr. Miller, a distinguished professor in the Theological Seminary at Princeton. An anecdote has been related of Dr. Breckinridge which admirably illustrates his sly humor. A clergyman, named Sparrow, one evening occupied his pulpit. When the congregation was dismissed a lady inquired of the Doctor who that preacher was. "That man's name is Sparrow," was the reply, "one of those birds spoken of in the Bible, of which two were sold for a farthing."

Dr. William C. Breckinridge was for many years my near neighbor. He was popular as a preacher, and was greatly respected as a courteous and well-bred gentleman. He was for a long time pastor of the Second Presbyterian Church of Louisville, and a short time before the Rebellion was called to the presidency of the University of Mississippi, from which, on the eve of the war, he removed, if I mistake not, to Missouri, where he soon afterwards died.

I cannot close my brief sketch of this family without saying a few words about the mother, from whom the sons evidently, in great degree, if not entirely, inherited their characteristic mental features. Mrs. Breckinridge was a woman of extraordinary powers of mind, with the determination, courage, and energy of a Cæsar. In 1841, while in attendance upon her son, Dr. John Breckinridge, I saw her for the first time. She had come all the way from Lexington, her old home, in a dilapidated family carriage, drawn by two horses, after a fatiguing journey of nearly four days. She was then far advanced in life, very fragile looking, and nearly blind in both eyes from cataract. She told me she was naturally very timid, and had never, in consequence, been able to trust herself upon a steamboat or railway car; and yet this little woman could be as brave as a lioness. Her husband had been the owner of many slaves, and being from home on a certain occasion, several of them determined to kill their mistress, rob the house, and flee the country. There was no white man at the time on the premises, and but for the fidelity of a young negro girl, who had become aware of the plot, the scheme would undoubtedly have been carried into effect. The moment Mrs. Breckinridge heard of it she confronted the ringleader, and told him if he did not behave himself and go about his business she would instantly shoot him. Her determined look and her readiness to defend herself at once arrested the diabolical plot, which, if she had been less courageous, would undoubtedly have cost her her life.

With the history of General John C. Breckinridge, a cousin of the three divines, everybody is familiar. Tall and well formed in person, and elegant in manner, I shall never forget the grace and dignity with which, as Vice-President during Mr. Buchanan's administration, he presided over the Senate. Mr. Breckinridge died in May, 1875, after a long and severe illness, caused by an abscess of the liver, which in time discharged its contents wholly through the lungs. When I saw him, at the request of some of his friends, eight or ten days before his death, with the family physician, Dr. J. R. Desha, Dr. Sayre, of New York, and Dr. Luke P. Blackburn, recently Governor of Kentucky, he was excessively emaciated, and laboring under terrible paroxysms of dyspnœa, momentarily threatening life, and painful to witness. The quantity of matter expectorated in the twenty-four hours varied, on an average, from a pint to a pint and a half, and its expulsion was attended with great fatigue and copious perspiration. It was agreed, in consultation, as a last resort, to make an outlet, if possible, for this fluid, so that it might drain off as fast as it formed, and for this purpose a trocar, in the absence of an aspirator, was pushed through the ninth intercostal space to the full length of the instrument without reaching the cavity of the abscess. As the operation was followed by considerable exhaustion, it was deemed best not to repeat it, and matters consequently remained *in statu quo.* Our conduct was harshly criticised by some of the public journals, but to their strictures I made no reply, conscious that we had done our duty. General Breckinridge succumbed a few days afterwards, completely worn out by his protracted suffering. It is to be regretted that owing to the wife's unconquerable objections a post-mortem examination was not permitted.

In 1849, broken down by overwork and malarial disease, I visited the Harrodsburg Springs on the Kentucky River, then a fashionable resort for invalids, kept by Dr. Graham, and now used as a government asylum for disabled soldiers. While here I saw a great deal of Mr. Poindexter, of Mississippi, an ex-Governor of the State and a United States ex-Senator, an astute lawyer, and a shrewd politician, familiar with all the tricks and devices of party, with an insatiable ambition for the spoils of office, a behemoth that did not hesitate to devour every beast that in any wise obstructed his path. He was much broken in health and spirits by a disease, for which he had been treated at a high fee by a Louisville charlatan. I refer to the case in this manner, because it was at that time known to every man and woman in the valley of the Mississippi.

For a while it was difficult to say which was the more famous, the patient or the physician.

Poindexter was a man of great ability, distinguished for his rhetorical powers, his sarcasm in debate, and the bitterness of his language. He was very aggressive—a man of whom everybody was afraid. Such a man has few friends, and when he can no longer be of use he is dropped by every one. This was the case with the ex-Governor of Mississippi at the time here referred to. He had outlived his usefulness; his party had no longer any need of his services; and his political friends had gradually, one after another, abandoned him. He keenly felt the peculiarity of his position. He was morose, irritable, even irascible. Every one pitied him, and still more his wife, a lovely woman, many years his junior. In his happier moods, when comparatively exempt from suffering, he was a most agreeable companion, with ready wit, an abundant amount of anecdote, and remarkable conversational powers. He had seen much of the world and of the good as well as the evil side of nature. Circumstances, the outgrowth of great talent, and of much personal magnetism in his younger and palmier days, had brought him in contact with the great men and women of the nation, and made him a tower of strength with the Democratic party. He was now old, and the recollections of his former triumphs served but as a poor compensation for his present forlorn and pitiable situation. He ably and successfully defended General Jackson in Congress, but they afterwards became bitter enemies, and this circumstance, added to a duel, in which he killed his adversary, served to estrange him still further from the world. His chief solace, while at Harrodsburg, was "Boaston" and scolding. After I left the Springs I saw Poindexter no more. He died at an advanced age in 1853.

In this year I was visited by a gentleman who had long occupied a distinguished position in the world of letters

and of politics.   I refer to Baron Friedrich Ludwig Georg
Von Raumer, of Berlin, the celebrated historian, politician, and statesman.   He brought me a letter of introduction from a friend in Philadelphia.   It was the Baron's
second visit to this country, the first having been made
in 1843, on which he soon after published a book—
America and the American People—which was translated
by Mr. Turner.   The object of his present visit was to
make himself more intimately acquainted with the nature
of our institutions and the character of our people, and
he brought with him his son, a quiet, reticent young man,
in order not only that he might afford him the benefit of
his experience in his travels, but have a constant companion and watchful friend in case of disease or accident.
The Baron called upon me early in the day, and learning
that his stay in Louisville was limited I invited some
friends to meet him in the evening.   As the hours advanced my wife said to him: "Baron, you must be a
relation of my father's family; my father was a German,
and I often heard him and my mother talk of the Von
Raumers; at school I was always called the 'Baroness,'
as all my schoolmates were familiar with my father's history, and thus, to tease me, gave me this nickname.   I
was then very young, and as my father died at an early
age at sea on his way to Europe, and my mother soon
after followed him to the grave, I have never been able to
trace the connection to a satisfactory conclusion.   Your
visit is a curious coincidence, and perhaps you can give
me some particulars."   The Baron was evidently disconcerted; he blushed, became embarrassed, and soon changed
the subject.   He called the next morning to take leave of
us, but did not once refer to the previous evening's conversation.   In 1868, during our visit to Berlin, we drove
to the son's house, but he was spending the summer at
his country residence.   Thus ended our acquaintance.
What gave point to the Baron's embarrassment at my

house was the fact that my wife's father was a collateral heir of the Von Raumer estate, and was on his way to look after his interests when he was accidentally lost at sea. To institute formal research after intricate titles would have been a useless procedure after the lapse of so many years.

Von Raumer was a profoundly educated man, of rare ability, industry, and perseverance. He was a copious writer, chiefly of historical and political works, and was for many years Professor in the University of Berlin; he was also a member of the German Parliament, and was at one time ambassador at Paris. In 1853 he retired from active life, and devoted the evening of his days to study, travel, and recreation. He was a man of small stature, an excellent linguist, and an agreeable conversationalist.

It was in the spring of 1853 that Mr. James P. Espy, widely known as the "Storm King," presented to me a letter of introduction from a gentleman who was then a colleague of mine—Dr. Drake, of Cincinnati. He was at the time a resident of Columbus, Ohio, and had come to Louisville on matters of business, but chiefly with a view of making some meteorological observations, a subject which had long deeply occupied his attention. I, of course, extended to him a warm welcome, and he did me the honor the following morning to breakfast with me. His conversation was animated, and was directed largely to the explanation of his famous theory of storms, which, while it had many adherents, had also some very powerful opponents. Being a man of positive temperament, he did not express himself in the mildest terms in regard to those who differed from him in opinion. He had made several appeals to Congress for pecuniary aid to carry his theories into effect, but without success, and this disappointment was a great, if not a constant, source of annoyance to him, serving to imbitter the evening of his life. He made himself so agreeable to Mrs. Gross and myself on the occasion here referred to that we were hardly aware when we rose from the table that two hours had passed since we had taken our seats, and when our distinguished guest rose to take his leave we both felt as if we were parting with an old acquaintance. Mr. Espy was a remarkably handsome man, tall, erect, well-proportioned, with a large head and a fine face, expressive of intelligence, and he had about him all the magnetism and characteristics of a well-bred gentleman. Born in 1785, in Western Pennsylvania, he was descended from a Huguenot family, with some of the sturdy blood of the Scotch Covenanters, and, like most men of genius, rose by dint of his own exertions from obscurity into fame. Owing to his father's poverty his early education was neglected, but this defect was gradually overcome by industry and perseverance; and, while still quite young, he became the principal of a classical academy at Cumberland, Maryland, showing that he had made good progress in learning.

Mr. Espy was an enthusiast. Whatever had possession of his mind was not easily dislodged by outside considerations. He was a firm believer in the idea that rain could be induced by keeping up large fires, scattered over large surfaces, and he even thought it possible by this means to maintain the navigation of the upper Ohio River during the dry season. Although Congress refused to give him money to carry out his wishes, he received, through the agency of the late Alexander H. Stephens, of Georgia, a warm personal friend, a government appointment as meteorological observer, an office from which emanated the first telegraphic weather reports ever made. Hence Espy may justly be regarded as the father of the system now in such successful operation in all parts of the civilized world. His death occurred at Cincinnati, in January, 1860, at the age of seventy-five years. Besides his work on storms, Mr. Espy published a treatise on the Will, a metaphysical study, and numerous essays on various subjects.

My recollections of Mr. John J. Crittenden are very vivid; as one of our leading statesmen I had, of course, heard and read much of him before I ever saw him, and when, after my removal to Kentucky in 1840, I met with him for the first time, he captivated me by his pleasant, genial, and frank manner. During my residence in Louisville I saw him frequently, either at the house of his son-in-law, Chapman Coleman, an eminent Louisville merchant, at my house, or at the houses of other gentlemen, and when or wherever I found him he was always the centre of attraction. He was generally beloved and admired, not so much because he was a great man as because of his many amiable qualities, his fine conversational powers, his sly humor, and his large fund of anecdotes. He had been so long in public life, and had been brought in contact with so many distinguished people, that he was a sort of encyclopedia of all public and international measures for half a century during one of the most stirring and interesting periods of our history. Born in 1786, in Woodford County, Kentucky, he was, like many of our great men, the son of a farmer, with no early educational advantages. At that time Kentucky was a new State, an offspring of Virginia; society was in a crude condition, with little of the culture and refinement which have since characterized it, and, as Mr. Crittenden himself told me one day in my parlor, he was fifteen years old before he ever put a hat on his head. A man of force of character can accomplish much by his own efforts, if he feels so inclined, and Mr. Crittenden was more indebted to himself for his education than to any aid derived from the schoolmaster. Kentucky at that period had no academies or colleges of any note. Dr. Marshall, a distinguished physician, brother of Chief Justice Marshall, and father of the celebrated Tom Marshall, was a famous teacher in that day, giving instruction in the classics, in mathematics, and in other branches of knowledge, to fit young men for college and the study of the various professions; but I am not aware that Mr. Crittenden availed himself of these advantages. However this may be, he studied law at an early age, was admitted to the bar, and soon achieved a high reputation as an astute and accomplished jurist. His popularity also rapidly increased, and the consequence was that he was soon called into public life; a life to which he always aspired as a youth, and which he afterwards followed with such distinguished success. From the State Legislature, Mr. Crittenden passed into Congress, thence to the Senate, and thence into General Taylor's cabinet as Attorney-General of the United States. When Mr. Fillmore succeeded to the Presidency, Mr. Crittenden was retained in office. In 1848 he was elected Governor of Kentucky. During his connection with the Senate Mr. Crittenden was the associate of Clay, Webster, Calhoun, Hayne, Benton, and other prominent men, who added lustre to their age and country. While a member of this body he became involved in the Graves and Cilley duel, which has been already mentioned in a former page, and he was unjustly blamed in consequence. The Kentucky Senator used all his influence to prevent a hostile meeting. Public sentiment was afterwards much mollified in regard to Mr. Crittenden's association with this miserable affair; and the same is true of his connection long afterward with the Matt Ward trial, detailed in another page. Here again the circumstances were such as absolutely to force Mr. Crittenden into the arena. As the lifelong and intimate friend of the young man's parents it was impossible for him to refuse to serve as one of his counsel. The public is not always just, and it certainly in this case arrayed itself on the wrong side.

Mr. Crittenden was an able orator, and some of his efforts in the Senate and on the stump are fine specimens of eloquence. His manner as a public speaker, however, was slow, unimpassioned, and unmarked by those higher flashes which characterized the oratory of Calhoun, Hayne, Tom Marshall, and other Southern debaters. His address on the Life and Character of Henry Clay, delivered at Louisville in the presence of an overflowing audience, the *élite* of both sexes, gathered from all parts of the country, soon after that great man's death, was, if not a failure, a feeble performance not at all in harmony with the occasion, or his own well-known ability. The day was uncommonly hot, the building in which the meeting was held was not well adapted to the object, and Mr. Crittenden's delivery was without its usual force and animation. Many of his hearers went away disappointed; and the report of the speech in the papers was not at all calculated to answer the expectation of the public, or of the orator's many friends. This was, if I mistake not, Mr. Crittenden's last public effort.

Mr. Crittenden was thrice married, each time to a beautiful woman. His last wife was the widow of General Ashley, of Missouri, who was celebrated as a great belle, with wonderful powers of fascination, but without any special accomplishments. She survived Mr. Crittenden only a few years. His sons—George and Thomas—were well-known officers during the war of the Rebellion, the former on the Confederate, the latter on the Union side. A life of Mr. Crittenden, in two volumes, was published some years after his death by his daughter, Mrs. Chapman Coleman, a woman of remarkable intellect, with many of the traits of her father and much of his force of character.

Mr. Crittenden was an excellent talker, with a large store of interesting and instructive information. He was fond of society, and was never so happy as when he was surrounded by his family and intimate friends, engaged in telling anecdotes, and in discussing public affairs, in which he always took a lively interest. His habits were sedentary. He was nearly six feet in height, with a handsome face, a good head, and expressive hazel eyes. He was fond of quoting passages from the Bible and the Pilgrim's Progress, the latter of which, as he repeatedly told me, he considered one of the most remarkable books ever written, and such, unquestionably, is the fact.   Mr. Crittenden died in July, 1863.

Mr. Fillmore's term of office expired on the 4th of March, 1853, and late in the following month he accompanied Mr. Crittenden to Louisville, where they were the guests for a short time of Mr. Chapman Coleman, Mr. Crittenden's son-in-law.   At a reception given in the evening of the second day after their arrival, at which all the prominent citizens of Louisville were present, the two distinguished gentlemen were the cynosure of all eyes.   Mr. Fillmore, until then a stranger in Kentucky, attracted special attention.   Tall, well proportioned, with a fine countenance, a large, well-formed head, animated by beautiful blue eyes, and the whole set off by the blandest smile and the most courtly and winsome manners, it is not surprising that he won all hearts and elicited the warmest admiration. When, in 1855, he was presented to Queen Victoria, her majesty declared that he was the handsomest and most elegant American gentleman she had ever seen.   In his youth he worked on his father's farm, and at the age of fifteen was apprenticed to a wool-carder and cloth-dresser. With a very limited school-education, he began the study of the law at nineteen, was in due time admitted to the bar, and rapidly rose to distinction as a politician and statesman, from one important position to another, until, on the death of General Taylor, he succeeded to the highest office attainable on this continent.   He passed through all the grades of office with a spotless private character.

I have many agreeable recollections of Mr. James Guthrie, one of Louisville's noblest citizens during my residence in that city, and one who took as much interest in its rise and prosperity as any man in it.   Born in Kentucky in 1792, he was educated at the Bardstown Academy, a celebrated Catholic seminary, and was early admitted to the Louisville bar, of which he soon became a distinguished member. He represented the city repeatedly in the State Legislature, and served it in various relations in developing its resources. The noble municipal buildings, erected at a great cost, owe their existence mainly to his influence and enterprise. He took a special interest in the establishment of the University of Louisville, of the medical department of which he was for many years President of the Board of Trustees, having succeeded Judge Rowan in that office. My connection with that institution brought me into frequent relation with Mr. Guthrie, and I always found him ready to listen attentively to any suggestions I had to offer in regard to the management of that school, at one time by far the most celebrated of its kind in the Southwest. When General Pierce, in 1853, was elevated to the Presidency, Mr. Guthrie was tendered the portfolio of the Treasury, and a better choice could not have been made. The Secretary remained in office until the expiration of Pierce's administration, when he returned to his old home, and spent most of his time in retirement and in attention to his private affairs, which had suffered more or less during his absence. In 1865 he was elected United States Senator, an office which he would have adorned by his learning, by his large experience as a legislator, and by his dignified and gentlemanly bearing, but which ill health, contracted during his residence at Washington, compelled him to resign before he entered upon the discharge of its duties. Death overtook him in 1869, at the age of seventy-six years.

Guthrie was a man of fine proportions, upwards of six feet in height, with a handsome face and a noble forehead. He was slow in his movements, slow of speech, deliberate in all his acts. His character was massive rather than brilliant, and he took hold of whatever he had to do with a giant's grip.   I had great respect for him as a gentleman and as an upright citizen.   The last time I ever met with him socially was the evening before he went to Washington, which he spent in my study stretched out at full length upon the sofa.

Among the more notable persons at my old home was Judge John Rowan, for seven years my opposite neighbor, remarkable for his intelligence, dignity of character, and urbane and gentle manners.   He was a gentleman of the old school.   Familiarly he was known as the "Old Monarch."   Even Mrs. Rowan, an amiable woman, loved so to call him.   The judge had seen much of public life, had served with distinction on the bench, and had been a member of the United States Senate in the days of its greatest renown.   His house in his later years was the resort of men of distinction irrespective of party, creed, or occupation.   Among others he was visited by his old friend, Martin Van Buren, soon after that gentleman retired from the Presidential office.   For nearly one entire week the "Monarch" and the "Sage of Kinderhook" were hobnobbing together, talking much over olden times, as well as over the present and future, and receiving calls from the more distinguished citizens of the place. No public or private receptions were tendered Mr. Van Buren, and I do not now recollect that he accepted any invitations to dinner.   His visit was strictly private.   He was a well-preserved, handsome-looking man, with all the airs and graces of the well-bred gentleman.   The character of Martin Van Buren for political intrigue is well known. He was a great pet of General Jackson, and lost his election for a second Presidential term on account of his short-sighted opposition to the admission of Texas as a State into the Union.   For once the "Sage of Kinderhook" had lost his head.   His defeat was the end of his political career.   One can appreciate after such a blunder the pithy remark of "Prince John"—"Why, father, the most distinguishing feature of your administration is that you are my father."

By a curious combination of circumstances it happened that I saw very little of Henry Clay during my residence in Kentucky; he rarely visited Louisville, and when he did, he seldom remained more than a day, often not so long. His oldest son, Henry, was for many years a member of the Louisville bar, and I purchased from him a part of the lot on which I built my house on Walnut Street. He was not endowed with intellect of a high order, and was killed at the head of his column in one of the battles of Mexico. His bravery was undoubted. His illustrious father I visited in September, 1852, during the meeting of the Agricultural Fair at Lexington. Accompanied by my elder son and several friends, I drove to Ashland, and had the good fortune to find Mr. Clay at home. Ushered into the parlor, it was only a few minutes before he made his appearance. He received us very cordially, and we soon found ourselves engaged in an animated conversation, the chief topic of which was the state of the country, which was then already foreshadowing the internecine war of 1861. Before we finished our visit, which lasted about half an hour, we had discussed the Roman republic and the natural tendency of states and empires to fall into decay after a longer or shorter existence, from the lawlessness and misgovernment of the people. Mr. Clay was not well, but he talked with great freedom and vivacity, like a man who was fully impressed with the truth of what he was saying. The day before this interview we saw him at the reception-room of the Agricultural Fair, with his daughter-in-law, Mrs. James Clay, leaning on his arm. He was about to enter, when the superintendent, decorated with his badge of office, for some reason refused him admission. An act so rude as this, an insult offered to so aged and distinguished a citizen, gave rise to not a few imprecations among the bystanders.   It was simply an outrage.

I saw Mr. Clay for the last time a year or two after this at Louisville, during the trial of the heirs of Miss Polly Bullitt, a maiden lady, whose will, involving a considerable estate, was disputed by Mr. Guthrie's children.   The ground of the suit was the alleged mental incompetency of the testatrix to make a will.   The case was long in dispute, and attracted more than usual attention.   Eminent counsel were employed on both sides.   Mr. Clay appeared for the defence.   He spoke for several days.   Many of the most distinguished ladies were in attendance.   I well recollect Mr. Clay's appearance.   He stood as erect as a flag-pole, spoke with great deliberation and distinctness, and held spellbound the attention of the judge, bar, and jury, as well as the crowded court-room.   His speech was a plain performance, devoid of any of the flowers of rhetoric.   There was no attempt at display.   He was attired on the occasion in a neat black suit, with a dress coat and a white cravat.   The case was decided, if I mistake not, in favor of the validity of the will.

The admirers of Mr. Clay cannot but regret the motives which induced him to spend his last days at Washington. It was a pitiful ambition which prompted him to forsake his family and his old friends to die at the capital of the country in order that he might have the *éclat* of a public funeral.   Broken down in health and spirits when he left his old home, unable to travel except by slow stages, he knew perfectly well that his days were numbered, and that he could never again see Kentucky.   How much more dignified would it have been if he had breathed out his once precious life in the bosom of his family and in the arms of the woman who for upwards of half a century had watched over his interests, reared his children with a fond mother's care, loved him with a true woman's love, and followed him, wherever he was, with her prayers and her blessings !

I have very pleasant recollections of many of the members of the Louisville bar, which has always been distinguished for its talents, learning, and gentlemanly bearing. I have already spoken of Mr. Guthrie. For Judge Pirtle, who was for years one of its leaders and a most amiable man, I had a warm regard; and Judge Ballard, who died suddenly and unexpectedly some years ago, was long my warm personal friend. He had a well-stored legal mind, and was one of the most conscientious men I have ever known—a man in whom there was no guile, and who was as incapable of bribery as Sir Thomas More or the purest man that ever lived. Judge Bullock was another man for whom I always had a warm personal regard. He is still living, at an advanced age, to adorn the bar and to witness the beneficent effects of his philanthropic labors. An upright judge and an honest man, he enjoys the respect, love, and admiration of his fellow-citizens, and the good-will of all who know him. Since I left Louisville its bar has been strengthened by the addition of numerous men, many of them still quite young, who have added influence and respectability to its ranks. The Louisville Law School has been a power in swelling the corps of educated lawyers in Kentucky and in the surrounding States. Originally in the hands of Loughborough, Pirtle, and Bullock, it is justly regarded as an institution of great value, as it is certainly one of great respectability.

The clergy of Louisville in my day were a pleasant set of men, not all of them noted, however, for their talent or learning. The most able of them, in point of erudition, was Bishop, afterwards Archbishop, Spalding, elsewhere referred to, a genial, pleasant gentleman, who rose to great eminence in the Catholic Church. Among the Protestant denominations I recall with much affection and respect the names of Jackson, Humphrey, Sehon, Craik, Stewart, Robinson, and Bishop Smith, who still survives, at a great age, to honor his Master, and to look back with complacency on the remarkable growth of the Episcopal Church in this country since he first put on the clerical robe, upwards of sixty years ago. All these men were my personal friends.

The society of Kentucky has always been noted for its intelligence, culture, refinement, and hospitality. Many of the most eminent men and women of the country have either been natives or residents of the State. There is no State in the Union which has produced so many beautiful women or so many tall and handsome men. Lexington was at one time called the "Athens of the West" on account of its elegant and brilliant society. Its bar, still respectable, was then generally acknowledged to be one of the ablest and most intellectual in the country. It could boast of a Wickliffe, a Woolley, a Bledsoe, a Menefee, a Breckinridge, a Robertson, and other great names. Holley was at the head of its university; and its medical department, with Caldwell, Dudley, and Yandell in its Faculty, was at the height of its prosperity.

CHAPTER V.

IN 1855 I was solicited by a member of the Board of
Trustees of the University of Pennsylvania to allow my
name to be placed before that body in connection with the
chair of Surgery, which had been recently vacated by the
resignation of Dr. William Gibson.   I was assured in the
most positive manner by my friend, a gentleman of influence and great respectability, Dr. René La Roche, that
the entire medical Faculty, with one exception — Dr.
George B. Wood, who soon after retired from the school—
had pledged themselves to support me, and to use their
best endeavors to insure my election.   Various reasons,
however, induced me to decline the offer; foremost among
which was the fact that the income of the department was
not equal to that of the University of Louisville, and the
next was the circumstance that, if defeated, I should be
subjected to more or less mortification.   When it became
known that I was inexorable, I wrote, at the request of
Dr. D. Hayes Agnew, a warm testimonial in favor of Dr.
Henry H. Smith, who was finally elected.

My election to the vacant chair in the Jefferson Medical College was unanimous, as had been my recommendation by the Faculty.   One of the members, the late Dr. Robley Dunglison, with whom I had for some time been personally acquainted, had previously addressed me upon the subject, as had also Dr. La Roche, asking me whether, in the event of my election, I would accept the chair.   The election came off sooner than I had expected, and I was therefore taken somewhat by surprise.   The truth is, I had a good deal of hesitation about abandoning my residence at Louisville, the more especially as my family were very averse to going away ; and hence, before I finally accepted, I visited Philadelphia, to ascertain more fully the precise state of affairs in reference to the school.   I soon found that it was in an eminently flourishing condition, and I therefore unhesitatingly accepted the chair which had been so flatteringly tendered to me.   My election came off early in May. I remained at Louisville until late in September, when, having disposed of my house, lot, and furniture, I removed with my family to my new home, not without many sighs, although without the slightest misgivings in regard to the future.

During the interval between my appointment and my removal to Philadelphia I was so fortunate as to rent Dr. Mütter's house and furniture, so that on our arrival we were not obliged to go to a hotel, everything being in readiness for our accommodation.   In fact, even dinner was awaiting us, and, to add to the gratification of the occasion, Dr. Dunglison had kindly sent us a bottle of champagne. I will here state that I paid Dr. Mütter two thousand dollars annually for his house and the use of his furniture, and that at the end of the second year I purchased the house and lot for twenty-five thousand dollars cash.   As the building was in bad condition, I was obliged to spend nearly two thousand dollars to put it in repair.   The offices especially showed marked dilapidation.   Everything was old and shabby; the walls had to be repapered, the ceilings cleaned, new bookcases erected, and new chandeliers hung. Mütter's library, left in the offices during the time I occupied the house as a rented one, was very small, not exceeding seven or eight hundred volumes, and of these many were obsolete. My own library, when I left Kentucky, consisted of nearly four thousand volumes, of which almost half the number were left behind in boxes, deposited for safe keeping in the University of Louisville. As I was about to go before my class on the 24th of December, during the first winter of my residence in Philadelphia, the janitor handed me a telegram. It was from the janitor of the University of Louisville, and ran thus: "The University was totally consumed by fire early this morning, including all your books and minerals." I need not say that this intelligence greatly shocked me, and that, as I proceeded with my lecture, the whole scene repeatedly rose up before me, rendering me nervous and uncomfortable. I regretted the disaster so much the more because it involved the loss of the finest and most extensive collection of books on the genito-urinary organs which had ever been brought together in this country. Many of the books were from the library of the late John C. Crosse, the eminent lithotomist, of Norwich, England, and can never be replaced. Besides, the books were not insured. As the situation of the University was completely isolated, such a step had not been deemed necessary. The cause of the fire was a defect in one of the flues, a cause which has occasioned the destruction of a vast deal of property throughout the world.

My Inaugural Address was delivered to a crowded amphitheatre of students, medical men, and citizens. It was well received, and was afterwards published by the class. The class that winter was very large, the income from each chair exceeding five thousand dollars. The number of students afterwards, until the opening of the war, fluctuated between four hundred and seventy-five, as the minimum, and six hundred and thirty-one, as the maximum, the latter being the largest class the college ever had. Mütter, after his resignation, was occasionally heard to indulge in sighs and exclamations about the future prosperity of the school, evidently imagining that his withdrawal would seriously damage it. But no such result followed; and I believe it may be laid down as an axiom that the withdrawal of any one man, however distinguished or popular, never seriously injures any school. When Professor Dunglison resigned it was reasonable to suppose that there would be a falling off of students, as he was widely known and highly appreciated as a teacher, and yet the school did not apparently suffer in the slightest degree. Boerhaave at Leyden, and Cullen at Edinburgh, were the great luminaries among medical teachers in their day, attracting pupils from all parts of the world; but that was long ago, when truly great and learned teachers were scarce. Nowadays everybody teaches, and one-man power has ceased to exert a predominant influence. It is the combined strength of a Faculty that gives a school preëminence and celebrity. Students at the present day care more for their diploma than for the names attached to it. A certificate to go forth upon their errand, that they may, like Samson, slay the people with the jaw-bone of an ass, is what most of them mainly covet.

During the war, and for several years after it was ended, there was, of course, a great decline in the number of students in all the Northern schools, while nearly all the Southern ones were suspended. Two-fifths of our students had for years been supplied by the Southern States. This supply was completely cut off, and the consequence was that our classes were for some time under three hundred. During the last few years, however, there has been a steady increase; and during the present session—1869-'70—our catalogue exhibits four hundred and seventy-five names, embracing representatives from every State and Territory in the Union, as well as from Canada, Nova Scotia, and various foreign countries. The prospect, therefore, is that the institution will again flourish, and will have again, as it had before the war, the largest classes in the United States.

It is proper here to state that as soon as it became known that there would be war nearly two hundred of our Southern students left us. This event, which was the first practical secession, occurred on the evening of the 23d of December, 1861, shortly after the secession of South Carolina. This conduct of the students caused great commotion in our school, as well as in the University of Pennsylvania, and in the city generally.

I was anxious that the Faculty should take some formal notice of this agitation, and that the dean should be commissioned to discharge this function as a part of his official duties. He, however, had great doubt of the propriety of the measure, and when at length he addressed the class it was evident that his remarks fell stillborn upon the ears of that portion of it which they were especially designed to influence and benefit. A strong appeal made at an early day might, I have always been of the opinion, have been of great service. The day before the exodus occurred I devoted fifteen minutes to the consideration of the subject, in which I strongly urged upon the disaffected students the importance of remaining to the end of the session in close attendance upon the lectures; but, although my address was well received, the most profound silence prevailing during its delivery, it failed of its object. Only a few of the Southern students had the good sense to complete their course of studies.

While this *émeute* was in progress letters were received from different Southern schools, as the Richmond, Augusta, Charleston, and Atlanta, offering to receive the seceders with open arms, and to give them their tickets, at the same time promising to graduate such as might present themselves as candidates. Governor Henry A. Wise made them a long speech of welcome on their arrival at Richmond, in the college of which most of them enlisted. I have often wondered what ultimately became of these young men, many of them the sons of wealthy and highly respectable parents, well educated, refined, and ambitious of distinction. That many of them perished during the war from accident and disease is unquestionable, and it is altogether probable that most of those that escaped with their lives were doomed to a worse fate—total demoralization and utter worthlessness!

I have now been in the Jefferson Medical College nearly fourteen years, and of the men who were my colleagues when I entered it only one survives. John K. Mitchell, crippled for several years by apoplexy, was the first to fall by the wayside, his death having been occasioned by an attack of pneumonia in the spring of 1858. A necrological notice of him from my pen is contained in the North American Medico-Chirurgical Review for May, 1858. Dr. Robert M. Huston, who resigned in 1857, on account of ill health, and who was succeeded in the chair of Materia Medica and Therapeutics by Dr. Thomas D. Mitchell, followed next in order; then came Professor Franklin Bache, in April, 1864; Dr. Robley Dunglison in April, 1869; and Dr. Charles D. Meigs in June following. Pancoast is thus the only survivor, all these sad changes having occurred within less than thirteen years. It should be added that Dr. Thomas D. Mitchell died in 1865, and was succeeded by Dr. John B. Biddle. Dr. Bache's successor was Dr. B. Howard Rand, and Dr. Dunglison's, Dr. J. Aitken Meigs. Dr. Mütter, my predecessor in the chair of Surgery, died at Charleston, South Carolina, in April, 1859. In 1873 Dr. Joseph Pancoast vacated the chair of Anatomy, which he had filled with distinguished ability since 1841, and was succeeded by his son, Dr. William H. Pancoast, he himself being appointed Emeritus Professor. In April, 1877,

Professor Rand resigned his chair on account of ill health, and was succeeded by Dr. Robert E. Rogers, for twenty-five years Professor of Chemistry in the University of Pennsylvania. The title of the chair was changed at my suggestion to ex-Judge James Campbell and Mr. Henry M. Phillips, two prominent members of the Board of Trustees, to Medical Chemistry and Toxicology. The college had groaned long enough under the teachings of high school chemistry, of little use to a medical student.

When I settled in Philadelphia there were four medical schools, which, in 1857-'58 had an aggregate class of eleven hundred and thirty-nine students. Of these, five hundred and one attended the Jefferson Medical College, four hundred and thirty-five the University of Pennsylvania, one hundred and forty the Pennsylvania College, and sixty-three the Philadelphia College. The number of graduates in the same institutions was four hundred and seven— two hundred and nine in the first named, one hundred and forty-five in the second, thirty-five in the third, and eighteen in the fourth.

It was the custom at that time for each professor to deliver a lecture introductory to his course at the opening of the session, the first week of which was always consumed in this absurd manner. To break up this system it took me four years, two of the schools having in the meantime perished from inanition. The University and Jefferson College, after repeated interviews upon the subject, finally agreed to have only one general introductory and to commence the didactic course the next day, the class thus gaining five days of valuable time, consumed under the other system mostly in idleness. I have always claimed some credit for having effected this important change. It was too bad that twenty-eight men should have wasted their time and talents in this manner. It was almost as hard to move the two Faculties of the schools in this matter as it would be for a regiment of soldiers to move the rock of Gibraltar, so completely steeped were they in fogyism.

During the late war I was seized, as was natural with one in my position, with a great desire to make myself practically acquainted with the nature and treatment of gunshot injuries, and for this purpose I visited the battle-field of Shiloh, in Tennessee, shortly after I received intelligence of that engagement. This, if I mistake not, was fought on the 6th and 7th of April, and I set out on my journey on the evening of the 10th. A heavy snow-storm prevailing in the afternoon and evening, the train was delayed about fifteen miles out of town, and we did not reach Harrisburg until late in the afternoon. When I arrived at Shiloh all the wounded had been placed upon government steamboats lying at the wharf at Pittsburg Landing. Upon one of these I took passage as far as Mound City, where, and at Cairo, accommodations had been provided for the unfortunate sufferers. On the voyage I examined and took notes of all the more interesting cases ; and I did the same in the hospital at Mound City during the six days that I remained at that then apparently God-forsaken village, in which there was not a dry spot for a man's feet to rest upon. The whole country for miles around was submerged, and, as the Ohio River was very high, the scene as witnessed from my lodgings in the hospital was frightful. During my sojourn in this delectable place, designed by its enthusiastic founders to become a great city and a great commercial and manufacturing centre, I received every possible attention and courtesy from the hospital physicians for the succcessful prosecution of my inquiries. The hospital contained many highly interesting and instructive cases, sketches of which were transferred to my note-book for future reference.

I must not forget to state that, in company with my son, Dr. S. W. Gross, Brigade Surgeon, I rode leisurely over the battlefield at Shiloh, and I became strongly impressed with the disadvantages of such a position. Most of the hard fighting took place on timbered ground, amidst ugly ravines and more or less underbrush, rendering the movements of both armies very embarrassing. The boat which carried me up to Pittsburg Landing had on board several military officers and a large number of medical men, intent, for the most part, upon seeing the battlefield and rendering such assistance as the occasion might demand. The evening before we reached our destination I delivered, at the unanimous request of my professional brethren, an extemporaneous lecture upon amputations and gunshot injuries, for which they tendered me a vote of thanks. I was absent from home nearly three weeks, and when I returned I felt fully compensated for the fatigue and expense of the journey.

In the spring of 1862 Surgeon-General Hammond offered me the post of Surgeon-in-Chief of the George Street Hospital in this city, an office which, as I had no fitness for it, I promptly declined, preferring to be placed in charge of the surgical ward, so as to be the better able to study gunshot injuries. The hospital was kept open for about nine months, and under the judicious administration of Dr. L. D. Harlow, who was appointed, at my solicitation, to the position originally offered to me, it effected a great deal of good; great attention was paid to cleanliness and ventilation, and the number of recoveries was proportionably gratifying. During my connection with the hospital I performed a number of important operations, such as amputation of the thigh and excision of the shoulder-joint, followed, in nearly every instance, by excellent recovery.

In the summer of 1862 I was appointed by Surgeon-General Hammond a member of a board of commissioners to examine into the merits of artificial limbs, with the view of furnishing our mutilated soldiers with a proper substitute. The board consisted of Dr. Valentine Mott, Dr.

Satterlee, U. S. A., Dr. Bache, U. S. N., Dr. W. H. Van
Buren, and myself. The meeting was held in New York.
Upwards of a dozen manufacturers were in attendance,
and they all with one accord assured the commission that
the flap operation, as it is termed by surgeons, left by far
the best stump for the adaptation and comfortable wearing
of an artificial substitute. I strongly advocated the use
of what is known as the peg leg, on account of its better
adaptation to the wants of the private soldier. In this,
however, I was overruled, every one of my colleagues
being in favor of supplying each man with the more elegant and costly, but far less durable, limb. I do not know
what the government paid for this luxurious article, but
the price of each could not have been much less than one
hundred dollars.

Immediately after the battle of Bull Run I went to
Washington City, Georgetown and Alexandria to inspect
the hospitals in those places and to study gunshot wounds.
At Washington, the day after the battle, everything was
in confusion; soldiers were lying in the streets in great
numbers, some on their knapsacks, others on the bare
earth, and horses and wagons were often seen in every
direction, apparently without any one in charge of them.
The whole city, indeed, seemed to be completely demoral-
ized. The next day I visited Arlington Heights, the late
residence of General Lee, and then drove over to Alexandria, in the hospitals of which every courtesy was shown
me by the surgeons in attendance. Whatever struck me
as of interest I took notes of, and afterwards embodied
some of the material thus collected in my System of Surgery. The treatment here, as well as in the hospitals at
Washington and Georgetown, was for the most part very
simple, consisting largely of cold-water dressings, with
great attention to cleanliness and ventilation. Before I
left Washington I called upon Mr. Cameron, the Secretary
of War, to offer my services to the government in any

capacity in which they might be useful; but no demand was ever made upon them, and the consequence was that I remained quietly at home in the bosom of my family, cultivating the arts of peace and attending faithfully to my practice. At that time our wise statesmen cherished the idea that the war would be at an end in less than ninety days. Any goose who had the slightest knowledge of Southern character might have known better. This stupidity came very nigh proving disastrous to the Government.

Soon after my arrival at Philadelphia, Dr. T. G. Richardson and I issued the North American Medico-Chirurgical Review, Messrs. J. B. Lippincott & Co. being the publishers. The understanding was that the patrons of the Louisville Medical Review should receive the new journal for the first six months to cover their subscription, which was five dollars a year. One of the peculiar features of the new, or rather substitute, journal was that each department of the sciences was intrusted to a separate contributor, whose duty it was to furnish an abstract of the current literature, so that it was always fully booked up in regard to the latest discoveries and improvements. The reviews were analytical and critical—sometimes quite caustic, although never discourteous or unjust. The Editor's Table was always interesting, as it gave a brief abstract of the latest intelligence. There were, besides, necrological notices and a bi-monthly bibliographical record. The original articles were often able and elaborate. One of our most learned, frequent, and exhaustive writers was Dr. John Bell. A dollar a page was the sum—and a meagre one it was—paid to the contributors. The work went on well until the war broke out, when all our Southern subscribers dropped off, and the publishers were compelled to abandon it at the close of the fifth year. It was a day of great rejoicing with me when I received the intimation that this step was required; for during the last twelve months of the existence of the journal really the whole drudgery of editing it devolved upon me, notwithstanding the original stipulation to the contrary—Dr. Richardson having moved to New Orleans more than three years previously as Professor of Anatomy in the University of Louisiana, and my son, Dr. Samuel W. Gross, who had acted as assistant editor, having gone into the army as a brigade surgeon. I had fretted under the editorial hardships, and was therefore charmed when I got rid of a task which had been, in some degree, forced upon me, for which I never had any taste, and which encroached altogether too much upon my time and patience. What was worse than all, when anything appeared in the pages of the journal that was in any wise offensive, either in reality or imagination, the whole burden was sure to fall upon me as the senior editor. To the abuse which I thus received I rarely formally replied, a note of explanation being generally deemed quite sufficient. I was determined never to involve myself or the journal in controversy, or to do anything inconsistent with professional, manly editorial dignity. Great regret was expressed at the discontinuance of the journal, and even long after that event—even, indeed, after the close of the war—letters reached me from various sections of the country with a request to send specimen numbers of the Review, the writers not knowing that it had long ago breathed its last. It was considered, although I say it myself, the best critical medical journal ever published on this continent, and for that reason, if no other, it was a source of regret with many practitioners that it was so short-lived.

I contributed to the pages of this journal a number of more or less elaborate reviews, as well as original papers, and it was made, during the greater part of its existence, the vehicle of the reports of my clinics at the Philadelphia Hospital and the Jefferson Medical College. In the July number for 1858 I furnished an elaborate paper of forty pages on the Nature and Treatment of Tuberculosis of the Hip Joint, illustrated by dissections. Fees for Professional Services was published in the Editor's Table at the end of the volume. One of the most careful articles furnished by me was a Sketch of the Life and Services of Ambrose Paré, covering twenty-four pages. It was my last contribution to the journal, with the exception of some necrological notices and the editorial valedictory.

In the autumn of 1857 I founded, along with Dr. J. M. Da Costa, the Philadelphia Pathological Society, of which I was elected the first President and Dr. Da Costa the first Secretary. Dr. René La Roche and Dr. Alfred Stillé were Vice-Presidents, Dr. Thomas G. Morton Assistant Secretary, and Dr. Addinell Hewson Treasurer. The meetings were held then, as now, once a fortnight, and consisted principally of the younger members of the profession. The idea of instituting such a society was first broached by myself to Dr. Da Costa, whose feelings were at once warmly enlisted in the matter; and within a few weeks after we had talked it over the preliminary meeting took place at my office. For a number of years the society occupied a room in the building on the Pennsylvania Hospital grounds, formerly used for the accommodation of West's picture of Christ Healing the Sick. After the completion of the new edifice of the College of Physicians an apartment was rented in it, which the Society has ever since occupied. It has been steadily increasing in prosperity and influence. Its Transactions, originally published in the North American Medico-Chirurgical Review, and afterwards in the American Journal of the Medical Sciences, is now issued in book form.

One of the chief motives which induced me to remove to Philadelphia was to get rid of a large and annoying family practice at Louisville and to write an elaborate System of Surgery, for the production of which my leisure in Kentucky was not sufficient. I had long contemplated such a work, and I knew that unless I changed my residence I should never be able to fulfil an object which lay so near my heart and was so intimately interwoven with my ambition and the great purposes of my professional life. Accordingly, upon my arrival in Philadelphia, I confined myself strictly to office and consultation business, to patients from a distance, and to surgical operations. A few families, nevertheless, attached themselves to me, despite my wishes; but, with these exceptions, I have rigidly carried out my original intention, and I have thus escaped a vast deal of hard work, especially night practice, which always causes so much wear and tear of mind and body. The income from my practice the first year amounted to four thousand dollars; from the school, a little upwards of five thousand dollars. My business after this rapidly increased, and the school also increased in prosperity until the outbreak of the war, when both declined, as we were cut off from Southern patients and Southern students, as I have already mentioned.

I had commenced the composition of my Surgery several years before I left Kentucky, and I now set vigorously to work to complete it. I had sketched the plan and adopted a title, both of which met with the approval of Messrs. Blanchard & Lea, who had agreed to publish it. I had determined to do my best to make it, if possible, the most elaborate, if not the most complete, treatise in the English language, and I therefore gave myself ample time for the labor. The heads of my lectures served me as a valuable guide, and I generally wrote with facility, as my knowledge of the subject, from long study, practice, and contemplation, was extensive, and, in the main, accurate. I generally spent from five to eight hours a day upon my manuscript, subject of course to frequent and sometimes annoying interruptions by patients. In the winter I commonly sat up till eleven and half past eleven o'clock at night. I then closed my study, and almost invariably took a walk down Chestnut Street as far as the State House, in order to obtain a little fresh air and to shake off my mind the subject upon which I had been so assiduously engaged. By this means I generally succeeded in obtaining a good night's rest with sound and refreshing sleep. Unless I was greatly interrupted, I seldom wrote less than from ten to fifteen pages of foolscap in the twenty-four hours, and I rarely retired until they were carefully corrected. It was not often I rewrote anything, although I not unfrequently interlined. In the winter, during the continuance of the lectures, my pen was less active than in the recess, but I nevertheless seldom failed to do a good day's work. I jogged along in this manner until early in the spring of 1859, when, the manuscript being ready, the printers commenced their task, and I the hard one of proof-reading. The preface was dated July 8th, 1859. Soon after, the work was issued in two portly octavo volumes, numbering, in the aggregate, two thousand three hundred and sixty pages, and profusely illustrated by engravings on wood. The mechanical execution was highly creditable to the publishers, printers, and artists. The edition comprised two thousand copies, and cost a large sum of money, enough, as Blanchard & Lea assured me, to have enabled them to open a respectable mercantile house on Market Street.

An author is not always happy when his labor is over. Like Gibbon, he may congratulate himself, or even thank God, that the last syllable has oozed from the point of his pen. But his self-complacency is short-lived, when, after the first night's repose, he reflects that his work has to pass through an ocean of criticism, and that every little cock-sparrow that sits upon an editorial tripod is ready to pounce upon him and pronounce judgment upon his writings, whether he knows anything of their merits or not. I had not to wait long for a verdict. First came the weeklies, then the monthlies and bi-monthlies, and finally the stately quarterlies, all testifying to the excellence of the work, and not a few of them declaring that it was the best system of Surgery in the English, if not, indeed, in any language. Of course, they said, it had faults and imperfections, but these were, for the most part, passed lightly over, and, in the main, I had great reason to be satisfied with the verdict of my countrymen. Abroad the work was equally well received, the reviewers bestowing upon it the highest encomiums, both as a scientific and literary production. My surgical brethren to whom I had sent complimentary copies, all, with one exception, and that a former colleague and one of my most intimate friends, at least confessedly so, bore testimony to the success of my labors. Although I have since repeatedly met the excepted gentleman and have seen in his study the identical copy of the work I sent him, he has never alluded to it in my presence. My philosophy has never been able to comprehend his reticence, the less so as he occupies, and that very deservedly, an elevated professional position.

The work has now—1870—passed through four editions, the last of which was stereotyped for six thousand copies. Each issue, excepting the stereotyped one, was a great improvement upon the preceding, the labor spent upon it having been excessive, in search of every available source of information, including always the results of my own ever-increasing experience and more mature reflection. The edition now in preparation has occupied all my leisure during the last four years, and has required an almost inconceivable amount of labor in the way of additions and modifications. The work will, in fact, be so thoroughly changed, and so greatly improved, as to constitute essentially a new production. Much of this labor has been rendered necessary by the extraordinary progress of surgery and the remarkable changes that have occurred in the treatment of accidents and diseases. It will be a long time before the laws of this department of the healing art will be as immutable as those of the Medes and Persians. This edition was issued in 1872, the last proof having been read the evening before my departure for Europe.

Bacon has remarked that "Some books are to be tasted, ... and some few to be chewed and digested." Mine, I fear, belongs to the former rather than to the latter class. It would take a man, even with the most excellent set of teeth, a long time to chew my big book, and a much longer time, even with the most powerful stomach, to digest it; and yet the work has had many readers; and so, judging from this fact, it must have been productive either of much good or much harm.

I have often been told that I have simplified surgery. A higher compliment could not have been paid me. Both as a writer and as a teacher my aim has always been to make myself understood, or, in other words, to express myself in clear, intelligible language, and to compress the greatest amount of matter into the smallest possible space. I was never satisfied unless I could give at least one exhaustive outline of the subject discussed. To leave a subject imperfect was, in my opinion, to mutilate it.

What compensation does the reader think I obtained for this hard work, this excessive toil of my brain, including original composition, the correction and improvement of new editions, and the proof-reading, in itself a horrible task, death to brain and eyes, extending over a period certainly not less than fifteen years? Eighty-five cents a copy, all told, and no extra dividends! Two dollars and a half ought to have been the price, or, what would have been more equitable, an equal distribution of the profits from the sale of the work. No wonder authors are poor and publishers are rich!

One of the most painful circumstances associated with authorship is the uncertainty connected with one's works, or, in other words, with the fate that may await them, the duration of their existence, and the estimation in which they will be held by posterity, should they be so fortunate as to reach it. "Literature," says Horace Walpole, "has many revolutions; if an author could rise from the dead after a hundred years, what would be his surprise at the adventures of his work!" Professional works, however erudite or scientific, are usually short-lived. Few survive their authors, and hardly one remains in active circulation beyond fifteen or twenty years.

The only review of my System of Surgery, at all worthy of the work, was given of the fifth edition in the Dublin Journal of Medical Science for 1874. It comprised nearly fifty pages of that periodical, and was at once able, critical, and analytical. The review thus concludes: "His work is cosmopolitan, the surgery of the world being fully represented in it. The work, in fact, is so historically unprejudiced, and so eminently practical, that it is almost a false compliment to say that we believe it to be destined to occupy a foremost place as a work of reference while a system of surgery, like the present system of surgery, is the practice of surgeons."

At the outbreak of the war I wrote a little Manual of Military Surgery, a kind of pocket companion for the young surgeons who were flocking into the army, and who for the most part were ill prepared for the prompt and efficient discharge of their duties. It was composed in nine days, and published in a fortnight from the time of its inception, having originally been designed as a leading article for the North American Medico-Chirurgical Review. The work embraced in outline the whole subject of military surgery and hygiene, and under the care of J. B. Lippincott & Co. passed through two editions of two thousand copies each. It was republished at Richmond, and was extensively cited by the Confederate surgeons during the war. This little book was far more profitable to me, in a commercial point of view, considering the time and labor bestowed upon it, than any other of my productions.   A translation of it in Japanese appeared at Tokio in 1874.

In 1861 I edited a work, an octavo volume of upwards of eight hundred pages, entitled Lives of Eminent American Physicians and Surgeons of the Nineteenth Century. It was dedicated to Dr. Samuel Jackson, an eminent physician of this city, formerly of Northumberland, Pennsylvania, and to Dr. John W. Francis, of New York, one of the great men of the country, full of wit, learning, and *bonhomie*.   It was designed to fill a void that had long been felt in our literature, the only productions of the kind being those of Thacher and of Williams, for the most part crude compilations, especially the work of the latter.   My list of collaborators embraced some of the ablest medical men in the country.   The two most elaborate as well as the two best articles were those on Rush and Physick, supplied, respectively, by Dr. Samuel Jackson and Dr. John Bell, of this city.   For the latter I paid one hundred dollars, and it was the only one for which any compensation was asked.   Bell was poor, and I could not refuse.   Altogether the work cost me upwards of two hundred dollars— a dead loss, as I never received anything for the copyright. I contributed myself only three sketches—Ephraim McDowell, the ovariotomist; Drake, the great Western physician; and John Syng Dorsey, the nephew of Physick and the author of the Elements of Surgery.   The book cost me much labor and vexation, and was, commercially speaking, a failure.   The undertaking was altogether a labor of love on my part.

In 1868, in the discourse which I read before the American Medical Association at its meeting at Washington, as its president, I called, among other matters, the attention of that body to a new method of appointing medical witnesses as experts in cases involving medico-legal considerations.   In 1869, at the meeting at New Orleans, an elaborate paper from my pen on the Training of Nurses was read, I myself being absent from unavoidable circumstances. The following year I read the same paper before the Pennsylvania State Medical Society, at its meeting at Erie. The paper attracted much attention, as it was the first ever published on that subject in the United States. Extra copies were printed, and a committee was appointed to bring the matter more prominently before the profession and the public; but it failed to act, and others have since done the work.

The publication of an American Medical Register, comprising a list of the names and residences of all the members of the regular profession, afterwards issued by Dr. D. G. Brinton, editor of the Philadelphia Medical and Surgical Reporter, had its origin in my suggestion.

In June, 1874, I read before the American Medical Association, at its meeting at Detroit, an address on Syphilis in its Relation to the National Health, in which I spoke of the deteriorating influence of this disease upon the human race, of its extensive prevalence, of the importance of enacting laws for its arrest, and of the identity, in many cases, of syphilis and what is known as scrofula. The address, comprising nearly fifty pages, afterwards published in the Transactions of the Association, occupied nearly two hours in its delivery, and received the highest commendation from the meeting,—from Dr. Sims, of New York, more especially, who in some eloquent remarks, called attention to its great value, and offered a resolution for the appointment of a committee to present the subject to the consideration of the legislatures of the different States and Territories. Extra copies were widely disseminated. The preparation of the address cost me much labor and thought. The unicity of the syphilitic poison was strongly insisted upon, and established by irrefragable testimony. The Detroit Free Press, of June 4th, 1874, in speaking of this address, says: "Dr. Gross delivered a long, learned, and deeply interesting discourse upon a

strictly professional subject, the nature of which forbids its
publication in a secular journal.'' This remark reminds
me of my boyish days, when, in certain rural districts,
over-modest dames used to blush when they spoke of Leg-
horn hats, and dressed the legs of the piano in pantalets;
it is an illustration of the old adage, ''Straining at a
gnat and swallowing a camel.'' The filthy quack ad-
vertisements in the same number of the Free Press
are in striking contrast with such squeamishness on the
part of its editor. The occasion was a most opportune
one for calling attention to a disease which is rapidly
undermining the health and life of the nation, and which
is a hundredfold worse in its effects than the fiercest
epidemic that ever struck terror into the hearts of a people.
In Great Britain and on the continent of Europe they generally call such things by their proper names. In this
country, which in this respect is less enlightened, we are
acquiring this habit gradually. Fanatics and hypocrites
cannot be taken by storm.

The following year I read before the same body, at its
meeting at Louisville, May 5th, 1875, a discourse on
Bloodletting Considered as a Therapeutic Agent. My
object in preparing the address was to recall the attention
of the profession to the importance of the abstraction of
blood in the treatment of inflammation. I asserted that the
operation ought to be performed more frequently, and that,
with proper care, it was calculated to be of immense benefit
not only in the treatment of inflammation, but in many
other affections attended with general vascular repletion
and local congestions. This paper was also well received,
and I flatter myself that it has already been productive of
much good. The announcement of the title of the discourse, One of the Lost Arts, excited much attention and
speculation previous to its delivery before the Association.

In October, 1875, I delivered two elaborate lectures introductory to my course at the college on the History of

American Medical Literature from 1776 to the Present Time. These discourses cost me much labor, occupying most of my leisure between my return from the meeting of the American Medical Association at Louisville and the opening of the winter session of the school. The design of the lectures, afterwards issued in book form, was to give a sketch, true and faithful, of the literature of the profession, holding up as in a mirror what each author had done to illustrate his respective department. The brochure occupies eighty-five octavo pages.

In the American Journal of the Medical Sciences for April, 1876, is an article, consisting of fifty-three closely-printed pages, from my pen on the History of American Surgery from 1776 to 1876. It is one of several papers by different writers illustrative of the progress of the different branches of medicine in this country during the period here specified, and it has since, along with these papers, been issued in book form as a kind of centennial souvenir. I need not add how much effort and thought this sketch cost me. It was written at the request of the editors of the Journal. Mr. Lea, the proprietor, paid me the magnificent sum of sixty-six dollars and twenty-five cents for my labor; that is, at the rate of one dollar and a quarter a page! Let me add, however, that pecuniary compensation did not influence me in preparing it for the press. The article will be read one hundred years hence, and that must be my reward.

Among other contributions which I have at various times made to medical and surgical literature, I may briefly refer to the following :—

A VALEDICTORY ADDRESS TO THE STUDENTS OF THE JEFFERSON MEDICAL COLLEGE: March 14th, 1860.

AN ACCOUNT OF A REMARKABLE CASE OF MELANOSIS, OR BLACK CANCER: from the North American Medico-Chirurgical Review for May, 1860.

PRACTICAL OBSERVATIONS ON THE NATURE AND TREATMENT OF

PROSTATORRHŒA: a paper read before the Medical Society of the State of Pennsylvania, at its meeting in Philadelphia, June, 1860, and published in the North American Medico-Chirurgical Review and in the Society's Transactions.

BRUNONIANISM, TODDISM, AND OTHER ISMS: a paper read before the Philadelphia County Medical Society, November 14th, 1860, and published in the North American Medico-Chirurgical Review, January, 1861.

NECROLOGICAL NOTICE OF JEDEDIAH COBB, M. D., formerly Professor of Anatomy in the University of Louisville: published in the same Review, January, 1861.

BIOGRAPHICAL SKETCH OF CHARLES WILKINS SHORT, M. D., formerly Professor of Materia Medica and Medical Botany in the University of Louisville, Kentucky: prepared by request of the American Philosophical Society.

THEN AND NOW: ADVANCES IN MEDICAL SCIENCE IN THE PAST FORTY YEARS: a Discourse Introductory to the Forty-third Course of Lectures in the Jefferson Medical College of Philadelphia in 1867. This address attracted much attention, and occupied nearly two hours in its delivery.

THE LIVE PHYSICIAN: Charge to the Graduates at the Forty-third Annual Commencement of the Jefferson Medical College in 1868.

A MEMOIR OF VALENTINE MOTT, M. D.: in 1868.

A MEMOIR OF ROBLEY DUNGLISON, M. D.: read before the College of Physicians of Philadelphia, October 20th, 1869.

In May, 1870, I contributed to the Medical Practitioner, issued at Louisville, an article on NATURE'S VOICE IN DISEASE AND CONVALESCENCE.

AN ADDRESS BEFORE THE ALUMNI ASSOCIATION OF THE JEFFERSON MEDICAL COLLEGE: March 11th, 1871.

ADDRESS BEFORE THE MEDICAL SOCIETY OF THE STATE OF PENNSYLVANIA AT ITS TWENTY-SECOND ANNUAL SESSION: June, 1871.

THE FACTORS OF DISEASE AND DEATH AFTER INJURIES, PARTURITION, AND SURGICAL OPERATIONS: a paper read before the American Public Health Association in Philadelphia, November, 1874.

THE GLORY AND HARDSHIPS OF THE MEDICAL LIFE: a Valedictory Address at the Forty-ninth Annual Commencement of the Jefferson Medical College, March 11th, 1875.

THE PROXIMATE CAUSE OF PAIN: an address delivered before the American Medical Association at its meeting at Chicago, 1877.

AN ADDRESS DELIVERED BEFORE THE KENTUCKY STATE MEDICAL SOCIETY AT ITS MEETING AT DANVILLE, IN 1879, AT THE DEDICATION OF THE MONUMENT ERECTED IN MEMORY OF EPHRAIM McDOWELL: published in octavo by the Society.

A MEMOIR OF DR. ISAAC HAYS, late editor of the American Journal of the Medical Sciences: published in the Journal, and separately in 1879.

THE SOCIAL POSITION OF THE DOCTOR: published in the New York Medical Record, March 13th, 1880.

In 1881 I prepared a memoir of John Hunter, entitled JOHN HUNTER AND HIS PUPILS, read in the same year as an anniversary discourse before the Academy of Surgery of Philadelphia, and published soon after as an octavo volume of ninety-six pages.

In 1882 I delivered the valedictory address to the graduates of Bellevue Hospital Medical College, New York: not published.

AN ADDRESS OF WELCOME BEFORE THE NATIONAL ASSOCIATION FOR THE PROTECTION OF THE INSANE AND THE PREVENTION OF INSANITY: January, 1883.

A paper on the VALUE OF EARLY OPERATIONS IN MORBID GROWTHS: read before the American Surgical Association at its meeting at Cincinnati, in May, 1883, and published in its Transactions.

THE IMPORTANCE OF HAVING TRAINED NURSES FOR THE SMALLER TOWNS AND RURAL DISTRICTS, AND THE PROPER METHOD OF SECURING THEM: published in the Philadelphia Medical News for September 15th, 1883.

OBITUARY NOTICE OF DR. J. MARION SIMS: prepared for the Medical News the evening after I received the intelligence of his death.

NOTE.—In addition to the contributions referred to, DR. GROSS a few weeks before his death wrote two important papers, in the preparation of which he had taken profound interest, and the proof of which he corrected during the pain and physical weakness incident to his last illness. Of these, the former —WOUNDS OF THE INTESTINES—was read before the American Surgical Association by his friend, Professor T. G. Richardson, of New Orleans, on April 30th, 1884; and the latter, entitled LACERATIONS OF THE FEMALE SEXUAL ORGANS CONSEQUENT UPON PARTURITION; their Causes and their Prevention, was read, two days after his death, by Dr. S. C. Busey, before the American Medical Association.—EDITORS.

During my residence at Cincinnati I was elected a member of the Cincinnati Medical Society, of the Ohio Historical and Philosophical Society at Columbus, and of the Medical Society of Louisiana at New Orleans. After I moved to Louisville, I became a member of the College of Physicians of Philadelphia, and of the American Philosophical Society. In 1868 I was elected a member of the Royal Medical and Chirurgical Society of London; and in 1869 of the Imperial Medical Society of Vienna. While in attendance at the British Medical Association at Oxford in August, 1868, I was made an honorary member of that body. I am a member of the Massachusetts Medical Society, of the New York State Medical Society, of the Academy of Medicine of New York, of the Philadelphia County Medical Society, of the Medical Society of the State of Pennsylvania, of the Kentucky State Medical Society, of the American Medical Association, of the National Association for the Protection of the Insane, of the American Public Health Association, of the Academy of Natural Sciences, of the Pathological Society of Philadelphia, and of the Medical Jurisprudence Society of Philadelphia. In April, 1870, I received the diploma of the Medico-Chirurgical Society of Edinburgh, composed of the most distinguished men in that city. I am also a member of the Medical Society of Christiania, and of the Royal Society of Public Medicine of Belgium. In April, 1874, I was elected a member of the Clinical Society of London; in 1876, of the Sociedad Medica de San Luis Potosi of Mexico; and soon after of the Medical Society of London.

In April, 1870, I was appointed president of the Teachers' Medical Convention, assembled at Washington City, to consider the improvements that might be suggested for a system of education for the American Medical Colleges. In June of the following year I was elected president of the Medical Society of the State of Pennsylvania, at its

meeting in this city.   In September, 1876, I was honored
with the office of president of the International Medical
Congress, held in this city—an honor which I greatly value,
the more because it was unsolicited, and unanimously bestowed both by the committee on nominations and by the
congress.   On the 19th of November, 1878, I was elected
an honorary member of the Pathological Society of London, a distinction which I highly appreciated, as I was the
first regular teacher of Pathological Anatomy in the United
States.

During my residence at Louisville I assisted in founding
the Kentucky State Medical Society, of which I was afterwards president; in 1863, I was elected president of the
Philadelphia County Medical Society; and, in 1867, president of the American Medical Association, a compliment
the more cherished because it was conferred at Cincinnati, my early Western home, upwards of a quarter of a
century before.   In 1880 I was made president of the Board
of Trustees of the Pennsylvania College of Dental Surgery,
and in 1883 I was made president of the Medical Jurisprudence Society of Philadelphia.

The Philadelphia Academy of Surgery was founded in
1879.   I was the originator of it, as I was also of the
American Surgical Association, instituted in 1880.   They
each did me the honor to make me president.   I had
myself long seen the necessity for two such associations,
one of a local and the other of a national character; and
when I formally broached the matter to some of my surgical friends, they at once offered me their coöperation.
The object of both these societies, as expressed in their
respective constitutions, prepared by myself, and afterwards adopted with certain modifications, is the cultivation and improvement of the art and science of
Surgery, and the promotion of the interest not only of
their Fellows but of the Medical profession at large.   Both
societies are already in a flourishing condition, and, if judi-

ciously conducted, cannot fail to contribute materially to the advancement and dignity of Surgical Science in the United States, which has already produced so many able and distinguished surgeons. It is no vain boasting when I declare that, in my opinion, the surgeons of this country are fully equal in learning, and in ability as diagnosticians, operators, teachers, and writers, to any in the Old World. This opinion is now, I am happy to add, generally accepted. Vast strides have been made in all these respects during the last twenty years; and that the two institutions under consideration will be instrumental in creating a spirit of generous and useful rivalry, especially among the younger members of the profession, cannot for one moment be doubted. I certainly anticipate great results; and, if my expectations be realized even in a comparatively slight degree, I shall be amply compensated for all the care and labor I have bestowed upon them. American surgery has given the world Ovariotomy and Anæsthesia, two of the greatest boons ever conferred upon humanity, and it is actively engaged in contributing its share in settling the great problems, therapeutic and operative, which are everywhere agitating the surgical profession. Where genius, industry, and talent are so conspicuously developed, the sceptre will not be likely to be monopolized by any one nation.

CHAPTER VI.

PROFESSIONAL INCOME AND FEES—TEACHING—KNOWLEDGE OF PATHOLOGICAL ANATOMY—AS A PRACTITIONER, PHYSICIAN, SURGEON, AND ACCOUCHEUR—AS A WRITER AND AUTHOR.

I LEFT Philadelphia a few hundred dollars in debt, notwithstanding I had parted a short time previously with my books, and it therefore took me some time after I settled at Easton to get a sufficient start to discharge my small liabilities. This was a source of great annoyance to me, and caused me some anxiety, although my creditors were very indulgent. At Easton I soon obtained practice, but as the charges were very low I made little beyond my expenses, so that when I left for Cincinnati I had, as stated in a previous page, less than two hundred and fifty dollars in my pocket. I cannot refrain here from referring more particularly to the subject of fees at Easton. A visit in town was fifty cents, and out of the town from one to two dollars, according to the distance, including a small charge for medicine, which it was the custom for the physician to put up himself, he being obliged for this purpose to keep a small supply on hand in his office. A consultation visit was five dollars for the first, and a dollar for each subsequent one. Bleeding in the spring and autumn was then very common, as a means, as was believed, of purifying the blood and relieving congestion. Sometimes a person would come with a request to be bled in the foot, on the assumption that it was a great remedy for headache! The quantity of blood lost for these and other purposes generally varied from sixteen to twenty-four ounces. Unless the loss was considerable the patient did not consider that he had received an equivalent for his money. These charges were beyond doubt very contemptible; but then it is to be borne in mind that rent, provisions, and clothing were much lower than they are now. A chicken, for example, could be bought at six to ten cents, and the best quality of beef at about eight to nine cents. The ordinary fee for an obstetric case was five dollars among the poorer classes, and from ten to twenty-five among the wealthier and more influential.

For the last eighteen months of my residence at Easton I enjoyed the office of surgeon to the recruiting barracks, with a salary of thirty dollars a month. This sum was of great importance to me in meeting my current expenses. I was indebted for this position to a former schoolmate, Lieutenant Perkins, of the army, a warm-hearted, generous fellow.

When I left Easton I disposed of my practice, along with the office of recruiting surgeon, to an early medical friend, and it was to this circumstance chiefly that was due my ability to remove to Cincinnati. The few hundred dollars which I received from this source were of very great advantage to me in my new home.

At Cincinnati the charges were also miserably low, the ordinary visit being one dollar and the consultation five. My practice the first year yielded me upwards of fourteen hundred dollars, and the Demonstratorship in the Medical College of Ohio about five hundred dollars, making an aggregate of nearly two thousand dollars. During the last year, my seventh, my books showed upwards of nine thousand dollars as the result of my practice, a considerable portion being consultation, which had rapidly increased during the last three years both in extent and influence. I also did a large share of surgical practice, and not unfrequently visited patients at a distance. I was, in fact, in the possession of a large field, worthy of cultivation, and in the enjoyment of a rapidly increasing reputation.

At Louisville the charges for professional services were much higher than at Cincinnati, and I soon began to accumulate money. My surgical practice and the income from the school made me independent, but not rich, and when, in 1856, I quit Kentucky I was hardly worth sixty thousand dollars, all told. I was now fifty-one years old, and had toiled in my profession, as few men have ever toiled, for upwards of a quarter of a century. I was, however, perfectly happy and contented, having never craved, much less worked for, riches. My family had no reasonable wants that could not readily be supplied, and they had the rare faculty of accommodating themselves to circumstances.

The largest fee I ever received was two thousand dollars, paid me for a visit which I made at Montgomery, Alabama, in 1865, to a rich planter affected with chronic cystitis. During my residence at Louisville I got one thousand dollars for a visit to another planter in North Alabama. I was absent one week, making the journey on a steamer, in which I employed nearly all my time in writing a Discourse upon the Life and Character of Dr. Drake, which I read soon after my return before the trustees, faculty, and students of the University of Louisville. Thus my time was spent quite profitably. The lectures which were lost in consequence of my absence I made up after my return. A few years ago I received one thousand dollars for an operation which I performed upon a rich sugar refiner of this city for the relief of neuralgia. I have repeatedly received five hundred dollars for operations.

Doctors are often defrauded of their fees. The law, as a principle, regards every man as honest until he is proved to be guilty, and so, in the medical profession, every patient is considered to be honest until the reverse is found to be the case—a contingency, I am sorry to say, by no means uncommon. I have done a large share of what in this country is called an office practice, or what in Great Britain is known as a chamber business, and I have never refused to prescribe gratuitously for any one, however poor or humble, provided he informed me beforehand that he was unable to compensate me for my services. On the other hand, I have often, after a laborious examination of a case, torn my prescription in the teeth of my patient when he told me, after the work was done, that he had no money, especially when he had about him any appearance of gentility. If he was dull or ignorant, or, to use a common expression, "did not seem to know better," I sometimes forgave the offence. "The laborer is worthy of his hire," and people have no right to steal the time and services of a physician any more than they have to steal groceries, drygoods, or any other commodity. The doctor must live by his labors ; and, although our profession is a liberal one, we ought to make a proper distinction between the poor, properly so called, and those who are able, without any inconvenience, to compensate us for our services. Boerhaave used to say that the poor are our best patients, because God is their paymaster. All this is very well ; but there comes a time when a man looks for something more substantial than a patient's mere "God bless you, doctor !" There are many persons in every community who would rather part with their eye-teeth than a five dollar bill in payment of a physician's fee. In my younger days, and, indeed, until after the age of fifty, I seldom neglected the call of a poor patient ; and in my capacity as a clinical teacher at the college I perform constantly an immense amount of gratuitous work, including many operations involving great skill, much anxiety, and vast labor during the after-treatment. I am sure I render thus every year, at the most moderate calculation, services to the value of several thousand dollars. It was a common remark of my wife, that at my office I was generally more polite and attentive to the poor than to the richer class of patients ; and I was induced to do this because a poor person's time is generally more valuable than that of one in better circumstances.

A well-dressed young man, of the blackleg order, with large rings on his fingers, and a big watch-chain on his breast, strutted one day, during my residence at Louisville, into my office, saying he had come from Indiana to get me to make a very careful examination of his case, adding that he had already consulted quite a number of physicians, who had all come to a different conclusion in regard to its character. After having handed him my prescription, he rose to take his departure, when I said, "You have forgotten my fee." "Oh!" he replied, "excuse me ; I have really no money with me." "You are then deliberately cheating me, are you?" And thus saying, I locked the door and rang my office-bell, which was promptly answered. "My servant will take care of your watch until you can get the amount of my fee." He went off, but returned in a few minutes with the money, which, of course, he had at the time in his pocket. The next day, in mentioning the circumstance to several of my more prominent professional brethren, I found that the fellow had consulted each of them, and had come off scot-free in every instance. If there were a proper *esprit de corps* among medical men in regard to a just appreciation of their services, there would be less cheating on the part of their patients, and the profession would be placed upon an incomparably better footing, as regards its own dignity and the respect due to it by the public. I have never turned away a poor patient from my office without prescribing for his ailments, often only after the most laborious and painstaking examination ; but I hate an impostor, and never allow myself to be imposed upon.

My professorships in the different medical schools with which I have been connected have, up to the present time—February, 1870—yielded me about one hundred and ten thousand dollars.

The income from my books has thus far been about eighteen thousand dollars, of which the greater portion has been derived from my System of Surgery. As I have already stated, the first edition of the Pathological Anatomy brought me nothing, in consequence of the failure of my Boston publishers. For the second edition Barrington & Haswell paid me twelve hundred dollars; and for the third I received one thousand dollars from Blanchard & Lea. The first edition of my Treatise on the Urinary Organs yielded me nothing; for the second, if I mistake not, I received one thousand dollars. For the work on Foreign Bodies in the Air-Passages, issued by Blanchard & Lea, and the American Medical Biography, published by Lindsay & Blakiston, I was not paid anything. The latter work, indeed, cost me at least two hundred dollars in the way of outlays of various kinds.

My first effort as a public teacher was a lecture on General Anatomy, which I delivered at the Franklin Institute, Philadelphia, in June, 1829, a little upwards of a year after my graduation. I had, the summer previously, as mentioned in a former page, published a translation of Bayle and Hollard's work on this subject, of which I had, moreover, made a special study in other ways, so that I was very well informed upon it; and, as no one had ever given any formal lectures upon it, I flattered myself, young and inexperienced as I was, that I could make myself sufficiently interesting to attract a good class. In this, however, I was mistaken. The Introductory was advertised to be given on a certain day; and, although it was highly complimented by several of my friends, the audience was so slim that I had no encouragement to proceed with the course. This was a sad disappointment to me; the more so, as I had hoped the occasion would afford me an opportunity of earning a little reputation. My great ambition at that time was to become a teacher of anatomy, a study to which I had devoted great attention during my student life, and which I cultivated for many years with unabated ardor and enthusiasm. Soon after my settlement at Easton a friend, without my knowledge, made an effort to procure for me the chair of Anatomy in the Washington Medical College at Baltimore, then recently organized; but, from some cause not now remembered by me, he failed to accomplish his object.

My next effort at public teaching was as Demonstrator of Anatomy in the Medical College of Ohio, in the attic of which, as stated in a former page, I delivered three lectures a week, for two winters, on visceral and surgical anatomy, and I have always thought that those were the most interesting and successful courses I ever gave upon any subject. I certainly never lectured with more force and enthusiasm at any period of my life.

In the Cincinnati College I lectured for four years on Pathological Anatomy, including the structure and functions of the tissues, and a general description of the viscera, with an account of their color, consistence, weight, and dimensions, as preliminary to the consideration of their morbid alterations. I lost no opportunity to investigate these topics, so important in their bearing upon the elucidation of my chair. These examinations, the results of which were afterwards embodied in my Elements of Pathological Anatomy, were performed with great care and patience; and although they were not conducted on so large a scale as some that preceded them, as, for example, those of Bouillaud on the heart and Sims on the brain, yet they embraced certain organs, as the pancreas and prostate gland, which, as far as my information extends, had never received any attention of this kind before.

When I received my appointment as Professor of Pathological Anatomy in the Cincinnati College, I was thirty years of age, and I was placed side by side with teachers of experience and acknowledged ability. I spared no effort to acquit myself in as creditable a manner as possible. During the four months that preceded the opening of the course I not only made full notes, but wrote out, nearly in full, a number of my lectures, which I afterwards delivered in great measure—indeed, often entirely—extemporaneously. After the first session I had acquired sufficient confidence to trust myself merely with "heads," as they are termed, and dispensed with manuscript altogether—a circumstance which gave me more ease and freedom, and greatly improved my power of utterance as an effective teacher.

I have now taught surgery for thirty years—1840-'70—and during all this time I have invariably spoken extemporaneously. The only didactic lecture, indeed, that I have ever written was one on scrofula, which I committed to the flames long ago. A man who understands his subject should never appear before his class with his manuscript. He should be so thoroughly imbued with it—should have everything so completely at his tongue's end —as to let it off as if it were so much steam, blowing and puffing, and throwing himself, heart and soul, into his matter, however trite or uninteresting it may be in itself. No man can talk so as to enchain the attention of his pupils, or make any permanent impression, if he reads his lecture. He is as one tied hand and foot, deprived of motion and power of expression. I can imagine no more painful situation.

It is a difficult matter for a man to form a just estimate of himself as a lecturer. Indeed, it may savor of vanity even to make the effort. I have, however, now been a teacher for upwards of a third of a century, so that I may reasonably be excused if I speak of myself in this connection. One evidence of my success as a teacher is that I have been a professor in not less than five medical schools, and that I had calls to nearly as many more. If enthusiasm constitutes one of the qualities of a successful lecturer, then I must have been successful, for I certainly have possessed this attribute in a very high degree; and I think I may truly affirm that I never went before my class without a thorough comprehension of my subject, or without previous study and meditation. In this way I always felt fresh, well booked up in regard to the latest additions and improvements. Order and system were among my more important attributes as a teacher. I never failed to begin at the first round of the ladder, and to go on gradually ascending until I reached the top. If a man has neither order nor system, he knows nothing of the duties of a teacher. They are essential elements in every discourse. But a person may have both, and yet be a dull fellow. Of this I think no one could ever accuse me. A lecturer is, of course, not always equal to himself. The fleetest horse sometimes "lets down," or comes out last. A certain amount of animation is indispensable to a teacher. He must be excited; he must show that he feels an interest in what he says and does. He must be fully alive. If he is dull or stupid, his pupils will feel the effect, and sink into listless indifference. I have sometimes thought that I am too boisterous and too excited; but this I cannot help; I must feel what I say, or I cannot proceed. I like to look my pupils in the face, to shake my fist at them, and to stamp my foot, as General Jackson did when he wanted to be emphatic and swore "by the Eternal," in order to impress upon their minds their duty, as students of a great, noble, and exalted profession. Rufus Choate was never more earnest in addressing a court and jury than I have often been in speaking to my class on questions of great and vital importance of a professional character. Who would not, inspired by the occasion, be eloquent when he is addressing himself to a body of ingenuous students, in quest of knowledge designed to heal the sick, to open the eyes of the blind, to make the deaf hear, to enable the lame to walk, and to loose the tongue of the dumb? I never enter the lecture-room without a deep sense of the responsibility of my office—without a feeling that I have a solemn duty to perform—and that upon what I may utter during the hour may depend the happiness or misery of hundreds, if not thousands, of human beings.

The opening portion of my course on Surgery has always been devoted to the discussion of principles, without a knowledge of which no student can possibly make any true progress. Not fewer than seven weeks have usually been given to this object, the topics embraced in it being inflammation and its consequences, syphilis, struma, tumors, and wounds. These topics being disposed of, I then lectured upon the diseases and injuries of particular regions, organs, and tissues, rapidly discussing each subject as it came up in proper order; so that by the end of the session the course may be said to have generally been a complete one. I never dealt in hypothesis, conjecture, or speculation. My plan has always been to confine myself as much as possible to matters of fact, and to make whatever I said my own, as if it were the result of my own experience, reading, and reflection. I am convinced that any teaching that does not rest upon such a basis is worthless.

Many teachers, American as well as European, think that they have done all that duty requires of them when they have instructed their pupils in practical and operative surgery. The principles of surgery are the principles of medicine, or, in other words, the principles of the art of healing, and therefore, unless a practitioner is fully acquainted with them, he is utterly unfit for his business. Most physicians and surgeons, for this very reason, are routinists. They leave the lecture-room with the merest modicum of information, which is never improved by subsequent training, observation, reading, or reflection.

When I die I wish no better epitaph than this—"A teacher of Principles."

A part of the first lecture of my course has always been employed in laying down a general plan of it, with an account of text-books, and the manner in which the student should deport himself in the amphitheatre. I never failed to lay down, distinctly and emphatically, my rules upon this subject, so that the class should fully comprehend my wishes. Punctuality, erect posture, and perfect silence were indispensable conditions. I never tolerated irregularity of any kind, lying down upon the benches, whispering, reading of letters, going out before the hour was over, or entering after the lecture had commenced. The class, in consequence of this precaution, was always most orderly, respectful, and attentive. The discipline of my room was perfect, and it was therefore a very uncommon thing for me to be obliged to rebuke a student. Claptrap of any kind I never could bear. Nothing was more offensive to me than applause as I entered the amphitheatre, and I never permitted it after the first lecture. I always said, "Gentlemen, such a noise is more befitting the pit of a theatre or a circus than a temple dedicated, not to Æsculapius, but to Almighty God, for the study of disease and accident, and your preparation for the great duties of your profession. There is something awfully solemn in a profession which deals with life and death; and I desire at the very threshold of this course of lectures to impress upon your minds its sacred and responsible character, that you may be induced to make the best possible use of your time, and conduct yourselves in a manner worthy of the dignity of Christian gentlemen."

Such appeals had always a most salutary effect; and, although I was a rigid disciplinarian, I am quite sure that I always enjoyed the esteem and affection of every member of my class. A teacher who cannot command the respect and attention of his pupils has no business in the lecture-room; he is out of place, and the sooner he quits the better.

This practice of applauding must have been borrowed from the stage. Henderson was wont to say that no actor could perform well unless he was systematically flattered both on and off the stage; and it is reported of Liston that he considered applause so necessary to good acting that he liked to see even a small dog wag his tail in approbation of his efforts.

The first element in the art of teaching is a thorough knowledge of one's subject, a complete mastery of what one is obliged to talk about; the next, the faculty of presenting it in a clear, agreeable, and satisfactory manner; and the third, the ability to keep alive the attention of one's audience. The last is often materially aided by the recital of an appropriate anecdote, or an illustrative case. In the former I never indulged much, and I have especially had a contempt for vulgar anecdotes, of which some teachers make such free use, and which are always out of place. Cases illustrative of particular points of practice never fail, if well told, to make a good impression, and are often more effective than the most interesting anecdotes. A lecturer is of no account unless he can move as well as instruct his pupils. If he cannot do this, much of his teaching must fall by the wayside upon barren soil.

A teacher should be neat in his habits, dress, and address before his class, choice in the selection of his language, and thoroughly systematic in the discussion of his topics. Slovenliness of mind and body has a demoralizing effect, and cannot therefore be too pointedly condemned. Dr. Charles D. Meigs, one of my colleagues, for many years Professor of Midwifery in the Jefferson Medical College, was one of the most attractive and charming of teachers, but rarely, if ever, systematic. George McClellan, the founder of the school, was always brilliant, always

interesting and instructive, but, like Meigs, superficial
and scattering, apparently without any definite aim, fore-
thought, or preparation.   Drake was a great lecturer;
but unfortunate with first course students, who could never
follow or understand him, because he always overshot his
mark, not having the faculty of adapting himself to their
comprehension.   Some lecturers are learned dunces.   They
think they must give an account of the opinions of everybody that ever wrote upon the subject they are discussing,
perhaps omitting their own, and in this way they are sure
to fall far short of being successful and agreeable teachers.
I have heard of a certain professor of surgery in a neighboring city who entertained his class four times a week,
for nearly two months, with an account of the different
operations for stone in the bladder, a subject which should
never occupy more than three lectures at the utmost in a
didactic course, such as we are restricted to in this country.
Dr. Short, the Professor of Materia Medica in the University of Louisville, a most amiable and excellent man, and
a most accomplished botanist, always read his lectures,
and, if he had occasion to extemporize, even for a moment,
he invariably raised his eyes over the heads of the class,
never, owing to some peculiar habit, or rather what may
be called sheepish modesty, looking them in the face.
Charles Caldwell, a man of noble presence and pedantic
style, was a model of a lecturer, walking to and fro upon
the rostrum like a caged lion.   He had practised oratory
before the mirror, possessed fine powers of elocution, and
had a mind well stored with professional and general information; and yet I doubt that he ever made a physiologist of any of his pupils.   He was a declaimer, a
speculator, not up to the existing state of the science,
notwithstanding his learning, and he was therefore a
miserable teacher.   Dr. John Esten Cooke always lectured
on his fingers.   Meigs never talked so well to his class as
when he was swinging his spectacles in his hand.

Eccentricity sometimes adds interest to a lecturer. Abernethy always lectured with his hands deeply buried in his breeches' pockets. McClellan could never talk without having hold of his watch-chain, or some other object, perhaps a knife or pair of scissors, much to the horror of the occupants of the first row of benches. William P. C. Barton was a coxcomb. He generally appeared before his class with two vests of different colors, which he never wore on two consecutive days, notwithstanding his poverty. A contemptuous smile, or curl of the upper lip, was one of his constant concomitants. He was always facetious, and generally interesting.

Dewees, an authoritative teacher, and a practitioner who delivered upwards of ten thousand women, was the type of an unrefined lecturer, abounding in coarse anecdotes and sayings which often disgusted the more cultivated members of his class; and yet he was a most successful instructor, every student swearing by him, for he was unsparing in his criticisms of the doctrines and practice of his predecessors and contemporaries, and most dogmatical in the assertion of his own views and opinions. He was by far the most positive teacher and writer on midwifery in his day in this country. He always lectured in the afternoon, after dinner, often, it was said, under the influence of vinous potations.

The dogmatic teacher is, in the main, the most successful teacher, the one most likely to impress himself effectually and indelibly upon the minds of young medical students. We like to listen to a man who speaks as if he were thoroughly saturated with his subject, as if there were no doubt of the truth of what he was uttering, as if he himself fully believed in the power and efficacy of what he is trying to instil into the brains of his auditors. No teacher ever caused a more profound sensation than Paracelsus when, seated in his chair at Basle, he deliberately burnt the works of his predecessors, sending their very ashes, as it were, to the infernal regions. The students stared, and the medical world was taken aback, as the news spread over Europe, carrying the fame of the eccentric professor into every nook and corner of the civilized world. It was an act most cunningly conceived and executed, and well calculated to arrest the attention, not only of medical men, but of mankind at large. Like Byron, Paracelsus woke up in the morning and found himself famous. If Dewees did not commit to flame the writings of his predecessors and contemporaries, he scorched them with the fire of his criticism and his sarcasm, and thus doomed them to a worse fate.

An Irishman's brogue has often made his fortune. His lisp and Scotch accent made Granville Sharp Pattison one of the most interesting lecturers of his day. Few men, in any age or country, ever enjoyed such widespread popularity as teachers of anatomy as this distinguished Scotchman, for one winter my colleague in the New York University. His lisp, his accent, his enthusiasm were irresistible. I have myself never entirely surmounted my German accent. I presume that it is at times very conspicuous in the lecture-room; but I have it also in ordinary conversation, so much so that when I visited Edinburgh, in 1869, Simpson, Syme, and others insisted upon it that I was a Scotchman. No man, perhaps, with any pretension to refinement and education ever had the Scotch accent in a more extraordinary degree than Dr. Chalmers. When the celebrated Edinburgh divine for the first time visited England he called upon Southey, who nearly fell into fits when Chalmers uttered the word "saxtain" for sixteen. The Lake poet, unaccustomed to such a horrible mutilation of the English language, was almost mortally shocked. He, however, speedily recovered from his depression; for when a few days after this event he heard Chalmers preach, he was so profoundly and so agreeably impressed by his eloquence and logic that he readily pardoned his

barbarous pronunciation. He had never before listened
to such pulpit oratory and enthusiasm.

A good, clear, resonant, well-modulated voice is a great
lever in a lecture-room, which seldom fails to command
attention. I have known a number of teachers to fail
because of their feeble voice. The object of the student
is to learn; but how can he understand what is said unless
the teacher has sufficient vocal power to make himself
heard over the entire lecture-room? Slow and rapid
speaking are both bad; the one fatigues and invariably
causes drowsiness, the other overwhelms and confuses the
listener. Few men can catch the happy medium; and
thoroughly successful and agreeable teachers are, and
always will be, scarce. Dunglison was always brimful of
his subject as he stood before his class, but he was monotonous, and did not sufficiently emphasize the great points
of his discourse. To make himself impressive a lecturer
must constantly italicize, and not unfrequently bring down
his fist, to give force to his utterance.

Many of our professors are slow of speech, mumbling
or muttering their words, and thus failing to make themselves heard and felt by their pupils. To such men, whom
God never intended for such positions, the language of the
great Hebrew legislator is eminently applicable: "O my
Lord," said Moses, "I am not eloquent, neither heretofore,
nor since thou hast spoken unto thy servant; but I am
slow of speech, and of a slow tongue." But these men
differ from Moses in this, that while he was, by the
special favor of Jehovah, assisted by his brother Aaron
as his spokesman, and was himself deputed to perform
miracles, they proceed in a stammering, halting, hesi-
tating way all their lives, much to the detriment of their
auditors.

Many teachers lecture well in a conversational style—a
style which I have myself never fancied, and which is only
effective when it is associated with a good, strong voice

and commanding presence, such as are combined, for example, in Wendell Phillips. The most noisy and earnest
lecturer I have ever listened to was Dr. Drake, and he certainly was one of the most interesting and fascinating men
in the presence of students whom I have ever heard. A
good voice in a lecturer is to a medical class what the
spur is to a rider, or a whip to a driver, calculated to keep
alive the attention of the student and to goad on the weary
animal. Drake's manner always reminded me of that
of an old Methodist preacher whom I was wont to hear
when I was a youth, and who seemed as if he were
wrestling with the Lord for a special blessing upon his
people. I, too, have been an earnest teacher, and I doubt
whether any one, as he stood before a medical class, felt
more keenly than myself the importance of what he was
saying and doing.

There is a wide difference between a good lecturer and
a good teacher. The distinction is important, but not
always well understood or clearly defined. A man may
talk well, and express himself in the most elegant and
scholarly manner, and yet may fail to impart his knowledge. The art of teaching is a peculiar one, not, like
poetry, exactly a gift of nature, and yet so nearly approxi-
mating it as to be almost equivalent to it.

Professor Samuel Jackson, of the University of Pennsylvania, was an excellent talker but a most uninstructive
teacher, "pleased with a rattle, tickled with a straw,"
and upsetting to-morrow the doctrines that he expounded
the day before. Dr. John Esten Cooke, on the contrary,
who was for many years Caldwell's colleague, made numerous converts to his doctrines and exercised a widespread
influence over the minds of his pupils, although he was one
of the dullest and most arid lecturers that could possibly be
imagined. He was a successful teacher. The seed which
he put in the earth sprang up and produced abundant
fruit—unfortunately, however, not of the best character.

My knowledge of pathological anatomy, acquired in early life, has been of immense benefit to me as a teacher, a practitioner, and a writer, and it is only surprising to me that there are so few practitioners in this country who have taken advantage of this study. I do not believe that I have ever delivered a lecture on surgery in which I did not freely avail myself of my knowledge of it as a means of illustrating every subject that I had occasion to discuss. A knowledge of pathological anatomy is the very basis of diagnosis; and when it is considered how important it is that a physician should be able to determine the nature of a disease before he institutes his treatment, it is not a little surprising that this department of medicine should be taught in so few of our schools. This omission is one of the crying sins of the present day. Everything, however irrelevant or useless, is taught to the exclusion of morbid anatomy. I only wish that every medical college in the country were compelled to introduce it into its curriculum of studies. To make room for it we might well dispense with some of the useless teachings in chemistry, materia medica, physiology, and even midwifery, so characteristic of the present day.

It takes many elements to make a great man, many to make a great teacher, writer, and practitioner; and there are few persons in whom these elements are so happily blended as to work out the desired result. Great genius is not by any means a necessary ingredient of these qualities. To accomplish great ends demands patience, perseverance, unwearying application, order and system, and a definite aim—in a word, talent rather than genius. Genius invents; talent applies. The only genius I possess is the genius of industry; if I have any other, I have not been able to discover it. The position which I have attained in my profession has been achieved by hard blows, by no special intellectual endowment, by no special gifts from God, by no special favor from man, but by my own unaided efforts, continued steadily and perseveringly through a long series of years, during which a kind Providence afforded me sound health, lofty ambition, and unflinching fidelity to my profession.

From the day on which I received my diploma, a period of forty-two years, I have been a most laborious and devoted student, true to the best interests of the profession, and one of the most faithful supporters of its honor, dignity, and advancement. My mind has ever been on the alert to gather information from every available source. I have been an incessant reader, and, I believe, not altogether a bad observer of nature. I have witnessed all kinds of diseases and injuries, have tried numerous remedies, and have performed many operations. My voice has often been raised in favor of progress. I have seen many abuses in my profession, and have passed through several revolutions of treatment, in which certain articles of the materia medica, at one time considered as most valuable and efficacious, have been abandoned as worthless, if not positively injurious; and yet, through all these changes, so singular in their character, I have never, I think I am safe in asserting, lost sight of common sense or the results of an enlightened personal and general experience.

Although I had a great fondness for surgery, my practice in the early part of my life was chiefly medical. The operations which I performed were few in number; nor were they of much importance until the latter period of my residence at Cincinnati, and during my residence at Louisville, when my reputation as an operative surgeon rapidly increased, and patients visited me from various sections of the country for relief.

I do not know that nature ever intended me for a great surgeon. I was the victim of a native timidity which was certainly at variance with such an assumption. The sight of blood was extremely disagreeable to me—so much so that on one occasion during the early period of my pupilage, while holding a basin for a fellow-student engaged in bleeding a patient, I came so near fainting that, if I had not abandoned my hold and sought refuge in the open air, I would, I am sure, have dropped down in a state of unconsciousness. It was some time before I could get rid of this feeling, and look with composure upon a surgical operation. Even now, after having performed thousands of operations, and spilled gallons of blood, I seldom feel comfortable as a looker-on at a great and protracted feat of this kind, however skilfully executed. I am naturally sensitive and sympathetic, and would rather at any time use the knife myself than see it used by another. In the one case I forget myself in the discharge of my duties, while in the other case my mind is absorbed in what concerns the poor sufferer. I recollect, when I was a boy not quite six years old, nearly fainting at the sight of the struggles of a sparrow which I had knocked down with a piece of corn-cob in my father's yard. I thought I had certainly killed the poor bird, and it was not until it recovered from the shock of the blow, and flew away, that I recovered my wonted equanimity.

Surgeons are often accused of being hard-hearted and unfeeling. My experience is that this is a great slander, entirely without truth. There are of course exceptions to all rules; but I am quite sure that the most skilful and accomplished surgeons in the world are men of the keenest sensibilities and the warmest sympathies. I never hear the word "butcher" applied to an operator without instantly resenting it. I recollect at one of my college clinics that a stout, tall Amazon made a remark of this kind, as she was handing her child to one of my assistants, preparatory to the performance of an operation. I instantly fixed my eyes upon her, and, addressing the class, said, "Madam, you do not know what you are saying; we are only butchers when we have to do with such a calf as you are;" and then I gave her a severe lecture upon her conduct, adding that, if she did not instantly retract her language, I should not operate upon her child.

I have always maintained that it is impossible for any man to be a great surgeon if he is destitute, even in a considerable degree, of the finer feelings of our nature. I have often lain awake for hours the night before an important operation, and suffered great mental distress for days after it was over, until I was certain that my patient was out of danger. I do not think that it is possible for a criminal to feel much worse the night before his execution than a surgeon when he knows that upon his skill and attention must depend the fate of a valuable citizen, husband, father, mother, or child. Surgery under such circumstances is a terrible taskmaster, feeding like a vulture upon a man's vitals. It is surprising that any surgeon in large practice should ever attain to a respectable old age, so great are the wear and tear of mind and body.

The world has seen many a sad picture. I will draw one of the surgeon. It is midday; the sun is bright and beautiful; all nature is redolent of joy; men and women crowd the street, arrayed in their best, and all, apparently, is peace and happiness within and without. In a large house, almost overhanging this street so full of life and gayety, lies upon a couch an emaciated figure, once one of the sweetest and loveliest of her sex, a confiding and affectionate wife, and the adored mother of numerous children, the subject of a frightful disease of one of her limbs, or, it may be, of her jaw, if not of a still more important part of her body. In an adjoining room is the surgeon, with his assistants, spreading out his instruments and getting things in readiness for the impending operation. He assigns to each his appropriate place. One administers chloroform; another takes charge of the limb; one screws down the tourniquet upon the principal artery; and another holds himself in readiness to follow the knife with his sponge. The flaps are soon formed, the bone severed, the vessels tied, and the huge wound approximated. The woman is pale and ghastly, the pulse hardly perceptible, the skin wet with clammy perspiration, the voice husky, the sight indistinct. Some one whispers into the ear of the busy surgeon, "The patient, I fear, is dying." Restoratives are administered, the pulse gradually rises, and after a few hours of hard work and terrible anxiety reaction occurs. The poor woman was only faint from the joint influence of the anæsthetic, shock, and loss of blood. An assistant, a kind of sentinel, is placed as a guard over her, with instructions to watch her with the closest care, and to send word the moment the slightest change for the worse is perceived. The surgeon goes about his business, visits other patients on the way, and at length, long after the usual hour, he sits down, worried and exhausted, to his cold and comfortless meal, with a mouth almost as dry and a voice as husky as his patient's. He eats mechanically, exchanges hardly a word with any member of his family, and sullenly retires to his study, to prescribe for his patients—never, during all this time, forgetting the poor mutilated object he left a few hours ago. He is about to lie down to get a moment's repose after the severe toil of the day, when suddenly he hears a loud ring of the bell, and a servant, breathless with excitement, begs his immediate presence at the sick chamber, with the exclamation, "They think Mrs. —— is dying." He hurries to the scene with rapid pace and anxious feeling. The stump is of a crimson color, and the patient lies in a profound swoon. An artery has suddenly given way; the exhaustion is extreme; cordials and stimulants are at once brought into requisition, the dressings are removed; and the recusant vessel is promptly secured. The vital current ebbs and flows, reaction is still more tardy than before, and it is not until a late hour of the night that the surgeon, literally worn out in mind and body, retires to his home in search of repose. Does he sleep? He tries, but he cannot close his eyes. His mind is with his patient; he hears every footstep upon the pavement under his window, and is in momentary expectation of the ringing of the night-bell. He is disturbed by the wildest fancies, he sees the most terrific objects, and, as he rises early in the morning to hasten to his patient's chamber, he feels that he has been cheated of the rest of which he stood so much in need. Is this picture overdrawn? I have sat for it a thousand times, and there is not an educated, conscientious surgeon that will not certify to its accuracy.

The terrible anxiety, the utter wretchedness, thus faintly depicted, often last, not merely for a night or a day, but for weeks, and even then the surgeon is not always rewarded with success. What other profession or pursuit is there that involves so much mental anguish, so much awful responsibility, so much wear and tear of mind and body? The physician and obstetrician certainly have their trials, and many sad and even bitter ones, but compared with those of the surgeon they are comparatively insignificant. The surgeon, like them, not only frequently necessarily loses his patient, but his patient, if in case of accident he should survive, is often literally a living monument of the surgeon's disgrace in consequence of his mutilated condition—a condition not seldom unjustly attributed to the attendant, although, unfortunately, only too often ascribed to him. The physician, on the contrary, either hides his bad skill in the grave, or, if his patient survive, no matter how crippled he may be, no blame is ascribed to the treatment. The hepatized lung does not, like the anchylosed joint or deformed limb, obtrude itself at every step upon the eye of the observer.

Although I have now practised surgery largely for upwards of a third of a century, and have earned some reputation in it, I have always thought myself a better physician than surgeon. My reasons for this conclusion are simply these: first, I had for many years an immense family practice, which necessarily brought me in contact with almost every variety of disease, common, specific, endemic, and epidemic; secondly, I was well acquainted with pathological anatomy and diagnosis, including auscultation and percussion; and, lastly, I have had an excellent knowledge of remedies and the requirements of the sickroom. A large share of my consultation business in Philadelphia, Louisville, and Cincinnati has been of a strictly medical character.

Of midwifery, practically speaking, I have never been fond, although I was at one time largely engaged in it in connection with family practice. As far as my recollection now serves me I have never lost but one woman by puerperal fever; and I never had occasion to apply the forceps in any cases originally under my care, a practice at present so disgracefully common as to be in danger of becoming, ere long, the rule instead of the rare exception, as it used to be in my early professional life. Stout, hale, young women, especially primiparæ, were generally bled early in labor; and this practice, along with the use of opiates, generally rendered the use of the forceps unnecessary, as under the influence of those remedies the parts usually became rapidly relaxed. Lacerations of the perineum were uncommon in those days.

Persons have often come to me saying they had understood that I was very fond of using the knife. Such stories are frequently propagated from selfish considerations by designing confrères, and the weak and credulous are only too prone to credit them. As for myself, nothing could be more untrue, or more unjust. I have never hesitated to employ the knife when I thought it was imperatively demanded to relieve or cure my patient; but that I have ever operated merely for the sake of display or the gratification of a selfish end is as base as it is false. I have always had too much respect for human life, for my profession, and for my own dignity, to be guilty of such an outrage. No man ever had a greater or more unmitigated contempt for the knife's-man, or mere mechanical surgeon and operator, than I, and I have never hesitated, in season and out of season, to denounce him in the most unmeasured terms.

I have performed many operations, and flatter myself that I possess at least some of the qualities of a good operator—a steady hand, an unflinching eye, perfect self-control, and a thorough knowledge of relative anatomy. I have rarely failed to accomplish what I had set out to do. The sight of blood, as I have said, was very disagreeable to me in early life; but it never appalled me in any of my great operations, and I do not believe that I ever trembled three times in my life when I had a knife in my hand. My hand and eye, so thoroughly trained in pitching quoits and pennies and practising with the bow and arrow in early boyhood, never failed me. I believe that I was always a safe operator, and if I ever committed any great mistake I am not aware of it. My knife was always guided by a thorough knowledge of the case, and, I have reason to believe, by sound judgment, strengthened and sobered by the light of experience and the dictates of common sense. I can say what few men, extensively engaged in practice, can say: "I have never lost a patient upon the table from shock or loss of blood."

It has been generally supposed, from the fact that I am a rather voluminous author, that I am fond of writing. Nothing is more true, and I should be very ungrateful if I denied it. Not only am I fond of writing, but writing has been one of the greatest solaces of my life. Many of my happiest days and nights have been spent with my pen, in the silence of my study, dead as it were to all the world around me, only enlivened by my own thoughts and reflections, in the midst of my books, the silent companions of my lonely hours, and the witnesses of my earnest efforts to contribute something that might be worthy of my profession.

I became a writer early in my professional life. I had hardly received my degree before, as I have said elsewhere, I began to translate French and German medical books, working generally, even at that early period, from six to eight hours a day at my task. Writing was not, at first, very agreeable to me. I composed with difficulty, and it was not until after much experience and great care that I at length overcame the obstacles which stood in my way to the attainment of a style which satisfied me. The art of composition can only be acquired by much effort and long practice, although with some persons it seems a natural gift. Let those who fancy that writing is an easy task read the anecdote of the visit of Lady Morgan to Rossini. "Ah," says she, "I have found you in a moment of inspiration." "You have; but this inspiration is thundering hard work."

In my earlier writings I was in the habit of doing a great deal of interlining and copying; but during the last twenty years I have seldom rewritten anything, generally trusting to the original draught. My style has always been characterized by simplicity; I have never been ambitious of ornament; my sole object has been to express myself in clear, intelligible language, adapted to the comprehension of the dullest intellect; and in this I believe I have generally succeeded. Indeed, medical writing does not need much display or embellishment. Medicine is a science of facts, which disdains all poetical license and meretricious ornament.

The only way to write well is to be thoroughly acquainted with one's subject. My invariable plan has been to outline my material beforehand, dividing and subdividing it in the most minute and thorough manner, and then to fill up, at my leisure, the groundwork thus sketched. In this way the task has been a comparatively easy and pleasant one. A large proportion of my works was composed in my carriage. My custom, when I was engaged upon a book, was to map out a certain amount of labor for the day; I would then jump into my buggy to attend to my morning rounds, and, while going from house to house, revolve the subject in my mind, amplifying and arranging it in proper, systematic order, and then, at the first leisure moment, sit down and commit it to paper. In this way I was not only never idle, but was able daily to perform a vast amount of useful labor. The exercise which I thus took on the streets was conducive to my health and vigor of intellect. I seldom allowed anything, unless it was more than ordinarily interesting, to distract my attention, and, on the other hand, I never in all my life neglected a patient in consequence of this mode of occupation. I have always been too conscientious knowingly to omit the performance of a single duty of any kind.*

In writing my books my practice has been to take up first such subjects as I was most familiar with, and in this way I often wrote the last chapters before the first. This, I think, is an excellent plan, calculated to facilitate progress, and enhance the pleasures of composition. A builder must necessarily begin at the foundation, and gradually proceed upwards. With an author it is different, especially when, as in the medical profession, the subjects are often independent one of another, and can therefore be worked out separately. The mind requires variety.

---

* I lately—1883—read a sketch of Charles Wesley, the celebrated Methodist divine, an author of numerous poems, from which it appears that "he composed on horseback, in bed, anywhere, on every occasion, and wrote his compositions as soon as he could get pen and paper." I have myself not unfrequently got out of bed at night to write a thought or sentiment that had occurred to me in a semi-dozing condition. A dream has sometimes served to solve an intricate mathematical problem, one that could not be solved in the waking state by the most powerful efforts of the mind.

To labor incessantly upon any one topic soon blunts one's ardor, and greatly retards one's progress.

Hazlitt, in speaking of the evanescent glory of a player's life, observes: "When an author dies it is no matter, for his works remain. When a great actor dies there is a void produced in society, a gap which requires to be filled up." The works remain! Where? Upon the shelf, in the dusty library, enveloped in cobwebs, or, as not unfrequently happens at the present day, they are sold to the ragman, as waste paper. Few works outlive their authors, or are handed down to posterity, as great repositories of learning, as fountains of knowledge, at which future generations may slake their thirst for information. A representative book, especially in the medical profession, is a rare production. Only a very few escape general oblivion, or they serve as milestones in after ages of the state of the science of which they treat. The author, like the poor player, whose fate is so sympathetically expressed by Shakespeare,

> "Struts and frets his hour upon the stage,
> And then is heard no more."

This death of an author's works before his own demise is almost as sad a doom as that which a parent is sometimes subjected to when he is obliged to witness the death of his own children, as one after another sinks prematurely into the grave, especially when his darling Benjamin, upon whose shoulders he had fondly expected to glide down to posterity by covering him with his mantle, is taken from him.

CHAPTER VII.

EVERY man has certain habits which are either peculiar
to himself, or which he shares in common with his fellow-
beings. Lord Chesterfield has said of himself that he
never laughed after he became a man of common sense,
evidently considering it rude and vulgar to give vent to his
feelings in such a manner. All the world knows that he
prided himself upon his good breeding, and yet in thus
suppressing his feelings he was guilty of violating one of
the natural laws of God. Of all animals man is the only
one endowed with this prerogative, and it requires no argument to show that its proper indulgence in nowise dero-
gates from his dignity. On the contrary, I have always
myself enjoyed a good hearty laugh. "Laugh and grow
fat" is an old proverb. Physick was hardly ever known
to smile, much less to laugh, and yet it has been said by
those who best knew him that he was, notwithstanding
his austere appearance and dignified deportment, a man of
very kindly feeling. He was naturally a man of few
words, who scrupulously shunned society and all places of
amusement, and was long the subject of bodily suffering,
well calculated to spoil the best temper in the world. It
is reported of him that, being asked on one occasion by
Dr. Dewees, who was fond of gayety and fun, whether he
would not go with him to the theatre to see a certain actor,
he replied, "No; it will not do for men occupying our
position to be seen at such a place. We must not make

ourselves so common." It is said even the devil laughs, and I am sure he would have few converts if he did not.

I believe I was constitutionally lazy, and I am not sure that indolence is not the normal condition of our nature. However this may be, I was very fond, as a boy, of sleeping late in the morning, and as I was somewhat of a favorite with my father I was often indulged until a late hour, long after all the other children were up. After my father's death, however, I acquired better habits, and became an early riser, a habit which has continued with me ever since. From six to half past six has been my usual time of rising for the last forty years, and I have seldom retired later than eleven to half past eleven, unless I was professionally engaged, out at a party, or intensely occupied in writing, when I sometimes, although rarely, encroached upon the early hours of the morning. My system has generally required from six and a half to seven hours' sleep. No man who wishes to live well or long should rob himself of his rest at night. Even if he cannot sleep, it is a great comfort to be able to stretch himself out upon his bed to relax his wearied muscles and his excited brain. Humboldt, the author of Cosmos, who was not a great sleeper, delighted to lie in bed for the sake merely of the pleasures of recumbency, and a man who can indulge in such a luxury deserves to be envied, for I am sure it must conduce not only to his happiness, but to the extension of his life.

I am one of those fortunate beings who can sleep anywhere, or almost in any posture. I verily believe I could, if at all fatigued, sleep soundly in the fiercest battle, amid the roar of cannon and the most terrible excitement. One of my habits for many years has been to take a short nap —from ten to fifteen minutes—upon my chair, on coming in from my morning rounds, while waiting for my dinner, and I know of nothing more refreshing and invigorating. The sleep thus obtained is a thousand times more salutary and sustaining than a dozen post-prandial naps, which generally leave the brain in a dull, stupid condition, unfit for active mental exertion during the rest of the day and evening.

A man is doubly fortunate if, when he retires at night, he can throw aside his business and compose himself to rest. In the medical profession this cannot always be done. The responsibility of our cases will not permit it. Like Banquo's ghost, they stalk into our presence, and even harass us in our dreams. I have spent many an uncomfortable night from this cause. When engaged in writing intensely, or studying out an important subject, I have occasionally been similarly annoyed; but commonly I have been able to shake off the matter from my mind, especially if I took a short walk before retiring, and thus obtained the necessary amount of refreshing sleep. Habit is a curious thing. As a physician and a surgeon I have often been obliged to visit patients in the country, compelling me to start early in the morning. Under such circumstances I have never been obliged to request anybody to wake me. On the contrary, I was always up in advance of time. I never missed a coach or train in my life in consequence.

For many years I have had few holidays, few days of positive relaxation and freedom of mind and body, and have always been unhappy when not actively or usefully employed. The grave is the only place where a man, bent upon the performance of good deeds, should seek repose. "Why don't you sometimes rest?" said a friend to Arnauld. "Rest! Why should I rest here? Haven't I an eternity to rest in?"

Regularity at one's meals is a source of great comfort, and not a little conducive to longevity. Much of the good health with which I have been blessed has been due to this cause. No man since the days of Adam and Eve has been more particular in this respect than myself. I have seldom, except when from home on a visit to a patient, or when dining out, taken a meal out of my own house, and I have the more carefully observed this conduct because it has seldom been in my power to meet my family at any other time. My breakfast has always been served, for the last forty years, at eight o'clock, summer and winter, my dinner at half past two, and my tea at half past seven, generally with the regularity of the clock. Late suppers I have always avoided, except when out at parties, when I never hesitated to indulge moderately, always sleeping better, and never feeling the worse on account of it the next day. A gentleman is to be pitied if, on such occasions, he is obliged, on account of his stomach, to fold his arms and look on the scene in silence. Such an organ is a great nuisance, only fit to be walked on in the morning, when empty, for the poor owner's health! I never drank wine, brandy, or whiskey until after I was upwards of twenty-five years of age; and even now I have a great aversion to all alcoholic drinks, except now and then a glass of hot whiskey punch, on a cold night, immediately before going to bed. The only wine I have really ever had a fondness for is champagne. In hot weather, for many years past, I have generally drunk claret, believing that it was highly beneficial to me. Sauterne and Rhenish wines are very grateful to me, and it must surely be a cause for congratulation that the use of these wines has, within the last ten years, become so common in this country. Of malt liquors I have never been very fond. Now and then I have been greatly refreshed by a glass of Scotch ale, and I have often recommended this drink with great advantage to my patients, on account of the large quantity of carbonic acid gas which it contains, in dyspepsia, asthma, inordinate insomnia, and various affections of the genitourinary organs. Champagne, provided it is of superior quality, is one of the very best, as well as one of the most grateful remedies in disorders of the digestive organs, whether acute or chronic, attended with flatulence, nausea, or vomiting. It is, in fact, a drink fit for the gods in such conditions, gently stimulating, refreshing, and exhilarating.

I have always been a hearty but temperate eater, and have never, in all my life, been intoxicated; although I have on several occasions felt the exhilarating influence of wine. Coffee I was able to drink twice and even three times a day with impunity until I was thirty-five years of age. It then produced dyspepsia, with acidity of the stomach, and I was obliged, notwithstanding my great fondness for it, to abandon its use altogether, employing black tea as a substitute. I believe, from much observation and experience, that the constant and inordinate use of coffee is productive of a great deal of evil, especially in nervous persons, in whom, I am quite sure, it is a fruitful source of indigestion, irritability of temper, and loss of sleep. Black tea as a daily drink is preferable to green, but both should be used in moderation and in proper season. I think I may confidently affirm that a cup of good tea is far better in relieving fatigue and preserving strength, when a man has to perform an undue amount of mental or physical labor, than a glass of wine, whiskey, or brandy. The British soldiers, both at home and in the Indies, have long acted upon this principle, and the result of our experience during our late terrible war was of a similar nature.

A proper mixture of vegetable and animal food is of great consequence in a dietetic point of view. The vegetarians, as they are called, with Graham at their head, are a singular class of bipeds, of American origin, who have done the race not a little harm by founding a practice so utterly at variance with the principles of sound sense and the laws of our being. Man is an omnivorous animal. It is impossible to view him in any other light. His teeth, his digestive apparatus, his appetites, and his wants, not to say anything of the world's experience, all concur in proving this fact. These vegetarians are generally enormous eaters. I knew one of them—a doctor—who during the peach season daily devoured a peck of that delicious fruit, and other vegetable matter in proportion! He was, of course, as thin as a herring in hot weather. When Dr. Reuben R. Mussey, a man of no mean reputation as a surgeon, a follower of Graham, settled at Cincinnati, I one day called at his lodgings to pay him my respects. A little chubby-faced boy, probably six or seven years of age, answered the knocker. Asking whether Dr. Mussey was within, he threw his face into a very quizzical shape and said, "Father is not at home." "You are Dr. Mussey's son, are you?" "Yes." "I suppose you are very fond of meat?" Looking again very quizzically, he replied, "I like the smell of it." I thank God most devoutly for the happy mixture.

If a man wants to be well, happy, cheerful, and comfortable, in the best possible condition for his day's work and night's rest, as it respects his brain and muscles, he must eat slowly, masticate his food thoroughly, and not crowd his stomach. This organ can bear a great deal, but there is a point beyond which endurance is impossible. A little rest after a hearty meal is a good thing, but it is not every man that can take it. In this country, where everything is done in hot haste, where persons become rich in a day and poor in an hour, people, especially merchants and mechanics, eat like so many wild beasts, swallowing their food without due mastication, and putting twice as much into the stomach as they can digest. Is it to be wondered at that we are a nation of dyspeptics, that we have bad teeth, that we are nervous, irritable, murderous, and short-lived? *Festina lente* should be the motto of every man when he sits down to eat. The venerable Charles Carroll, when asked what means he employed to preserve his health in such perfect condition, replied, "I always leave the table hungry;" and the good Bishop

David, of Kentucky, upon being asked a similar question, rejoined that he always carried his physician with him. Upon being requested to tell who that physician was, he answered it was "hunger."

The Code of Health of the School of Salernum, founded in the ninth century, comprises some excellent general rules in regard to the use of food and drink, which should be more widely disseminated than they have hitherto been. The elegant translation of this code, recently published by Dr. Ordronaux, of New York, will no doubt be followed by very good results in popularizing these rules.

> "Without the habit, suppers never suit ;
> Shun then strange meals and drinks and fish and fruit,
> And frequent revels, of disease the root.
> Take wine for health's sake after every course,
> And those who can let them this rule enforce.
> Drink not when needless; eat not out of mood ;
> For thirst and hunger tonic powers include,
> While surfeits bring of direst ills a brood.
> Note *when* you drink, that you may not fall ill ;
> Note *what* you drink; drink after baths your fill.
> 'Tis heavy, not light, suppers that give pain,
> As common sense and doctors both maintain.
> Unless compelled, you never should combine,
> At one meal, divers sorts of food or wine ;
> But if constrained, then take the lightest cheer ;
> From wine and milk a lepra will appear.
> Routine before and after meals demands
> Water, dispensed to wash convivial hands.
> With wholesome dishes be all paupers fed ;
> Let supper close our calls for daily bread.
> Curb appetite and thus prolong your breath—
> Temp'rance, the doctors tell us, laughs at death."

These rules, in the main excellent, are not all unexceptionable. The Salernians were evidently too fond of wine. Young people should never use wine of any kind, and it

is equally important that they should abstain from con-
diments, as pepper, mustard, pungent sauces, and hot
dishes, as they unduly excite the appetite, and thus lead
to repletion, indigestion, and bad health. Persons who
are naturally weak, the aged, the infirm, and the overworked will be benefited by a glass of generous wine, or
a little whiskey, brandy, or ale, at dinner. A man, as the
Apostle says, should occasionally take a little wine for the
stomach's sake. Water, too freely drunk during, or soon
after, a meal, is bad, as it interferes with healthful digestion. Any severe exercise of mind or body soon after a
full meal is equally prejudicial.

The voice of the stomach should not be disregarded in
eating and drinking. As a general rule, whatever the
stomach craves may be accepted as an indication as to
what is wholesome. There are, of course, enough exceptions to prove the rule. Some physicians, otherwise apparently sufficiently wise, are fools in this respect. They
seem to be incapable of interpreting nature, no matter
how loudly or energetically she makes her demands. One
of my daughters had been terribly ill for several weeks;
she was much exhausted by nausea and vomiting; everything she took was promptly rejected, and her life was in
imminent peril. I was summoned to her bedside early in
the morning; she was extremely feeble, and in constant
retching. "Is there nothing that you would like to eat
or drink? Have you no craving for any particular kind
of food or drink?" "Yes, I have been dying for the last
few days for champagne, but my physicians have obsti-
nately interdicted its use." Her husband was immediately summoned, a bottle of the much-desired article was
brought to the bedside, and from that moment convalescence commenced. This is only a type of a hundred similar cases in the experience of every enlightened and observant practitioner. The voice of the stomach, under
such circumstances, is emphatically the voice of God—

the voice of suffering Nature. Some years ago I published
in Dr. Yandell's American Practitioner an elaborate paper
upon the Cravings of Nature in Disease. The subject had
never, as far as I know, been treated of before, but it has
since attracted wide attention. Practically, indeed, it is
a very important one.

When I was a boy I tried hard to learn to smoke and
chew, but after various efforts abandoned the attempt in
disgust, on account of the nauseating effects of tobacco
and the disgusting habit of spitting which its use so generally engenders. A pinch of snuff is occasionally a good
thing, as it serves to clear a man's brain by the impression
which it exerts through the mucous membrane of the nose
upon the sympathetic nerves. It has always been a source
of surprise to me that a genteel woman could tolerate an
habitual chewer and smoker, and yet I have heard many
ladies declare that the odor of a cigar was more agreeable
to them than the fragrance of a delicious flower. A mouth
covered with tobacco-juice is anything but ornamental.
Of its fragrance I cannot speak from personal observation.

I have all my life, with the exception of my early childhood, been a hard, earnest worker. Whatever I had to do
I did with all my might, never putting off till the afternoon what could be done in the morning, or until to-
morrow the labor of to-day. I always liked to be fully
up to time, or even a little in advance of it. In my professional engagements I have been a very strict observer
of punctuality. I have never in my life wilfully made
a professional brother wait for me in a consultation. I
have always considered that no man has a right to rob
another of his time, and therefore, while I have myself
been a most scrupulous respecter of the interests of others,
I have never allowed any one to trifle with my own.

Every man that is a man—that has the slightest pretension to manly qualities—ought to feel that his destiny is
in his own keeping, and that he can hold the world, as it

were, in his grasp. The brain can perform wonders; so can the spade, the pickaxe, and the hammer. Every human being, even the idiot, has talents that may, if properly applied, work out useful results. The architect may display genius and talent in the erection of a house; the coachmaker, in the construction of a carriage; the cook, in the preparation of his dishes. Every pursuit in life requires aptitude, and aptitude is nothing but genius or talent properly applied. Neither is worth anything if unaided by industry and perseverance, along with a definite aim, or a well-digested ulterior object, to the accomplishment of which a man's whole soul must be bent, alike in his waking and in his sleeping hours.

To owe no man has been one of the great maxims of my life. It has been an invariable rule with me to pay on the spot for whatever I buy, or as soon thereafter as possible. My servants have never been obliged to wait a day for their wages. Tradespeople have seldom, if ever, been obliged to present their accounts twice.

Hard work and annoying cases have sometimes rendered me irritable, and made me occasionally indulge in a hasty or unguarded expression, for which I was afterwards sorry. Naturally I am of an amiable temper, as prompt to forgive as to resent an insult. It has fallen to my lot to have a few enemies; but they were not made so through my own agency or conduct. They rose up in consequence of my position as a professional man, and as a natural result of a large and diversified practice, which brought me in contact with all kinds of people—good, bad, and indifferent. I never spoke ill of a professional brother, or did anything, directly or indirectly, to undermine his standing with his patients, the profession, or the public. On the contrary, I have often gone out of my way to sustain and defend him—sometimes, I fear, when silence might have been the correct course. I have on several occasions prevented patients from instituting suits for malpractice against members of the profession ; I saved two of my own pupils in this way, and both became afterwards my enemies.

I occasionally visit the theatre to see a great tragedy or an interesting comedy, and to get a good laugh, to break the dull monotony of my life, and to prepare me the better for new exertion, on the principle of "All work and no play makes Jack a dull boy." The opera I have never enjoyed, and have sometimes fallen asleep during the performance, especially if I was much fatigued. The circus has always afforded me genuine amusement. I have attended only three horseraces. I have never witnessed a cockfight, and have seldom been present at a political meeting. In politics I have always sided with the candidate whom I supposed to be the most honest, and have consequently seldom voted a full ticket. The first vote I ever cast was for General Jackson for the Presidency. I believed him to be an honest man, and therefore gave him my suffrage. Immediately before the war I supported Bell and Everett, and afterwards Mr. Lincoln when he became, for the second time, a candidate for the Presidency. I was actuated by the belief that he would do all that any mortal could do to promote the rapid reconstruction of the rebellious States. His assassination, which took place only a short time after his inauguration, was a great calamity, a national evil. He was a good, nay, a great man, governed by principle and the kindliest feelings of our nature.

I doubt, however, whether he had the slightest conception of the gigantic character of the war at its commencement. The fact that his proclamation called for only seventy-five thousand volunteers has always satisfied me that he thought the war would soon be over, and that the seceded States would rapidly fall back into their places in the Union. I was greatly disappointed on reading the proclamation, and observed at the time to my family that if the President had had a proper appreciation of the

Southern people and the reasons which induced them to go to war, he would have called out at the start not less than five hundred thousand men. Such a call would have exercised a most powerful influence upon Southern politicians by showing them that the Federal Government was in earnest to put down the rebellion—to crush it in its infancy.

Of late years I have frequently remained away from the polls, having rarely found a candidate whom I regarded as worthy of a vote. Besides, it is not pleasant to have one's vote neutralized by a scamp immediately in front of or behind one.

I have always had a sovereign contempt for doctors who meddle in politics, and my contempt has hardly been less keen for men who combine the practice of medicine with preaching. Politics may well be left to the care of politicians. A man has quite enough to do when he is a physician or a preacher, without mixing the two callings. My motto has always been, *Ne sutor ultra crepidam.*

I recollect, many years ago, hearing an anecdote of an old Virginia physician, Dr. Cabbell, who had long been at enmity with one of these preaching-doctors. The two had not spoken for many years, when Cabbell one day was brought home in a state of unconsciousness from having been pitched head foremost over the neck of his horse. The preaching-doctor, considering the occasion a favorable one for a reconciliation, anxiously approached the couch of the dying man, who by this time had completely regained his senses. "Good-morning, Dr. Cabbell." Dr. Cabbell, raising himself off his pillow, exclaimed, "What the d—l brings you here? Begone! begone! I can bear anything, everything but a preaching-doctor and a tripping horse." Every honest physician will indorse this sentiment.

I have always been particular in my friendships. I have never attached myself to any man of coarse mind, rough manners, or bad habits. If I have ever toadied to anybody, I am not conscious of it. On the contrary, I have often in my practice made the rich give way to the poor.

It has been said, not without truth, that youth is a blunder, manhood a struggle, and old age a regret. My life is an exception to this rule. That I was guilty of some indiscretions in my youth is probable ; but few youths, perhaps, were ever more moral or more conscientious. My manhood was a period of courageous self-reliance, full of work and hard knocks, but also full of hope and confidence. It was the seedtime of my professional life, without one misgiving, if my life should be spared, of ultimate success. Am I old at sixty-four ? I do not feel that I am. If my vigor has in any degree abated, I am not conscious of it. I have just finished my thirtieth course of lectures on surgery. If I ever lectured better, with greater enthusiasm, or with more point and effect, with more ease and unction than I have this winter, I am not aware of the fact. Always punctual to the minute, I invariably filled the hour in a sustained and easy manner, keeping fully alive the attention of my class until the janitor's bell announced that the time had expired. If my old age has not been a triumph, it has been one of great tranquillity and of unalloyed happiness, with an amount of work, mental and physical, just sufficient to keep me comfortably occupied. I am, on an average, three to three and a half hours in the streets each day, in making my professional rounds, and the exercise which I am thus compelled to take in the open air acts as a safety-valve to my constitution, which might otherwise sink into a state of sluggishness incompatible with sound health.

Few if any physicians or surgeons have ever been more tormented with letters, upon all kinds of subjects, than myself. To answer them has been to me a grievous task, and yet there have hardly been any that could be safely overlooked or neglected. Many of them have been addressed to me by my professional brethren, and more especially by graduates of the different schools with which I have been connected, asking advice respecting the nature and treatment of their cases. These letters could not be slighted without the risk of making these men my enemies, and thus positively injuring myself as well as the institution with which I might at the time be connected.

The writer perhaps tells me that he has a man laboring under a tumor or morbid growth, concerning which he earnestly desires my opinion, adding, it may be, that his diagnosis, if I can confirm it, will be the making of his reputation. Now, much as I like to assist my professional brethren in their troubles, I never lose sight of the fact that I owe something to myself. I therefore always answer that, inasmuch as I have not seen or examined the case, I cannot be supposed to know anything about it. To give an opinion in the dark, founded solely upon the statement of another, perhaps not overly wise, would indeed be the height of folly. It is certainly what no sensible man should do.

A professor is thus a dependent creature. If his pupils are his friends they send him patients, and his school students; if his enemies, they withhold both, and thus give other physicians and other colleges their patronage. A graduate then has a professor greatly in his power. The same remark applies to advice concerning the purchase of books, instruments, and apparatus.

I have often been asked to give my opinion upon points of professional etiquette; and also to act as umpire in cases of disputes between two professional brethren—no very enviable office, certainly, and yet not always avoidable, especially in the case of old pupils, or of good friends, whose wishes were law with me. Where there are no such bonds, my advice is to steer clear of the responsibility implied in such requests.

I am not unfrequently obliged to give my testimony as an expert in suits for malpractice, in behalf of practitioners of whom I have not the slightest personal knowledge, and who perhaps live at a great distance from me. Such calls I seldom decline if I find that the defendant is a worthy person, as I consider it my bounden duty always to defend a professional brother when he is, as so generally happens, unjustly prosecuted. These suits have, unfortunately, been exceedingly common in this country during the last twenty-five years, and, from what I know of them, there is reason to believe that they are generally instigated by dishonest and designing medical men, intent upon the ruin of the defendant, who is thus often subjected to great trouble, vexation, expense, and even loss of character. What is worse than all, no physician or surgeon, however exalted his character or position, is exempt from them. There are at this moment—February, 1870—three suits of this kind pending in our courts against three highly respectable practitioners in this city. A verdict of three thousand dollars was rendered against the late Dr. Paul B. Goddard for an operation on an eye; and Dr. Horner, for many years Professor of Anatomy in the University of Pennsylvania, only escaped by his death a trial for malpractice. These suits are not peculiar to this country, though they are much more common among us than they are in Europe. The celebrated case of Bransby B. Cooper, the nephew of the great Sir Astley, is famous in medical history, on account of the respectability of the defendant and the outrageous character of the prosecution.

Some idea of the extent of my correspondence may be formed when I state that my paper, envelopes, ink, and postage-stamps cost me nearly one hundred dollars annually. This cost, however, is a trifle compared with my time and labor. Fortunately, I long ago learned the proper way of dealing with such communications—by short answers; and yet short answers will not always suffice.

A man must do himself justice, especially when he gives a professional opinion; otherwise he must bear the risk of misrepresentation and its ill effects upon his business as a sensible, educated, scientific physician.

The most laconic answer I ever returned to any person was the following: A medical man wrote to me about a case of prolapse of the iris consequent upon a wound of the cornea in a young child. The mother would not allow the iris to be replaced, fearing the effects of chloroform. At the end of twelve days the physician wrote to me to know whether he should make an effort at reduction or snip off the protruding portion. To this I simply replied, "Snip," and the operation, as I subsequently learned, was successful.

I am often asked for testimonials of character, or recommendations of qualifications, a thing I never grant unless I have some personal knowledge of the applicant, or he comes fully indorsed by one in whose judgment and honesty I have full confidence. To act otherwise would be highly culpable.

No man has probably been more frequently tormented than I have been about testimonials for all kinds of things from a nipple-shield to an electric battery, and for every intermediate contrivance that can be conceived of, including cod-liver oil, vegetable extracts, toothpicks, and even blacking. The importunities that have accompanied these petitions have sometimes been very great; but I have invariably had the firmness to resist them; and if, after I am dead and gone, my name should appear in connection with any such document, I hereby declare that it was forged; for I never gave a testimonial for such a purpose. A newspaper is occasionally sent to me with a quack advertisement, in which the writer has had the impudence to refer to my name, of course without my knowledge or authority. These things will happen, and they are not a little annoying, as they have a tendency to place one in a false position, both with the public and the profession.

Swaim, an illiterate, cunning charlatan, made his fortune with his "Panacea" on the strength of the testimonials given him by Chapman, Dewees, Hare, and Gibson, Professors in the University of Pennsylvania. How these men could have deliberately committed such an outrage upon their school and the profession has always been a mystery to me. Nothing could have been more unwise, undignified, or unprofessional. Physick, who had been solicited to unite with them, would rather have burned off his right hand than have been guilty of such an act. He had a higher and nobler sense of what was due to himself and his profession. Some men seem to have a special fondness for such things. Dr. Mütter at one time gave his name to all kinds of testimonials, evidently from a sheer desire for notoriety. I have now before me a pamphlet, entitled Concentrated Extract of Pinus Canadensis, a quack medicine, indorsed by one of the most eminent gynæcologists of the day and a former President of the American Medical Association; and there are hundreds of just such men in this country who, apparently for the sake merely of seeing their names in print, do not hesitate to sacrifice their professional dignity and degrade their noble calling.

No profession can sustain itself long in public estimation unless it is largely composed of gentlemen, men of mental culture, refined taste, general intelligence, and courtly bearing. Unless this high standard is sedulously maintained, loss of caste and decline of influence will be no less conspicuous than deplorable. Of nothing do I feel more profoundly assured than this: that there can be no salutary leadership which is not based on sound morals and good breeding, and that no barrier of protection should be thrown down by any one—be he physician, clergyman, or lawyer—who wishes to secure an honored and a lasting reputation.

The medical man should be a thorough gentleman. I have heard of a physician losing a wealthy lady patient because he cleaned his nails in her presence, a thing which of course no well-bred gentleman ever does. Walking roughly across the floor of the sick-chamber, loud talking, and an angry or impatient tone of voice, are sure to be commented upon, and not unfrequently lead to unpleasant consequences. In consultations, which always take place away from the patient, the business should be scrupulously confined to the matter in hand. Any irrelevant talk, if overheard, as is not unfrequently the case, is often interpreted to the disadvantage of the attendants, on the ground that they do not take sufficient interest in the welfare of the patient; and in truth there is some reason for such a conclusion.

I always had private pupils during my early professional life, and have reason to believe that most of them remained ever afterwards my warm friends. A few, whom I most befriended and assisted to important positions, became lukewarm and apparently indifferent, thus affording another illustration of the old adage that "The more you do for a man the less he likes you." Some of my pupils have become distinguished teachers, writers, and practitioners, and have thus reflected credit upon me as their preceptor. Having experienced but little benefit from private instruction myself, I spared no pains to advance the interests of my pupils, and to use every effort to inspire them with an honest zeal for their studies. My practice always was to examine them at a certain hour regularly every other day, or thrice a week, as long as they were under my charge, not with book in hand, as had been the custom with my own preceptor, but extemporaneously, often explaining matters in the form of familiar lectures, interspersed with apt questions, a mode of instruction which commends itself by its great simplicity and effectiveness, as it interests the student much more than any other practice with which I am acquainted. One and a half to two hours were generally consumed in this exercise. The teaching was always conducted in the most systematic manner; the pupils were obliged to be punctual in their attendance; and whenever it was in my power, I showed them cases and illustrated the application of bandages and apparatus. The regular fee for private tuition was one hundred dollars a year; but, although I had altogether a considerable number of private pupils, I am sure I never made three thousand dollars in this way, as there were many who never paid me anything for the pains I took in instructing them. Now and then I was decidedly a loser, as some of them borrowed money of me which they never returned. Not many of these men have risen to eminence, although a number of them were endowed with excellent talents, and would doubtless have succeeded in acquiring reputation if they had not been deficient in these most important of all the elements of greatness—industry and perseverance. The two who have thus far most distinguished themselves are Dr. T. G. Richardson, Professor of Surgery in the University of Louisiana at New Orleans, and Dr. Nathan Bozeman, who has earned a large reputation—American and European—as a gynæcologist. Of the pupils who have attended my public lectures many have become distinguished teachers and practitioners of surgery, and not a few occupy highly respectable positions in the army and navy.

My residence in Cincinnati, as stated elsewhere, was one of hard work, with an income gradually increasing, but at all times sufficient for my slender wants. My family was small, and my wife and I economized as much as we could. At Louisville I made a great deal of money, but my expenses were proportionably great, and when I left, my property all told was probably not worth sixty thousand dollars. I have made some money since my residence here, but I am not rich—only in very easy, comfortable circumstances, the best condition, perhaps, in which a rational being can be. The acquisition of money has never been my aim or desire. I have lived solely for my profession. If I had been less of a student, I might, and probably would, have been a richer man. I have never engaged in any speculations. I have made by hard work every dollar I possess. My library, although not very large, has cost me a considerable sum; and when I was young I sometimes bought books when I could ill afford the purchase. My personal habits have never been expensive. In my dress I have always endeavored to be neat; my equipage has been very plain; and my study has always been simple, without any extravagance. I have never attempted any parade, or been guilty of ostentation or display. In riding about the city I have never been so happy as when I was seated in my buggy, with reins in hand, behind a respectable, well-broken, trustworthy horse. In 1867 I bought a coupé, but it was a long time before I felt at home in it, or became reconciled to its requirements. Even now, after a trial of nearly three years, I frequently feel lost and uncomfortable in it.

In religion I have been for the greater part of my life a Unitarian, although I was brought up, in conformity with my mother's wishes, in the Lutheran Church, and at the age of fifteen was confirmed and took the sacrament, after having learned nearly the whole catechism by heart. As I grew older I threw aside the narrow sectarianism of my childhood, and adopted what I believe to be the most rational doctrine that has ever been proclaimed. In this faith I have lived, and in this faith I hope to die. My respect for the Christian religion has always been profound. Even apart from the disputed doctrine that Christ is God, it is the most sublime religion that has ever prevailed among men; and it has done more to civilize, refine, and humanize our race than all other schemes that have ever been devised for our salvation, temporal and eternal, put together. In my younger days I was a regular attendant at church; but for many years past I have been so much occupied, professionally, on the Sabbath that it has seldom been in my power to be there more than perhaps half a dozen times a year. This I have always sincerely regretted. As it was, I should have gone much oftener if it had not been utterly repugnant to my feelings to enter my pew when the service was half over, or to struggle during a prosy sermon against sleep, brought on by excessive mental and bodily fatigue incurred in the exercise of my professional duties.

Many of the most distinguished men that ever lived were Unitarians, or upheld Unitarian doctrines. In our own country Unitarianism has been indorsed by Channing, Parker, Emerson, and other leading minds; in Germany it found a warm sympathizer in Herder; and Dr. Robert Knox, the great Scotch anatomist and anthropologist, believed in it. Sir Isaac Newton, John Milton, and John Locke were Unitarians, together with many of the noblest intellects in English history. I am therefore not ashamed of the faith that is in me. To err is human; to forgive divine. One part of my religious creed is to be charitable to all men, of whatever faith, provided it does not lean to idolatry. No human being can tell with any degree of certainty who is right or who is wrong. There is probably no religion that has not some godliness in it as its basis. "The fool hath said in his heart, There is no God." A greater truism never was uttered.

I hold it to be unwise, if not positively criminal, for a physician to thrust his religious views upon his patients. If his views differ from those of the people around him, especially of those who give him their confidence in sickness and in sorrow, it is little less than brutal to disturb their belief. It is better, a thousand times better, to remain silent, and to intrust all such matters to the clergy, to whom they properly belong. The opinion uttered upon this subject by Dr. John Gregory, of Edinburgh, a hundred years ago, coincides so fully with my own that I cannot refrain from quoting it: "A physician who has the misfortune to disbelieve in a future state will, if he has common good-nature, conceal his sentiments from those under his charge with as much care as he would preserve them from the infection of a mortal disease."

I have naturally, as all men must have, an instinctive horror of death, not because of any fear about the disposition of my soul, but because my life has been a pleasant one, and I would therefore be glad to hold on to it. I have often thought that our lives are too short for the amount of labor we are obliged to perform. Just as we begin to know how to live, and become comfortably settled, we are obliged to go hence, whither exactly we know not. What my soul is God has not revealed to me. Whatever it may be, He will, in His good mercy and great kindness, take care of it. I have doubtless many sins, but more of omission than of commission. I have never believed in original wickedness. Man is only man; he is weak and frail by nature, and he must therefore do a great many things that are displeasing to his Creator. Imperfection is his great characteristic.

When I am dead I should like to be burned. It is not to me a pleasant idea to be put six feet under ground, without the possibility of ever again reaching the surface. I have a great respect for urn burial, and hope the day is not distant when it will come into general use. I know of no more disagreeable sight than a graveyard, especially in a city. It is amazing that civilization should ever have tolerated such a nuisance. To me nothing is more distasteful or disgusting. It is a relic of barbarism of the worst kind. I want to be useful when I am dead, which

I cannot be if I am stuck away six feet into the earth. If I am burned, my body will enter again into new creations, and thus be subservient to some useful purpose. It may assist in animating a flower, in ornamenting the plumage of a bird, or in directing the movements of a caterpillar. I prefer anything rather than to be obliged to decay in the earth and lie forever idle.

If I am obliged to be buried as other people are, I wish to lie in some spot where birds may sing over my grave, and where occasionally a friendly hand may deposit a flower, as a memento of respect and devotion to my memory. An immortelle is worth all the chiselled marble that was ever erected over a man's tomb.

There is some choice in regard to a man's death. If I could have my own way, I should select apoplexy as the most desirable mode of exit. It does its work quickly, and generally very gracefully, very much like an anæsthetic, without the consciousness of the individual. The Litany contains a prayer against sudden death, considering it as a great evil; but this has reference solely to a man's religious preparation. It assumes that a slow death affords a person a better chance to get ready for the kingdom of heaven. A sensible man should always be ready. His motto should be, *Nunquam non paratus.* I have seen so much of chronic death, as it may be called, that I pray God to preserve me and mine from its appalling affliction. What can be more horrible, more truly agonizing than death from consumption or cancer? When my hour comes I hope the Destroyer will do me a friendly act by extinguishing life in the twinkling of an eye, and thus save me from the pangs of gradual dissolution. "Oh, that my life may go out like the snuff of a candle!"

Few persons can look upon death with the same composure as Mrs. Barbauld, who in her old age composed the following beautiful lines:

"Life! we've been long together
　　Through pleasant and through cloudy weather;
　　'Tis hard to part when friends are dear;
　　Perhaps 't will cost a sigh, a tear;
　　Then steal away, give little warning,
　　Choose thine own time;
　　Say not ' Good-night,' but in some happier clime
　　Bid me ' Good-morning.' "

The practice of medicine leaves one little leisure for the study of the classics or the cultivation of the fine arts. A physician who has little or no business is in a sad condition; one who is overwhelmed with it is, if possible, still worse off, for his mind and body are on a constant strain, affording him no opportunity for recreation, for domestic enjoyment, or for the charms of literature. It is reported of the celebrated Dr. Matthew Baillie, of London, that when he was at the height of his practice he often came home so much exhausted that if a member of his family made a sign to approach him, he would motion him back with uplifted hands, and sink down in the first convenient chair to rest himself.* Many, many times have I experienced similar feelings after I had been up all night with a sick patient, had performed a tedious and delicate operation, or had held a protracted clinic, attended with more than ordinary labor and anxiety. No man in such a condition wants to be troubled with company, idle talk, or light reading. What he needs is substantial repose of mind and body, to reinvigorate his exhausted powers. It is certainly highly desirable that every physician should know something outside of his own profession; that he should have a general acquaintance with art, science, geography, travel, poetry, and history, in order that he

---

* On one occasion Baillie was paying a visit to a lady affected with some trivial complaint; she had plied him with all sorts of questions, when, tearing himself away, he ran headlong down the stairs. " Stop!" said the unrelenting creature; " may I eat oysters ?"　" Yes," was the reply, " shells and all, madam."

may appear before the world at least as a man of some culture and general information. It is not necessary that he should be profoundly versed in any of these things. Such knowledge can be obtained only at the expense of his profession, to which he owes his first duty, his best allegiance, and which, if properly cultivated, allows him but little time for extraneous work. I have frequently found that physicians who pride themselves upon their classical attainments, their knowledge of literature, or their scientific proficiency, are poor practitioners, who seldom contribute any useful facts to the stock of their profession. They are like meteors, very brilliant, but of little use as practitioners of the healing art. There was a time, as in the days of Radcliffe, Mead, and Johnson, when medical men, even if in large practice, had an abundance of leisure, a portion of which at least they could devote to social enjoyment and to the attractions of literature. But things are different nowadays. Medicine has become a great and complex study, and he who would excel in it, whether considered merely as an art or as a science, must be wide awake, and give himself up, soul and body, to its interests. No half measures will suffice. She is a zealous mistress, and will not put up with evasive coquetry.

It has been said of lawyers that he who preserves his honor unspotted deserves a place in the calendar of saints, so rarely, it would seem, do they pass unscathed through the fiery ordeal of professional life, a life beset with so many temptations. I would fain hope that such a sentiment is a slander upon the members of the bar. However this may be, I am quite sure that the remark does not apply to medical men. Faults undoubtedly we have, and there are, it is equally true, many bad men among us; but, in the main, physicians are high-toned, upright, conscientious, and honorable men, who practise their profession not so much for the love of gain as for the opportunities it affords them of doing good. It is rarely that we hear of a patient being neglected, overcharged, or in any wise ill treated. The secrets which are confided to them in their professional intercourse are seldom revealed; and if, now and then, there is a gossip among them, he is commonly short-lived, the community soon fixing a brand upon him by which all men shall know him. I am often told that the professional standard is lower than it was forty or fifty years ago. Certainly it is low enough, but this is a great slander. Physicians at the present day, without being more refined, or without having any better preliminary education, are more highly educated than formerly; our means of instruction are far greater, and the instruction itself is of a much higher order. The time will come when this matter will regulate itself, when a higher standard will be demanded both of brains and of preparatory knowledge, and when our instruction will be better systematized, and the student required to study a much longer time and to make better use of his opportunities than he now does. Meanwhile, some of our schools at least do the best they can. It is unfortunately only too true that many of the young men of the present day study and practise merely as a trade, or as a means of obtaining a livelihood. Our examinations for the doctorate are too lax, and the candidate is let loose upon the world without that practical knowledge of his profession so necessary to meet the emergencies of daily life. Our opportunities for the acquisition of this knowledge are as great and varied here as they are anywhere in the wide, wide world. But our young men are too impatient to benefit by them. They are in hot haste to break through the shackles of student life, and to embark upon the rough sea of practice without a due appreciation of the quicksands that lie in their path, and upon which so many are wrecked.

Industry does a great deal towards building up a practice and laying the foundation of an enduring reputation. Dr. William Stokes, of Dublin, who attained to the highest pinnacle of reputation long before he died, made this entry in his diary at the age of twenty-two: "I rise early, write until breakfast, then go to the dispensary, where I sit in judgment on disease for an hour; then to the hospital, where I go round the wards attended by a crowd of pupils; from the hospital I return home, write again till two, and then go round and visit my patients through different parts of the town, attended by a pupil. Many of my patients have one great defect, viz., that, instead of giving money, they too often, unfortunate beings, have to solicit it from their medical attendant; and who, with the heart of a man, would refuse to relieve their sufferings when he has a shilling in his pocket? A poor woman whom I attended long, and who ultimately recovered, said, 'Oh, doctor, you have given me a good stomach, but I have nothing to put into it.'" Thousands of young practitioners, who are in search of practice in a large city, and who must be content, often for years, with the scum of the alleys and byways, can indorse the truth of this statement of the Irish physician. My heart has often ached and my pocket opened under such sad circumstances.

Mungo Park, the celebrated traveller, who was educated to the profession of medicine, declared that he greatly preferred the life of an explorer in the wilds of Africa to the drudgeries of practice among the hills, moorland, and heaths of Scotland, his native country. He mentions that he rode one day a distance of forty miles on horseback, sat up all night in attendance upon a woman laboring under the throes of parturition, and received as his fee a roasted potato and a glass of buttermilk. It is not every obstetrician that can boast even of such a grand reward. I myself, in my earlier days, on more occasions than one, put up with less.

It may be well for me here to enumerate briefly some of my labors and original contributions to medicine and surgery, apart from authorship :

Experiments on dogs and rabbits, in 1833, during my residence at Easton, to illustrate the subject of manual strangulation. A full account of these experiments was published in Drake's Western Journal of Medicine, vol. ix., and an abstract of them will be found in Beck's Medical Jurisprudence, vol. ii.

Experiments upon excretion, to ascertain the rapid transit of certain articles, when taken into the stomach, through the blood by the kidneys. For this purpose rabbits were selected, to which, after having tied both renal arteries, protoxide of iron was administered. The animals were killed within thirty minutes, and upon applying a solution of cyanide of potassium to the urine, well-marked traces of iron were invariably found in that fluid.

During my residence in Cincinnati I spent much time in weighing and measuring healthy organs, as well as in studying their color and consistence, with a view of determining the more readily their changes in disease. The results of these examinations were embodied in my treatise on Pathological Anatomy. My examinations of the prostate have been fully quoted by Sir Henry Thompson and others.

My experiments on the nature and treatment of wounds of the intestines are referred to on a previous page. They occupied fully two years of my leisure time, and were performed soon after I entered the University of Louisville.

In my Pathological Anatomy I have given an account of a number of dissections of specimens of false conceptions, or uterine moles, as they are termed—the first account of them in the English language, as far as I know.

During my residence at Easton, I took, with the greatest possible care, fifty observations on the temperature of venous blood in healthy persons of both sexes, the result being an average of 96° Fahr. The results of these investigations were published, in 1835, in the Western Medical Gazette, vol. ii.

Deep stitches in wounds of the wall of the abdomen, to prevent hernia or protrusion of the bowel after recovery. As far as my reading extends I know of no work on surgery in which this subject was placed in its true light, or, indeed, any light prior to the publication of my monograph on wounds of the intestines. Of course every surgeon speaks of it now.

The invention of an enterotome for the treatment of artificial anus, intended to supersede the clumsy contrivance of Dupuytren.

A tracheotomy forceps, for the extraction of foreign bodies from the air-passages, favorably mentioned by writers on surgery.

Wiring the ends of the bones in dislocations of the sterno-clavicular and acromio-clavicular joints, taught originally in my lectures in the University of Louisville soon after I took charge of the chair of Surgery in that school. Since successfully practised by the late Dr. Cooper, of San Francisco, and by Dr. Hodgen, of St. Louis.

Blood catheter, an instrument for drawing off the urine, when mixed with blood, or when the openings of the ordinary catheter become obstructed with blood, as it is passed along the urethra.

An arterial compressor—a peculiar pair of forceps— for arresting hemorrhage in deep-seated vessels not accessible to the ligature or amenable to torsion or acupressure, as in the perineum after lithotomy.

A tourniquet, or compressor, constructed in the form of a clamp, for compressing the vessels of the extremities in amputation, now superseded by Esmarch's bandage ; still of use in compressing the axillary artery in amputation at the shoulder joint.

An instrument for extracting foreign bodies from the nose and ear, found in nearly every pocket-case in the country.

Modification of Pirogoff's amputation at the ankle joint, unjustly ascribed to Dr. Quimby of Jersey City.

Laparotomy in rupture of the bladder.

Direct operation for hernia by suturing the pillars of the ring.

Mode of operating for inverted toe-nail.

Apparatus for the transfusion of blood.

First account of Prostatorrhœa.

Description of a new form of neuralgia of the jaws in old persons.

Pododynia, a disease of the foot, first described by me.

I was the first to describe the use of adhesive plaster as a means of making extension in the treatment of fractures of the lower extremity. The account was published in my work on Injuries and Diseases of the Bones, in 1830. The case in which this treatment was originally employed was one of compound fracture in the practice of my first preceptor, Dr. Joseph K. Swift, of Easton, Pennsylvania.

When I settled in Philadelphia the practice among the more distinguished physicians was to administer morphia and quinine in very small doses, the former generally in about the one-eighth of a grain and the latter in about a grain, repeated every two, three, or four hours. A quarter of a grain of morphia was considered a very large dose, and half a grain was rarely ventured upon in any case. When in my didactic lectures and at the clinics I spoke of half a grain as a minimum dose in inflammation, and of one grain as a proper dose in severe pain, many of my new confrères held up their hands in holy horror, and yet now this very practice is quite prevalent among us. Does not common sense teach that a small anodyne in violent suffering is worse than useless? So of quinine : what use is there in small doses in cases of emergency, as in neuralgia and intermittent fever? In a duel which is to decide the fate of a nation, it would be folly to oppose a pigmy against a giant, or to fight with a pistol against a chassepôt. The dose must be such as to meet the exigencies of the particular case. Of course, there are proper limits in all things, which no man of sense will lightly disregard.

As far as my reading extends, I was the first to suggest the use of ergot in the treatment of diabetes. The case was that of a woman—a patient of Dr. Shearer, of Sinking Springs, Berks County, Pennsylvania, who afterwards published an account of it in the Philadelphia Medical and Surgical Reporter. Although the case was a bad one, the quantity of water discharged in the twenty-four hours being very large, perfect recovery took place, entirely ascribable to the use of the ergot. Since then the article has been employed in very numerous instances with great success in this affection. A full account of this treatment is contained in the late Dr. Napheys's Therapeutics.

Many years ago I suggested a new method of treating ganglia of the hand and foot by the subcutaneous division of the cyst, comminuting it most thoroughly by means of the tenotome, and then making firm compression with sheet-lead and a compress and bandage—a plan now generally pursued in this country, if not also in Europe.

The opening of chronic abscesses is, as is well known, when practised by the ordinary method, almost invariably followed by high constitutional reaction, or hectic irritation. To prevent this occurrence I have been in the habit —at least for a quarter of a century—of placing the patient immediately under the full influence of opium, and keeping up the impression for at least five or six days, by the end of which time the system has usually fully accommodated itself to its new relations. I have never known any bad effects to arise, even when the opening was very free, in the most depraved constitution, where this treatment was properly carried out. If this practice is not original with me, I have never seen any account of it, and must therefore claim some credit for it.

The inflammatory origin and vitality of tubercle of the lungs and other structures were for a long time doubted by most pathologists in this country and in Europe. These doctrines, so directly in harmony with common sense and the results of accurate observation, I taught with great emphasis in my lectures in the Cincinnati College and afterwards in my work on Pathological Anatomy, and they are now the accepted doctrines of the schools. The vitality of tubercle is, of course, very feeble, and hence, after a certain period, it is sure to undergo softening and degeneration.

The propriety of amputating in senile gangrene has long been a disputed question. If the operation be ever proper, and there are certainly cases in which it is, it should invariably be performed, as I have reason to believe I was the first to teach, at a great distance from the seat of the disease, after a very perfect line of demarcation has formed. The disease, as is well known, is dependent upon calcification of the arteries, leading to the formation of emboli, or fibrinous clots, in their interior, with consequent obstruction of the circulation, followed by the death of the parts thus deprived of blood. As the degeneration of the arterial tissues often, if not generally, extends a considerable distance beyond the gangrenous structures, there is every reason why, if amputation be performed, the limb should be removed at a great distance from the affected parts to prevent a recurrence of the disease. Thus, for instance, in gangrene of the foot, amputation should be performed only a short distance below the knee, and in gangrene involving the ankle or lower part of the leg, nearly as high up or quite as high as the middle of the thigh.

If I was not the first to suggest, I was certainly the first, at least in this country, to sew together the ends of an accidentally divided tendon of the hand. The ends were refreshed, and united by wire suture. The parts did well, and an excellent cure was the result. The operation has only of late years begun to attract attention.

In my lectures on surgery for many years I have taught that what are usually called scrofulous diseases are nothing but remote forms of syphilis, in which the latter disease has lost its distinctive features. The more I see of such cases the more I am convinced that I am right. My views upon this subject are fully set forth in the address which I delivered at Detroit, in 1874, on Syphilis in its Relation to the National Health.

CHAPTER VIII.

I HAD long been desirous of visiting Europe for the purpose of becoming better acquainted by personal observation with her people and her institutions, but more particularly for the opportunity that would thus be afforded me of meeting some of the distinguished medical men with whose names and works I had been familiar, and with many of whom I had been for years in correspondence. I had wished to see the practical working of the medical schools and the hospitals of the Old World, and the magnificent museums with which some of the larger British and Continental cities are enriched. I had longed to visit the scenes of the early struggles and triumphs of a Haller, a Hunter, and a Cooper, and to compare European with American medical science. In 1868 the severe indisposition of my wife demanded entire change of scene and air, and accordingly in May of that year we set sail for France. It is not my purpose, nor would it be my pleasure, to give a detailed sketch of this visit. The unusual facilities now enjoyed for reaching Europe, and the great number of works annually published as the result of foreign travel should alone preclude my undertaking such a task, even if want of space were not pleaded as an excuse for the rather disjointed way in which portions of this visit are related. Accompanied by my son, A. Haller

Gross, who joined us in Paris, and who had already been for some time on the Continent engaged in study and travel, we spent several delightful months.

Some of the pleasantest recollections of this visit are connected with Berne, the city of the bears, where the chief attraction for me was the house in which Von Haller, the great physiologist, lived for so many years, and in which he finally died.* A young, well-dressed, ladylike woman responded to the old knocker, and with a polite courtesy bade me enter. Telling her that I was an American physician, I explained the object of my visit, and to my great delight found that she was a connection by marriage of the Von Haller family. When I told her that my son, then present, was named for Haller, it seemed as if she could not do too much for us. The house, an old two-story stone structure with a deep basement, is situated upon an elevated street, almost immediately opposite to, and only a very short distance from, the mouth of the river Aar, a fierce, tumultuous stream rushing down from the Alps, which, with their snow-capped summits, are in full view of this classic residence. One of the principal objects which attracted my attention was a marble tablet in the wall of the hall inscribed with the date of Haller's birth and death. My kind cicerone evinced great pleasure in showing me the apartment which had once formed the study and library of this great and good man; and upon taking my leave of her she presented me with a beautiful rose from a small parterre on the veranda overlooking the Aar. Of this flower I sent some petals to my good friend, the late Professor Robley Dunglison, whose work on physi-

---

* It is related that on one occasion an English traveller wended his way to the house of the great physiologist that he might worship at his shrine. Some time afterwards, meeting with Voltaire, he was surprised to hear the distinguished Frenchman refer to Haller in terms of praise and admiration, adding, "Haller does not speak so well of you." "Alas! possibly we are both mistaken," replied Voltaire, with great coolness and a shrug of the shoulder.

ology may justly be regarded in our day in the same light in which Haller's was in his—a monument of erudition and of stupendous industry, worthy of any age or country.

From my earliest professional life I had been a warm admirer of the character and writings of the Swiss physiologist. During my pupilage I had read his First Lines of Physiology; and soon after I obtained my medical degree I was so fortunate as to secure the German edition of his great work, in eight duodecimo volumes, a *résumé* of all that had been published upon the subject up to the time of its appearance, near the middle of the eighteenth century. This work is not a mere compilation. While it partakes largely of this character, as every work of the kind professing to give a full history of the science necessarily must, it embodies a great amount of original matter, the results of the experiments of Haller and of his pupils, many of whom afterwards became distinguished men, worthy of the fame of such a master. This work passed through many editions, was translated into the principal languages of Europe, and will be referred to in all time to come as a true and faithful exponent of the science and literature of physiology up to the time of the death of its illustrious author.

Haller was, in every respect, a wonderful man, many-sided, endowed with a lofty genius. He was a hard worker, a lover of nature and of art, with an inquisitive mind incessantly bent upon the acquisition of knowledge, a skilful interpreter of science, and, in the truest sense of the term, a seeker after truth. He was, as is conceded by all, the most learned man of his day. What Erasmus was in the sixteenth century Haller was in the eighteenth. He spoke with great fluency nearly every living language of Europe, and was a thorough master of Greek and Latin. Born in 1708, his childhood was passed in constant study, in which he made such marvellous progress that when, in his tenth year, he was examined for admission into the

gymnasium, he performed the self-imposed task of translating his German exercises into Greek, instead of Latin, as
he had been requested to do. He had already, at this time,
prepared brief sketches of the lives of more than two
thousand distinguished men, and made some progress in
the study of Hebrew and Chaldaic. It is asserted by one
of his biographers that he wrote Latin like Tacitus. He
had the merit of introducing a new era into German literature. Excepting Luther, no man perhaps ever did more
than he to advance its interests, or to invest it with so
much respect. For more than half a century the German
language had lost caste among the higher orders of society,
and had been effectually banished from the German courts,
which, in their imbecility, abjured their mother-tongue and
substituted for it the French language, which few of them
spoke with fluency and none with accuracy. Haller, whose
literary tastes were of a high order, and whose researches
penetrated into almost every branch of knowledge—science,
theology, statesmanship, politics, and even law—did much
to correct this state of things by the labors of his pen,
which was never idle. His style was always graceful and
dignified, and he knew how to express his ideas in the
fewest words and in the simplest language. Incredible as
it may seem, he wrote several thousand reviews of important works, prepared constantly new editions of his
own treatises, and for nearly half a century kept a diary
of the things and events which transpired around him.
His poems, of which a copy has long been in my library,
passed through thirty editions, of which one was in Latin,
one in English, one in Italian, and eight in French. His
biographer tells us that when Schiller left Stuttgart he
carried with him only two works, Shakespeare and Haller.
Haller was a born poet; for he wrote poetry when he was
a mere youth, his first efforts being translations of Ovid,
Horace, and Virgil, followed by imitations of Lohenstein,
and of the Psalms of David. His poetical effusions are

pervaded by a religious tone, which shows that he was a firm believer, not only in the existence of God, but in the fundamental truths of Christianity, as understood and practised in his day. His piety is beautifully shown in his Letters on the Truths of Christianity, a small volume addressed to his daughter. His library consisted of upwards of twelve thousand volumes, and comprised the choicest works in the various languages of Europe. Humboldt, no mean authority, pronounced him the greatest naturalist of his day.

Haller was the founder of modern physiology, as Vesalius, two hundred years before, had been the founder of modern anatomy. Both of these great men found these branches of study a mass of jargon, unworthy of the name of science, and erected them upon a solid and substantial basis. Vesalius was the first to dissect the human subject and to teach anatomy practically; Haller the first to place physiology upon an experimental footing. Both rendered immense service to the interests of science, and infused into the minds of their pupils the fire of their genius. Haller studied the higher mathematics under the illustrious Bernouilli, and medicine under the great masters of his time—anatomy under Winslow and Albinus; botany under Jussieu; and theoretical and practical medicine under the immortal Boerhaave. He had not been long in the profession before he discovered the irritability of the muscles, traced the development of the heart and blood in the embryo, and entered upon that course of experimental physiology which has left its impress upon succeeding ages. His labors were no child's play; he worked earnestly, early and late, in season and out of season. In botany he wrote an elaborate treatise, containing descriptions, with drawings, of two thousand four hundred and eighty-six Swiss plants, and contributed several thousand articles to the Göttingen Cyclopedia. Independent in worldly matters, he practised medicine only for the first few years after his return from his foreign travels, and then abandoned himself to study and the observation of nature. At Berne he established an anatomical theatre, and instructed small classes of students. At the age of twenty-seven he was elected to the professorship of Medicine and Botany in the University of Göttingen, a chair which he occupied for seventeen years, attracting pupils from all parts of Europe, and imparting to that school a popularity never attained before or since. During his residence in that city he was treated with princely consideration. Francis I., Emperor of Germany, raised him to the rank of nobility; and Count Orloff, of Russia, used all his influence to entice the great man to St. Petersburg. On his retirement from Göttingen he settled permanently at Berne, where, in the midst of learned friends, the greetings of illustrious men of science, and light but genial labors, he died near the close of the sixty-ninth year of his age, regretted by the world, and mourned by Switzerland and Germany. On the 12th of December, 1877, Berne celebrated in a manner worthy of her citizens the hundredth anniversary of his death. Deputations from all the Swiss schools and from a number of the German, French, and Italian medical schools and medical societies, as well as many illustrious men of science and distinguished statesmen, attended on the occasion, the interest of which was still further enhanced by the presence of Haller's descendants. An elaborate address, commemorative of the life and character of Haller, was delivered by Professor König.

We left Venice near midnight on the 1st of July, in the train for Vienna. We were fortunate enough to have a coupé allotted to ourselves, so that we had an abundance of room; but the night was cold and wet, and the consequence was that we were more or less uncomfortable, despite the liberal use of our wrappings. At six o'clock in the morning we found ourselves at the village of Nabresina, where, after partaking of a warm breakfast, we became somewhat thawed, so as to be in a better condition to enjoy the remainder of our journey, which embraced some of the most glorious views upon which it is possible for the eye to rest. The road across the Alps from the foot of Lake Lucerne to St. Gothard, full as it is of the grandest and wildest scenery, presented few objects of greater sublimity than the pass over the Tyrolese Mountains by the Semmering Railway, two thousand feet above the level of the sea. After travelling some distance the road formed a series of curves and semicircles flanked by deep valleys, which it made one almost shudder to behold. The train as it swept along resembled a huge anaconda, whiffing and blowing as if it were ill at ease with itself and the majestic mountains over which it was drawn at the rate of thirty miles an hour. Cold as the day was, with only now and then a gleam of sunshine, the ride was one of unalloyed enjoyment; and although we were not a little fatigued, we were sorry when we found, late in the afternoon, that we were rapidly approaching the environs of Vienna. A short ride from the depot soon brought us to one of the principal hotels, where we passed the next four days, visiting meanwhile some of the more important objects of interest, more especially the Imperial Royal Picture Gallery, the Lichtenstein Gallery, and the Church of the Capucines, in the vault of which are contained the bodies of upwards of seventy emperors and empresses. Among the latest contributions to this curious receptacle of royalty was the sarcophagus of Maximilian, who played for a short time so conspicuous a part in Mexican politics, and whose career met with so sad a termination. The fresh flowers upon the sarcophagus showed that the young prince had left behind him tender and loving hearts. What the destiny of Mexico might have been if Maximilian had been permitted to remain permanently upon its throne is of course a matter solely of conjecture;

but it was generally, and I believe correctly, thought that it would have been greatly improved. Judging from the wily and treacherous character of its people, it was easy to foresee that he would sooner or later be hurled from his seat, and that he would never leave the country alive. Of all this I was myself at the time thoroughly convinced, and often so expressed myself. In a corner in this narrow house, in an unadorned coffin, lies, at the special request of the Empress Maria Theresa, the body of the Countess Fuchs, her early and faithful instructress. It is eminently creditable to this great woman that she was capable of appreciating merit wherever she found it. The remains of her physician, the famous Van Swieten, whose celebrated Commentaries may still be read with profit, and to whom Austria is indebted for her system of universal education, lie in the vault of the Church of the Augustines, near the tombs of the Emperor Leopold II. and of the illustrious General Daun.

Few strangers visit Vienna without taking a walk to the Kärnthnerstrasse to look at the famous post leaning against the wall of the house No. 1079, in what is now the very heart of the city. This post is said to be the trunk of a tree which once belonged to the Wienerwald, or ancient forest, and is an object of uncommon historical interest from the fact that it is bound round with iron hoops to prevent it from falling, and so completely riddled with nails that there is no room for any more. For centuries, it seems, it was the custom of the apprentices of Vienna, after serving out their time, to perfect their knowledge of their trades by visiting foreign countries. Before setting out on their journeys each made it his business to drive a nail into this post, in order to propitiate the Fates, or, in other words, to secure good luck.

The morning after our arrival in the Austrian capital I made my way to the Allgemeines Krankenhaus, upwards of a mile and a half from our lodgings, to shake hands

with the renowned pathological anatomist, Professor Karl
Rokitansky, a man of world-wide reputation. We had
previously interchanged letters, and on handing him my
card he extended to me a cordial welcome. At the moment of my entrance into his workshop, for such it was,
he was surrounded by his pupils, engaged in the dissection
of the body of a man who had been murdered the previous
night. After the examination was completed he washed
his hands and showed me his collection of anatomical
preparations, one of the richest of the kind in the world,
and the product solely of his own patient and protracted
labors. As Professor of Pathological Anatomy, and Cura-
tor of the Imperial Pathological Museum, it is his duty to
examine the bodies of all persons dying in this great hospital, and to keep a full record of the results. In addition
to this vast work, he is obliged, by virtue of his office of
coroner's physician, as it would be called in this country,
to examine the bodies of all persons found dead under sus-
picious circumstances in the city, and to report the results
to the public prosecutor. Rokitansky has been a liberal
contributor to the periodical press; but his principal production is his Manual of Pathological Anatomy, issued, in
five volumes, between the years 1842 and 1846, the first
having appeared last. This work, which embodies the
results of the dissection of upwards of thirty thousand
cadavers, and upon which the posthumous fame of this
great man will mainly rest, was translated soon afterwards
by the Sydenham Society of London, and republished in
this country, where, as well as abroad, it has enjoyed an
extensive circulation. How many cadavers he has examined since the first appearance of this work I am unable
to say; but if his dissections have been anything in the
ratio that they were before, it is reasonable to conclude
that they amount to fifty thousand, a number probably
thirty or forty times greater than were ever made by
any other anatomist. Such an amount of labor implies

vast industry, and I was therefore not surprised to learn
from Rokitansky's own lips that he is an early riser, and a
persistent, systematic worker. Notwithstanding this, he
finds leisure to frequent the opera and the concert, and to
give social entertainments at his own house, especially
musical *soirées*, being very fond of music and a good
performer upon the flute.

At the time of my visit Rokitansky was sixty-four years
of age, having been born in 1804. He is a native of
Koniggrätz, in Bohemia, and took his medical degree at
Vienna in 1828. After having served for several years as
assistant in this institution, he was appointed in 1834
Professor of Pathological Anatomy; in 1849, Dean of the
Medical Faculty; and in 1850, Rector of the University of
Vienna. He is one of the court physicians; and since my
visit, in 1868, he has been elected a Councillor of State
and a member of the Austrian Parliament. A few years
ago he retired from the University as a public teacher. In
stature Rokitansky is six feet high, well proportioned, with
a good forehead, and a face beaming with intelligence and
benevolence. He is a slow talker, and as a lecturer not
particularly attractive. As a writer, many of the passages
in his works are so obscure as to render it difficult to grasp
their meaning; and the translation of his Manual of Pathological Anatomy must therefore have been a laborious
task. In conversing with him in German I noticed that
he constantly used the word "bissel" for "wenig," an
Austrian provincialism. His German was a broad brogue.

Rokitansky has done for Austria what the lamented
Bichat did for France. He laid the foundation, broad and
deep, of pathological anatomy for its medical profession,
and diffused a taste for its cultivation, the happy effects of
which have been felt in every nook and corner of the civilized world. His Manual is a vast storehouse of precious
knowledge, although it is no longer used as a text-book,
owing mainly to the fact that it is defective in microscop-

ical details, which now figure so largely in all productions of this kind.

The Vienna School of Surgery has long been celebrated for its great men. Vincent Kern, who for many years occupied the chair of Surgery in its University, and was widely known as an able teacher and a successful practitioner, was particularly distinguished as a lithotomist, and was one of the first to call attention to the use of cold water in the treatment of gunshot wounds. He greatly simplified surgical dressings, and was the author of several monographs on medical and surgical subjects. George Joseph Beer, a contemporary of Kern, may be regarded as the father of scientific ophthalmology. He contributed numerous papers upon the subject, and enjoyed for more than a third of a century an unrivalled reputation as an oculist. His principal work was a treatise, in two volumes, entitled Lehre von den Augenkrankheiten, issued in 1818. A synopsis of this work was published soon afterwards by the late Dr. George Frick, of Baltimore. The fame of the chair of Surgery in the University of Vienna was long upheld by the labors and genius of Rust, a dexterous operator, an excellent pathologist, and an erudite writer. He was distinguished for his advocacy of the actual cautery in the treatment of chronic diseases of the joints. Dr. Franz Schuh, a celebrated surgeon and teacher, and the author of an admirable work entitled Pathologie und Therapie der Pseudoplasmen, was the first to recognize epithelioma as a distinct form of carcinoma. He died in 1865, and was succeeded by the present incumbent in the University, Professor Billroth, a man who has achieved a world-wide reputation, although he is still comparatively young. A pupil of Von Langenbeck of Berlin, Billroth was for some years Professor of Surgery at Zurich, whence, upon the death of Schuh, he was called to Vienna, where I met him in 1868. Somewhat above the medium height, he has an immense frame, with a marked inclination to stoutness, large head, and a good, open, frank, and intelligent face, with dark hair and eyes. As a lecturer his style is conversational rather than forcible; his voice and manner are agreeable, and he keeps thoroughly aroused the attention of his class. The second day after my arrival at Vienna I heard him deliver an admirable discourse upon lymphatic tumors, illustrated by microscopical drawings and wet preparations, and with frequent references to the blackboard, he being, as is well known, a ready draughtsman. As an operator he is fearless and bold almost to the verge of rashness. The principal operation which I saw him perform was excision of a carcinomatous rectum—a tedious procedure, attended with great loss of blood, the patient, an elderly man, being under the influence of chloroform. Upon asking him the following morning how his patient was, he replied, with a significant shrug of the shoulder, "He is moribund," and passed on. Billroth has lately twice exsected the larynx, the patient in one of the cases surviving several months in comparative comfort with the aid of an artificial substitute. What he may do in the way of heroic surgery it would be difficult to foretell. Possibly his next feat may be the extirpation of the liver or of the stomach! Billroth is a good liver, fond of society, a composer, and a superior pianist; in a word, a remarkable person, such as is rarely found in any profession. In this country he is known principally by his work on Surgical Pathology and Therapeutics, translated by Dr. Charles E. Hackley, of New York, and by his achievements as a bold, dashing operator.

Billroth's lecture-room is always well filled with attentive pupils, a circumstance which is in striking contrast with the slim attendance at Dumreicher's clinics in another part of this immense hospital. In looking at Dumreicher, and following him through his wards, one is not slow in discovering the reason of this difference in the popularity of the two men. Dumreicher, as his name implies, is a

dull, drowsy sort of a man, an old fogy, without energy or
life, and without the faculty of interesting his pupils.
Billroth, on the contrary, is full of soul, always busy, instructive, and full of resources under the most trying difficulties; a live man, a great pathologist, a good talker, and
a great operator. Arldt, the ophthalmologist, a tall, slender man, impressed me very favorably; he was surrounded
by a group of interested students, and evidently knows
what he is about. Hebra, the dermatologist, had hardly
half a dozen attendants; he is a short, thick-set man, with
dirty fingers and a dress a good deal the worse for wear;
in a word, he is anything but neat in his person; and
during the hour I spent in his ward I did not become at
all pleasantly impressed by his manner or his appearance.
Of his skill as a diagnostician everybody must be convinced,
seeing how great is his experience; but, from what I have
seen of his writings, I have no hesitation in saying that he
has done more than any living authority to confuse the
study of skin diseases. His treatment, moreover, of many
of those affections seems to me to be too purely local, or,
in other words, not sufficiently addressed to the constitution, upon the derangement of which they so often depend.

An opportunity was afforded me during my short stay at
Vienna of renewing my acquaintance with Dr. Neudörfer,
Surgeon-in-Chief of the Austrian army in Mexico. I had
met him a year or so previously in Philadelphia, and had
it in my power to show him some attention, which he
kindly reciprocated on this occasion. I found him in a
small room in the suburbs of the town, busily engaged
upon his work on Military Surgery, embracing an account
of the results of his observations in Mexico, one volume of
which had already appeared. I called at the residence
of Professor Von Pitha, joint editor with Billroth of the
Handbuch der Allgemeinen und Speciellen Chirurgie, a
great work still in course of publication, but found to my

regret that he had gone to some watering-place in search of health and recreation.

The physicians and obstetricians of Vienna rank among the most illustrious medical men of the past and present generation. The names of Skoda, Oppoltzer, Türck, Czermak, Braun, Sigmund, and many others are known everywhere in association either with important discoveries or with the advances of scientific and practical medicine. Hyrtl is widely recognized as a great anatomist. His celebrated museum, the work of a lifetime, and now in the possession by purchase of the College of Physicians of Philadelphia, abounds in specimens of the choicest character, displaying an amount of labor and patience in their preparation of an almost miraculous nature. The dissections of the internal ear alone must have cost him years of toil. His treatise on Surgical Anatomy, one of his later productions, is highly appreciated for its sterling excellence. It is by the exertions and genius of such men that the University of Vienna has achieved a reputation surpassed by no medical school in the world.

My recollection of the Austrian capital will always be green and pleasant; for, although it was not in my power to accept any hospitalities, I was brought into contact with men with whose reputation and deeds I had long been familiar, and whom, therefore, I was glad to see. Several years prior to my visit the Royal Medical Society of Vienna had done me the honor to elect me an honorary member. A notice of my treatise on Pathological Anatomy had preceded me.

The General Hospital is an immense edifice, founded by the Emperor Joseph II., arranged in quadrangular form, supplied with all the means and appliances for efficient clinical teaching, and capable of accommodating more than three thousand patients. The number of admissions annually amounts to nearly thirty-five thousand, embracing, of course, all kinds of diseases and accidents to which flesh is heir. Such an enormous field, properly cultivated, cannot fail to produce useful results in developing great practitioners of the healing art, and in throwing vast light upon pathology and therapeutics. Connected with this establishment, indeed forming a part of it, is the celebrated Lying-in Hospital, one of the largest of the kind in the world, and one which has educated many of the ablest and most distinguished obstetricians and gynæcologists of the present century. The number of women and children annually admitted is enormous. Vienna is famous for its illegitimate births; and one, if not the principal, reason of this is the fact that no questions are asked of any of the women upon their entrance into the institution. They may enter veiled or masked, and even their names need not be known, unless they are in danger of dying, when their names are inclosed in a sealed envelope to be opened only by their nearest relatives. No persons, except the physician and nurse, are admitted to them, and when their confinement is over they are discharged in the usual manner, leaving the child behind them to be bound out at a certain age, if not called for. Such conduct on the part of the authorities is, in my opinion, anything but praiseworthy, inasmuch as it affords a powerful incentive to the grossest immorality. All that a bad woman has to do, when she gives way to her passion, is to conceal her shame in such an asylum, and to repeat the offence at the next opportunity, satisfied that her family, her friends, and the public will remain alike ignorant of her conduct. It is said that the principal purpose of this secrecy is to prevent infanticide, which would otherwise be of very frequent occurrence!

The Military Hospital at Vienna is a large, old building, capable of accommodating several hundred patients. It is a government institution, devoted exclusively to the treatment of wounded soldiers, and affords a fine field for the study of military surgery, especially in times of war. Pitha and Neudörfer have each a service in this hospital.

We left Vienna, July 7th, for Dresden, crossing the Danube, a shallow, quiet river, a little wider than the Schuylkill at Philadelphia. The country for many miles along the route was flat and highly cultivated, and everywhere studded with fields of wheat, rye, and oats. The people were busily engaged in harvesting, and we noticed that many of the laborers were women, reminding us of what was formerly so common in harvest time in the German settlements of Pennsylvania. The cradle and the sickle were the only agricultural implements employed. Of reaping-machines we saw no sign. A considerable portion of our road passed through Moravia and Bohemia, and as the train whirled along, generally at a rapid pace, we were struck with the paucity of horses and cattle. The houses for the most part had a very common appearance, and there were no barns such as one is accustomed to see in Pennsylvania. At eleven o'clock at night we reached Aussig, a small village on the Elbe, and on the next morning at half past six we embarked on a miserable little steamer for Dresden. The Elbe, a small river, with a gentle current, is fringed with high mountains, many of which are very prominent and imposing. We passed many towns and villages, some castles, and some fine private residences, especially as we neared Dresden. The railway from Prague, which we passed early in the evening, runs along the left bank of the river. We were glad when, at two o'clock in the afternoon, we reached our destination, for despite our wraps we suffered much from cold, as the air was very damp, and the sun did not show itself during any part of the day.

Dresden, apart from its great beauty, its elegant society, its china manufactories, its opera-house, its art galleries, and its museums, presents no objects of special interest to the medical man. There is no medical school, and the hospital I did not visit. The citizens, like those of Vienna, indulge much in beer-drinking, and for this purpose and for social intercourse they generally, on a pleasant afternoon, assemble in crowds at one or more fashionable coffee-houses, where many of them often remain for hours together in the open air listening to music and talking over the news of the day. What interested me most in this city was the Armory, or Military Museum, containing the most extensive collection in the world of all kinds of weapons, accoutrements, armor, trappings, and relics of ancient knights and distinguished warriors. In looking at the display of pistols one is forcibly impressed with the conviction that Colt must have visited the armory and borrowed from it the idea of his celebrated revolver, a weapon in use in Europe nearly two hundred years previously. With the exception of the lock, there is not the slightest difference between the foreign and the American revolver— another proof that there is nothing new under the sun. The knights in armor, seated upon their fiery steeds with lance in hand, must have been fierce-looking fellows. In the same room are to be seen the coronation robes of Augustus II., King of Poland, a man of gigantic strength, with his cuirass, weighing one hundred pounds, and his iron cap of twenty-five pounds, along with the horse-shoe which he broke with his fingers. One does not forget to visit the Schloss, or royal palace, to examine its numerous works of art, its vast collection of jewels, which in one room alone amount in value, it is said, to fifteen millions of dollars, and the crowns, sceptres, and diamonds worn by departed sovereigns. A lover of the sublime and beautiful in art might profitably spend at least three months in studying the objects of interest that wealth and taste have accumulated in this little Saxon city. Although the price of living is by no means cheap, yet such are the varied attractions of the place, in a social, educational, and æsthetic point of view, that a number of American families have for many years past made it their permanent home.

The country between Dresden and Berlin is as flat as a pancake. The soil is very sandy, and the general aspect is such as to remind one forcibly of the Atlantic borders of New Jersey. Here and there we noticed a strip of woodland, covered chiefly with pine trees and small oaks. Wheat, rye, and oats were the principal field products. Potatoes were growing in abundance, and in a few fields there was evidence of an effort to raise corn, which, however, was very diminutive. Why the people do not cultivate watermelons and cantaloupes is a mystery, unless it is explained by the shortness of the summer. The soil is certainly admirably adapted to the object. Immediately beyond Dresden we passed several small vineyards. Very few orchards skirt the road, but the cherry tree is of common occurrence, and the fruit is said to be of superior quality. The windmill is seen in every direction: at one place there were as many as seven in close proximity one to another.

Reaching Berlin late in the afternoon, we took lodgings at Meinhardt's Hotel. Early on the following morning we found ourselves on the train for Potsdam, where, in company with Dr. and Mrs. James R. Wood, of New York, we spent the entire day, visiting Charlottenhof; the palace of Frederick the Great; the palace of Sans Souci, the beautiful grounds ornamented with fountains and magnificent shrubbery and orange trees; the marble equestrian statue of the great king, a glorious work of art; the towers of Pfingstberg, commanding an imposing view of the river Havel, of Babelsberg, and of the surrounding country, with Berlin in the distance; the Russian colony, now greatly diminished in numbers; the house, situated on a little island in an artificial lake, in which the father of Frederick the Great used to smoke and to hold his drunken orgies; the old palace, containing the writing-table, chairs, and dining-table of the famous king; the Lutheran church, in which, in a marble sarcophagus, lie the remains of this extraordinary man; and, in short, everything of interest to the inquisitive tourist. The day was bright and genial, and one of the most delightful and enjoyable of our lives. No traveller should fail to visit this beautiful spot, so full of historical associations.

Many anecdotes are told of Frederick the Great. His fondness for his dogs and his warhorse led him to make a request that he should be buried with them—a request which the good taste of his friends prevented from being carried into effect. The story of the windmill has become classical. The king, wishing to extend his pleasure-grounds near the palace of Sans Souci, offered to purchase it. The miller, however, was obstinate in his refusal, and the consequence was that the matter was carried into court, in which his majesty was defeated. After the trial was over the king replaced the old windmill with a more stately one as a monument to Prussian justice. The descendants of the original proprietor, having become financially embarrassed, offered to sell the property, but the king, upon learning the circumstance, relieved their necessities, saying that the windmill belonged to Prussian history.

There were three professional men in Berlin whom, as their names had long been familiar to me as household words, I was most anxious to see—Virchow, Langenbeck, and Graefe. Accordingly, early in the morning of the second day after our arrival, I went to the Allgemeines Krankenhaus in search of Virchow, the illustrious pathologist and accomplished statesman, a professor in the University of Berlin, and a member of the German Parliament. The great man, upon my entrance, was in the midst of his pupils, engaged in a post-mortem examination. As my presence attracted some attention, especially on the part of several Philadelphia students with whom I was personally acquainted, I deemed it my duty, although the moment was not the most opportune, to pass my card to the professor, at the same time apologizing for the intrusion. He at once saluted me with a gracious bow, and, shaking me cordially by the hand, introduced me to his pupils and expressed his gratification at seeing me. After a few minutes spent in conversation, he resumed his knife and completed his examination. He showed me his laboratory, his lecture-room, and many of his more interesting pathological specimens, most of them prepared by his own hands. His collection of diseased hearts of children, the result of inherited syphilis, is the largest in the world, and as he explained specimen after specimen, he became not only enthusiastic but eloquent. He also showed me a large number of preparations of infantile syphilitic livers, exhibiting the ravages of a poison which has taken deep root in the human family, and which, if effectual means be not speedily adopted for its eradication, is sure eventually to sap the very foundations of the best society in all parts of the globe.

The laboratory, or work-shop as it may be termed, of Professor Virchow is a model in its way, admirably adapted to the wants of the student for improvement in the use of the microscope and the examination of morbid specimens, which are passed round in jars or on plates on a neat little railway carriage, so that every one may have a full opportunity of inspecting them. Microscopes are provided in great numbers, and, in fact, every facility is afforded for the acquisition of knowledge. If the student does not become the wiser for his labors it is his own fault, not the fault of his teacher. Such a room with the necessary appliances ought to exist in every well-organized medical institution in the United States. An abundance of material for the successful study of pathological anatomy is found in all our larger cities; and it is only necessary that we should go to work and use it properly for the edification of the profession and the advancement of medical science.

Virchow is a most patient and laborious investigator, and yet he never seems to be in a hurry. His dissections seldom occupy fewer than two and a half to three hours each. Every organ of the body is thoroughly explored. For years past his habit has been to open, every Monday morning, a cadaver in the presence of his private pupils with a view of instructing them in the art of conducting autopsies—holding the knife, using the saw, and taking notes, the whole being supplemented by microscopic inspections of the more important diseased structures. In these dissections he is, if possible, more patient even than Rokitansky, his great Viennese prototype. For exposing the spinal cord, Virchow employs a double sickle-shaped saw, eight inches in length—an instrument, I believe, of his own designing. A work from his pen on the subject of autopsies was lately issued at Berlin. On Wednesdays and Saturdays he devotes two hours before his class to the illustration of pathological anatomy.

Virchow is a thin, slender man, about the medium height, with a fine forehead, although the head is not large, and handsome black eyes, concealed by a pair of glasses. He is deliberate in his movements, a good talker, very affable, courteous, and warm-hearted—in a word, a gentleman of the higher type. In his general appearance there is nothing at all striking. As a lecturer he did not especially impress me. His voice is good, and, while his delivery is graceful, he seemed to me to be rather sluggish; at all events, without that enthusiasm which one might expect in so renowned a teacher. In age, at my visit at Berlin in 1868, he was probably about fifty. In his political feelings he is thoroughly republican, and it is said that Bismarck is more afraid of him than of any man in the German empire. Early in life, indeed, he was banished from Berlin on account of his political proclivities,

but his great reputation at length induced the government
to recall him, and to reinstate him in his former chair.
Virchow is a hard worker, a close observer, and a philosophical reasoner.   He is a good sleeper, and does not trouble
himself about early rising.   At his lectures, he is often
behind time, and does not always occupy his hour.   He
is a voluminous author, and he may be regarded as the
founder of a new school of pathology and pathological
anatomy.   His work on Cellular Pathology and his Lectures on Tumors, two productions abounding in original thought and investigation, translated into different
languages, and republished in this country, have acquired
for him a world-wide celebrity.   Whatever it touches his
pen adorns.   He is a member of numerous domestic and
foreign societies, an associate of the French Institute, and
a member of the German parliament.   Europe and America
acknowledge him as the first pathologist of the age.

The evening before leaving Berlin I had the pleasure of
meeting Virchow at his own table, at his elegant residence
in a fashionable part of the city.   The gentlemen who were
invited to meet me were, among others, Professor Von
Langenbeck, Von Graefe, the famous oculist, Donders, the
celebrated ophthalmologist of Utrecht, and Dr. Gurlt, Professor of Surgery in the University of Berlin.   Our time
was occupied in agreeable and instructive conversation.   At
ten o'clock the folding-doors were thrown open, and we sat
down to a bountiful repast.   After the viands were pretty
well disposed of, our host, availing himself of a lull in
the conversation, drew forth a large volume from under
the table, and rising he took me by the hand, and made
me an address in German, complimenting me upon my
labors as a pathological anatomist, and referring to the
work, which happened to be the second edition of my
Elements of Pathological Anatomy, as one from the study
of which he had derived much useful instruction, and one
which he always consulted with much pleasure.   I need

not say how deeply flattered I felt by this great honor, so unexpectedly and so handsomely bestowed upon me by this renowned man. I felt that I had not labored in vain, and that the compliment was more than an equivalent for all the toil and anxiety which the work had cost me.

Of Von Langenbeck I saw much while in Berlin. His kindness to me was uninterrupted, and was shown in a great variety of ways. From the cordial welcome which he extended to me I felt at once as if I had met with an old and well-tried friend. He invited me to his house, showed me everything about his hospital, introduced me to his class, and took special pains to perform upon the dead subject some operations in which he had acquired unusual distinction. A nephew of the celebrated Langenbeck of Göttingen, he settled early in life at Berlin, where, after the death of Johann Friedrich Dieffenbach, he speedily rose to the topmost round of the ladder. As an operative surgeon, he enjoys an unrivalled reputation on the continent of Europe ; and it is questionable whether he has ever had a superior in this branch of the healing art anywhere—Dupuytren, Lisfranc, Mott, Liston, Syme, and Fergusson not excepted. His record is one of which any surgeon may justly be proud. In his appearance he is remarkable. His forehead, without being uncommonly high, is well formed, but the occipital region, near what is supposed to be the organ of philoprogenitiveness, is of extraordinary bulk, almost amounting to deformity. He is tall and rather slender, and his lower limbs are disproportionately long ; his eyes are blue, and his features are expressive of intelligence and courtly breeding. He speaks English and French fluently, rides in his carriage, and lives in elegant style in the upper and newer part of the city, a short distance from "Unter den Linden." Like Virchow he is a hard worker. During the summer session of the University he invariably meets his private classes at the General Hospital at six o'clock in the morning, before many of the respectable citizens of

Berlin have rubbed the dew off their eyes. He generally
passes two hours with his classes several times a week, instructing them in the operations on the cadaver, either
using the knife himself, or seeing that it is properly employed by others. One of the mornings that I spent with
him was devoted to excisions of the joints, every one of
which he performed for my special benefit, pointing out
whatever there is peculiar in his methods. His pupils are
all very fond of him—a circumstance not at all surprising
when we consider the pains he takes to instruct them in
operative and mechanical surgery.

The name of Von Langenbeck is associated with many
of the most wonderful exploits in operative surgery. His
resections, of which he has performed a great number, are
distinguished by their simplicity, by the superiority of the
dressings employed in the after-treatment, and by the fre-
quency with which they are followed by the reproduction
of osseous tissue—due doubtless to the fact that he always
saves the largest possible amount of periosteum. In visiting his wards he pointed out to me three cases of excision
of the shoulder, two of the elbow, one of the wrist, one
of the hip, one of the knee, and two of the ankle, together with one of the shaft of the humerus and one
of both bones of the leg, the pieces removed being
three inches and a half in length. Of ankle-joint resections he had had, as he informed me, altogether eighteen
cases, of which nine were traumatic, with one death, and
nine pathological, of which one ended fatally and two required amputation. In all such operations, as well as in
recent fractures, whether simple or compound, he applies
at once a very thick, immovable plaster of Paris splint,
provided with fenestra for facilitating drainage. In the
case of the knee he employs a posterior iron splint, with a
handle in front for lifting and moving the limb—a very
useful contrivance, worthy of general adoption. At the
time of my visit he had performed, with good results, four

amputations of the thigh, with the periosteum drawn over
the end of the bone, one of the cases being under treatment
at the time. In flap amputations he uses stitches, but no
plaster or bandage, and places the stump upon a hollow
cushion of gum elastic, inflatable at pleasure, the dis-
charges being received underneath in a plate filled with
powdered charcoal. He showed me a child, five and a
half years old, in whom he had successfully closed, two
weeks before, a large fissure in the hard palate by lateral
flaps; and also a young man from whom he had removed
a retropharyngeal polyp through the upper jaw, dividing
this bone through its ascending process and immediately
above the roots of the teeth, along with the zygomatic
process of the temporal bone, an oval flap of skin having
previously been reflected towards the temple. Although
but little blood was lost, the patient looked very bad,
and his life was in imminent jeopardy. Langenbeck informed me that he had performed excision of the rectum
in sixteen cases, and in only one of these had life been
prolonged to the end of the fifteenth month.

It struck me as extraordinary that a surgeon so judicious, experienced, and well-read should prefer the high
or suprapubic operation for stone in the bladder; and yet
he informed me that it had hitherto been his favorite
method, as he had performed it altogether thirty times.
"Inasmuch, however," he significantly added, "as I have
lost all my adult patients from pyæmia, at periods varying
from eight to twelve weeks, I no longer resort to it except in
children." He cut a child eighteen months old according
to this vile method, making an incision at least three
inches in length along the middle, and dividing some of
the fibres of the straight muscles to relieve tension. The
bladder was opened very cautiously, an index finger was
inserted into the organ, and the calculus, which consisted
of uric acid, one inch long by five-eighths of an inch in
diameter, was extracted with the scoop. Having introduced

a narrow strip of muslin into the wound with one end protruding, he sewed up the skin and sent the little patient to bed. A small boy who had been lithotomized by this method nearly two months before was still suffering under an open wound at the time of my visit. Had he been subjected to lithectasy, or to the ordinary lateral section, I venture to say that the poor little fellow would have been on the street weeks sooner. The reason why he prefers the suprapubic method is that, as he alleges, it prevents incontinence of urine and injury to the ejaculatory ducts— two ridiculous and fanciful objections according to my own experience and that of the profession generally. He candidly confessed that the wound is always very long in healing.

In conversing with this great surgeon respecting extirpation of the tongue for the relief of cancer, he told me that he had had one case, that of a man sixty years of age, in which he removed the entire organ, excepting a little of its posterior border, the patient surviving the operation for two years, during which he enjoyed excellent health with the power of articulation and tolerable speech. The operation included the division of the symphysis of the jaw and the removal of the sublingual and submaxillary glands, the former on both sides.

During the late Franco-Prussian war Von Langenbeck acted as Surgeon-in-Chief of the Prussian army, and added new lustre to his name. Although no longer young, he is a man of wonderful activity, both physical and mental. He has long been the editor of what is known as Langenbeck's Archiv für Chirurgie, and he has been a copious contributor to the medical press, although he has not published, as far as I am aware, any express treatises on surgery. He is a member of many learned societies, both native and foreign, Surgeon to the Emperor, and Professor of Surgery in the University of Berlin. He has been the recipient of numerous decorations.

Albrecht von Graefe, whose acquaintance I made the second day after my arrival at Berlin, but who, much to the regret of all Germany and of the medical profession generally, died in July, 1870, within two years after my visit, was one of the remarkable men of his day. As an ophthalmic surgeon and as the inventor of certain operations, now in common use, he was for years without a rival in Europe, attracting patients and pupils from all parts of the civilized world. Tall and slender, yet gracefully built, he was a man of winning manners, amiable in a high degree, with the simplicity of a child. His countenance had so mild and benevolent an expression that he was known in the streets of Berlin as the Christus, in reference to his resemblance to some of the pictures of Christ by the older masters. Every one loved him. Although he was hardly forty years of age at the time of my interview with him, his hair, which he always wore long, was already white, and his whole appearance indicated that he was incessantly overworked, and destined, as the result has only too clearly shown, to be short-lived. He had about him an appearance of everlasting unrest. He was quick in all his movements, almost as nimble as a cat, and was never longer than a few minutes in the same place. Up early in the morning, and until a late hour at night, driving like a Jehu through the rough streets of Berlin, and performing daily an astonishing amount of labor, it was evident alike to friend and stranger that he could not long endure such wear and tear of mind and body; that sooner or later he must sink under their effects. Expostulation and reasoning were of no avail. He was a doomed man. The only recreation which he ever took was a brief visit to Paris, or to some watering-place, where, it is true, he always obtained a change of air and scene, but no substantial repose for his exhausted powers. Pulmonary phthisis, the result probably of an hereditary taint, at length overtook him, soon after the close of the forty-second year of his age.

Graefe was of Polish descent, a native of Berlin, and a son of Carl Ferdinand von Graefe, a celebrated professor and practitioner, long a resident in the Prussian capital, and the surgeon who, next after Valentine Mott, tied the innominate artery. It is said that the son early in life distinguished himself by his literary, mathematical, and scientific attainments. In 1856 he was appointed Professor of Ophthalmology in the University of his native city. He also gave private instruction, had a large eye clinic, and was the author of numerous papers upon his specialty, published mainly in the Archiv für Ophthalmologie, issued at first in his name, and subsequently with the assistance of Arldt and Donders.

As a lecturer, Graefe was entertaining and instructive. He talked rapidly, but connectedly, and constantly referred to his blackboard and to his cases to illustrate his remarks. His students, nearly one hundred and fifty in number, were very attentive, many of them being engaged in taking notes. On the day preceding my last visit to his clinic I saw him operate six times for strabismus, and extract six cataracts and one cysticerce, the specimen of which, put up in diluted alcohol, he kindly presented to me, and which is, after many years, still in my possession. The subject of this singular disease was a married woman, pregnant, twenty-nine years old, whose sight had been gradually diminishing for more than eighteen months. The entozoon, without the aid of a magnifying-glass, was distinctly visible in the lower part of the posterior chamber of the eye, and appeared to be a large opaque body, the movements of which could be plainly seen with the aid of the ophthalmoscope. Latterly it had occasioned a good deal of pain. The operation was performed under chloroform, and was attended with great difficulty, as Graefe was obliged, so to speak, to fish for the entozoon. The case happened to be his one hundred and twenty-first. Professor Donders, the celebrated ophthalmologist of Utrecht,

who was present, said that he had never met with this kind
of entozoon in Holland. In Prussia, on the contrary,
where the common people eat a great deal of badly-cooked,
almost raw, pork, it is found quite frequently.

Von Graefe told me that he had extracted nearly three
thousand cataracts, with a loss only of from three to three
and a half per cent. He often operates on both eyes in
immediate succession. He fixes the organ with a screw
speculum, pinches up the conjunctiva with a toothed
spring forceps, held by an assistant, and performs what is
known as the upper section with a very small knife, the
sclerotica being embraced in the incision; separates the
lids, and drawing out a piece of the iris, snips it off with
the scissors; removes the speculum and forceps, lacerates
the capsule, and presses out the lens with a curette; adjusts
the edges of the wound with the greatest possible care,
all blood having previously been removed, not only from
between them, but also from the anterior chamber of the
eye; finally, the eye is covered with a layer of gauze or
cribriform muslin, upon which is piled a mass of soft
charpie, confined with a narrow flannel roller, drawn quite
firmly. At a late hour of the night, generally from ten to
twelve, the operation in summer being usually performed
from four to six o'clock in the afternoon, Graefe invariably
visits his patient and takes off the dressings to see that all
is well—a proceeding nowhere practised in this country.
Such interference, indeed, would be regarded among us as
eminently officious or meddlesome. No anodyne, as a
rule, is administered after the operation, which, in his
hands, is seldom followed by unpleasant nervous symptoms.

Graefe was the inventor of iridectomy for the relief of
pain in glaucoma and the prevention of undue inflammation after the extraction of cataract. At first sight it
seems revolting to one's sense of propriety to mutilate so
important a structure as the iris for such an object, and
yet the operation for cataract is now so generally per-

formed after this method that its benefits must be fully conceded. As an earnest and successful cultivator of ophthalmology, it is impossible to lay too much stress upon the labors of this wonderful man. He found ophthalmology nothing but a mass of blind empiricism, and at the end of twenty years, the close of his useful life, he left it a science and an art in advance of every other branch of surgery. Graefe was not only a great worker, but he possessed the happy faculty of inspiring his pupils with unbounded enthusiasm, which, carried away with them to their homes in different parts of the world, has been productive of incalculable good.

Dr. Gurlt, who was of the party at Virchow's, is a son of the Director of the celebrated Veterinary College of Berlin, and the author of a valuable work on fractures and of an atlas of hospitals and ambulances. He is one of the professors of surgery in the University, and a man of mark, although in point of reputation he is not equal to any one of the illustrious triumvirate above noticed. He is a short, stout man, of prepossessing appearance, and a hard worker. At the time of my visit he was engaged upon the composition of an exhaustive treatise on pyæmia.

Donders, whose name is so well known in this country in connection with his able work on refraction and accommodation, is a most genial, pleasant gentleman, cordial in his manners, tall, with fine, expressive features, black hair and eyes, and a hale, robust frame. He is an excellent talker, and speaks German, French, and English fluently. He was said to be fifty years of age, although, judging from his looks, one would not suppose him to be over forty.

Of the physicians of Berlin the only one whom I saw was Dr. Frerichs, the Professor of Clinical Medicine in the University, and the author of the celebrated treatise on Diseases of the Liver, translated by Dr. Murchison, and published under the auspices of the Sydenham Society of London. He is a man of medium stature, with a good, intelligent face, and a ready talker, apparently deeply interested in his subject. At his clinic, which I attended one morning, I counted one hundred and ten students, many of whom were busily engaged in taking notes. The case which the professor was expounding was one of cardiac disease attended with ascites and swelling of the lower extremities. The examination was a thorough one, and impressed me very favorably with Frerichs as a clinical teacher. The room in which the exercises were conducted was small and badly lighted, and the seats were not sufficiently raised for seeing.

The medical department of the University of Berlin has forty-eight instructors of different grades, many of them being simply assistants, while others are private teachers, delivering lectures to small classes of students. In point of fact these young men occupy pretty much the same rank as what are known among us as "quizzers," except that they are much better educated. Some of the lectures are delivered in a large building, formerly the palace of Prince Henry, brother of Frederick II. On the opposite side of the street, in the grounds belonging to the great hospital of La Charité, is the pathological museum in charge of Virchow. The hospital is one of the largest in the world, and annually admits more than ten thousand patients. Every facility is afforded by the public authorities to the medical attendants for the study of disease and injury and for the thorough instruction of the medical students.

The University of Berlin, founded in 1810, is one of the greatest educational institutions in Europe. Its corps of teachers numbers nearly two hundred, and embraces many of the ablest scholars and scientists of the present day. Indeed, the University has been a kind of centre around which have revolved during the present century many of the master-minds of Germany. In medicine the world has produced no greater or more illustrious men than Schönlein, Jüngken, Müller, Dieffenbach, Langenbeck, and Virchow; or than Humboldt, Mitscherlich, and Ehrenberg in natural science; Schleiermacher and Neander in theology; Savigny and Gans in jurisprudence; Von Raumer and Ranke in history; Encke in astronomy; or than Fichte, Hegel, and Schelling in speculative philosophy. Art too has found a new home in this beautiful city. Many of the finest pictures in Europe are to be seen in its galleries; and the Egyptian Museum contains the richest collection of its kind to be found anywhere. The Royal Library embraces upwards of five hundred thousand volumes, and the University more than one hundred thousand, for the special use of the professors and students. With such facilities for the acquisition of knowledge, it is not surprising that Berlin, comparatively young as it is, should, in a literary, scientific, artistic, and educational point of view, be one of the first cities in the world. The more modern portions contain many beautiful private residences, some of them of almost palatial grandeur. The most fashionable street, called "Unter den Linden," although very broad, and nearly a mile in length, presents few attractions, as many of the houses are old and dirty-looking, and most of the trees from which it is named have a withered appearance. With the exception of Philadelphia, I know of no city that is worse paved. Berlin owes much of its architectural beauty to the taste and genius of Schinkel, Rauch, Winckelmann, and Schadow, whose services are commemorated by marble statues placed under the portico of the Museum of Antiquities. The equestrian statue of Frederick the Great is in "Unter den Linden," opposite the emperor's palace. It is of bronze, is of colossal size, and is one of the most magnificent monuments in Europe.

An excursion to Charlottenberg, which few tourists omit, brings one to the small Doric temple, in a lovely garden, in which repose the remains of Frederick William III., and of his beautiful queen, Louisa, buried thirty years earlier. Their persons are represented by marble figures with folded hands, lying side by side upon marble sarcophagi, the whole being regarded as among the masterpieces of the celebrated Rauch. At the feet of the group is the heart of Frederick William IV., inclosed in a marble casket, and on each side is a white marble candelabrum, that on the right representing the three Fates, and that on the left the three Muses. A walk through the pines and the orangery affords additional interest to the scene, and serves to dispel the melancholy occasioned by the contemplation of the royal monument.

During this visit it was my pleasing duty, as President of the American Medical Association, to be the bearer of a letter from that body to Professor Christian Gottfried Ehrenberg, congratulating him upon the fiftieth anniversary of his entrance upon his professional career as a physician, and upon his wonderful achievements as a scientist in developing and extending our knowledge of insect life, which until his time had been an untrodden field. Unfortunately, however, he was out of town for change of air on account of ill health, and I therefore missed the pleasure of seeing him. This circumstance compelled me to write him a letter, which was afterwards published in pamphlet form, along with another addressed to him by Agassiz, Gould, Dana, Torrey, and other distinguished scientists, and also with a short poem from the prolific and facile pen of Oliver Wendell Holmes. Professor Ehrenberg acknowledged my own communication in a letter written in German, of which I subjoin a translation:

MUCH HONORED PRESIDENT: BERLIN, March 30, 1869.

SIR: The congratulations sent to me by my colleagues in North America, on the occasion of my fiftieth anniversary as a physician, should have long since induced me to return you my particular thanks in writing. It is true that last year I requested Mr. Bancroft, your Minister at Berlin, to return to you my thanks preliminarily; but now that fortunately, by the help of our healing art and science, I am again enabled to write for a longer time, I shall not omit to send you a few words of thanks in my own handwriting for your indulgent opinion of the doings of my life. To you and your whole fatherland, so full of liberal and fresh thoughts, I wish a success ever increasing in strength and health. May God bless all those who, in profound research ever augmenting, and with a clear, ruling, godly spirit, join in the universal effort, and endeavor to obtain blossoms and fruit, though they should be fully enjoyed only by coming generations.

With thankful regards, your most obedient

DR. C. G. EHRENBERG.

S. D. GROSS, M. D.,
President of the American Medical Association.

The following is an extract from my letter: "Your fame as a great scientific discoverer and as an indefatigable student of nature has long been familiarly known in the United States, and has produced for you numerous followers. In your hands microscopic researches first assumed a definite and distinct character, and revealed to the admiring gaze of the world many new fields of inquiry, since so successfully trodden by others. The infusoria, under the influence of your plastic genius, became for the first time in our knowledge a new link in the scale of animated beings, and a new source of wonder and admiration of that great and beneficent Being who holds the universe in the hollow of His hand, and who is the Creator alike of the smallest atom of matter, invisible to the unassisted eye, and of our glorious globe, the abode of myriads of human beings."

At the time I sent my letter to Ehrenberg he was afflicted with blindness.

CHAPTER IX.

THE ride between Berlin and Frankfort-on-the-Main is long and fatiguing, occupying from ten to twelve hours. As far as Weimar, which is passed in the early part of the day, and which has been rendered famous as the residence of Wieland, Schiller, Goethe, and Herder, the country exhibits very much the same aspect as between Dresden and Berlin, being flat and sandy, and not particularly attractive. Beyond Weimar it becomes gradually more undulating and fertile, and so continues as far as Frankfort. We passed many fields covered with yellow wheat nearly ripe for the sickle, and as we approached Frankfort the sight was greeted with beautiful meadows, in some of which we occasionally noticed a stork, a large, dignified, apparently self-possessed bird, with a long neck and beak, well adapted to get the better of a fox in eating out of a bottle. Frankfort, one of the oldest cities of Germany, is celebrated as having been the favorite residence of Charlemagne. Here were crowned its emperors. It is noted for its numerous banking houses, its great wealth, its educational institutions, its splendid dwellings, and its magnificent promenades, unequalled in Europe. In the Judengasse, an old, narrow, dirty street, is the house in which Rothschild, the father of the great bankers, lived; and not far away is the house in which Goethe was born, both

247

objects of deep interest to the tourist. The monument of
Gutenberg, erected in 1858, stands in the Rossmarkt, and
is in itself worthy of a visit to this ancient city. There
are three principal figures, the central one being that of
Gutenberg, supported on the right by Faust and on the
left by Schöffer. Dannecker's Ariadne is universally admired as one of the most chaste and beautiful productions
of modern art. A statue of Goethe, erected by Schwan-
thaler, stands in the Goethe square, and is said to be an
excellent likeness of the great author and philosopher.
The most noted public building is the Römer, or council
house, an old edifice, celebrated as the place in which the
election of the German emperors was held. The walls of
the banqueting hall are decorated with portraits of all these
worthies, forty-six in number; and in the election chamber, as it is termed, is the "Golden Bull" by which the
election of the emperors was regulated.

The house in which Goethe was born is regarded by the
city of Frankfort as one of its most sacred objects, and,
like that of Shakespeare, it will no doubt be preserved with
scrupulous care to the latest generation. Considered by
itself, it is of no account, as it is simply an old, two-story
building, without any architectural beauty, or any special
comfort or convenience. The rooms are small, and the
ceilings very low. Among the relics of the great man
that remain, a leather-covered chair and a few old, well-
worn books are shown. It was from the upper front
chamber of this house that the youth was in the habit of
communicating by signs and other means with Gretchen,
a girl in the humbler walks of life, his first and for a long
time his only love. The father of the poet was the son of
a tailor. By his talents, probity, and industry he rose to
a prominent position among his fellow-citizens, and spared
no pains to give his boy all the educational advantages
afforded by his own and foreign countries. The mother,
too, was a person of more than ordinary intellect. Order,

quiet, and strong common-sense were her characteristics; and it is not improbable that the son inherited from her a large share of the genius which made him the first literary man of his age.

It was with feelings of no ordinary kind that we left Frankfort for Homburg, to enjoy a week of absolute repose at that charming watering-place. We had been constantly on the wing for more than two months, and as we had suffered a good deal from the heat, especially during the last fortnight, we were very anxious to get to a cool, quiet spot. A ride of thirty minutes over a pleasant, undulating country, nearly all the way in sight of the Taunus Mountains, brought us to our destination. Homburg, a town of nearly ten thousand inhabitants, is celebrated for its mineral waters, its elegant bathing establishments, its handsome residences, and its beautiful and picturesque promenades. The Kursaal is a large, elegant edifice, superbly furnished, and surrounded by beautiful grounds, enlivened by excellent music. It was the resort for years of fashionable people from all parts of Europe, especially of invalids in search of health by drinking its various mineral waters. Numerous gamblers made the Kursaal annually their headquarters; and for many years, much to its discredit, the government received a large revenue from this source from the lessees of the establishment. Since our visit, in 1868, the gambling-saloons have been closed, and the house and grounds have assumed a more respectable character. Notwithstanding that many of the people who resort to Homburg possess great wealth, there was a remarkable dearth of fine equipages, although it was the height of the season. It was interesting to watch the gaming-tables, attended indiscriminately by men and women, old and young, and to observe their countenances as the little ball whirled around the insatiate wheel, bringing joy to some, and grief to others. None appeared more excited than the old ladies; none picked up their ill-gotten gains more eagerly; and none looked more disconcerted when they found themselves slighted by Fortune. Considered all in all, it is difficult to conceive of a more lovely spot as a summer residence than Homburg.

As the distance from Frankfort to Heidelberg is only fifty-four miles, we could not resist the temptation to visit a city so celebrated as the seat of one of the most renowned universities of Germany, to say nothing of its many romantic associations. The journey, which occupied only two hours, extends through a beautiful and highly cultivated country, covered with fields of wheat partly in shocks, and numerous patches of tobacco in a remarkably flourishing condition. The soil seemed to be very rich, and the general aspect of the country reminded me forcibly of Lancaster County, Pennsylvania. Ten miles from Frankfort we passed through the old city of Darmstadt, and farther along, on our left, a high range of hills, with now and then an ancient castle. The day—the 23d of July—was hot and sultry, and the dust annoying.

Heidelberg is situated on the left bank of the Neckar, a stream about the width of the Schuylkill, and contains nearly twenty thousand inhabitants. Its position is remarkably picturesque, being bounded on the one side by the river, and by high hills on the other. The main street is very wide, well shaded, nearly two miles in length. The modern parts of the city contain many beautiful private residences. The University, founded in the fourteenth century, is a very old, unprepossessing edifice, which, but for the many classical and endearing associations which cluster around it, might well be replaced by a better and more suitable structure. As it was vacation season, there were scarcely any students about it. The library contains nearly two hundred and fifty thousand volumes, and is particularly rich in antique works, and in books on theology, jurisprudence, and philology. It has also many manuscripts. The conveniences for carrying on all kinds of studies—literary, professional, and scientific—are on an ample scale. The number of students is not nearly so great now as formerly. Its medical department, especially in the days of Chelius, Tiedemann, and Gmelin, was at one time one of the most famous in Germany. That, too, has gone to naught. What agency the fighting element in the "Burschenshaften," resulting in frequent duels, has exerted in bringing about this result is a problem which it is not hard to solve. The conduct of the authorities who permitted such flagrant outrages cannot be too severely censured. The ultimate effects upon the prosperity of the University could not be for a moment doubted. The practice was a relic of barbarism, of the most revolting character. In the mean time, while the custom was sanctioned, and the institution was suffering from its consequences, other universities sprang into notice, and naturally attracted students of the better class. Heidelberg has educated immense numbers of great men; and some of our own most distinguished scholars, such as Everett, Bancroft, and Longfellow, are among its alumni. There seems to be a fatality in the affairs of scholastic and scientific institutions as there is in the affairs of families, of communities, and of nations.

The Hirschgasse, the house in which the duels take place, is situated on the opposite bank of the Neckar, a short distance below the city. Curiosity led us to visit it. There is nothing peculiar about it, or anything that would suggest the idea that it was the frequent scene of such disreputable rencounters. The fighting is usually done with swords, which are always kept in the best possible condition for the purpose. When it takes place on account of feuds existing between different corps, of which there are not less than six or eight, the combatants wear thick, heavy caps, and thick bandages round their necks as a means of protection; but when they engage on their own account these trappings are dispensed with, it being considered dishonorable to employ them. Terrible gashes, leaving unseemly scars for the rest of life, are often inflicted, especially upon the face, and now and then a mortal wound. The man who receives the least number of cuts is declared the victor. Sometimes the combat, after having lasted for an indefinite period, without resulting in a satisfactory manner, is renewed at a future day, as soon as the parties are sufficiently recovered from the effects of their injuries.

Next in interest to the University is the Castle of Heidelberg, noted for its antiquity, its picturesque situation upon a high hill, its architectural magnificence, and its historical associations. Originally it was occupied both as a fortress and as a palace. In the latter part of the seventeenth century it was sacked and partly burned by the French, and in 1764 it was struck by lightning. It was an immense structure, and if all is true which is said of its wine-cellars it must have been the seat of princely hospitality. Only two of the original thirteen casks remain. The celebrated Heidelberger Fass, as it is called, is said to hold eight hundred hogsheads, or nearly three hundred thousand bottles of wine. The capacity of the other is sixty thousand gallons. Close by the larger of these casks is the wooden statue of the court-fool Porkes, who daily, on an average, drank from fifteen to eighteen bottles of wine, and never went to bed sober. On the wall of the cellar, near the famous Fass, is a box, upon touching the spring of which a fox's tail flies out. It is one of the original relics of the place, and, together with the court-fool, must have been a source of merriment to the people of the castle.

The Museum, known as the Kunst und Alterthum Halle, a short distance from the city, interests one very much. It is filled with ancient curiosities, and is particularly rich in instruments of torture. A prominent object is a chair, of peculiar construction, in which the criminal used to sit while his head was being struck off with a broadsword.

The signal for the blow was the ringing of an old hemi-spherical bell, which was suspended from the wall, and which emitted a gruff, dolorous sound befitting the occasion. There is a rack, shaped like a cross, on which the criminal was stretched beyond his natural length; and another for crushing the body and limbs. There are several speci-mens of thumb-screws, an iron thorn for tearing the flesh on the back, a whip for flogging persons, and a wheel for crushing bones. There is also a curious figure with a face in the shape of a violin, with a hole in the top for the neck and two perforations for the arms, used for punishing liars and thieves, who were thus driven through the streets as a chastisement. Compared with these the whipping-posts of our Delaware neighbors are playthings. In the armory in the upper room of the museum I noticed two revolvers, each with a lock and flint, manufactured more than two centuries ago. In looking at these weapons one could not help exclaiming, "Long live Colt!" Among other curiosities in this remarkable building are garments of an old robber, who killed twelve soldiers before he was captured by the elector's guards.

A visit to the Molkenkur, a large house upon the sum-mit of the high mountain back of the castle, for treat-ing invalids with buttermilk, repays one by the charming views which it affords of Heidelberg and the surrounding country,—the Neckar, as it winds for miles, like a ser-pent, towards the Rhine; the two banks of that beautiful river clothed with verdure and magnificent graperies; the Rhine itself at a great distance; the grand old bridge across the Neckar almost in the heart of the city; and the hills and fertile plains as far as the eye can see. A drive of two miles brings one to the Wolfsbrunnen, where, as the story goes, the enchantress Jetta was torn to pieces by wolves—a romantic spot, more famous at the present day for its fine trout dinners than for its witches and wild animals.

Before bidding adieu to this delightful city I spent an hour with the eminent surgeon Maximilian Joseph Chelius, with whose name and fame I had long been familiar, and between whom and myself there had been an interchange of civilities. He received me with courtly dignity, and soon entered into an animated conversation, in which he particularly inquired after Dr. Gibson and Dr. Mütter, with whose scientific labors and contributions he seemed to be perfectly familiar. His residence, near the bank of the Neckar, is almost palatial, and is surrounded by beautiful grounds and shrubbery, the whole exhibiting great taste and refinement. Without asking him, he told me that he was seventy-four years of age, that he had resigned his chair in the University several years ago, and that he was now living in retirement. For the last forty years, he said, he had spent a part of every summer at Baden Baden, within three hours' ride by rail of Heidelberg. Tall, erect, with a handsome, benevolent face, and black eyes, he was remarkably well preserved, and looked as if he might live to a very old age. My expectations were not disappointed. In August, 1876, the telegraph brought me an account of his death, at the age of eighty-two years. The obituary notice states that he was a native of Mannheim, in the Grand Duchy of Baden, where he was born in 1794. He was elected to the chair of Surgery at Heidelberg in 1819, at the age of twenty-five, and in 1843–'45 published his celebrated Handbuch der Chirurgie, translated into numerous languages. An English version by the late Mr. South, of London, enriched by extensive additions, was republished in Philadelphia many years ago under the supervision of the late Dr. George W. Norris. Besides this work, Chelius produced at an early period of his life a Treatise on the Eye, and he was also a copious contributor to the periodical press. He was one of the great pillars of the medical school of Heidelberg. He obtained his medical degree

when he was only eighteen years of age. Before he settled
at Heidelberg he had practised his profession in different
towns, and was for a time physician to the hospital at
Ingelstadt in Bavaria. His experience was greatly extended by accompanying the German army into France,
and by visiting the hospitals and universities of Vienna,
Göttingen, and Berlin. Owing to his great accomplishments as a surgeon and as a physician, and to his high
social position, he attracted around him for nearly half a
century much of the best practice in Northern Germany.
During the illness of the young Prince Imperial he was
summoned to Paris to consult with Nélaton and others
respecting the nature and treatment of his disease. When
I rose to depart, the veteran surgeon warmly pressed my
hand and thanked me for my visit.

The ride from Frankfort to Mayence by rail occupies
twelve minutes and extends over a pleasant, highly-cul-
tivated country, which, in the neighborhood of the latter
city, is one great field of grapevines; from these are manufactured the sparkling Hock and Moselle, so celebrated
throughout Europe. Taking our passage on board the
Mayence and Cologne steamer, a small boat with an open
upper deck, somewhat like what one sees in the United
States, we floated down the Rhine as far as Coblentz, where
we disembarked to view that venerable city, as well as
Ehrenbreitstein, perched upon a high and rugged hill
immediately opposite, the two being closely connected by
a bridge of boats nearly four hundred yards in length. On
our right, as we descended the river, was pointed out to
us the celebrated castle of Johannisberg, the residence of
Prince Metternich, to whom it was presented by the
Emperor of Austria. It is here that the famous Johan-
nisberger wine is made, the vineyard covering only thirty-
eight acres. About three miles farther down, on the same
side of the river, is Rüdesberg, also celebrated for the excellence of its wine. The grapes grown at these two spots

owe their superior quality, it should seem, to the fact that, in pleasant weather, the sun from the time it rises until it sets never leaves them, thus giving to the soil the warmth and fertility so essential to the culture of this fruit.

Coblentz, founded a short time before the Christian era, is situated at the confluence of the Rhine and Moselle, and abounds in historical associations. It is the seat of a palace occupied as a summer residence by the emperor, and has the finest wine-cellars in Germany. The streets are, for the most part, narrow and uninviting. Some fine private dwellings are to be seen in the newer parts of the city, and there are several excellent hotels on the river bank opposite Ehrenbreitstein. Every stranger of course visits the Church of St. Castor and the celebrated Castorbrunnen, erected in 1812 by the French prefect in commemoration of the French campaign against Russia, and rendered famous by the sarcastic inscription of the Russian General St. Priest, who recaptured the city in January, 1814. Close by is a fine view of the Moselle and of the beautiful valley through which it meanders just before it empties into the Rhine.

Ehrenbreitstein, often called the Gibraltar of the Rhine, is so famous in history and romance as to be of itself almost worthy of a visit on the part of the American tourist. Everybody, far and wide, has heard or read of it in novels and the illustrated annuals which were once so fashionable. The officer in charge, learning that we were from the United States, the land of Washington, was particularly courteous and communicative. He pointed out to us every object of interest in and about this celebrated fortress, and the spots whence we could behold to the greatest advantage the surrounding country with its glorious scenery and its two beautiful vine-clad rivers lying immediately at our feet, with the fertile valleys through which they run, and the numerous villages, hills, and mountains which dot the landscape in every direction as far as the eye can see. Our visit was made on a bright afternoon in July, and the very atmosphere seemed to be redolent of joy, so genial and pleasant was everything around us. Two more agreeable or happy hours I never spent.

The next morning, Sunday, at nine o'clock, we found ourselves on the steamer on our way to Bonn, intending to stop there a few hours, and then to proceed to Cologne. As we passed along we found the shores lined with people, and at one of the towns we saw a large Catholic procession with a boy carrying the Host before him upon a high pole. I never witnessed a more merry company. Song and mirth in various forms were evidently the order of the day, and the Saviour, represented by the image, was treated in the most unceremonious manner. Just here a little discovery was made which completely changed our plans for the day. One of our party, much to her consternation, found that she had left her purse, freighted with gold coin, at the hotel under the pillow of her bed. Embracing the earliest opportunity to go ashore, she took the train which soon after came along for Coblentz, and within less than an hour reached the Giant, where she had slept the previous night. Making known her loss, the chambermaid was summoned, the fact disclosed, and the purse with its contents restored, greatly to the joy of all concerned. I am induced to mention this circumstance simply to confirm, what I believe is generally known, that the servants at the German inns are, as a rule, very honest and trustworthy.

Bonn, nearly midway between Coblentz and Cologne, is interesting chiefly on account of its old Minster Church, its well-organized University, its splendid avenues shaded by double rows of horse-chestnut trees, and its scientific and literary society. The University, founded by the King of Prussia in 1818, is one of the most celebrated in Germany. Its Faculties are extremely able ; and the number

1—33

of students is considerably over one thousand. The building, which was formerly occupied as a palace, and in which
are commodious and well-arranged lecture-rooms, is nearly
a quarter of a mile in length. Attached to it are a museum
of Rhenish antiquities and a library of nearly two hundred
thousand volumes. At the time of my visit, preparations
were in progress for the celebration, on the 2d of August,
of the fiftieth anniversary of the University. The medical
department has long been in a flourishing condition, and
a number of the teachers enjoy a well-earned reputation.
It was my good fortune to meet, among others, one
of the most distinguished members of the Faculty, Dr.
Busch, the Professor of Surgery and the Director of the
Surgical Clinic, with whom I passed a very pleasant hour,
the conversation relating chiefly to medical education in
Germany and the United States. On taking my leave he
kindly placed in my hands a number of brochures and
pamphlets, written by himself, upon various subjects connected with surgery. The great composer, Beethoven,
was a native of Bonn, and a beautiful bronze monument
is erected to his memory in the heart of the city. Bonn
affords a fine view on the bank of the river of the villages
of Königswinter and Drachenfels, especially of the latter,
situated, as the name implies, upon a rock, nearly nine
hundred feet above the level of the Rhine. The slopes
of the rock are covered with vineyards, one of which contains the cavern once occupied, as the story goes, by the
dragon slain by Siegfried, the hero of Holland, who,
having bathed himself in the monster's blood, became
invulnerable. The wine yielded by the grapes grown upon
Drachenfels is known as the Dragon's blood.

The Rhine beyond Bonn loses its interest. Its banks are
flat and destitute of beauty. It was late in the evening
when our boat, crowded to excess, landed at Cologne.
Soon after we left Bonn the moon rose in all her grandeur
and threw her bright rays in beautiful images upon the

water. The passengers were merry, and while many of them engaged in loud conversation, not a few amused themselves with singing religious or national songs.

Arriving at Cologne, we selected the Hotel du Nord as our temporary resting-place, and, after an early breakfast, the next morning we sallied forth sight-seeing. The chief objects of interest in this old city, now containing nearly one hundred and fifty thousand inhabitants, inclusive of seven thousand soldiers, are the Cathedral, Dom, or Minster of St. Peter, St. Ursula, the Gürzenich, the iron bridge across the Rhine nearly fourteen hundred feet in length, the Museum of Roman Antiquities, and the botanical and zoological gardens. The Cathedral, one of the finest specimens of Gothic architecture in the world, although begun in the middle of the thirteenth century, is still unfinished, notwithstanding several millions of dollars have been expended upon it during the last fifty years by the German rulers and the friends of the church in different parts of Europe. Numerous workmen were busily engaged upon it at the time of our visit. The structure, which stands upon a slight eminence a short distance from the river, is more than four hundred and fifty feet in length by one hundred and forty in width, the portion appropriated to divine service occupying an area of seventy thousand square feet. The two towers when completed will each be five hundred feet high. What the good citizens of Cologne want with so gigantic an edifice it would be difficult to conjecture, unless it is their desire to be considered the most holy people in the world, a thing which every one who has had any dealings with them would find it hard to believe, since, even as respects the special liquid prepared in the city, all tourists are cautioned to buy at one house only, the article sold by all the rest being declared to be spurious.

St. Ursula is one of the wonders of the world, a perfect Golgotha, literally a place of skulls and other bones, arranged in cases in every nook and corner round the church. The sight is not only horrid, but excessively disgusting, even to an anatomist accustomed to the handling of dead bodies. These hideous relics are said to be the bones of eleven thousand virgins, who accompanied St. Ursula, daughter of the King of Brittany, on a pilgrimage to Rome, on returning from which they were foully murdered by the Huns. How these bones were prepared for this unique museum is a mystery. The church in which they are contained was erected at the beginning of the twelfth century. In the choir is a monument in honor of St. Ursula, who was shortly after her death enshrined as the patron saint of Chastity. It would be very difficult, if not impossible, at the present day, to get together such a collection of virgins in any part of Europe or this country. Other relics are to be seen in this remarkable place, such as earthen vessels used by the Saviour at the marriage in Cana; a part of the chain with which St. Peter was bound; and a fragment of the garment worn by Christ at the crucifixion.

The hospital at Cologne is a large, well-arranged edifice, in charge of the Sisters of Charity. It is surrounded by handsome grounds, set out in shrubbery, and is under the supervision of an able staff. On the road to Aix-la-Chapelle I saw a man who, twenty years previously, on account of a railway injury, had one arm and both legs amputated at the same time by Dr. Fischer, the eminent surgeon of Cologne, the fellow recovering, as he told me, without a bad symptom. This result, of which there are several cases on record, among others one by the late Dr. Koehler, of Schuylkill Haven, Pennsylvania, is a triumph of surgery. As if to cap the climax, Dr. Begg, of Dundee, Scotland, in 1869 amputated all the extremities of a young woman, the subject of embolic gangrene. She not only rapidly recovered, but is able to walk with the aid of crutches and to earn a livelihood by knitting and by various other kinds of work. She feeds and dresses herself, and even writes an excellent hand! Is there really any use for hands and feet?

Aix-la-Chapelle, a beautiful old town, with many handsome modern improvements, is celebrated as the birthplace of Charlemagne, as the city in which for several centuries the German emperors were crowned, and as a watering-place, famous for its hot sulphur springs and bathing establishments. Persons suffering from gout, rheumatism, neuralgia, and constitutional syphilis resort to it from all parts of the civilized world in quest of health. The water is strongly impregnated with sulphur, and as it issues from the wells is disagreeably hot. The new Kursaal is close by, and is provided with pleasant grounds and promenades. It is a curious as well as a sad sight on a fine day to see the cripples hobble about, some on sticks, some on crutches, and others on disabled limbs, wincing and writhing under their aches and pains as they go along. The Cathedral, an old massive structure, remodelled in the present century, contains the tomb of Charlemagne and numerous sacred relics—such as a robe of the Virgin Mary, the leathern girdle of Christ, a part of the true cross, and the bloody cloth in which the body of John the Baptist was wrapped after his execution. These relics are publicly exhibited every seven years with great pomp and ceremony, and attract vast crowds of people, by whom they are regarded with sacred awe. Among other objects of interest in this church are the skull of Charlemagne, one of his leg bones, and his hunting-horn. Evidently the German people have a great fondness for storing away and looking at dead men's bones. In the United States all such objects are regarded with well-merited disgust. Even Byron's celebrated drinking-cup would here find few admirers and still fewer purchasers.

The country between Aix-la-Chapelle and Rotterdam is mostly flat, especially that part of it which lies at some distance beyond the former city, and it is, in the main, quite uninteresting. From Antwerp to Rotterdam the journey is made partly by rail and partly by boat, on the river Meuse, and occupies four hours and a half. The track rests upon sandy soil, upon a dead level, the whole bearing a strong resemblance to that between Camden and Atlantic City or Cape May. The steamboat was small, dirty, and uncomfortable, without any of the conveniences found upon our Delaware or Hudson River vessels. The Meuse is a wide, deep, magnificent stream, abounding in fish, especially salmon and sturgeon, both of which are taken in large quantities. The harbor of Rotterdam reminds one of that of New York. It is of considerable extent, and at the time of our visit it contained a number of large and small vessels, which gave the wharf a very lively appearance. It is a notorious fact that Rotterdam has not one respectable hotel. The house at which we stopped, said to be the first in the place, was decidedly untidy and unattractive, and would hardly have compared favorably with the meanest hotel in any of our inland towns. Rotterdam is a seafaring place, overrun with sailors, and this is probably the reason why the accommodations are so indifferent. The two objects worthy of special notice in the entire city are the house in which Erasmus was born, and the monument erected to his memory in the market-place. The figure is that of a student in gown and cap, with an open book in hand.

The ride by rail from Rotterdam to Amsterdam occupies two hours and twenty minutes, and extends over a level country dotted by windmills and intersected by numerous dykes, not a fence being visible on the entire route. The fields were enlivened by numerous cattle and sheep, many of the former being white and black, and comparatively few being brown. The crops consisted chiefly of oats, buckwheat, and potatoes—wheat and rye being rarely observed. Beautiful fields of red clover, similar to our own, also greeted the eye. Very few trees, and those generally of small size, were seen. Amsterdam affords a great contrast to Rotterdam. The latter is barren of interest; the former abounds in it, and the tourist consequently leaves it with regret. In many respects Amsterdam strongly resembles Venice. It is a city emphatically built upon piles, intersected by canals and covered with bridges, the latter numbering nearly three hundred, many of them being handsome and costly structures. The hotels, unlike those of Rotterdam, are on a large and elegant scale, and an entirely different atmosphere pervades the place. Many of the streets are wide, and flanked by fine dwellings built in the modern style; while nearly all the older residences are faced with gables, similar to the houses one still sees at Albany and other Dutch towns in New York. The harbor is excellent, and covered with ships trading with all parts of the world, and returning laden with the harvests of other climes. Amsterdam is one of the richest cities in Europe. The manufacture and sale of diamonds are carried on here on a large scale by the Jews, of whom there are not less than twenty thousand, living chiefly in the more dirty and obscure parts of the city. Some of the finest pictures in the world, chiefly by Dutch and Flemish artists, are to be seen here. The Banquet of the Civil Guard by Van der Helst, in the Museum, comprising twenty-five lifelike portraits, is of itself worth a visit to Holland. The older Dutch masters excelled in the delineation of animals and birds. Many of these portraits are so true to nature that we are literally entranced by the sight, and ready to affirm that the real object is before us. The lion roars, the tiger growls, the wolf grins, the fox looks stealthily at his victim, the turkey struts and gobbles, and the peacock, proud of his plumage, expands his tail and erects his head. The scene is enchanting, and the eye, as it turns away, instinctively looks back to take another glance.

Amsterdam is celebrated for its many educational and charitable institutions. The Royal Academy of Fine Arts, founded in 1820, has a large number of pupils, and has been of great service in diffusing a taste for painting and sculpture. In passing through the streets one is struck with the remarkable absence of poverty and dissipation. A ragged child or a drunken person is a rare sight. Among the great men born in this city may be mentioned Spinoza, Swammerdam, and Admiral De Ruyter, who burned the English fleet at Chatham. Swammerdam, who was born in 1637, was one of the greatest anatomists and entomologists of his day; and the works of few philosophers are better known or more highly appreciated than those of the Dutch philosopher. The tombs of De Ruyter, and of Van den Vondel the famous Dutch poet, are in the New Church, as it is called—a grand structure, founded at the beginning of the fifteenth century. The house in which the admiral was born stands on the wharf. A statue of Rembrandt is situated in a conspicuous part of the city.

One of the great objects of interest to me at Amsterdam was the Public Hospital, one of the neatest and best ventilated establishments of the kind I have ever seen. It contains more than six hundred beds, most of which were occupied. The floors were singularly clean, and there was an entire absence of odor. Every ward has a gallery—an arrangement, I believe, peculiar to this institution, and of course necessitating a high ceiling. The surgical ward was under the charge of Professor Telanus, a tall, elderly, agreeable gentleman, assisted by his son. He seemed to be much interested in his patients, and took great pains to point out to me the more important cases. Among others he showed me two of elephantiasis: one was just admitted; the other had been for a fortnight under treatment by compression of the femoral artery with a ten-pound weight kept up for half an hour at a time thrice daily, the effect being a marked diminution of the size of the limb. He also showed me a case of recurring chondroma in a boy thirteen years of age, situated on the left side of the face, for the cure of which he had, two years previously, amputated the upper jaw. The lad was very pale and greatly emaciated, and the countenance horribly disfigured, the mouth being drawn towards the right side and the left eye completely out of its socket. Death would have been a great relief to the poor fellow.

The Medical School of Amsterdam, in which Dr. Telanus is the Professor of Surgery, was founded about forty years ago, and does not seem to be in a flourishing condition, as the classes are very small. It has a respectable pathological museum, and ample material for thorough instruction in clinical medicine and surgery. The centres of medical teaching in Holland are Leyden and Utrecht; the former at one time had the most celebrated medical institution in the world. Holland in the seventeenth and eighteenth centuries produced a number of great anatomists, physicians, and surgeons, as well as many distinguished medical teachers. Herman Boerhaave, born in 1668, was one of the greatest physicians that ever lived. Able, learned, eloquent, and of indefatigable industry, he acquired at a comparatively early age a world-wide reputation, and attracted to Leyden a large number of students from all parts of Europe, and not a few also from America. As an evidence of his great celebrity, it is recorded that a letter written in China with the simple superscription, "Herman Boerhaave, Europe," readily reached its destination. Among his more illustrious pupils, the disseminators of his doctrines and practice, may be mentioned Haller, Van Swieten, Gaubius, and Van Haen.

Amsterdam has several large bookstores, in which I found translations of the works of Prescott, Motley, and other American authors. I am indebted to Holland for a translation of my System of Surgery, made by Dr. I. D. Sachse, a naval surgeon, the first part of which was issued at Nieuwediep in 1863.

The great attraction at Antwerp is the Cathedral, one of the grandest church edifices in Europe, nearly five hundred feet in length by two hundred and fifty in width, with a steeple variously estimated at from three hundred and fifty to five hundred feet in height. It is said that nearly eighty years were occupied in its erection. Apart from its vast size and architectural elegance, it is famous the world over for containing Rubens's wonderful picture of "The Descent from the Cross," the *chef-d'œuvre* of that artist. The figures are drawn with matchless force and expression, and the whole scene is placed so vividly before the eye that one is almost compelled to regard it as a reality. Rubens was a native of Antwerp, and the house in which he was born was long preserved as an object of curiosity. A beautiful monument of the artist is contained in the Cathedral. The figures in his "Holy Family" are said to represent himself, his two wives, his son, his father, and his grandfather. On each side of the picture is a statue in white marble of one of his female descendants, who died, respectively, in 1834 and 1835. In a retired part of the great church a young man, born without arms, and holding his brush between his toes, was busily engaged in copying the Holy Family, working, apparently, with facility. The picture was not completed, but promised well, and the artist is regarded as an excellent painter. The city is celebrated for its many magnificent churches, all containing paintings by such Flemish artists as Van Dyke, Rubens, Jordaens, and others. Many choice specimens are also found in the Museum, one of the most celebrated in Europe.

The fortifications of Antwerp are two miles or more in extent, and the harbor is one of the finest in the world. During its best period, in the fifteenth and sixteenth centuries, it was visited by a greater number of vessels of large tonnage than any other city in Europe. The principal street, called Rue de Mère, is lined by magnificent shade-trees, and is noted for its elegance. The older houses are all built with the gables towards the street, and many of them present a fine appearance. The stranger, in passing along the wharves, is attracted by the sight of many enormous draught-horses, almost of gigantic stature, and of Normandy descent, and he asks himself the question, "Why is this breed of horses not introduced extensively into the United States?" Such animals, which by the way are a great curiosity to a foreigner, could not fail to be of immense service, especially in our larger cities in connection with heavy dray-work.

A ride of one hour, on July 30th, carried us from Antwerp to Brussels, the distance being only twenty-seven miles. The country along the route is quite level and highly cultivated. It is covered with rich fields of clover, wheat, potatoes, and various kinds of vegetables, exhibiting a superior style of farming and of horticulture. Brussels, as everybody is aware, is one of the most beautiful cities in the world, a second Paris in miniature. The older streets are narrow, and the houses are built in the Dutch or Flemish style; but the new streets are noted for their width, and the modern dwellings for their elegance. The population is rapidly increasing, commerce is uncommonly active, the people are refined and cultured, and there are few signs of idleness and intemperance. The University, founded in 1834, is one of the best organized institutions of the kind in Europe. Its four departments of literature—or belles-lettres, law, medicine, and science—are supplied with able teachers, many of whom enjoy a wide celebrity. The observatory is one of the finest in the world. The public library contains more than two hundred thousand volumes. The botanical gardens are large, attractive, and beautifully situated,

affording charming promenades in pleasant weather. The
Medical School annually educates a considerable number
of young men, who receive their clinical instruction at
two large and well-arranged hospitals, the St. Pierre and
St. Jean, under the supervision of eminent professors. The
examinations for the degree of doctor of medicine, which
were going on during my visit, are conducted with great
rigor—the requirements, like those in Paris and in Europe
generally, being of a high standard. The St. Pierre contains three hundred and fifty beds, and is remarkable for
its cleanliness and thorough ventilation. Dr. De Rue, in
charge of the surgical ward, was kind enough to point out
to me many cases of deep interest. I had felt a great desire to see Professor Uytterhoeven, between whom and
myself some letters had passed several years previously;
but, much to my regret, he was out of town. I was
anxious to see the lithotomist who had extracted the largest
calculus ever removed from a human subject; and although
the man died on the eighth day after the operation, I
have always considered the case as one of the triumphs
of surgery. It is worthy of notice that the stone weighed
more than two pounds, and that it was nearly seven inches
in length by four in breadth, and nearly two and a half in
thickness. It was extracted by the suprapubic method.

One of the most interesting objects in Brussels to a
medical man is the bronze statue of Vesalius, erected under the auspices of Leopold I., in the Place des Barricades.
The figure is beautifully posed, and is arrayed in a flowing
robe, with pen in hand and a folio volume under the left
arm. Underneath, on the pedestal, is the inscription:
"Andreæ Vesalio, Scientiæ Anatomiæ Parenti:" (To Andrew Vesalius, the Father of the Science of Anatomy.) It
is an honor of no ordinary character that a king, absorbed
in the cares and duties of statecraft, should have turned
aside to prompt the erection of such a memorial in honor
of a member of the medical profession. The history of Ve-

salius is remarkable. Born at Brussels in 1514, he studied medicine at Louvain, Montpellier, and Paris, paying especial attention to the structure of the human body, of which his knowledge was so vast that when scarcely twenty-six years of age, he was appointed professor of Anatomy in the University of Pavia, from which he was soon afterwards called to that of Bologna, and finally to that of Pisa. In 1543, at the age of twenty-eight, he published his great work on anatomy, entitled De Corporis Humani Fabrica, pronounced by Senac as the discovery of a new world, and by Haller as an immortal production, which completely revolutionized all that had been written and published upon the subject. The story of his residence at Madrid, where he was physician to the emperor, Charles V., and afterwards to Philip II., is well known. Having, it is said, opened the body of a nobleman, one of his patients, he found to his own horror, as well as to the horror of those around him, that the heart was still pulsating. The report was at once carried to the court; and thence to the Inquisition, which denounced him as guilty of murder; and it was only through the intercession of powerful friends that his life was spared, and then only on condition that he should perform a pilgrimage to the Holy Land. However this may be, a story at best of a very doubtful character, it is certain that he visited Jerusalem, and that on his return he died of starvation in the island of Zante, as is generally supposed, the vessel on which he was a passenger having been wrecked in the Mediterranean. A more reasonable conjecture, I think, is that he went to the Holy Land of his own accord, being incited thereto by his roving, restless disposition, combined with a strong religious sentiment tinctured with a spirit of fanaticism peculiar to the period in which he lived. His death occurred in 1564, at the age of fifty years.

Brussels was at one time largely engaged in the book-publishing business. Works issued in Paris were extensively reprinted, and, on account of their cheapness from the absence of copyright, met with a rapid sale. An appeal by the authors, whose rights were thus seriously infringed, induced the French government to put a stop to the practice by the establishment of an international law. The effect of this wholesale piracy must have been highly prejudicial to the development of native writers. Of late years the literature of Belgium has assumed a very creditable rank in nearly all the pursuits of life, and its Academy of Sciences is doing a great deal of useful work.

I must not forget to mention that before leaving for England we spent a most charming day in visiting Waterloo, the scene of the great battle which decided the fate of Europe.

CHAPTER X.

OXFORD—THE MEETING OF THE BRITISH MEDICAL ASSOCIATION—STRATFORD-ON-AVON—CAMBRIDGE—THE UNIVERSITY—NORWICH—THE BRITISH ASSOCIATION FOR THE ADVANCEMENT OF SCIENCE—THE NORFOLK AND NORWICH HOSPITAL — MR. PARTRIDGE — LONDON HOSPITALS — LEEDS — YORK — EDINBURGH—JAMES SYME—JOHN BROWN—SIR JAMES Y. SIMPSON, BART.—THE UNIVERSITY—GLASGOW—COURTS OF JUSTICE—NORMAN MACLEOD.

WE left Brussels on Tuesday, August 5th, for London, by way of Calais. The Channel was crossed in two hours on a miserable little boat, but as the sea was perfectly smooth there was hardly any seasickness. As for ourselves, we escaped completely, notwithstanding our remarkable predisposition to it—a circumstance due in some degree to the fact that we remained perfectly quiet, and for the most part recumbent during the passage. A great crowd awaited us at the wharf at Dover, and some time elapsed before we could be transferred to the train. The Chalk Cliffs, rising several hundred feet above the level of the water, appeared unique and interesting. The track was bounded on each side for many miles by immense fields of hops, cultivated for the London breweries; but as we neared the great city these were replaced by fields of grain and vegetable gardens in a high state of improvement. The soil, in the hop region as it may be called, is underlaid by beds of chalk, with frequent outcroppings, which impart to the surface a singular aspect. Soon after reaching the Victoria Station we took the train for Oxford, where we arrived at half past nine in the evening. As I was a delegate to the British Medical Association, which met the day before, I immediately sent my card to Professor Acland, the president, who in his reply begged me to join the Association at breakfast, at eight o'clock the next morning, in one of the public halls. Upon entering I found nearly all the seats of the large room occupied, every man being fully intent upon his knife and fork. The entertainment, viands and all, was cold and formal, without conversation or hilarity, the merest matter of business imaginable, at four shillings a head. The meeting was largely attended—a number of prominent Continental and American physicians, among others J. Marion Sims and J. Fordyce Barker, being present. I presented my credentials in due form. During the morning two elaborate papers were read—one, the address in medicine, by Sir William Gull, of London; and the other, the address in physiology, by Professor George Rolleston, of Oxford. The opening discourse, by Professor Acland, had been delivered the day before, and had elicited much applause. The Sections were well organized, and performed a great deal of useful labor.

The same day I dined with Dr. Leighton, the Vice-Chancellor of the University of Oxford, in company with a number of distinguished gentlemen, such as Dr. Locock, the Queen's accoucheur; Professor Syme, of Edinburgh; Mr. Thomas Curling, Sir James Paget, Professor Acland, and the Rev. Dr. Liddell, Dean of Christ Church—in all about twenty. There were many dishes, and an abundance of choice wine, all well served. The conversation was animated and discursive, but rather staid, as perhaps became the occasion. In the evening I attended an immense party given by the citizens of Oxford to the members of the Medical Association at the newly-erected Museum, a grand edifice surrounded by beautiful grounds. There must have been present fully fifteen hundred persons of both sexes, besides many distinguished strangers. The hall was crowded to excess. Everybody seemed to be full of happiness. The refreshments were simple, consisting of ice-cream, water-ices, and cake, enlivened by the wassail-bowl, charged with claret punch, and circulating freely from mouth to mouth, a custom more honored, one would suppose, in the breach than in the observance. The occasion was one long to be remembered. Of the Museum in which this meeting took place mention will be made in another part of the volume.

The anniversary dinner of the Association came off on Thursday evening in the great banqueting hall of Christ Church. The entertainment was rendered particularly dignified and impressive by the old pictures hung everywhere upon the walls, and representing many of the dignitaries in church, in state, and in literature of bygone days. Professor Acland occupied the chair, and in a few remarks, after the cloth was removed, referred in handsome terms to the foreign delegates. I had the good fortune to be seated upon the platform next to Sir James Paget, and immediately opposite Professor J. Hughes Bennett, of Edinburgh, the author of the celebrated treatise on clinical medicine. A number of speeches were made, most of them concise and in good taste. The best of all was that of Sir James Paget, one of the most ready and felicitous speakers I have ever listened to. As the senior of the American delegates, it devolved upon me to reply to the toast offered by the chair in honor of our profession, a duty which I performed with much diffidence, surrounded as I was by so august and learned an assembly. During my remarks I spoke of the efforts that we were making to establish a national medical literature, and to the obligations we were formerly under in this and other matters to our European brethren. As I proceeded I heard "Hear! hear!!" on every side, and I was happy to find that my little speech was well received. In the exercises of the evening were included songs from a choir, in which many of the company joined; and the hilarity was kept up until a late hour of the night, every one going away well satisfied with himself and with the occasion. Not fewer than two hundred and fifty sat down at table, each paying a guinea. Among the distinguished gentlemen present were William Stokes, of Dublin, Locock, Syme, Sir William R. Wilde, and the venerable Dr. Jelf, formerly Principal of King's College, London, with many of the more prominent younger members of the English, Scotch, and Irish profession.

On Friday evening I had the pleasure of dining with Dr. Church, a Fellow of one of the colleges, and one of the physicians of St. Bartholomew's Hospital, a gentleman rapidly rising in his profession. The company was small, and among the guests were Duchesne, of Bologne, the writer on nervous diseases; Professor Rolleston; and Dr. Victor Carus, of Dresden. It was near midnight when we found ourselves on the way to our lodgings, the evening having been a most charming one.

From Dr. Rolleston, the Professor of Physiology in the University, we received much kind attention. He lives in a beautiful and retired part of Oxford, in an elegant house, surrounded by large and pleasant grounds, and furnished with a choice library. His amiable and excellent wife is the daughter of Dr. John Davy, and a niece of the great Sir Humphry.

Having spent six days very pleasantly at Oxford, we next went to Leamington, a ride of two hours by rail, intending on the morrow to visit Warwick Castle, Kenilworth, and Stratford-on-Avon, the birthplace of the "deer-stalker." The sun rose bright and beautiful, and after an early breakfast we were soon on our way to visit scenes with which we had been acquainted through reading alone. Everything pertaining to these places is replete with interest and instruction, but to attempt any connected narrative of them after the numerous accounts that have been published would be absurd. Warwick is well worth a visit, if it were only to look at its many splendid paintings by some of the great masters of the seventeenth and early part of the eighteenth centuries; and Kenilworth, as everybody knows, has been sung in poetry and immortalized in prose. It is a grand old relic, whose broken, ivy-covered walls alone remain to remind one of its former greatness and diversified fortunes. The day was still young when we reached Stratford-on-Avon, and after refreshing ourselves at the famous Red Horse, the principal hotel, we sauntered forth to take a look at the house in which Shakespeare first saw the light. The entrance fee was six-pence for each. What interested us most was the inscriptions of the names of visitors on the walls and on the low ceilings, grouped so closely together in most places as to leave hardly anywhere a white spot the size of a grain of wheat. It seems as if every fool that comes along must leave his mark, and America is not behind the rest of the world in this respect. Shakespeare died in April, 1616, and was buried in the chancel of the little church near the bank of the Avon. The stone placed over his grave bears the following inscription:

"GOOD FREND FOR JESUS SAKE FORBEARE,

TO DIGG T–E DUST ENCLOASED HEARE:

BLESTE BE $\frac{E}{Y}$ MAN $\frac{T}{Y}$ SPARES THES STONES,

AND CURST BE HE $\frac{T}{Y}$ MOVES MY BONES."

One can hardly suppose that this injunction of the great poet was dictated by fear of falling into the hands of the resurrectionists. Anatomy was little cultivated in that day, and such men as body-snatchers were unknown.*

---

* In 1883 an attempt was made to obtain possession of Shakespeare's skull with a view of forming some estimate of the size of his brain, and the effort, so degrading in its character, was foiled only by the interference of the mayor and town council of Stratford.

The Red Horse is now familiarly known as the Washington Irving Hotel, from the fact that the author of The Sketch Book spent some days there. In the parlor is the arm-chair in which he sat while a guest in the house; his name engraved on a brass plate. Another object of interest is the poker with which he stirred the coal in the grate.

The next objective point of our tour was Cambridge, and we were fortunate on reaching Oxford to find that we should have Professor Humphry of the former city as our travelling companion. Our ride extended over a country of no special interest, and we were glad when we reached our lodgings at the famous Bull, the principal hotel of Cambridge. The day after our arrival we dined with Dr. Humphry and his family at his country residence a mile beyond the town, and had a delightful evening, diversified by conversation and music. The doctor is Professor of Anatomy, human and comparative, in the University, and Lecturer on Clinical Surgery at Addenbroke Hospital, so called in honor of its founder. It was opened in 1770, supports one hundred and thirty beds, and is beautifully situated on the main street. The front yard is adorned with shrubbery and flowers, and everything about and within it indicates care and neatness. Dr. Humphry showed me through his wards, and pointed out to me many cases of interest. His treatment is characterized by simplicity. He gives very little medicine, and he possesses great judgment and dexterity as an operator. He has had forty-nine resections of joints. He mentioned to me a case in which he cut a man five times for stone in the bladder. A sixth operation was performed upon this patient at Norwich, but with a fatal result. He often applies no dressings whatever to wounds made in operations, trusting altogether to drainage and cleanliness for success.

The medical school of Cambridge, like that of Oxford, is very small, the number of pupils hardly reaching thirty annually. This is due to the overwhelming competition of the London colleges. Most of the Cambridge students are University graduates, and very few of them remain longer than one year, at the end of which they go to some metropolitan school to attend the hospitals and to take their degrees. The Anatomical Museum contains many valuable preparations of healthy and morbid structure, the former having lately been augmented by the collections of Dr. MacCartney, of Dublin, and Dr. Robert Lee, of London. The specimens of Dr. Lee comprise the elaborate dissections of the nerves of the heart and of the uterus, in the preparation of which that gentleman spent many of the best years of his life.

The great attraction of Cambridge is of course its University, made up of seventeen colleges and halls. Of these colleges Trinity, "the noblest institution of the kind in the kingdom, if not in the world," was founded by Henry VIII. in 1546, and has educated some of the greatest scholars, statesmen, philosophers, poets, prelates, and scientists in Great Britain, such as Newton, Bacon, Raleigh, Dryden, Barrow, Porson, Byron, Macaulay, Peacock, Sedgwick, Whewell, and Tennyson. The building is arranged in the form of a quadrangle, and occupies an immense space. The origin of the University, according to some writers, dates as far back as 630; but this is probably a mistake, as the oldest college, Peterholme, was not opened until 1257. The University Library, a beautiful edifice, contains about four hundred thousand volumes, with a great number of manuscripts, and is said to be particularly rich in early English works. Its interior is adorned by a number of busts of illustrious men, and by a beautiful statue of Byron, which is famous alike as a work of art and as having been rejected by the University of Oxford on account of his lordship's supposed immoral character.

Cambridge is situated on the river Cam, whence its

name, and is embosomed in stately trees, which almost conceal it from the surrounding country. It has a population of about thirty thousand. Besides its college buildings it has a splendid Senate House for the use of the University, and the Fitzwilliam Museum, which contains valuable pictures and a collection of antique marbles, plaster-casts, coins, manuscripts, and other objects of interest well worthy of a protracted visit.

In walking through the suburbs of this beautiful town one afternoon my attention was attracted by a large engraving which, upon further inspection, proved to be a rare print illustrative of the Revolution of Paris in 1793. The owner asked six shillings, which I promptly paid, for what I justly considered a treasure. It represents some of the scenes which occurred when the *canaille* of Paris broke into the wine-cellars of the wealthy citizens, and drank to such excess that, in their wild delirium, they poured the liquor into one another's throats, hung one another to lamp-posts, and chopped off one another's heads.

The distance by rail from Cambridge to Norwich is two hours. The country between the two cities is a flat agricultural district, abounding in Southdown sheep with black faces and in ordinary cattle. We passed Ely, the see of the bishop of that name, and saw many windmills, which became more numerous as we approached our destination. Norwich, with a population of eighty thousand, is the capital of Norfolk County, and is situated on the river Wensum near its junction with the Yare. The site is very hilly, and the streets are short and narrow. The evening of our arrival was signalized by the opening meeting of the British Association for the Advancement of Science in the large town hall in the presence of an immense audience, the retiring president, the Duke of Buccleugh, occupying the chair. His grace made a dull, stupid address. He was followed by Dr. Hooker, the president-elect, in an elaborate and learned paper, miserably read.   A great deal of interest was manifested in the meeting, which extended over four days.   More than forty Continental delegates were present, and much good work was done in the different Sections.   The old city was arrayed in holiday garb; and booths and tents, filled with country produce and all kinds of knickknacks, were seen in every direction.

Norwich is famous for its Hospital, known as the Norfolk and Norwich.   It was opened in 1772, and is celebrated on account of the great number of calculous patients admitted into its wards.   It is situated upon a small eminence, on fine grounds, and is one of the neatest establishments of the kind imaginable.   The beds are each provided with a foot and side drawer, the latter being on the right side, near the head, an arrangement affording great convenience.   The museum connected with the hospital is a model of its kind, not large but very neat, and kept in the best order.   The walls are adorned by portraits of Dalrymple and Crosse, the famous lithotomists, the latter of whom immortalized himself by his excellent treatise on Stone in the Bladder.   Both of these men were dexterous operators.   The collection of calculi exceeds one thousand specimens, the product of nearly that number of operations; these are well preserved, carefully labelled, and placed in appropriate cases with glass doors.   The largest calculus in the collection weighs fifteen ounces; it was removed by Hamer, and is described and figured in Gooch's Surgery.   The patient recovered.   There is another of six ounces, of an ovoidal shape, which was expelled spontaneously from the bladder through the vagina, and was followed by recovery.   I was shown a specimen of cystic calculus, formed upon a small oxalate of lime nucleus; it was of very soft consistence, and readily crumbled under pressure.   The man was thirty-three years old, and had been subject to attacks of cystic hemorrhage; the disease recurred, and another operation was performed four years

after the first. There is a specimen of hypertrophied prostate gland, weighing twenty ounces. The patient, an old
man, was in the habit of relieving himself with the catheter, and one day he pushed the instrument behind the
enlarged organ, between it and the rectum, causing infiltration of urine and death. The collection is rich in specimens of all kinds of renal and vesical disease.

Two days after my arrival at Norwich I was invited,
with Sir James Y. Simpson, J. Hughes Bennett, Broca,
Baker, Humphry, and others, to witness three operations for stone at the Hospital—one by Mr. Nicholls on a
boy nine years of age; and the other two by Mr. Cadge
on old men. One of the latter was cut by the median
method; the stone, which was fully two inches in length,
was brought away easily, but the wound bled, and had to
be plugged. In the other case of Mr. Cadge the stone was
very brittle, and broke into numerous fragments, thus
prolonging the operation. Lister's tube was used in all
the cases except the boy's to conduct off the urine and prevent spasm. Both operators used narrow-bladed knives.
All the patients, although fully chloroformed, were tied,
for what reason I was unable to ascertain. Mr. Nicholls
and Mr. Cadge, the latter a pupil and former assistant of
Robert Liston, have each operated nearly one hundred
times with great success. Mr. Cadge occasionally performs lithotrity, but never upon children. He has repeatedly practised median lithotomy; the largest calculus
which he has removed by this method weighed four ounces
and three-quarters. The patient, aged sixty-three, recovered with a rectal fistula. The first operation for stone in
the Hospital was performed by Mr. Donne in 1772, very
soon after the institution was opened.

Nearly all the calculous patients heretofore admitted
into this Hospital were from Norfolk and Suffolk counties,
especially from the former; and most of them were adults
and elderly persons. These counties lie along the seacoast,

and are underlaid with chalk. The air is very raw and damp, especially in winter; and rheumatism is a prevalent complaint. Many of the inhabitants habitually void lithic acid.

During my sojourn in this good old town I dined with Mr. Nicholls in company with Broca, Baker, Bennett, Hughlings Jackson, Richardson, Rolleston, Bateman, Robertson, and others, a large and intellectual company; lunched with Mr. and Mrs. Cadge, a cousin of the Quains of London; and breakfasted with Dr. Bateman, one of the physicians to the Norfolk and Norwich Hospital. I had met most of the gentlemen who were present at the Nicholls's dinner the day preceding. I attended a dinner at Dr. Eades's; and a breakfast was given to me by Mr. Allen, whom I had met shortly before at Oxford. In fact, I never experienced greater hospitality anywhere. The physicians and citizens vied with one another to entertain their visitors.

From the list of professional gentlemen of London to whom I was indebted for much kindness in 1868, I must not omit the name of Mr. Partridge, Professor of Anatomy in King's College, and one of the surgeons of King's College Hospital, a genial, pleasant gentleman, of courtly manners and great intelligence. In stature Mr. Partridge is about the middle height, with black eyes, a gentle expression of countenance, and a head not indicative of great intellect. As a lecturer, he is popular but not brilliant, and always commands the attention of his pupils. He has contributed numerous papers to the medical press; and his articles in Todd's Cyclopedia of Anatomy and Physiology are all able productions, mostly of an exhaustive nature. Mr. Partridge was one of the surgeons who went to Italy to examine Garibaldi's ankle which had received a gunshot wound at the battle of Aspromonte in 1862. His attendants, unable to find the ball or to heal the wound, had abandoned the case in despair.

Mr. Partridge was equally unsuccessful in his search, and was so unfortunate as to express his conviction that no ball was present. The friends of Garibaldi, not being satisfied with the views of the English surgeon, sent for Nélaton. This gentleman, who stood at the head of the surgical profession in Paris, before setting out upon his mission consulted an eminent French chemist to ascertain whether it were possible to devise an instrument which, when rubbed against lead, would receive the characteristic stain of that metal. The result was the now famous porcelain probe—that is, a metallic rod tipped with this substance. Upon introducing this instrument into the bottom of the wound, and rotating it roughly upon its axis, the operator was delighted to find, upon withdrawing it, a bluish spot upon the porcelain knob, clearly denotive of the existence of the long-lost missile. The sinus was at once enlarged, and the ball extracted. The operation was followed by a rapid cure, with of course permanent anchylosis of the affected joint. Thus, what one man gained in reputation the other lost; and it is not too much to say that Mr. Partridge never entirely recovered from the effects of his blunder. The Frenchman, as might have been expected, went home elated, with an additional ell to his stature, and thenceforth the name of Nélaton was in the mouth of everybody.

One afternoon late in August, Mr. Partridge was kind enough to call for me at my lodgings to drive me to Shooter's Hill, six miles from London, to examine the Herbert Military Hospital, erected by Sir Sidney Herbert during his connection with the British cabinet as Secretary of War. The hospital, arranged on the pavilion plan, is a fine structure, erected at great cost, and provided with six hundred beds, designed exclusively for the accommodation of sick and disabled soldiers. The grounds are large and attractive; the wards are thoroughly ventilated and kept in perfect order; and everything indicates the care bestowed by a great nation upon its defenders. The hospital is a monument alike to the memory of Sir Sidney Herbert and to the munificence of the British government.

I met with Mr. Partridge again in August, 1872, at Birmingham, during the sitting of the British Medical Association. He sat with me upon the platform, and looked as well as I had ever seen him, but he took no part in the proceedings. Some time after my return, I learned that he was in declining health, and not long afterwards that he had died. Judging from his appearance, he must have been my senior by at least six or seven years.

From Mr. Henry Smith, author of a small work on the Rectum, I received many courtesies during my sojourn in London, repeatedly meeting him at his own house at King's College Hospital, of which he is one of the surgeons. I saw him perform a number of operations, among others lithotomy. I was struck with the ability with which he used the knife. On one occasion he brought before the class a lad with stone in the bladder. Previously to cutting him he introduced the sound, but he was unable to find the stone, although he had several times detected it before. He handed the instrument to me and to one or two others; but as we equally failed, the boy was sent away until the following Saturday, when the concretion being found, he was successfully lithotomized. Mr. John Wood, another of the surgeons, since appointed as Fergusson's successor, I also saw several times, and I witnessed one of his operations, now numbering more than one hundred, for the radical cure of hernia, in the treatment of which he has earned great reputation, although the operation must, I doubt not, from its very nature, be followed by many relapses. I was surprised to find at this and other London hospitals a can of hot water still in use for warming adhesive plaster. On this side of the Atlantic the practice has been long discontinued—alcohol or chloroform applied upon a sponge having taken its place. In this way the plaster is instantly softened, and the patient incurs no risk of being scalded, as he was by the old method.

At Guy's Hospital I was kindly received by Messrs. Cock, Hilton, Bryant, and Le Gros Clark, the last of whom took special pains to show me the surgical wards, the lecture-rooms, and the grand museum, illustrated by the labors of Sir Astley Cooper, Hodgin, and a host of able and enthusiastic workers in the interest of healthy and morbid anatomy. The collections are especially rich in preparations of the different varieties of hernia, fractures, and dislocations, and of affections of the mammary gland. Clark has added many interesting dissections of the descent of the testis, and Bryant numerous specimens removed from the living subject with his knife. At the time of my visit, Cock had opened the bladder through the perineum upwards of forty times for retention of urine. Truly a really skilful surgeon might have done better than this! The old hospital building has a dirty, dilapidated appearance, with low ceilings, and should be replaced by a new one. The annual income of the institution is nearly half a million of dollars. A bronze statue of Guy stands in the front yard of the hospital.

We bade adieu to London on the 8th of September, and took the train for Leeds, where we arrived at three o'clock in the afternoon. The day was cold and cloudy, and the country through which we passed not particularly inviting to a stranger. I had been induced to visit Leeds mainly at the instance of Mr. Nunnelly, the eminent surgeon, whose acquaintance I had formed at Oxford at the meeting of the British Medical Association, and with whose writings and reputation I had long been familiar. His work on Erysipelas, the ablest ever published on the subject, had served to make his name widely known in the United States. The occasion of my visit was rendered the more interesting by the fact that the town was full of strangers

attracted thither by a great fair held for the benefit of the
Leeds Hospital, an immense establishment, erected at an
expense of nearly one million of dollars.   No pains had
been spared to render the fair, which was held in the new
edifice, a success, and yet, while it was perfect in all
its details, it was, I was told, pecuniarily a failure.   Many
of the finest paintings in the kingdom were on exhibition, and the display of water-colors by Turner and his
school was indeed most beautiful.   Halle, the morning
after our arrival, gave a grand concert, which was largely
attended by a select audience.   During the day Mr. Nunnelly exsected a mammary gland, an operation in which,
instead of ligatures, he used small compressing forceps for
arresting the flow of blood, four of the instruments being retained in the wound to be removed at the end of forty-eight
hours.   He informed me that he had adopted this plan
for several years, in nearly all cases involving extensive
dissection, and that the results had been highly flattering.
In the afternoon he drove me through the town, and
showed me, among other objects of interest, the Leeds
Medical School, one of the best provincial colleges in
England.   The building, although small, was well arranged and well equipped, and seemed to be well adapted
to its purposes.   We also visited the old Infirmary, the
scene for so many years of the labors and achievements
of the elder Hey and of the elder Teale, men whose
mantles rest gracefully upon the shoulders of their sons.
Bidding farewell to Mr. Nunnelly and his family, we left
Leeds, after a sojourn of two days, for Edinburgh, stopping
on our way to take a glance at the ancient city of York,
so interesting on account of its numerous historical associations, its grand cathedral founded in 625, Clifford's Tower,
the ruins of St. Mary's Abbey, and its pretty museum
filled with various Roman and Saxon remains.   Here we
again had the pleasure of meeting Dr. and Mrs. Acland,
who, like ourselves, were engaged in examining the con-

tents of this old curiosity shop, as York, from the great variety of its ancient treasures, may not inappropriately be called. The day was delicious, and we enjoyed every moment of it.

We reached Edinburgh at early twilight, Friday, September 10th, and took lodgings at the Edinburgh Hotel, Princes Street, near the station. My first object the next morning was to call upon Mr. Syme, the celebrated surgeon, whose acquaintance I had made at Oxford nearly two months previously. Fortunately he was already in his consulting-room. As the servant opened the door he was standing with his back toward a large fire—for the morning was unusually chilly for the season—evidently absorbed in deep meditation; but the moment he espied me he approached and extended his hand, cordially welcoming me to Edinburgh. After an interchange of a few civilities Mr. Syme said, "Dr. Gross, what are your plans for to-day?" In reply I said, "I have come to Edinburgh to pay you my respects and to see you perform some operations, to inspect the more interesting objects in your beautiful city, and to make the acquaintance of the author of Rab and His Friends." "Very well; tell Mrs. Gross I shall be at your hotel at twelve o'clock to drive you round Arthur's Seat; and if you will dine with me at six o'clock this evening you shall see the author of Rab and His Friends." Punctually, almost to the minute, the carriage, drawn by two beautiful gray horses, with a servant in livery, was at the door of the hotel. The next three hours were spent in pleasant drives and delightful conversation, Mr. Syme taking particular pains to point out to us every object worthy of notice, especially the ruins of Holyrood Abbey, with whose melancholy historical associations we had of course been long familiar, but which, now that we stood upon the very spot itself, were invested with new and increased interest.

The dinner hour having arrived, we found ourselves at

Millbank, the country residence of the great surgeon, two miles from Edinburgh, in a beautiful and quiet spot, situated upon a sloping hill, laid off in well-arranged terraces, ornamented with trees and shrubbery, and furnished with ample conservatories. Dr. John Brown had already arrived, and the conversation at once assumed a free and easy character, without any of the restraint so common even among well-bred persons who are brought together for the first time. Mr. and Mrs. Syme presided with dignity, and the two hours during which we sat at the table passed rapidly and pleasantly. Dr. Brown was quite agreeable, and conversed fluently upon a variety of subjects, but without any brilliancy, wit, or humor. He was, in fact, rather sedate than otherwise, as if he might have been somewhat jaded by the labors of the day; he talked well, and nothing more. In stature he is nearly six feet, rather stout, with a lofty but too receding forehead, and a countenance literally beaming with benevolence. He well deserves the title of "Good Doctor John," by which he is generally known among the poorer classes of Edinburgh, many of whom he attends, pay or no pay.

The story of Rab and His Friends has been widely read and much admired, and has made the name of John Brown familiar on both sides of the Atlantic. A beautifully illustrated edition of it was issued some years ago in Boston. It is said that the entire story was composed at one sitting, and I can readily believe the statement; for a man who could write so prettily must have been brimful of his subject. Altogether it is one of the most pathetic and interesting books in the English language, written in a style at once elevated and vivid. No one can read it without feelings of admiration for the noble dog, the warmest respect for James, and the deepest sympathy for poor Ailie. The surgeon who figures in the story is no other than Mr. Syme, John Brown's preceptor and particular friend. Before leaving Edin-

burgh the author kindly called at our lodgings with a copy
of this work inscribed, "Mrs. Gross, with the author's
compliments, September, 1868." Dr. Brown has written
many stories besides Rab and His Friends, but none which
have been more admired, or which display a finer literary
taste or more happy descriptive powers. His collected
writings are comprised, for the most part, in his Horæ
Subsecivæ, published in 1858, and embrace a large
amount of valuable and interesting matter, presented in
an agreeable and graphic style. A strain of piety which
well befits the son of a Scotch clergyman pervades all his
writings.

But it is high time to return to our dinner, which,
although now cold, was well served, and, if not seasoned
with wit and humor, was set off with some choice fruit
from Mr. Syme's extensive conservatories. The peaches,
with a skin as soft and delicate as the finest satin, were
delicious, large, juicy, and high-flavored, such as I had not
met with before in Europe; and the pineapples would
have delighted the palate of a refined epicure. The banana was not in season, but oranges and lemons graced
the table and hung in beautiful clusters upon the trees.
Mr. Syme was proud of his exotics, and spent daily more
or less time in his greenhouses, which must have been a
source of not a little expense to him. Millbank, when he
purchased it in 1840, was a comparatively unsightly spot,
but taste and money soon improved it, and eventually
converted it into a paradise, fit for the occupancy of the
family of such a man. It was here that he delighted to
entertain his friends, generally limiting himself to a few
choice spirits; for, owing to his retiring disposition, he
disliked large parties. Prominent strangers, especially
members of the medical profession, always found a welcome seat at his table.

Mr. Syme occupied a conspicuous place among his contemporaries. In surgery he had no superior, not merely as

an operator, or as a man skilled in the use of the knife, but as a surgical pathologist, diagnostician, and therapeutist. With his great contemporary, Robert Liston, he shared the honor of reviving the flap amputation, originally suggested by Lowdham, of Oxford, towards the close of the seventeenth century ; and with another not less illustrious man, Sir William Fergusson, the honor of reviving excision of the joints, until then almost forgotten. He was the first to perform Chopart's operation in Great Britain, and he is exclusively entitled to the credit of pointing out the practicability and safety of amputation at the ankle-joint, now an established procedure in surgery. He revived, and successfully practised in numerous cases, the perineal section for the cure of callous or impassable strictures; and he was the first in modern times to lay open the sac of a carotid, an iliac, and a gluteal aneurism, to turn out the clots, and to apply a ligature to each end of the diseased vessel—achievements until recently without a parallel in the annals of surgery. The only operation which I saw Mr. Syme perform during my sojourn in Edinburgh was that of trephining the tibia for an abscess in its cavity, in a middle-aged man who had for fourteen years been a victim to severe neuralgic pain. The instrument was not in good order, and the operation was therefore more than ordinarily tedious, although successful.

As a writer, Mr. Syme was felicitous, his thoughts being always well chosen, and conveyed in a clear, terse, vigorous style. He is best known by his Principles of Surgery, which was published soon after his entrance into the profession, and which was enlarged and improved in each succeeding edition. The best edition of his works, embracing a complete collection of his monographs, was issued by J. B. Lippincott & Co. of Philadelphia, in 1866, under the editorial supervision of a former pupil, Dr. Donald Maclean, the present Professor of Surgery at Ann Arbor Uni-

versity, Michigan. As a contributor to the periodical press
his pen was seldom idle, and he was for some time editor
of the Edinburgh Medical and Surgical Journal. Early
in life he had a decided taste for chemistry, and made the
important discovery that distilled coal-tar is a ready sol-
vent of caoutchouc, a discovery which was soon afterwards
utilized by Mackintosh in the manufacture of waterproof
cloth. Many distinguished honors were conferred upon
Mr. Syme both at home and abroad. He was Surgeon-in-
Ordinary to the Queen in Scotland, member of the General
Medical Council, and for nearly a third of a century Professor of Clinical Surgery in the University of Edinburgh.
In stature he was about the middle height, well-formed,
with a countenance somewhat indicative of melancholy.
In his younger days he must have been a handsome man.
It has been said that Mr. Syme was not amiable, and, considering the many quarrels in which he was engaged, we
find some ground for such a statement. His biographer,
Dr. Robert Patterson, asserts that he was a somewhat
peculiar man, with much acuteness and sagacity, and
quite obstinate. It must be remembered that the medical
polemics of the Scotch capital was for a long time in the
worst possible condition; that there was often great jealousy among rival candidates for office; and that Mr.
Syme was not unfrequently a target for bitter and un-
founded innuendoes. Surely, under such circumstances,
one's temper must sometimes give way. A man who loves
children and flowers cannot be unamiable, much less bad,
and Mr. Syme loved both. He was at all times rather
reserved in his manner, but when warmed up by the occasion he was an agreeable companion. His friends and
pupils were greatly attached to him, and loud in their praise
of his virtues, his intelligence, and his accomplishments.
John Brown, who was his devoted follower and life-long
admirer, in inscribing to him one of his publications, has
pithily portrayed his old master's chief characteristics—

Verax, capax, perspicax, sagax, efficax, tenax. He adds: "It has been happily said of him that he never wastes a word, or a drop of ink, or a drop of blood; and his is the strongest, exactest, truest, immediatest, safest intellect, dedicated by its possessor to the surgical cure of mankind, I have ever yet met with." Death overtook the great surgeon in June, 1870, in the seventy-first year of his age, in consequence of a second attack of apoplexy.

Soon after the death of Professor Syme his old pupils and friends took active measures to raise a suitable memorial to him. Among these friends, the most enthusiastic, perhaps, was Dr. Charles Murchison, of London. Knowing the warm regard which I felt for his former preceptor, this gentleman addressed to me a letter upon the subject. He begged me to interest myself with the principal surgeons of the United States in furtherance of the object, and forwarded to me at the same time copies of a printed circular, fully setting forth the wishes of the London committee in charge of the matter. The design was to make the memorial international. Altogether I obtained about twenty subscribers, each contributing ten dollars. The memorial consisted of a marble bust of Mr. Syme, placed in the hall of the University of Edinburgh, and of a scholarship of one thousand pounds.

I cannot help subjoining the touching words of the good John Brown of Syme's last days: "I was the first," he says, "to see him when struck down by hemiplegia. It was in Shandwick Place, where he had his chambers— sleeping and enjoying his evenings in his beautiful Millbank, with its flowers, its matchless orchids and heaths and azaleas, its bananas and grapes and peaches; with Blackford Hill, where Marmion saw the Scottish host mustering for Flodden, in front, and the Pentlands, with Cairkelton Hill, their advanced guard, cutting the sky, its ruddy porphyry *scaur* holding the slanting shadows in its bosom. He was, as before said, in his room in Shandwick

Place, sitting in his chair, having been set up by his faithful Blackbell. His face was distorted. He said, 'John, this is the conclusion;' and so it was, to his and our and the world's sad cost. He submitted to his fate with manly fortitude, but he felt it to the uttermost—struck down in his prime, full of rich power, abler than ever to do good to man, his soul surviving his brain, and looking on at its ruins during many sad months. He became softer, gentler, more easily moved, even to tears; but the judging power, the perspicacity, the piercing to the core, remained untouched. Henceforward, of course, life was miserable. How he bore up against this, resigning his delights of teaching, of doing good to men, of seeing and of cherishing his students, of living in front of the world—how he accepted all this only those nearest to him can know. I have never seen anything more pathetic than when, near his death, he lay speechless, but full of feeling and mind, and made known in some inscrutable way to his old gardener and friend that he wished to see a certain orchid which he knew should be then in bloom. The big, clumsy, knowing Patterson, glum and victorious—he was forever getting prizes at the Horticultural—brought it in without a word. It was the very one—radiant in beauty, white, with a brown freckle, like Imogen's mole, and, like it, 'right proud of that more delicate lodging.' He gazed at it, and, bursting into a passion of tears, motioned it away as insufferable."

John Brown was a worshipper of James Syme. He evidently looked upon him as a superior being, as one worthy of the love and admiration not only of his pupils, but of mankind at large—as one endowed with the noblest attributes of human nature, and yet, perhaps, not wholly free from some of its failings.

I had been in Edinburgh more than two days before I had the good fortune to fall in with Sir James Y. Simpson, whose acquaintance I had made a short time previously at

Norwich during the meeting of the British Association for the Advancement of Science. I had called at his house, but as the day was Sunday I did not succeed in seeing him until Monday morning when he visited us at our lodgings; and after that time he was all kindness and attention during our week's sojourn, inviting us to breakfast, luncheon, dinner, and tea, so that we saw him generally several times a day. On these occasions there were always some agreeable and intelligent people at table; sometimes distinguished strangers from a great distance, or from foreign countries. The morning before we left he had at breakfast, to which he had kindly invited us, two Egyptian doctors, who had come purposely to Edinburgh to form his acquaintance. In fact, at his house there was a constant round of unostentatious hospitality. Sir James always had at command a fund of interesting anecdotes, and every guest felt quite at his ease. As a talker he was one of the most charming of men, always brimful of accounts of great personages, ghosts, murders, and church affairs. He seemed to be at home upon every subject. His house was a perfect caravansary, open at all times to everybody. How Lady Simpson bore all this strain was a marvel. One would suppose that it would have required the patience of a Job and the strength of a giantess to preside at such a board, and to undergo the incessant labor of pouring out the tea and of doing her share in entertaining. The house, without being elegant, was spacious and well arranged, and afforded a beautiful view of the city and of the Frith of Forth. Several rooms were set apart for the reception and examination of patients, who came to Sir James from all parts of the country, the Continent of Europe, the United States, and even the antipodes. Several hours in the morning and afternoon were generally spent in his consulting-rooms, where he was aided by one of his more advanced pupils and a well-trained female nurse. As might well be supposed, he was often called to patients at a distance from home. It was very common for him to run up to London and to return on the same day. Occasionally he went to Paris and to other Continental cities, always travelling in haste to economize time, so precious to a man of his active temperament and incessant occupation. For these excursions he usually received liberal fees; and yet I doubt whether, with all his large income from his practice, he left much of an estate. His family expenses must have been great. Besides, money was not his idol. He worshipped gods of a far more genial character.

In his appearance Simpson was as extraordinary as he was in his social and professional relations. The moment I cast my eye upon him at Norwich I recognized him from his strong resemblance to the photographs I had seen of him. He was of medium stature, with an enormous head, well covered with flowing locks, a light complexion, bright blue eyes, a well-shaped mouth, a short, thick neck, and broad shoulders, the whole set off by a countenance indicative of benevolence and intelligence. A glance was sufficient to convince us that we stood in the presence of a great man—a man who would have attained a conspicuous rank in any pursuit to which he might have devoted himself. Few men in any walk of life ever attained such eminence in so short a time, led so successful a career, or died so universally regretted. Born at Bathgate, Linlithgowshire, Scotland, in 1811, of humble parentage, he was, like many other illustrious men, the architect of his own fortune, and rose rapidly in public and professional favor until, in 1840, eight years after he received his medical degree at Edinburgh, he was elected Professor of Midwifery in his Alma Mater, a position which he filled with distinguished *éclat* up to the time of his death in 1870. During all this period, in which he stood side by side with such men as Syme, Bennett, Christison, and Goodsir, there was no one who did more than he to uphold the fame of that great and ancient school. He taught Midwifery as it had never been taught before at Edinburgh, and imparted to it an impulse felt throughout the civilized world. He placed gynæcology upon an elevated platform, and invested it with new resources. His contributions to both of these departments, mostly in the form of essays, are everywhere recognized as standard productions, and have been republished in this country and translated into different languages. In everything he undertook he was progressive, often original, always bold and decided. When the news reached him that ether had been used in America as an anæsthetic he at once employed it in his midwifery cases, and within a twelvemonth, solely by the aid of experiment, discovered the anæsthetic properties of chloroform. With such a mind as his, so active, so vigorous, so restless, it was impossible for him to be idle, or indifferent to the needs and improvements of medicine. Not content with the exactions and labors of his own profession, and deeply impressed with the truths of Christianity, he often spent the Sabbath in preaching and in other religious exercises; took an especial interest in the temperance cause, and busied himself in various ways in ameliorating the condition of the poorer classes. He devised a new process, known as acupressure, for the suppression of hemorrhage after surgical operations, upon which he published a learned and exhaustive treatise. Antiquarian researches occupied at one time much of his attention. Hospitalism, a term introduced by him to designate the hygienic conditions of hospitals, formed the subject of a series of elaborate and valuable papers among the later contributions from his prolific pen.

Simpson, like Syme, was the recipient of many honors, native and foreign. Every prominent medical and scientific society was anxious to enroll him among its members. In 1853 he was elected a foreign associate of the French

Academy of Medicine, which, three years later, awarded him the Monthyon Prize of two thousand francs for his discovery of the anæsthetic properties of chloroform. In 1868 the University of Oxford conferred upon him the degree of D. C. L. The Town Council of Edinburgh voted him the freedom of the city; and since his death a monument has been erected to his memory—an unnecessary undertaking for a man whose name is immortal. Knowing that he and Syme had long been on ill terms, I took good care not to mention in the presence of the one the name of the other. How their misunderstanding originated, I never learned. Syme detested Professor Miller, another of his colleagues, and a most estimable man.

Mr. Spence, the Professor of Surgery, received me very kindly, gave me a handsome luncheon, showed me the University buildings and some of his morbid preparations, and altogether impressed me as an amiable and estimable man. He was an excellent surgeon, but not a brilliant lecturer. He performed the hip-joint amputation nearly, or quite, a dozen times. His recent work upon surgery has not added anything to his reputation, owing to the fact that it is in arrear of the existing state of the science. Laycock, the professor of medicine, was out of town; and Professor Turner, an able anatomist and accomplished teacher, I had met at Oxford, at the table of Professor Rolleston. At the Royal Infirmary I saw Dr. Heron Watson perform lithotomy upon a middle-aged man, and was struck with the immense length of his external incisions. Upon inquiry, I found that this, unlike our own, was the ordinary Edinburgh practice.

Professor Christison, now a veteran in our ranks, whose great work on Poisons has given him a world-wide reputation, was, much to my regret, out of town. The late J. Hughes Bennett was also absent. I had, however, met him a short time before, first at Oxford, and subsequently at Norwich, where, in the medical section of the British Association for the Advancement of Science, I heard him read an abstract of his paper embodying the results of the experiments performed jointly by himself and others, known as the Edinburgh Committee, on the effects of mercury as a cholagogue. The subjects of these experiments were dogs, and the conclusion reached by the Committee was that mercury, in every form in which it is administered, fails to act upon the liver as a stimulant of the biliary secretion. It was my privilege to reply to some of the statements of Professor Bennett on the occasion, and, if I convinced no one else, I was myself perfectly satisfied that the inferences of the Committee were entirely fallacious as applied to the human subject. Every intelligent and observant practitioner on this continent knows that calomel will increase the secretion of bile, whatever effect it may produce upon the inferior animals. Bennett, who was a man of undoubted talents, an original observer, a good teacher, and an able writer, did not enjoy the reputation of being an amiable person. He was irritable, haughty, captious, overbearing, and quarrelsome—whether from constitutional vice, or as the result of ill health, of which he was long the subject, I am unable to say.

My visit to Edinburgh brought me into contact with several of the younger members of the profession, particularly Mr. Joseph Bell, a great-grandson of the celebrated Benjamin Bell, and Mr. Thomas Annandale, both men of surgical promise. Dr. James Miller, for a number of years Professor of Surgery in the University of Edinburgh, and the author of two excellent works on surgery well known in this country, had died only a short time before my visit, leaving behind him a son destined, it is hoped, to follow in the footsteps of his distinguished father.

The University of Edinburgh, founded by James VI., in 1582, has long been known as a great centre of medical science and medical education. In the last century it was rendered famous by the Monros, father and son, by Cullen,

1—38

and by Black, and in this century it presents a galaxy of names which the world will not willingly let die. Benjamin and John Bell, although never connected with the University, wrote and practised surgery here; and Barclay and Knox were great extramural teachers of anatomy. It was in the Scotch capital that that great triumvirate in surgery, Robert Liston, James Syme, and William Fergusson, laid the foundation of their future renown. It was here that Thompson first taught military surgery and wrote his immortal work on Inflammation; and it was here that, under the inspiration of the prelections of John Bell, Ephraim McDowell conceived the idea of the practicability of ovariotomy. It is worthy of note that the first professor of medicine in the University of Edinburgh was appointed in 1685. The University has recently augmented its reputation, owing mainly, I think, to its great clinical advantages, and now commands immense classes, students flocking to it from all parts of the world.

One of the great events during our stay at Edinburgh was the visit of General Lord Napier, the hero of Magdala, at the instance of the Town Council, who voted him the freedom of the city, and extended to him a public reception. The city was crowded with strangers, and the day was given up to amusement and recreation, most of the stores and public places being closed in honor of the occasion.

A singular fatality seems to have attended the families of two of our most distinguished Edinburgh friends. Within less than two years after our visit Mr. and Mrs. Syme and Sir James and Lady Simpson were numbered with the dead.

From Edinburgh to Glasgow the ride, which occupies only about two hours, extends over a somewhat hilly and unattractive country. We selected Maclean's Hotel. The next morning my son and myself sallied forth in quest of objects of interest, with Dr. George H. B. Macleod, the author of the well-known little work entitled Notes on the

Surgery of the Crimean War, republished by J. B. Lippincott & Co., of Philadelphia. Our first stopping-place was
the old Royal Infirmary, famous on account of the exploits
of Lowrie, Buchanan, and other surgeons, and as the
building in which Professor Lister, since transferred to
Edinburgh, first put in practice what is now known as his
dressing. From thence we walked to the University of
Glasgow, then to the Hunterian Anatomical Museum, and
finally down St. Giles Street to the city court-rooms in
order to see the judges and lawyers in their gowns and
wigs and to get a sight of the lower classes of people.
As we wandered along this celebrated thoroughfare, we
passed crowds of filthy, noisy persons, indulging in loud
talking and obscene language, and we were therefore
not a little glad when we found ourselves in a quiet and
orderly part of the city. Entering the court-room, we
were politely shown to seats, and an opportunity was thus
afforded us of observing the proceedings at our leisure. The
presiding judge, arrayed in his wig and red gown, was an
elderly man, who seemed to be thoroughly acquainted with
his business. The case before him was that of a young
man and his wife, who had been caught a few days before
in a crowd in St. Giles Street in the act of stealing a watch
worth probably ten or fifteen shillings. The evidence was
unmistakable, and the judge, without further ceremony,
gave each eight years in the penitentiary. Upon asking
one of the lawyers whether the sentence was not a severe
one, he said, "Not at all; both the prisoners are old jail-
birds." Other cases came up in rapid succession, mostly
of denizens of the famous street through which we had
passed only a short time before. The judges of this court
lodged at Maclean's Hotel, which, strange to say, was
guarded while they were in the house by several armed
men in uniform. In the morning they were carried away
in their wigs and robes in carriages, similarly guarded, and
brought back in the same manner after the adjournment

of the court.   Upon inquiry as to what all this meant, the answer was, "It is the custom."   "Are the judges in any danger of being assaulted or waylaid?"   "Certainly not."

The Hunterian Museum, the gift of the celebrated Dr. William Hunter, of London, is of itself worthy of a visit to Glasgow.   It is especially rich in anatomical preparations, in dissections of the healthy and gravid uterus, and in specimens of the fœtus and of the full-grown child, healthy and diseased.   It also contains a good collection of books, coins, pictures, and objects of natural history and comparative anatomy.   William Hunter was a brother of the great John Hunter, and a pupil of Dr. William Cullen— three illustrious names in medicine.   He was a native of Scotland, and for some time studied divinity, which, at the instance of Cullen, he abandoned for medicine, graduating at the University of Glasgow in 1750.   His career in London was successful.   He devoted himself chiefly to the practice of midwifery, in which he rapidly rose to distinction.   He was physician to the Queen, President of the College of Physicians, Fellow of the Royal Society, and Associate of the Academy of Medicine of Paris.   Besides his Medical Commentaries, published in 1762-'64, he left a work upon the Human Gravid Uterus, which was illustrated by splendid plates engraved from his own dissections.   He died in 1783.   It is said that the immediate cause of his death was exhaustion brought on during the delivery of an introductory lecture at a time when he should have been in his bed.   The effort was too great; he fainted, and never rallied.   Turning to a friend as he was passing away, he observed, "If I had strength enough to hold a pen, I would write how easy and pleasant a thing it is to die."

Having heard much of the Rev. Dr. Norman Macleod as a preacher, and having occasionally read a number of Good Words, Mrs. Gross, my son, and myself were desirous of seeing him in his own pulpit.   We accordingly went the Sunday after our arrival to Barony Parish Church, his brother, Dr. George H. B. Macleod, having, on the previous evening, kindly engaged seats for us in the family pew. The service was just beginning as we entered, the divine giving out the hymn in a voice at once clear, distinct, and euphonious. A devout prayer followed, then another hymn, and finally a sermon of great strength and beauty, full of strong, common sense, and delivered in the sweet persuasive tone so characteristic of the man. There was no attempt at oratory, no declamation, no excitement. The words, as they rolled from his mouth, in elegant and impressive sentences, fell gently and pleasantly upon the ear, and sank deeply into the heart and mind of the hearer. Looking at the preacher as he stood before his large congregation, earnestly expounding the great truths of the Gospel, one could not fail to be struck with his magnificent physique, his immense head, well covered with silvered hair, his well-formed mouth, and his noble features, denotive of the highest order of intellect and of the warmest, gentlest heart, in full sympathy with the whole human family. When the services were concluded he walked directly from the pulpit to our pew, shaking each of us cordially by the hand, and expressing much pleasure at seeing us. He added that he had many kind friends among my countrymen, and had received much attention during his late visit to America.

Norman Macleod was one of Christ's noblest ambassadors, a man of great versatility, full of knowledge, and a fine scholar. He was always engaged in benevolent enterprises, particularly among the poor, always liberal and tolerant, yet consistent and loyal to his own church. My heart warmly sympathized with his countrymen when, in 1872, the press announced the unwelcome news of his death. A great man had fallen in Israel, and Israel was clothed in sackcloth and mourning. He died at the age of sixty.

He was associated, as author, editor, and contributor, with many literary undertakings, and at the time of his death was chaplain to the Queen for Scotland. His Good Words enjoyed a wide circulation, and served an important purpose as an educational organ, especially with the more humble classes. An excellent Life of this good man was published in 1876 by his brother, Rev. Donald Macleod.

Of the influence which Macleod wielded over his congregation some idea may be formed from the fact that on one occasion, during the disruption controversy in Scotland, in 1843, he spoke to it for three hours and a half. "Not a soul," he says, "moved. Never did I see such an attentive audience." During the same year he wrote to his sister Jane, "I am very *dowie* and cast down—not because I am alone, for I love the bachelor life every day more and more, and delight in the independence with which I can rise, eat, read, write when I like!"

I had corresponded with Dr. George B. H. Macleod before I had the pleasure of making his personal acquaintance, and I had the gratification several years previously of announcing to him his election to membership in the College of Physicians of Philadelphia. At the time of my visit he was one of the surgeons of the Royal Infirmary of Glasgow, and Professor of Surgery in the Andersonian University, from which, since the appointment of Mr. Lister as the successor of Syme at Edinburgh, he has been transferred to the University of Glasgow, a more enviable and influential position. Like his late brother, he is a giant in mind as well as in body, of handsome appearance, upwards of six feet in height, well proportioned, an excellent operator, a popular teacher, and a clear, vigorous writer—one, in short, of those men who know how to perform every duty incumbent upon them. Frederick the Great would have given half of Silesia for a regiment of such men as the Macleods.

Since the above was penned I had the pleasure, in 1881,

of extending a warm welcome to Dr. Macleod at my own house, and of entertaining him along with a small number of friends invited to greet him. He was making a rapid tour of the country, with which and its wonderful enterprise, everywhere discernible, he expressed himself greatly delighted. He is unquestionably one of the strongest men in his particular sphere in Scotland.

In connection with my visit to Scotland I must refer to a circumstance which has always been to me a source of annoyance. Professor Pirrie, of Aberdeen, a great man, recently deceased, did me the honor to transfer from my work on Surgery to his a whole page, *verbatim et literatim,* of my remarks on the bite of the rattlesnake; and he did this without one particle of acknowledgment. Why he should have done it has always been to me a mystery, the more especially as he is an excellent writer, and thoroughly versed in the literature of the art and science of surgery. I should not have mentioned the matter at all in this autobiography were it not for the fact that others, not acquainted with it, might suppose me, and not my Scotch contemporary, to be at fault. An asterisk would have rendered such a reference unnecessary.

CHAPTER XI.

LEAVING Glasgow after a sojourn of three days, during
which we visited Loch Katrine and Loch Lomond, full
of weird associations and romantic scenery, we took the
steamer late in the afternoon for Ireland, passing down
the beautiful Clyde, and crossing the Irish Channel during
the night, reaching Belfast by daylight the next morning.
Taking an early breakfast we hurried off to the train for
Portrush, where we arrived after a ride of nearly three
hours over a dreary country, with now and then a fine
field and respectable house to break the monotony of the
sad sight. Hiring a jaunting-car, a one-horse vehicle
peculiar, I believe, to the Emerald Isle, we drove rapidly
over a pleasant road, much of it lying along the seacoast, to the Giant's Causeway, that wonderful natural
curiosity which is so well worthy of a visit, and which
has been so often and so well described by tourists. Many
romantic stories are told about this singular basaltic prom-
ontory, consisting, it is said, of nearly four thousand columns, each presenting the form of a crystal, with a smooth,
polished surface, three-sided in some, and nonagonal, or
nine-sided, in others. How far these columns extend in
depth is hardly a matter even of conjecture. The scene
is one of sublimity, and it is therefore not surprising that
in the estimation of the vulgar it should have been regarded as the work of the giants—whence its name.

Belfast presents few objects of interest to the medical tourist. Apart from its immense flax and cotton factories it is little known out of Europe. It has a beautiful botanical garden, and a large museum, worthy of inspection on account of its rich collection of Irish antiquities. Queen's College is a well-organized institution, embracing faculties of arts, science, literature, and medicine. The medical school has a convenient edifice, well arranged and equipped for efficient courses of instruction, and several of the professors are men of eminence. Dr. McCosh was for a number of years professor in its literary department; and it was fortunate for Princeton and the United States that he was decoyed away from an institution in which he had no opportunity of exercising those remarkable executive abilities which have raised Nassau Hall, within less than ten years, from a third-rate or fourth-rate seminary to one of the most respectable colleges in the land.

The Belfast Hospital is an old edifice, but its interior is kept in excellent condition, and the medical and surgical staffs are men of ability, intent upon the performance of their duties. Before leaving the city, I called upon Mr. William MacCormac, a promising and highly-educated young surgeon, whom I met a few weeks previously at Oxford at the meeting of the British Medical Association, and who extended to me a genuine Irish welcome.

The journey from Belfast to Dublin occupies nearly three hours and a half, the distance being one hundred miles. The road passes over a lovely rolling country, interspersed with numerous towns and villages, and the views impress one favorably with the industry and resources of the Irish people. On arriving in the Irish capital an American traveller almost instinctively tells the coachman to drive to the Shelbourne, which is a clean, well-kept hotel, and situated immediately opposite Stephen's Green, or what in Philadelphia would be called Stephen's Square, convinced that he will meet with some of his countrymen, with whom the house is a great favorite. Dublin is admirably situated, and in point of beauty is inferior to no city in Great Britain, Edinburgh not excepted. To an American it is quite attractive, apart from the elegance of its many private residences, for the very atmosphere is full of historical associations. Trinity College, founded in the reign of Elizabeth, is known the world over as a great Protestant educational institution, the Alma Mater of thousands of distinguished scholars, representing all the learned professions, politics, statesmanship, the army and navy, poetry, wit, humor, and authorship. A degree from this college has always been esteemed a high honor. Its medical department has embraced many able men. Indeed, Dublin has long been celebrated for its physicians, surgeons, and obstetricians, constituting what is known everywhere as the "Irish School"—not, I think, excelled by any learned body in the world. Among the famous living representatives at the time of my visit, in 1868, were Stokes, Kennedy, Jacobs, Robert Smith, Adams, Beatty, Sir William R. Wilde, Churchill, O'Farral, Sir Dominic John Corrigan, Bart., Tufnell, Butcher, George Porter, MacDonnell, and Maurice Collis. The dead embrace a long list of illustrious names, such as Carmichael, Colles, Wilmot, Crampton, Graves, Harrison, William H. Porter, Rynd, Macartney, Houston, Marsh, Montgomery, and Bellingham. The medical press of Dublin has been prolific in meritorious productions. The works of Robert J. Graves and William Stokes alone are sufficient to impart a distinctive character to any medical school. Carmichael and Colles laid the foundation of much of our knowledge of the nature and treatment of syphilitic diseases ; Montgomery and Kennedy have excellently illustrated the diagnosis of pregnancy ; Robert Smith has written the ablest monograph on fractures of the joints, and Robert Adams the best on rheumatic gout, in any language ; the works of Collins and Beatty on midwifery are largely quoted by contemporary writers. Sir William R. Wilde's treatise on aural diseases was for a long time the most scientific work upon the subject ; the work of William Henry Porter on the larynx is consulted by everybody in quest of information respecting the affections of that organ. In medical journalism Dublin occupies a high position. The Dublin Journal of Medicine has enjoyed a brilliant career, and comprises much of the best periodical literature that has appeared in Great Britain during the present century. The ablest men in the Irish profession have contributed to its success. It may be observed, in general terms, that the works which have emanated from the Dublin school are characterized by originality, by force of expression, and by elegant scholarship. The treatises of Graves and Stokes are specimens of the highest class of authorship.

In the treatment of aneurism the Dublin surgeons are entitled to the highest praise. Until near the middle of the present century no advances had been made of any really important character in the management of this disease since the days of John Hunter. In 1847 appeared the monograph of Dr. O'Bryen Bellingham, entitled Observations on Aneurism, and its Treatment by Compression —a work which speedily imparted a new impulse to this branch of surgery. Mechanical compression by means of well-constructed clamps in great measure superseded the use of the ligature, and led to other important modifications of treatment, especially digital compression and forced flexion, by which numerous cases of this disease, even aneurism of the abdominal aorta, have since been cured. It had occasionally been employed prior to the period in question ; but it remained for the Dublin surgeons, especially Bellingham and Tufnell, by a course of carefully-conducted, philosophical observations, to place the treatment upon a scientific basis.

Dublin abounds in hospitals. The principal ones are Stevens's, the Richmond, Meath, Mercer's, Sir Patrick

Dun's, and St. Vincent's, the last being in charge of the Sisters of Charity. Stevens's Hospital, founded in 1720 by Dr. Stevens, contains three hundred and fifty beds, and is situated near the insane asylum founded by Dean Swift; Stella having been a contributor to it, and the Dean himself having, if I mistake not, been for a while an inmate. The Meath Hospital, so celebrated as the theatre of the labors and observations of Graves, Stokes, Cusack, Crampton, W. H. Porter, Maurice Collis, and others, is an ordinary-looking building, situated in the outskirts of the city, on a lot originally belonging to the Earl of Meath, whence its name. It has one hundred and fifteen beds, and is provided with a well-arranged lecture and operating room. It was in this hospital, a few years ago, that Maurice Collis, an eminent young surgeon, the author of an excellent work on cancer, in removing a scirrhous mammary gland, accidentally received a wound on his finger which caused pyæmia and death. The Richmond Hospital is connected with what is known as the Carmichael School of Medicine, and is an old but well-managed institution. The younger Stokes, who, instead of following in the footsteps of his father, is rapidly building up a surgical reputation, and Dr. Robert Adams, at the time seventy-four years of age, but still hale and vigorous, showed me everything of interest. The operating-room is small but convenient. The museum contains many valuable pathological specimens, among others one in which both femoral arteries had been tied in the same subject after an interval, if I mistake not, of seventeen years. It is particularly rich in preparations and casts of chronic arthritis, from which Mr. Adams copied the admirable drawings and plates which illustrate his work upon that disease. Sir Patrick Dun's Hospital was founded by a noted physician of that name, who bequeathed to it his large fortune. The building, situated in the vicinity of Trinity College, has a granite front, and is one of the neatest institutions of the kind in the metropolis.

Connected with the hospital is a training-school for nurses, under the supervision of Miss Probyn, who gave me much useful information upon a subject in which I felt at the time deeply interested, and presented me, on parting, some valuable printed documents.

Of the eleemosynary institutions in Dublin none interested me so much as the Rotunda, or Dublin Lying-in Hospital, kindly shown me by Dr. Evory Kennedy, the attending physician, or, as he is generally called, the Master. It is a noble edifice, extending along one of the principal streets one hundred and twenty-five feet, and it is provided with every comfort and convenience for the treatment of destitute parturient women, the number of admissions annually being upwards of two thousand. The rooms, although not spacious, are neat and well ventilated, and are frequently whitewashed. In fact, every possible precaution is used to keep them in a salubrious condition. The result is that the mortality is uncommonly slight. The Master is assisted by six resident students and by eight female obstetricians—the latter of whom, in addition to the duties of the house, attend to out-door patients. The hospital, owing to the manner in which it is managed, enjoys a wide reputation; and numerous pupils, both native and foreign, are drawn here by the four courses of obstetric lectures which are annually delivered by the Master in virtue of his official position. Dr. Evory Kennedy, widely known by his writings, is an accomplished obstetrician. He is a tall, slender, elderly gentleman, with a fine head and face, and of winning manners. It was my good fortune to renew my acquaintance with him in 1872, at the meeting of the British Medical Association at Birmingham, and it was not easy to resist his tempting and urgent solicitations to accompany him to his home in Dublin. The Rotunda was founded in 1751 by Dr. Mosse, a wealthy and benevolent gentleman, whose marble bust is in the hall.

Dublin has an excellent ophthalmic hospital, founded by Sir William R. Wilde, under whose direction it was for a long time mainly managed. It has room for thirty-six beds, and is provided with a neat operating and lecture room and all the requisite conveniences for the examination and treatment of diseases of the eye. Sir William continues to extract cataract by the old method, looking upon Graefe's process by iridectomy as an unnecessary and absurd innovation.

It will be seen from the foregoing remarks that not fewer than four of the Dublin hospitals were founded by medical men, three of whom—Stevens, Mosse, and Sir Patrick Dun—devoted their entire estates to their endowment. Such noble benefactions deserve the highest praise, for who can estimate the amount of good which they are daily doing to the sick poor? Nearly all the hospitals in the Irish metropolis are connected with medical schools, and hence they are in no small degree contributory to the advancement of scientific medical and surgical education. The rivalry which must necessarily exist among them is in itself a powerful incentive to a generous ambition and salutary exertion. As the classes are generally small, the teaching and the opportunities for improvement must be more effective than in larger institutions. Is not this the reason why Dublin has so many excellent physicians, surgeons, and obstetricians? Every man connected with such a hospital, if he is good for anything at all, becomes at once an observer of disease and a teacher of youth— two powerful factors in the acquisition of reputation. There must be considerably more than one hundred men in Dublin who are daily occupied in this manner of receiving knowledge and imparting it to others.

I am indebted to Mr. George Porter for an opportunity of inspecting the museum of the Royal College of Surgeons, situated in a beautiful part of the city, directly opposite Stephen's Green. The building is in the Doric style, with a granite front, and is surmounted by the statues of Minerva, Hygeia, and Æsculapius. The hall is adorned with excellent busts of Dease, Cusack, Colles, Carmichael, Kirby, Crampton, Charles Hawkes Todd, William H. Porter, Bellingham, Power, and other surgeons. The library comprises more than twenty thousand volumes; and the museum, contained in three separate rooms, the largest of which is eighty-four feet long by thirty in width, is rich in valuable specimens, exhibiting healthy, pathological, and comparative anatomy. There is also a fine collection of wax preparations, the work chiefly of French artists—the gift, I was told, of the Duke of Northumberland. The lecture-rooms and the dissecting-rooms are among the best I have ever seen. Many prominent physicians and surgeons of Dublin have been teachers in this institution. It was incorporated in 1784, and, although it received liberal aid from Parliament, its success was mainly due to the influence and labors of the late Dr. Renny, Director-General of Military Hospitals. The College of Physicians has a fine edifice, a good library, and excellent rooms, adorned with portraits of some of its more noted members.

We happened to be in Dublin during the meeting of the clergy to consider the question of Mr. Gladstone's bill for the disestablishment of the Irish church. The meeting, presided over by the Archbishop of Dublin, was held in a large edifice near Stephen's Green, and was attended by persons of the highest respectability from all parts of Ireland. There was a great deal of speaking, but little which was good, or which seemed to me to be to the point. Questions as to order were of frequent occurrence, and occasionally there was a great deal of merriment, interspersed with hisses and loud and even boisterous talking. Much confusion often prevailed, and it was, apparently, almost impossible for the chairman to preserve order. The meeting was in session nearly a week.

The passage of the Premier's bill hardly disappointed any one out of Ireland. To show the folly of feeding the Irish clergy, as had been so long the practice of the English church, I may mention that I met at dinner at the house of a friend one of these gentry from the interior of the country, who had for more than forty years received annually more than three thousand dollars for his charge of a parish which had never had at any one time as many as twenty communicants. To use his own expression, his parish was "steeped in Catholicism." It was distressing, of course, to throw such a man out of employment, and hence it is not surprising that he and hundreds of others in similar circumstances should have died hard.

I had met Sir William R. Wilde at Oxford some time before my arrival in Dublin, and was therefore glad to renew my acquaintance with him at his own house. A more generous, warm-hearted man it would have been hard to find in her Majesty's three kingdoms, or any one who possessed more general intelligence, or had acquired a higher position as an aurist and an oculist. He was a steady worker, an enthusiast in everything he undertook. His writings, whether in book-form, or contributions to the periodical press, whether relative to general medicine, to his own specialties, or to purely literary or scientific investigations, are scholarly productions, evincing unusual powers of observation, patient research, and critical acumen. His treatise on the ear is a classical work. His statistics of deaf-mutism were collected with great pains, and had the effect of bringing his name prominently before the British government, as well as before the different nations of Europe. It was in consideration of the time, labor, and talents bestowed upon this important subject that the Queen was induced to confer upon him the honor of knighthood, without however a baronetcy. Many of his leisure hours in the latter part of his life were devoted to antiquarian researches, in which he made some important discoveries. The discourse upon the Antiquities of Ireland, which he delivered before the British Association for the Advancement of Science at its meeting at Belfast in August, 1874, attracted much attention, on account of its learning, the force and elegance of its diction, and its philosophical deductions.

Sir Dominic John Corrigan, Bart., occupies a high position in Dublin as a physician and as a man of intellect. Soon after my arrival he kindly invited me to dine with him at his country residence some miles from the city; but a previous engagement prevented me from accepting his courtesy—a circumstance which I much regretted, as the company which I was to meet was a select one, composed of prominent doctors and Irish gentlemen. Sir Dominic is a baronet, a man of wealth, and is in large practice. He has a noble physique. Besides his lectures on the Nature of Fever, and some minor publications, he has been a large contributor to Forbes's Cyclopedia of Practical Medicine and to the periodical press. As a writer he is clear and full of his subject, and on occasion a sharp critic. In his address on Medicine delivered before the British Medical Association at its meeting at Dublin, in 1867, he indulged in some harsh and unjust remarks respecting the American medical profession, which at the time led to caustic comments on this side of the Atlantic, and for which we have hardly yet forgiven him. Some years ago a strong effort was made to secure Sir Dominic a seat in Parliament, either as a representative of the medical profession or of the Irish universities; but, although the medical press and a number of the more prominent secular papers of the Irish metropolis strongly advocated his claims, he was not elected. Had he succeeded, he would have proved a powerful champion in promoting the interests of medical reform and of the public health. His ability, his experience, his strong common-sense, and his independent bearing would have well fitted him for such a task.

During the meeting of the British Medical Association at Oxford, in 1868, I made the acquaintance of Dr. William Stokes, a man of world-wide reputation as an author and as an original observer, and occupied a seat near him on the platform at the annual dinner. Called upon to reply to a toast, he rose slowly, passed his hand over his "gastricism," and said, "Mr. Chairman, I am very much in the condition of an American Indian,—'belly full, head empty.'" And, true enough, the learned doctor, the great physician, the LL. D., and the recently made D. C. L. of Oxford, had nothing to say which was not commonplace. His remarks were quite dull, and his manner was devoid of everything that might have been expected from an Irishman. I take for granted that Dr. Stokes was never a great lecturer, although he has unquestionably been a superior teacher. He took his degree at Edinburgh in 1825, and appeared to be a well-preserved gentleman. I presume that he is one of those men who are never idle. His numerous works show him to be a man of uncommon industry, of close observation, and of great powers of analysis. As a diagnostician and medical practitioner it is but just to say that he has no superior. His work on Diseases of the Chest, his treatise on Diseases of the Heart, his lectures on the Theory and Practice of Medicine, and his lectures on Fever are characterized by sterling excellence, and form an enduring record of his ability. He is the most prolific medical author Ireland has produced ; and everything he has written is based essentially upon the cases treated by him in the celebrated Meath Hospital.

We returned from Europe on the 15th of October, 1868, after an absence of five months. We hardly touched the shore before I was told that my medical friends, graduates of the College, chiefly young men, had determined, as a testimony of their affection and esteem, to give Professor Pancoast, who had been absent nearly one year, and myself a public reception in the foyer of the Academy of Music. As all the arrangements had been made before the news was divulged to us, it was in vain to remonstrate, and the reception accordingly came off on Saturday, October 24th. Dr. Ellwood Wilson, the well-known obstetrician, was chairman of the committee, and Dr. Frank F. Maury, secretary. The greeting was presented in an able address by Dr. Addinell Hewson. Several hundred ladies and gentlemen were in attendance, such as J. Marion Sims, Eliott, Sayre, the Flints, Dalton, James R. Wood, John L. Atlee, Askew of Delaware, and Kinloch of Charleston. A number of distinguished physicians had come from New York, Pennsylvania, and other States. There were also present prominent members of the bar and pulpit, representatives of the navy, of the press, and of the mercantile community. Hassler's band discoursed sweet music; the Academy was admirably lighted; the ladies were in their best toilettes; and the whole scene was one of great beauty and brilliancy. After the addresses were over an elegant and costly supper was served. An abundance of champagne added greatly to the hilarity of an occasion which, while my family and friends fully appreciated it, I shall never forget. The compliment was as flattering as it had been unexpected; and I was as glad to share it with Pancoast and his family, as, I know, he was glad to share it with me and my family. No jealousies ever existed between that good man and me. We had worked together shoulder to shoulder for thirteen years for the good of the school, and no unkind word had ever passed between us. Our pupils knew this well, and the compliment they had in store for us was therefore so much the more gratifying to all concerned.

The Public Ledger of October 27th, in giving a report

of this flattering reunion, uses the following language: "It was graceful, because it was an appropriate tribute to high merit, an unmistakably sincere expression of deep regard from their professional brethren, not only of this city but of our great sister cities, and a heart-warm token of affection from student to teacher, from the entered apprentices of the healing craft to the great masters of the science. The festival was also graced by the presence of ladies, whose brilliant costumes and brighter faces gave a charm to the occasion that could have been produced in no other way. The whole affair had heart and meaning in it."

In response to an address of welcome by Dr. Addinell Hewson, I spoke as follows:

"Allow me, Mr. President, to thank you most cordially for the kind words just addressed to me through your eloquent spokesman, and for the enthusiastic manner in which they have been received by your distinguished guests. Such a welcome is eminently grateful to our feelings, and it is difficult for me to find language to express my own sense of gratitude. The announcement, soon after my arrival from Europe, that it was the intention of the alumni and pupils of my Alma Mater to give my colleague, Professor Pancoast, and myself a public reception took me, I confess emphatically, by surprise. I was wholly unprepared for such an honor. Now that I stand in the presence of this large assembly of my fellow-citizens, members of the learned professions, the mercantile community, and the various walks of literature, the arts, and sciences, the question naturally arises, What have I done to merit this distinguished honor? Is it because I was temporarily absent in Europe? Is it because of anything good or great that I did before I went abroad? If I were a great general, just returned from the battlefield covered with glory and crowned with laurels, I could readily comprehend the reason for such a mark of your attention. But I am neither a warrior nor a statesman, and have not been in any battle, nor did I during my absence negotiate any treaty of peace, of amity, or of commerce with any foreign power. I went abroad and returned as a common citizen, proud, it is true, of my profession and of my country.

"But although I am neither a warrior nor a statesman, nor able to lay claim to any great discovery or improvement in my profession, I may confidently assert, without fear of successful contradiction, that there is no man who has watched that profession with a more jealous eye, or who has taken a deeper interest in its prosperity, its honor, and its dignity than I have. My loyalty and devotion have never flagged. In all my intercourse I have never wilfully wronged any human being, or done aught to cast discredit upon its escutcheon. What Strabo said of the poet is equally true of the physician; no bad man can be the one or the other. I have ever scrupulously respected the Hippocratic oath.

"It was but a few weeks ago that I had the pleasure of witnessing the proceedings and ceremonies attendant upon the presentation of the freedom of the city of Edinburgh to General Lord Napier, with whose exploits in Abyssinia, in asserting the supremacy of the British army, every one is familiar. It was pleasant to see the enthusiasm with which this distinguished soldier was welcomed, and the kindly feeling which was from all sides showered upon him. Though he could not lay claim to the honor of being a native of the city, he was nevertheless greeted as a countryman, and the highest civic distinction in the gift of the Scotch metropolis, so renowned for its illustrious citizens, was freely awarded to him for the great and signal services he had rendered his native land. The swelling emotions which animated the breast of the hero of Magdala as he stood before that grand audience assembled to do him honor were not greater than those which I experience upon this occasion. The wreath which entwined his brow was not dearer to him than this free offering of your esteem and kindness is to me. I have accepted this honor at your hands because, as was so gracefully expressed in the invitation of your gifted young secretary, it was designed as an exhibition of the love and veneration felt for me by my professional brethren, especially by the alumni and pupils of a great medical college with whose interests and prosperity my own have been closely identified for the last thirteen years; an institution which may boast of a noble parentage—of belonging, in fact, to one of the 'first families,' the daughter of a school of which any land might justly be proud. I refer to the University of Pennsylvania.

"I have accepted this honor because it is the highest tribute which a man can receive from his fellow-citizens and from the members of our own profession. I need not say how deeply sensible I am of your kindness. I rejoice to be again in the midst of those with whom I have so long labored to uphold the honor and dignity of our noble profession, and in whose personal success I shall ever feel a deep, nay, let me add, a parental interest. It is to me no less gratifying than it is true, to be able to say that, during my visit abroad, where I had an opportunity of seeing many of our most distinguished brethren in the Old World, I saw no more able, learned, or skilful practitioners, teachers, and writers than are assembled here to-night. I think, sir, that if a traveller learned nothing more than to appreciate fully his country's greatness, he would be amply compensated for the peril and expense of his voyage across the Atlantic. As God made woman more beautiful and perfect than man, because He created her last, so He endowed this continent—this last and best gift to the human race—with beauty and perfection nowhere visible in the Old World.

"Every one acknowledges with a hearty free will the extraordinary activity and enterprise of our physicians and surgeons and the rapid strides which we are developing in our national literature. Chassaignac, the great French surgeon, said to my honored colleague and myself, in one of our visits to the famous Lariboisière Hospital, 'You have just reason to be proud of your country. America at this moment wields the surgical sceptre of the world.' Our military surgeons have no equals. The reports of the Surgeon-General of the United States are read with avidity, and American works on medicine and surgery are used in the medical libraries of Europe.

"Although it would not be fair to judge a man's knowledge by the number of books he reads, yet there can be no doubt that the more labor of this kind which he performs, the more likely is his intelligence to be complete. It was pleasing to hear our profession spoken of in terms of high respect and commendation. As a nation, America commands admiration. The works of Kent and Story are in every lawyer's library in Great Britain; and the writings of Barnes, Hodge, Channing, and other divines are to be found on the shelves of England, Scotland, and Ireland.

"It may be recollected that I was commissioned at the last meeting of the American Medical Association at Washington to represent that body in the British Medical Association at its meeting last August at Oxford. That meeting was largely attended; many of the members were men of great eminence and learning, and every opportunity was embraced by them to speak in the kindest manner of their American brethren. Our delegates received a hearty welcome, and everything was done to make them comfortable and happy during their sojourn at that great seat of learning. From what transpired, there is reason to believe that the Association will now be annually represented on this side of the water.

"There is one thing that strikes an American in viewing the great literary and scientific and charitable institutions of Europe with admiration such as he cannot feel for his own. It is the respect which is everywhere shown to the memory of their great and good men. Portraits, busts, and statues adorn alike the halls of learning and of legislation, the courts of justice, the gallery, the hospital, and the medical school ; and thus serve to inspire the visitor not only with a love for his particular pursuit, but an ambition to excel in good works, and an admiration for a people who know how to reward their servants while living, and to cherish the memory of their virtues after they are dead.

"In the hall of Christ Church College, Oxford, at the great dinner of the British Medical Association, I felt, in responding to the toast kindly offered in compliment to the American delegation, as if every portrait in the large and majestic room were watching me and saying, 'Hear! hear! hear!' and felt as if ten centuries were looking down upon that grand and learned assembly. In our city, so distinguished for its charitable, literary, and scientific institutions, there is a singular absence of everything of this kind. We have not one solitary monument of a great man, not even of Washington or of Franklin, to inspire our youth with ambition or to warm the heart of a stranger as he walks along our streets.

"But I must not prolong these remarks. Already I have trespassed too much upon your patience. However, before I take my seat, permit me again, Mr. President, to thank you, and through you this large assembly of good and great men, for the honor they have done me in coming here this evening. I have been the recipient of perhaps as many compliments as a man of my age and of my humble position could expect, but of all that have been bestowed upon me, this is the most precious to my feelings, and the one which will be most cherished by my family long after I shall have gone to 'that undiscovered country from whose bourne no traveller returns.'"

CHAPTER XII.

EARLY in May, 1872, I received a letter from my friend,
Professor Acland, of Oxford, informing me that, if I could
be present on Commemoration Day, in June, the Univer-
sity would confer upon me the degree of D. C. L. He said
that, if it had been known in time that I would be at Oxford in August, 1868, during the meeting of the British
Medical Association, when that degree was conferred upon
Sir James Paget, Sir Thomas Locock, Sir William Gull,
Sir William Jenner, Professor James Syme, and Professor
William Stokes, I would have been included in the list.
As my dear wife was in poor health, rendering it probable
that change of air would be of great service to her, I had
thus a double motive for visiting Europe a second time.

My wife, my son A. Haller Gross, and myself left
Philadelphia on the 26th of May, having previously engaged our passage on the steamer Russia, which sailed
the next day from New York. Nothing of importance
occurred during the voyage except that the vessel en-
countered some rough weather, and that we were all
three seasick, a fate which we experienced during our first
visit. The vessel reached Liverpool on Friday, June 7th.
The next day we were off for Oxford, where we arrived
late in the afternoon in a cold, drenching rain, Professor

Acland being kindly in waiting.   The commencement exercises of the different colleges took place the following week.

On Wednesday the one-thousandth Commemoration Day of the University was celebrated.   Shortly after half past eleven o'clock the officers of the institution entered the Sheldonian Theatre, headed by the mace-bearers, and immediately followed by the Vice-Chancellor, the Rev. Dr. Liddell, the doctors and the heads of houses, the proctors and registrar bringing up the rear.   My son and I had secured good positions, so that we had a full view of the procession.   "The organ struck up as the great gates were flung open, and 'God save the Queen' was sung lustily while the grave and reverend seigniors took their places."   The Vice-Chancellor, a man of splendid physique, well known in this country as one of the authors of Liddell & Scott's Greek Dictionary, a work of wide celebrity, then explained in a Latin speech that the object of the convocation was the delivery of an oration in accordance with the will of that excellent benefactor, Lord Crewe, followed by the recitations of the prizemen.   Although the amphitheatre for nearly two hours before the procession entered was a bedlam of uproar and rude disorder only equalled by the noise and confusion in the House of Commons when some unfortunate wight rises to speak, from the moment the Vice-Chancellor took his seat till he uttered the final words, "Dissolvimus hanc convocationem," not a sound was heard except the ordinary applause enthusiastically given at the conclusion of each recitation.   The audience was large, and comprised many fashionable and influential persons of both sexes, a large number of whom came from a distance.   The exercises, on the whole, did not impress me favorably.   They were cold and formal, and not at all in harmony with what we witness on like occasions on our side of the Atlantic.   The undergraduates, the lords of the gallery, behaved more like rowdies than civilized beings. It was evidently their "free day," on which they felt at liberty to do pretty much what they pleased. Hardly any person entered without being cheered, and not a few were hissed. "The lady in blue," "The lady in black," "The lady with the white ostrich feather in her hat," "The lady with the cashmere shawl," and similar expressions resounded from every part of the large theatre. That all this noise should have been succeeded by profound silence upon the entrance of the heads of the University was astounding, and yet such was the fact.

On Thursday, June 13th, at eleven o'clock, a special convocation was held at the Sheldonian Theatre for conferring the honorary degrees upon the following gentlemen :

1. His Highness Prince Hassan, son of the Khedive of Egypt.

2. George Burrows, M. D., Caius College, Cambridge, President of the Royal College of Physicians of London, and formerly President of the General Medical Council.

3. Sir Benjamin Brodie, Bart., M. A., late Professor of Chemistry.

4. Samuel David Gross, M. D., LL. D., Professor of Surgery in the Jefferson Medical College of Philadelphia.

These were the only exercises performed on the occasion. Each candidate as his name was called was addressed in Latin by the usher, after which he mounted the platform and shook hands with the Vice-Chancellor ; and thus ended a ceremony which to most persons must have seemed very tame. No diplomas were issued to the recipients of these honors. Each candidate, arrayed in the customary red gown, with white gloves, and a four-cornered hat in hand, was cheered as his name was announced. I may add that a special day was chosen for these exercises, because the year before the authorities had great difficulty, on Commemoration Day, in securing order, and it was apprehended that there might be a recurrence of the turbulence.

In the evening the Commemoration Dinner was given in the great dining-hall of the University, the Vice-Chancellor, Rev. Dr. Liddell, occupying the chair, supported on the right by Dean Stanley and on the left by Lord Roseberry. My seat was in front of the Vice-Chancellor's, and on my right sat Sir Thomas Gladstone, brother of the Premier, a member of Parliament, and a large landholder in the north of Scotland, his residence. Several speeches were made, the best of which was that of Dean Stanley; and the entertainment was to me, stranger as I was, a very pleasant one. My neighbor, Sir Thomas, was quite chatty. He made some complimentary remarks respecting the United States, and gave me a cordial invitation to visit him at his home in the Highlands, to see his lands and especially his sheep, of which, he said, he had large flocks of the choicest varieties. About one hundred gentlemen sat down to dinner.

A few evenings after the anniversary, Prince Hassan gave a splendid entertainment to the heads of colleges and to the citizens of Oxford. Many invited guests were present, and the occasion was one of general merry-making. Temporary buildings were erected under canvas for the accommodation of the immense crowd; the choicest flowers were everywhere seen in profusion; dancing commenced early and was kept up until a late hour in the morning; and ices and fruits were served during the entire evening. The whole affair was brilliant, worthy of the son of a great prince rolling in wealth and luxury. Young Hassan, I was informed, spent his money lavishly while a member of the University, and this, added to his gentle manners, was doubtless the secret of his popularity. In his appearance there was nothing whatever of a prepossessing character. He was of small stature, with a rather dark complexion, and his countenance showed no evidence of intellect or special culture. He was simply a clever youth, using the word in the

American, not the English, sense. It was his father's
desire that, on leaving the University, he should spend
several years in travel and foreign study. In 1877 I
learned to my surprise that the young Prince, after having
acquired a military education at Woolwich and Berlin,
had been made Commander-in-Chief of the Egyptian con-
tingent on the Danube, and had already acquired some
experience as a soldier. It is related of him that, being
taken prisoner by King John of Abyssinia, a large cross
was, as a punishment, tattooed on the back of each of
his hands. In vain did he seek after his release the advice
of the most skilful physicians to rid him of these disagreeable reminders of his capture, and rather than take the
advice of the dervish who suggested the unique remedy of
the amputation of both hands he is said to seek to hide
the blemishes by wearing gloves.

There is much in and about Oxford to interest a stranger. The town itself, with its ancient wall, its quaint
buildings, its botanic garden, and its charming situation
upon the banks of the Cherwell and the Isis, is well
worth a visit; but the interest is vastly increased when
we remember that the city is the seat of the greatest University, not only in Great Britain, but in the world—embracing within less than a mile and a half in diameter
upwards of twenty separate college edifices, many of them
dating back six to eight centuries, all erected on a grand
scale, with ample accommodations for their pupils and fellows, and surrounded, for the most part, by spacious
grounds, embellished with trees, shrubbery, and flowers.
The very atmosphere exhales a classical odor. It is the
place where, above all others, one would like to be educated and to pursue one's studies in after-life. Lately
several new colleges have been added, so that the number
of colleges and halls at present is not fewer, if my memory
serves me, than twenty-four. Among the more interesting
objects to the visitor to Oxford are its libraries and Uni-

versity Museum. The Museum is a noble quadrangular edifice in the mediæval style, situated upon a large lot of ground, and was opened in 1868. It contains already an immense collection of specimens in the various branches of natural history, botany, and zoology, and is provided with numerous lecture-rooms for the efficient teaching of the natural sciences. Indeed, the object in erecting this vast building was that it should serve as a great school for the study of the natural sciences under the leadership of separate professors—men devoted to the cultivation and illustration of specialties. To the disinterested and arduous exertions of my friend, Professor Acland, the institution is much indebted for the success which has attended it since its opening. Unfortunately the outlays have been very heavy; and I have recently learned that the management is somewhat crippled for the want of funds to place the Museum upon a proper footing.

Of the four principal libraries at Oxford, the most noteworthy is the Bodleian, opened in 1602, and comprising at present nearly three hundred thousand volumes. The Radcliffe Library, founded in the eighteenth century, was endowed under the will of Dr. John Radcliffe, who left forty thousand pounds for that purpose, besides one hundred pounds a year for its increase, and one hundred and fifty pounds as a salary for the librarian. The collection, which has been steadily growing in extent and value, was originally largely composed of works on medicine and natural history. In addition to this munificent bequest, Radcliffe left a large sum of money for the establishment of an observatory, with a dwelling-house for the resident, and a lecture-room furnished with all the means and appliances necessary for the study and illustration of astronomy. It is flattering to one's vanity to know that a physician—one who rose to great distinction by the force of his own genius — did all these things for this noble institution. Radcliffe was emphatically the architect of his own fortune. Born in 1650, he entered University College, Oxford, at fifteen, became B. M. in 1675, and M. D. in 1682, and soon acquired an extensive, lucrative, and influential practice. Before he had attained middle age he removed to London, where he soon laid the foundation of the large wealth which he so wisely devoted to educational purposes. Although he possessed more than ordinary talents and attainments, he was coarse and brusque in his manners, sometimes indeed almost brutal, often indulged in ill-timed jests, and probably said more rude things than any physician before or since his day. His remarks to King William were characteristic. It is related that when his Majesty, showing him his swollen ankles, which formed a striking contrast to his emaciated body, asked him, "Doctor, what do you think of these?" "Why, truly," said he, "I would not have your Majesty's two legs for your three kingdoms."

Radcliffe is not the only physician whose name and munificence are indissolubly associated with this great institution. Dr. Thomas Linacre, born nearly two centuries previously, endowed two lectureships on medicine in Merton College, Oxford; and another in St. John's College, Cambridge. He was distinguished for his learning and practical skill, and immortalized himself as the founder of the Royal College of Physicians of London. An eminent Greek scholar, he was the first Professor of Greek in the University of Oxford, in which he delivered lectures on medicine; and he furnished an elegant translation of the works of Galen. After his removal to London he rapidly rose in reputation and influence, and was appointed court physician by Henry VIII.

What Linacre and Radcliffe did for Oxford Dr. John Kaye, more generally known by his Latinized name of Caius, did for Cambridge. Born in 1510, he was successively physician to Edward VI., Queen Mary, and Queen Elizabeth; enjoyed great distinction as a practitioner, au-

thor, antiquarian, Greek and Latin scholar; and founded
Caius College, Cambridge, which, to use the language of
another, "is to this day the chief medical college in that
celebrated University." To these great men England, it
is said, is greatly indebted for important advances in her
literature soon after the revival of learning; yet Shakespeare caricatured Caius in his Merry Wives of Windsor,
very much as Aristophanes caricatured Socrates in his
play of the Clouds.

During our sojourn at Oxford constant attentions were
showered upon us by prominent citizens and by members
of the University. Among these none were more kind and
considerate than the Acland family, who, from the moment of our arrival until the time of our departure, more
than a fortnight after, could apparently not do enough
for us. We were welcome in this family alike at breakfast, dinner, and at tea, as well as at every hour of the day
and evening. At the social gatherings of the Vice-Chancellor and of his accomplished wife and daughters we met
many distinguished personages; and at Professor Rolleston's I had the pleasure of dining with Dr., now Sir,
George Burrows, President of the Royal College of Physicians of London, and with Mrs. Burrows, a daughter of
Mr. John Abernethy, the celebrated London surgeon, who
rendered such important services to his profession, and of
whom so many odd sayings and curious anecdotes have
been related. The presence of the daughter, a charming
woman, served to recall to us, during and after the repast,
the vivacity and flashes of genius of her illustrious father.
Mrs. Rolleston is a daughter of Dr. John Davy, and a
niece of Sir Humphry. Her husband, a fine conversationalist, an accomplished scholar, an eminent scientist,
and a follower of Darwin and Huxley, is Professor of
Physiology in the University.

One of the most interesting persons I met with at Oxford was Dr. Pusey, one of the authors of the celebrated

Tracts for the Times. He had been confined for some weeks by a species of felon upon one of his fingers, for which he was attended by my friend Acland. Having heard me express a strong desire to see so celebrated and learned a personage, one who had acquired so great a reputation by his controversial writings, that gentleman kindly took me, early one morning, to Dr. Pusey's room. We found the divine seated in his arm-chair, in a dreamy mood, unshaved, and not particularly neat in his toilet. He was an old-looking man, of medium height, with a pleasing countenance shaded by heavy eyebrows, and a soft, agreeable voice. The conversation turned upon the topics of the day, in which he seemingly took little interest. After having sat for about fifteen minutes, during which we carefully inspected the disloyal finger, and offered some suggestions respecting its treatment, we took our leave. I had seen in person the author of Puseyism, and that was something to be proud of. At the time of this interview Dr. Pusey was seventy-two years of age, having been born in 1800. He looked decidedly older; hard mental labor and mental excitement had evidently made serious inroads upon his constitution.

I had been entertained at the house of Dr. Acland four years previously during the meeting of the British Medical Association, and it was therefore a source of no little gratification to me to greet him again. Of all my English friends there is not one for whom I cherish a warmer attachment. Of a highly respectable family, the son of Sir Thomas Acland, of Devonshire, his name has long been intimately associated with the interests of the University of Oxford and of the medical profession in Great Britain. For many years he has been Regius Professor of Medicine in the University, and at the time above referred to he was President of the British Medical Association, and of course presided at the annual dinner. Much of what he has written of late years relates to sanitary medicine; and there is no physician in England, with the exception of Mr. Simon, who has done so much as he has to popularize that branch of science. Since my last visit, Dr. Acland was appointed President of the General Council of Medical Education, a government office of which any man might justly be proud, as it is one of the highest positions to which he can aspire. He has a large and influential practice, and is Honorary Physician to the Prince of Wales, whom, in his visit to this country in 1860, he accompanied as medical adviser. I may add that he is emphatically a friend of progress, and a live man in every sense of the term.

Sir Benjamin Brodie, who was associated with me in the D. C. L. decoration, is a son of the famous surgeon, the late Sir Benjamin Collins Brodie, who occupied for nearly half a century so large a space in the professional and public eye of Great Britain, and whose writings, surgical and physiological, have been so widely disseminated and highly appreciated on both sides of the Atlantic as to render his name a household word. The son, not having imbibed any taste for surgery, has not followed in the footsteps of his father. He has sought out other paths for the exercise of his talents. Soon after I left Oxford the public journals announced that he had resigned the chair of Chemistry which he had so worthily filled for a number of years in the University. My dear wife, my son, and myself brought away with us pleasant recollections of the evening we spent with his charming and accomplished family at his beautiful villa near the banks of the Isis. I learned that Sir Benjamin had been an industrious worker in his laboratory, and had lectured with much acceptableness to his pupils. Daubeny, the great botanist, had died some time before our visit. His humble tomb, bearing a simple inscription, is in the courtyard of one of the colleges, a short distance from the garden in which he spent so much of his time and wrote some of his ablest works. No flowers decorated his grave. He was a bachelor, and bachelors are soon forgotten. Professor Phillips, the eminent geologist, a small, old, delicate-looking man, rather inclined to reticency, I met several times, but was not particularly impressed with his appearance, manners, or conversation.

The medical schools of Oxford and Cambridge, although officered by some very able men, as, for instance, Acland and Rolleston in the former, and Humphry and Paget in the latter, are small, as stated in a former page, most of the graduates of the University preferring to seek their medical knowledge in London and Edinburgh, owing to their greater facilities for the study of anatomy and clinical medicine. Botany, zoology, and comparative anatomy are included in the curriculum of both institutions; and in each there are a number of competitive scholarships. At Oxford a Radcliffe travelling fellowship of two hundred pounds is annually competed for, to enable the successful candidate to continue his medical pursuits abroad. The period of study is three years.

We left Oxford for London in June and went into lodgings at No. 8 Princes Street, opposite the Hotel Brunswick, a fashionable part of the city. On Saturday, the 22d, through the courtesy of the American Minister, General Schenck, I was able to attend the levee of the Prince of Wales at St. James's Palace, having previously been supplied by the Secretary of Legation, Mr. Moran, with a ticket of admission, accompanied with a short sword and a chapeau, articles always required on such occasions. The event was to me as novel as it was interesting. The ceremonies commenced at two o'clock in the afternoon. The Prince stood in the centre of a long room, leaning with his back gently against a kind of railing, and each gentleman as he approached him made a respectful bow and passed on. His familiar acquaintances shook hands with him and exchanged more or less cordial salutations.

In the procession I was immediately behind Dr. Liddell, Vice-Chancellor of the University of Oxford, his former preceptor, and he of course was cordially greeted. The assemblage was a large one, and was made doubly interesting by the attendance of the foreign ambassadors, arrayed in their national costumes. The Chinese, Japanese, and East India representatives attracted especial attention by their gay colors and flowing robes. The Prince himself was dressed in the plainest manner, and looked just as if he wished the thing was over.

A few weeks after this levee I met the Prince at a garden party at Lauderdale House, Highgate, six miles from London, on the occasion of the opening of the grounds as a retreat for the convalescent patients of St. Bartholomew's Hospital, the generous gift for seven years of Sir Sidney Waterlow. A large company was present, including the Princess of Wales, a number of the nobility, and many prominent citizens. The Prince, who accepted the gift in behalf of St. Bartholomew's Hospital, made a brief but pertinent address, which elicited rapturous applause. The meeting then adjourned to the grounds, where refreshments were served in abundance, enlivened by conversation and music, while in a large mansion near by the Prince and Princess received their friends. Through the courtesy of Sir James Paget I had the honor of being personally presented to the Prince and of talking with him for some time, during which he was kind enough to refer to my Oxford degree, then recently conferred, and to speak in complimentary terms of his visit to this country in 1860. One of the queerest persons present on this interesting occasion was Lady Burdett-Coutts, the wealthy philanthropist. She patiently waited near the gate for the arrival of the royal party, and the moment they approached her she made a courtesy so profound that her knees must have almost touched the pavement.

We dined on Monday, June 24th, with Sir Francis and

Lady Drake, the proprietors of Nutwell Court, South Devon, and other hereditary estates, once the property of Sir Francis Drake, the great navigator in the reign of Queen Elizabeth. Lady Drake is the daughter of Lady Douglas, a first cousin of my wife. Sir Francis and Lady Drake always pass the season in London, and of course live in elegant style. The dinner on this occasion was a handsome one. Before we took our leave they extended to us a cordial invitation to spend a week with them in July at Nutwell Court.

On June 25th, at nine o'clock, I breakfasted with Sir Henry Holland, at his residence on Upper Brook Street. My first interview with him occurred during the visit of the Prince of Wales to this country, in 1860, at a dinner given to him at the Philadelphia Club by the British Consul, Mr. Kortright. Only a few gentlemen were present. Dr. Robley Dunglison had been invited, but was unable to attend on account of indisposition. It was, if I mistake not, Sir Henry's fifth visit to the United States. The conversation during the dinner was of a discursive kind, but the principal topic was the Prince, then quite a youth— his general bearing, his sagacious observations as a tourist, his keen remarks, the dignity of his demeanor, and matters of a similar nature, all expressive of admiration of His Royal Highness. The laudations of Sir Henry, who accompanied the Prince as Physician-in-Chief, were especially emphatic; so much so, indeed, as to savor somewhat of snobbism. How I might have been impressed if I had been an Englishman I do not know; but looking at the matter from an American standpoint it was impossible to interpret his language in any other manner. The dinner in the main was a dull affair, and of short duration, as Sir Henry had a pressing engagement, and the evening was already far advanced when we sat down at table. I did not meet with him again until I saw him at his own house in 1872. When I called he was out; but late in the afternoon he sent me a note, inviting me to breakfast the following morning at nine o'clock, adding that Mr. Froude, the historian, would be the only other person present, apart from his family, which, I found, consisted of himself and of two maiden daughters. I do not know whether I should include in this enumeration a favorite lap-dog, of which one of the ladies in particular seemed to be extremely fond. Mr. Froude did not arrive until the breakfast, consisting of tea, toast, eggs, and mutton-chops, was more than half over, saying, by way of excuse, that he had been buttonholed by an old friend whom he had not seen for a long time, and from whom he could not extricate himself sooner. The meal was, in all respects, an informal one, and therefore quite free and easy. Sir Henry inquired with special solicitude about the health of his old friend, Mrs. Gilpin, whose guest he had been during some of his visits to this country, and about the condition and prospects of our colored people, in whose welfare he appeared to take more than ordinary interest. Mr. Froude, who had very little to say, addressed himself principally to the ladies, the elder of whom presided with great dignity at the head of the table. Precisely as the clock struck ten Sir Henry excused himself and rose, saying he was obliged to fulfil an engagement. The rest of us sat a little longer, when, after an interchange of the civilities usual on such an occasion, we took our leave. At the door, at parting, I said to Mr. Froude, "I understand you are coming to Philadelphia; if so, it will afford me pleasure to renew my acquaintance with you, and to tender to you the hospitalities of my house." It happened, however, that I did not meet with him, as he was constantly on the wing during the delivery of his lectures in New York and Philadelphia. His lectures failed to attract large audiences, and my impression is that he went back disappointed, as he came on a pecuniary speculation. Great writers are not always, or even generally, good speakers; and a lecturer, if he has not some oratorical ability, may as well be silent.

Sir Henry had none of the characteristics of a great man in his personal appearance. In stature he was scarcely of medium height, and his head exhibited no marks of extraordinary intellectual development. Yet he was a man of decided ability. He had great powers of observation, united with all the advantages of a classical education, high culture, and high social position. Taking his degree in medicine at Edinburgh at the time when that school was in the height of its glory, he soon after settled in London, where he rapidly acquired practice, and ultimately rose to the highest professional eminence. Knighted, and appointed physician to the Queen, honors, foreign and domestic, were showered upon him, and he became literally a child of Fortune. That he was an accomplished practitioner, full of resources in cases of emergency, is well known; and his Medical Notes and Reflections, published at an early period of his career, show him to have been an able thinker and a vigorous writer. Much of his professional labor was consultation practice among the nobility and the higher circles of London society. For many years during his summer vacation he spent regularly from two to three months in travelling, visiting many countries, some, such as the United States, repeatedly, and thus making himself personally familiar with the habits and customs of the people with whom he was brought into contact. The income from his practice during these years rarely, as he himself informs us, exceeded twenty thousand dollars annually. His work, entitled Recollections of a Professional Life, issued a few years before his death, reflects but little credit upon his taste or judgment. It is a kind of diary, written by a man who seems anxious to show himself off as a man of the world, and to tell us the names, if nothing more, of the distinguished people with whom chance had made him acquainted.

His wanderings in distant lands were of great advantage to him. They afforded him thorough relaxation from the cares and anxieties of practice, invigorated his mind and body, and enabled him the better to perform his arduous work during the coming months. He always, immediately on reaching home, resumed his wonted professional labors. "The new methods of intercommunication since steam and electricity have held empire on the earth often," he says, "enabled me to make engagements for the very moment of my return. I recollect having found a patient waiting in my room when I came back from those mountain heights, more than two hundred miles from the frontier of Persia, where ten thousand Greeks uttered their joyous cry on the sudden sight of the empire. The same thing once happened to me on returning from Egypt and Syria, when I found a carriage waiting my arrival at London Bridge to take me to a consultation in Sussex Square; the communications in each case being made from points on my homeward journey. More than once, in returning from America, I have begun a round of visits from the Euston Station."

The Sunday before we left London for South Devon I saw Sir Henry for the last time, apparently somewhat feeble, but full of animation and cleverness. We were spending the evening with Sir James Paget and his family, and he came in at a late hour to take leave of them, prior to his departure, a few days after, for the Cape of Good Hope. My wife had a long conversation with him about the Princess Caroline, but he was, perhaps properly, entirely non-committal. The voyage, I believe, was of some benefit to him; but he never completely regained his strength, and died in October, 1873. He was twice married. His last wife was a daughter of Sydney Smith, a woman of high culture and great intellect. A portrait of her father graced the wall of our breakfast-room.

This evening, June 25th, at seven o'clock, Dr. Thomas

Bevill Peacock gave me a dinner. As he is a widower, no ladies were present. Among the guests were Dr. Barker, Mr. Gay, Mr. Croft, Liebreich, Weber, MacCormac, Hutchinson, and my son. The repast was select and enjoyable. Dr. Peacock, an excellent gentleman and physician, had dined with me, but quite informally, a few summers before in Philadelphia, and I therefore appreciated this compliment all the more. As an author he is well known; his works and monographs on malformations and morbid conditions of the heart have given him a world-wide reputation. In the London Hospital for Consumptives, Victoria Park, of which he is one of the physicians, there is a large and valuable collection—the result mainly of his own labors—of specimens illustrative of these disorders. Our appreciation of Dr. Peacock on this side of the Atlantic will be better understood when I state that he was recently elected a member of the College of Physicians of Philadelphia.

On June 26th my wife, my son, and I lunched with Mr. and Mrs. Erichsen, after which I accompanied Mr. Erichsen to University College Hospital to see him excise the wrist-joint of a young girl according to Mr. Lister's method, a complicated and tedious procedure. He was followed by Mr. Berkley Hill with a resection of a knee-joint. The hospital is kept in excellent condition.

At five o'clock in the afternoon I went to the Royal College of Physicians to listen to the Harveian oration, delivered by Dr. Arthur Farre. Dr. George Burrows, the president, in his robes, was in the chair. The oration, which was excellent, well worded, and well delivered, gave an account of Harvey's works and of his views on generation. The audience was not large but attentive, and the address elicited frequent applause. It is one of the requirements of the college that such an oration be delivered every three years, and a prominent Fellow is always selected for that purpose. After the exercises were concluded, Dr. Burrows showed me Harvey's preparations illustrative of the circulation of the blood.

In the evening I was present at the anniversary dinner given by Dr. George Burrows, as President of the Royal College of Physicians, at his residence, No. 8 Cavendish Square, to some of the more prominent Fellows. It was in every sense a handsome and enjoyable entertainment. Invitations to about thirty Fellows, including the heads of the army and navy, had been sent out a fortnight previously. Among the guests upon whom all eyes were centred was one who has achieved a vast reputation as a scientist—Richard Owen, the naturalist, a tall, noble figure, in whose presence most men, whatever their professional stature may be, feel insignificant, and yet who is so gentle and so modest that any one unacquainted with him would take him for an ordinary man. Sir Thomas Watson had been expected to be at the dinner, but a day or so before it took place he lost his brother, and I was thus deprived of the pleasure of seeing him. Dr. Burrows is one of the three gentlemen with whom I received the degree of D. C. L. at Oxford a few weeks before he gave this dinner, and the Queen, one of whose physicians he is, conferred upon him several years afterwards the honor of knighthood with a baronetcy. Sir George occupies a high position as a practitioner, writer, and scholar.

On June 29th my son and I breakfasted at ten o'clock with Mr. Mowbray, Member of Parliament for Oxford, at Onslow Gardens, a pretty suburban residence at least three miles from our lodgings, a long and disagreeable drive. We found the family very agreeable, chatty, and cordial. Mr. Mowbray was most kind to us in showing us through the two Houses of Parliament, and pointing out to us the more prominent members. He presented us to Sir Roundell Palmer, afterwards distinguished as Baron Selborne, who had just returned from the Geneva Arbitration, and with whom we had a pleasant conversation.

At two in the afternoon I drove to King's College Hospital, where I saw Henry Smith, my old friend, resect the elbow-joint of a young man on account of gelatinoid degeneration; and afterwards Sir William Fergusson perform staphylorraphy, an operation in which he has earned reputation as the great English pioneer. The patient, a young man, only partially under the influence of chloroform, struggled very much, and bled profusely. The operation involved the hard palate; Thomas Smith's gag was used.

In the evening, at a quarter to eight, I dined with Sir James Paget. The company consisted of sixteen persons, Dr. Tilbury Fox being the only medical man present. I talked a great deal about America with Lord Blatchford, a very intelligent gentleman. The entertainment was agreeable. The learned host and hostess were especially courteous.

At ten o'clock I went with Sir James to a *conversazione* at the hall of the College of Physicians. The attendance was large, and there were present many eminent medical men of London. I was introduced to Carpenter, Gull, Bowman, Balfour, Martin, and others. An ingenious electric bullet forceps, the invention of Dr. John Taylor, was exhibited, and attracted much attention. Tea, coffee, cake and ices were served. The hall was hung with portraits of Harvey, Jenner, Hewson, and many other great men, whose name and fame are indissolubly associated with the progress of medicine in England.

Mr. John Gay was, as usual, most hospitable. He kindly insisted upon my dining with him and his charming wife at their beautiful villa at Hampstead, six miles from London. My son and I accordingly went out on Sunday, June 30th, Mrs. Gross being too indisposed to accompany us.

On July 2d I went with Mr. Joseph T. Clover, the London chloroformist, to witness an ovariotomy by Mr.

Graily Hewitt. The operation was dexterously performed, without parade, and with as few words as could well be imagined. If I were to say, "without unnecessary words," my meaning would be more accurately conveyed. Mr. Clover informed me that he had now administered chloroform with his peculiar apparatus between eight and nine thousand times without a solitary accident. His ordinary fee for this service, I am told, is two guineas. Mr. Hewitt's reticence reminds me of what I have often noticed—that there are generally not enough quiet and composure on the part of our surgeons and their assistants during operations, especially those demanding great skill and self-possession. There should be no conversation, no unnecessary movements, no appearance of haste or of indecision; all the necessary arrangements should be made beforehand; the assistants should be thoroughly instructed in their duties, and every means adopted to anticipate and meet emergencies. A display of instruments is always out of place, and cannot be too pointedly condemned. Nothing savors so much of charlatanism.

During our sojourn in London we met with unceasing attention from our old friends. On the 4th of July I dined with the Fellows of the Royal College of Surgeons at their anniversary dinner, and had a pleasant time. Sir William Fergusson presided, and the meeting did not break up until near midnight. I was of course called upon to make a speech. Fergusson spoke with grace and dignity, and in every respect acquitted himself well. More than two hundred Fellows were present.

We also dined with Mrs. Douglas Douglas, of Orsett Terrace, a cousin of my wife; with Mr. John Croft, the eminent surgeon and genial gentleman, whose wife is also a cousin; and with several other persons of distinction. Mr., now Sir Joseph, Fayrer breakfasted with me at my lodgings early in July. He had recently returned from Calcutta after an absence of twenty years, and he told me many things of interest respecting India, among others that fully twenty thousand people are annually destroyed in that country by poisonous snakes, and that many besides are killed by lions, tigers, and elephants. This statement might seem incredible were it not vouched for by authentic statistics. Mr. Fayrer is now engaged upon the composition of an elaborate work upon the snakes of India, of which he has kindly promised to send me a copy. He was Professor of Surgery in the Medical College of Calcutta, and is the author of a valuable work on surgery, besides numerous contributions to our periodical literature.

During this visit I attended, through an invitation kindly extended to me by Mr. John Croft of the surgical staff of St. Thomas's Hospital, the distribution of the competitive prizes in that ancient and celebrated institution in the chapel of the new and magnificent edifice on the west bank of the Thames, almost immediately opposite the Parliament Houses. A large assembly was in attendance, including many gentlemen and ladies of distinction. The meeting was presided over by the Archbishop of Canterbury, who opened it with prayer. As the name of each successful candidate was announced he was presented to his grace by one of the hospital staff in a neat little address setting forth his merits and offering kind words of encouragement. These exercises were followed by an address by the Archbishop, of about half an hour's duration, in which he spoke in the most kind and feeling manner of the medical profession, of its divine character, and of the vast benefits which it is daily and hourly conferring upon the human race. Next to his own profession, he said the medical occupied the loftiest position in its power of doing good, and in the exalted character of its members. He dwelt with peculiar emphasis upon the hardships of the medical life, and of the unrequited ser-

vices of medical men, adding that they must not always
expect their reward in this world but have higher aims
and aspirations. Towards the close of the address, which
was listened to with great attention, and which was delivered in a very plain, gentle, and parental manner, his
grace extended a cordial invitation to the students who
attend the summer classes to visit the grounds of Lambeth
Palace, within a few squares of St. Thomas's, for exercise
and recreation—a kindness worthy of the greatest praise
and of the pure and benevolent character of the head of the
Anglican Church.

St. Thomas's Hospital, one of the largest institutions
of the kind in the world, is worthy of passing notice. It
was originally an almshouse, situated opposite Guy's Hospital and founded in the early part of the thirteenth century. Its site is one of the most desirable in London.
The new building, the erection of which occupied more
than seven years, cost three millions of dollars, and is
provided with every convenience and comfort for the accommodation of patients and for efficient clinical teaching.
A most agreeable feature of the very commodious and
thoroughly ventilated wards is the display of engravings
upon the walls, illustrative of scenes in the Bible and in
general history, well calculated to interest and gratify the
inmates and to divert their attention from their sufferings. The little stands were covered with flowers. The
medical school connected with this Hospital has educated
many of the most distinguished men in the kingdom; and
the hospital staffs, who perform the teaching, have always
been very able. In the days of the Clines and Sir Astley
Cooper the schools of St. Thomas and of Guy were united,
and the great works of the latter on Hernia, the Testes,
and the Mammary Gland, all immortal productions, were
based upon observations made by him in the two institutions. In 1868, during my first visit to London, the surgical staff consisted of Solly, Le Gros Clark, and Simon;

the medical, of J. R. Bennett, Peacock, and Bristowe; and the obstetrical, of Barnes—names widely known in this and other countries. In 1872 I found that Sydney Jones and my friends John Croft and Mr. MacCormac, formerly of Belfast, all excellent operators, had been added to the surgical staff, the first two after having for a number of years acted as assistants. Some changes, owing to death and resignations, had also taken place in the medical staff. The teaching in the medical school is conducted on a large scale, and there are two sessions, in each of which clinical instruction occupies an important place.

When the services were ended I was invited into an adjoining room, where I was presented to the Archbishop and Mrs. and Miss Tait, three tall persons, his grace being more than six feet in height, and, withal, very slender, not in the least denotive of the good living which so generally falls to the lot of even the ordinary clergy, to say nothing of those in high life, who always live upon the fat of the land. He is evidently very amiable, conscientious, and pious, but hardly any one would suppose him to be a great man. His liberal principles have greatly endeared him to the English people. As primate of all England and the first peer of the realm he necessarily exerts much influence in the House of Lords as well as in the Church. The interest which he showed in 1877 in the passage of what is called the Burial Bill, by which dissenters shall be permitted the privilege of burial in parish grounds, was a move, as it would be considered in this country, in the right direction, and gives him a warm claim to the gratitude of a large and deserving class of people. It is amazing that in an age so enlightened as this is such prejudices should have been tolerated so long. Every citizen of England is taxed for the support of the Church, and it would therefore seem to be only right that every man should have an interest in its burial grounds, and not be treated like a dog when he knocks for admission to rights to which he is plainly entitled. The passage of the bill in the House of Lords was evidently due to the great personal and official influence of the Archbishop.

There was a singular story in circulation during my visit to England in regard to the manner in which Dr. Tait obtained his appointment. The Queen, it seems, was much attached to him, and having learned that he had been plunged into the very depths of affliction by the loss of several of his children in rapid succession, she concluded that she could show her sympathy in no better way than by elevating him to the Archbishopric of Canterbury.

My wife having promised a visit to her cousin, Lady Douglas, of Dawlish, South Devon, we left London on the 9th of July and reached our destination at four o'clock in the afternoon. We had a cordial welcome. Everything was in readiness for us at her pretty residence, known as Bursledon House, and no effort was spared to contribute to our happiness during the week in which we were her guests. Excursions were made throughout the neighborhood, and among other places of interest we visited Exeter Cathedral, a grand old structure, of which Lady Douglas long ago made so thorough a study that she is perfectly familiar with the minutest details of its history; she proved a most instructive guide to us. Almost every day some persons were invited to join us at meals; and on the third day after our arrival an elegant luncheon was given us by the Vicar of Bryanstone, the Rev. Mr. Clark, an intimate friend of our hostess; followed at half past seven by a dinner party at Bursledon House.

Of Lady Douglas, with whom I have long carried on a correspondence, my wife entered the following note in her memorandum-book: "She is different from any one I have ever known, with great ability, learning, and wonderful powers of conversation. She has given up the world and society, and seems to maintain over herself a rigid disci-

pline and watchfulness. She is devoted to the church.
Exeter Cathedral is her especial delight; and she has rendered important service in deciphering and explaining the
old inscriptions and bosses on the arches. She has given
money towards the restoration of the building, and some
years ago she contributed a beautiful chalice-veil to St.
Paul's in London at the convocation there. She is very
religious, and I cannot but respect the self-denial to which
she subjects herself." I might say much more of this
noble-hearted woman; I might speak of her remarkable
learning, of her inquisitive mind, of her great refinement,
of her artistic tastes, of her unaffected piety; but if I were
to do this, I should, I am sure, incur her displeasure.

Our next visit was to Nutwell Court, where, as at
Dawlish, we spent one week as the guests of Sir Francis
and Lady Drake. Nutwell Court is one of the places
of mark in English history. It is a beautiful spot, with
large grounds and a noble old hall, a present of the
English government to Sir Francis Drake, the great sailor
who saved England by destroying the Spanish Armada
in the reign of Queen Elizabeth. The house abounds
in relics. The library contains a fine collection of the
works of English and foreign authors, mostly in quarto
and folio editions of the sixteenth century. Among other
books is Sir Francis Drake's Bible in black letter and a
copy of the Bishop's Bible, with the inscription on the fly-
leaf, "All around ye world." His sword, belt, and chapeau, and the trumpet used by him at sea are preserved
with scrupulous care. Among many curiosities are the
bedstead, a beautiful piece of carved and inlaid work,
which belonged to the admiral of the Spanish Armada,
and a full-length portrait of "Queen Bess," a present from
her Majesty to Sir Francis in token of her admiration of
his character and as an acknowledgment of his great services as a navigator and warrior. There are also, in good
condition, the green silk scarfs fringed with gold given

him by the Queen, and six red silk flags which used to float on his vessel as it was proudly plowing the waves in pursuit either of discovery or of victory. The walls of the house are hung everywhere with portraits of distinguished personages, some of them by the older artists, and nearly all procured at great cost. Much of the furniture is old, and the plate, which is of silver and gold, is very valuable. There is also some Sèvres ware of rare pattern. The grounds of this palatial residence are very extensive and are kept in excellent order. The gardens and conservatories are large; and the orange, lemon, banana, and pineapple are grown in more or less profusion. The stables are supplied with fine horses and carriages, and attached to them is a riding-school for training purposes and for exercise in inclement weather. The country around affords beautiful drives. After a certain hour in the morning horses and carriages are constantly at the door for the accommodation of visitors. Nutwell is situated on the river Exe, and almost directly opposite the park and residence of the Earl of Devon. It is, like some of the other possessions left by the old navigator, an entailed estate.

Having passed most pleasantly the week for which we had been invited, and during which we received not only the unbounded hospitality of Sir Francis and Lady Drake, but many marks of attention from prominent citizens of the neighborhood, we reluctantly took our departure for Torquay. We stopped on the way at Exeter to lunch with Canon Cook and his charming and accomplished wife, both of whom we had met at Nutwell Court, and who had kindly invited a number of their friends to meet us. Mrs. Cook is a cousin of Lady Drake, and a Douglas. Canon Cooke is one of the Queen's chaplains, noted for his piety and learning, and is one of the divines selected for revising the Bible.

We visited Torquay solely on account of Mrs. Gross's health, impaired by long suffering from severe neuralgia.

We remained there nearly one month, during which she greatly improved in flesh and strength, and enjoyed her sea baths and excursions in the neighborhood. The walks and drives in and around this town, perched as it is upon high hills, on almost every side in view of the ocean, are enchanting; and we availed ourselves of every opportunity to make the best of our time. We found here, as everywhere else, agreeable and hospitable people. Dr. and Mrs. Blake were especially kind to us; and Mr. Vivian spared no pains to point out to us every object of interest in regard to the history of the town. Mr. Vivian is one of the founders of the Torquay Museum, containing a valuable collection of organic remains found in and about the town, especially in what is known as Kent's Hole—a natural cave in which have been found the bones of hyenas, tigers, bears, elephants, and other animals no longer seen in Great Britain. Intermixed with these remains have been discovered some fragments of human bones. The passage has been explored to a distance of six hundred yards; and everything goes to prove that human beings must have dwelt in its vicinity at least two hundred thousand years ago.

The bathing at Torquay is not good; the water is shallow, without surf, and cold even in August. The women and men bathe separately, the former in the morning, and the latter in the afternoon—in machines, as they are called, or two-wheeled carriages. After they are undressed, the bathers are pushed into the water, and hauled out when they have completed their toilet. The best season for visiting Torquay is the autumn; at that time many invalids resort thither, and not a few pass the winter there. The air is delicious, the market excellent, and the charges reasonable. Flowers, including the fuchsia, the geranium, and the heliotrope, bloom in the open air until late in the season.

During my stay at Torquay I had an invitation from the

Lord Mayor of London to attend his annual dinner; and also one from the Mayor of Brighton to dine with the British Association for the Advancement of Science, at the Pavilion, in that city, the former residence of George IV. Owing to unavoidable circumstances I was obliged to decline both of them. I was, however, able to go to Birmingham to attend the meeting of the British Medical Association, which met in that city Tuesday, August 6th. I went there as the guest of Mr. Thomas H. Bartlett, one of the surgeons of the Birmingham Hospital, an eminent practitioner, and a gentleman of agreeable manners. The Association met the next morning, and was largely attended, the president, Mr. Alfred Baker, in the chair. His *soirée*, which cost him, it was said, more than six hundred pounds, was a great success. More than twelve hundred persons were present, and all enjoyed themselves. At the annual dinner nearly four hundred subscribers sat down. As the senior American delegate, it devolved upon me to tender thanks in behalf of my countrymen. This I did in a brief speech, which was kindly received with three rousing cheers. The address in medicine, by Dr. Wilks, of Guy's Hospital, London, and that in surgery, by Mr. Oliver Pemberton, of Birmingham, were able productions, eliciting much commendation. During my stay in this busy and hospitable city I dined with Mr. Baker, the President of the Association; with Mr. Berry, father-in-law of my host; and with Mr. Pemberton. Mr. Fernwick Jordan, Professor of Surgery in Queen's College, invited me to breakfast with him at the Queen's Hotel, with a company of sixty gentlemen, many of them of professional prominence. He was kind enough to assign to me the seat of honor at the table. The morning after this I met at breakfast, at the same hotel, the Temperance League, nearly one hundred members and invited guests being present. The object of the meeting was to elicit the views of the medical gentlemen in regard to the necessity or uselessness of alcohol in the treatment of disease and injury. There was much diversity of sentiment expressed upon the subject. Some denounced its use *in toto;* while others, including myself, strongly advocated it, in certain conditions of the system, as a most valuable, if not indispensable, remedial agent. I must not forget to state that soon after the opening of the meeting of the British Association I was elected an honorary member, and that a similar compliment was bestowed upon Ricord and Demarquay, of Paris.

I had long been anxious to visit Lichfield, the birthplace of Samuel Johnson, the Goliath of English literature, and finding that it was only eighteen miles from Birmingham, I determined to gratify my wishes. I was particularly desirous to see his statue illustrative of events of his early childhood. In my journey I was accompanied by Mr. Wilcox, a friend of my host, who contributed greatly to the enjoyment of the occasion.

Although a man of masculine mind, Johnson was naturally superstitious, and this feeling never forsook him even in his riper years. His statue at Lichfield stands in the little market square, and was erected by the Rev. Chancellor Law at his own expense, at a sum of four hundred pounds. The figure represents a young man in the sitting posture, the head resting on one hand, with a book in the other, in a studious, contemplative mood. The countenance is singularly sensuous, animal-like, the lips being thick and round, the nose broad, and the chin rather long; indeed, there is an entire absence of refinement about it. There are three *basso-relievos.* The first represents Johnson as a boy riding upon the shoulders of two of his companions with another behind pushing all three onward; the manner in which, it is said, he used to be carried to school. The second represents him as an infant astride his father's shoulders, listening to one of the Rev. Dr. Sacheverell's sermons. The third, as a boy, shows him doing penance in the marketplace for having told a story, his mother standing behind, and the magistrate in front of him. As a piece of art, the statue has nothing to boast of; it is an awkward, clumsy performance. Those who are familiar with his early life will recollect that Johnson, when hardly two years old, was carried by his parents to London to be touched by Queen Anne for the king's evil—a scrofulous disease; and that, young as he was, he distinctly recollected her majesty's pearl necklace, showing what a wonderful memory he had even then.

Not far from this famous marketplace, in a print shop, is Johnson's arm-chair, an awkward, unseemly piece of furniture, and also his cane, a very long one, made of bamboo wood, surmounted by an ivory head, quite loose from long use. At the town museum I saw his beer-mug, salt-cellar, snuff-box, and silver shoe-buckles—precious relics, preserved with religious care. Portraits of Johnson, Garrick, and Darwin, the author of Zoonomia, and grandfather of the evolutionist, adorn the interior of the building. Before I left I bought two photographs, one representing Johnson's statue, and the other a portrait of him by Reynolds.

Lichfield is situated upon a dead level, with a population of seven thousand; it has a magnificent cathedral, and had at one time a famous grammar-school, in which Johnson, Addison, and Garrick laid the foundation of their greatness. Mr. Wilcox and I greatly enjoyed our visit. We returned early in the afternoon; and on the following morning, with a heart full of gratitude to my host and hostess for their kind attentions to me, I retraced my steps towards Torquay, mindful that I should never be able to repay the good people of Birmingham for their hospitality. This word hospitality naturally recalls the viands and markets of the people from whom we were at all times the recipients of unbounded kindness, and it may therefore not be inappropriate for me here to state that the shooting season of game in England begins, for

grouse, August 12th ; for black cock, August 22d ; for
partridge, September 2d ; for pheasant, October 2d ; and
for hare, October 30th.   Venison is freely eaten as early
as August.   The London fish-market is very superior ; the
salmon is a standard dish in its season, and white bait is a
bonne bouche not to be despised.   The beef, mutton, ham,
and poultry are excellent ; but, excepting mutton, not any
better than our own, while our lamb is not surpassed in
tenderness and flavor.   Much cold meat is eaten, especially
at breakfast and luncheon.   Vegetables are not nearly so
numerous as with us.   When I told an English lady, at a
dinner party in London, that in the garden of one of my
sons-in-law near Baltimore there were at that moment
twenty-six culinary vegetables growing side by side, she
threw down her fork, raised her eyes like a duck in a
thunder-storm, and almost audibly said, "That is not true !"
English eating is not bad, but America is the paradise of
good living, although the cooking of the lower and even
of the middle classes is often wretchedly bad.   Our markets are supplied with an abundance of delicious venison, quail, pheasant, grouse, snipe, plover, woodcock, rail,
reed-bird, and duck, including the canvas-back and red-
head—neither of which, nor the terrapin, our English
brothers ever get, except as presents from their friends
on this side of the Atlantic.

On the 20th of August we took leave of our friends at
Torquay, and three days thereafter embarked in Liverpool on the Russia for home, all the better, and not a little
the wiser, for our three months' residence among people
from whom we had received great kindness, and whom,
in turn, we had learned to love and honor.

CHAPTER XIII.

ON March 4th, 1873, I went to New York to attend
the public banquet given by citizens at Delmonico's to
Professor John Tyndall, the scientist, who has been engaged during the last few months in delivering a series
of lectures in the principal cities of the Union. The
number of guests was upwards of two hundred, embracing
many of the most distinguished members of the various
professions and prominent citizens of all classes from different sections of the country. The occasion was designed
to be a grand one, and the result did not disappoint expectation. Mr. William M. Evarts occupied the chair,
supported by Dr. John W. Draper, Rev. Henry Ward
Beecher, Parke Godwin, Frederick A. P. Barnard, of Columbia College, Dr. Andrew D. White, of Cornell University, and the Rev. Dr. H. W. Bellows. Speeches were
made by all these gentlemen except the last; the best and
most felicitous of all was by Draper, who had for his subject the toast, " English and American Science." Evarts
made a few happy remarks; and the speeches of Tyndall,
Beecher, and White were good, but not brilliant. Godwin
and Barnard were tedious, and every one was glad when
they took their seats. Their long-winded speeches reminded one forcibly of Presbyterian prayers of bygone

352

days. An after-dinner speech, to be at all tolerable, must be short and pointed, and well seasoned with wit and humor. Notwithstanding these drawbacks, the heated atmosphere of the room, and the indifferent *menu*, served by indifferent waiters, the occasion was one not soon to be forgotten. The compliment was well merited by Tyndall, and was highly creditable to New York. Such an array of great men as graced this banquet is rarely witnessed anywhere.

Tyndall was born at an obscure village, near Carlow, Ireland, in August, 1820, received a limited education under the direction of his father, and evinced at an early age a marked tendency to the study of the physical and chemical sciences, in a knowledge of which he perfected himself chiefly in the most celebrated laboratories of Germany, notably those at Marburg and Berlin. His progress was rapid. The articles which he contributed during his foreign residence secured him admission into the Royal Society of London; and soon after his return he was honored with the professorship of Natural Philosophy in the Royal Institution, in which, in 1866, he succeeded Faraday. In 1872 he came to this country on a lecture tour, from which he realized more than fifteen thousand dollars. This money he generously placed in the hands of an American committee as a fund in aid of students who devote themselves to original research. I heard Mr. Tyndall lecture in this city, at Horticultural Hall, to a crowded audience, not one of whom in fifty, I am sure, understood what he said. The subject of the discourse was Heat. His language would have suited a scientific audience, but was far too abstruse for a promiscuous one. His manner was pleasant enough, but not striking. He had none of the Irish brogue or any of the English mouthing about him. In private life his manners were genial and agreeable. I met him for the first time in my own parlor at a meeting of the Saturday Evening Club, of which I was at the

I—45

time a member, having called a few days previously at his lodgings without finding him.

The writings of Mr. Tyndall embrace a great variety of topics, and are chiefly in the form of essays and contributions to scientific journals. His pen has been particularly prolific in matters connected with light, heat, electricity, and the formation of the glaciers of the Alps. The Universities of Oxford and Cambridge have honored him with their degrees; and it is not too much to say that he is decidedly the foremost scientist in Great Britain, if not in the world. He has been a great worker in original research, and his mind is cast in the finest philosophical mould. He is a firm believer in the evolution theory; and a few years ago he attracted universal attention by his proposition to submit the efficacy of prayer in the cure of diseases to a scientific test. In person Mr. Tyndall is tall and rather slim, with a large mouth and nose, a good but not capacious head, heavy brows, and a thoughtful expression of countenance.

December 9th, 1873.—Among the kind friends who welcomed me and my family on our arrival in Philadelphia in 1856, there was no one who received us more cordially than Charles Macalester, whose death occurred this morning at his residence on Spruce Street, at the age of seventy-five years. His health had been failing for some time; his gait had become feeble, much of his accustomed vivacity had vanished, and it was evident to his many friends that his life was gradually ebbing away. The immediate cause of his demise was pneumonia, the bane of old age, which yearly slays so many thousands. Exposure to cold, a severe chill, and in a few days, often not more than three or four, the work is done, and death is the victor!

Charles Macalester was no common man. Descended from a good Scotch stock, he was endowed with a strong mind, highly improved by early education and a life-long contact with many of the best and most distinguished men

of the country. Friction of mind with mind strengthens
and improves every one, and this was strikingly true of
my friend. He saw much of the world, and greatly profited
by his intercourse with it. His great business capacity
was recognized by his appointment, in early manhood,
as a director of the United States Bank, a government
office; and he subsequently served the public in various
other capacities of trust and honor. He was intrusted with
the management of many large estates, performed much
gratuitous work, was liberal in the bestowal of his charity, and was often consulted by persons in distress on account of his wide experience, superior judgment, and correct business habits. Many a widow and orphan had cause
to bless his bounty and his unselfish acts. His death
brought great sorrow upon this class of our citizens.
Reared in the Presbyterian Church, he was long an elder
in it, as well as a trustee of the General Assembly. "In
all these relations to the church," says one who knew him
intimately, "he was faithful, wise, and sagacious, giving
his time and his means freely to the furtherance of the
various schemes of benevolence." Among his charities
was one of fifty thousand dollars for the endowment of a
college at St. Paul, Minnesota, which now bears his honored name.

Mr. Macalester was famous for his hospitality. No man
in his day in Philadelphia entertained more frequently
or more elegantly than he. His house on Spruce Street,
and his residence at Torresdale on the bank of the Delaware, twelve miles above the city, were long the resort of
refined and cultivated persons of both sexes, native and
foreign. Distinguished strangers were always sure of a
cordial welcome. His viands and his wines were of the
best quality, and served in the best style. His daughter,
Miss Lily, afterwards Madame Berghmans, and at a later
period Mrs. Laughton, always presided at these entertainments, and by her grace of manner, ready wit, and power

of repartee, added greatly to the enjoyment of the guests. The host himself could always be depended on for well-timed and well-told anecdotes. Broad and liberal in his views, he invited to his table all classes of people—the Presbyterian, the Quaker, the Episcopalian, the Baptist, the Unitarian, and the Catholic; the statesman and the politician, the actor and the actress, the cabinet minister and the soldier, the physician and the apothecary, the lawyer and the scrivener; the professor and the scientist, the littérateur, and the journalist. The party seldom exceeded a dozen or fourteen; and the honored host never sat down when, in consequence of an unavoidable absence, there was an uneven number of guests. On such an occasion death was always warded off by pressing some one— generally a member of the family or a near neighbor—into the service, or by retiring some one of the company. His belief in this old Scotch prejudice had evidently been inherited; or, at all events, had taken deep root in his mental organization. The people of note whom I most frequently met at Mr. Macalester's dinner parties were Edward Everett, George Peabody, Mr. and Mrs. Henry D. Gilpin, Rev. Dr. Shields, Rev. Dr. Beadle, General Van Vliet, Daniel Dougherty, John W. Forney, George W. Childs, and Dr. Emerson. The last was an *habitué*, a dry old stick of a man, not without intelligence, but the quintessence of stinginess. He ate many rich meals at the houses of his friends, but never gave one in return. All that any of them ever received from him was half a dozen peaches sent from his farm in Delaware.

Everybody knew Mr. Everett. What a sweet and gentle disposition he had, how gifted he was, and what a genial influence he shed upon all with whom he came in contact are too well known to require comment. But it was very different with Mr. Peabody. He too could smile, but he was a dull, heavy, stalwart man, hard to arouse, and when aroused uninteresting. Of the anecdotes told me of this money king by Mr. Macalester none astonished me more than an incident which occurred during his last visit to this country. He had reached New York early in July of that year, and he immediately telegraphed for his friend to meet him. Mr. Macalester found him suffering greatly from the intense heat. Upon inquiry he ascertained that the great banker had not doffed his winter flannel. "Why don't you send out and get thin underwear?" was asked. Mr. Peabody replied, "I shall be at Danver, Massachusetts, in a few days, where plenty of thin underwear awaits me." It is difficult to appreciate such economy. Here was a man worth many millions, all devoted to charitable objects, and yet he stinted himself in his personal comfort for the sake of a few dollars. It was said of Johns Hopkins, the founder of the great university of that name, that he was too mean to wear decent clothes. Is not ostentation at the bottom of such conduct? What else can it be? Mr. Macalester was long intimate with Mr. Peabody, and was one of the trustees of the Peabody Fund for the advancement of education in the Southern States. At the time of his death he was President of the St. Andrew's Society of Philadelphia, and presided with his usual grace and dignity at its annual meeting only a few days before the sad event. He was buried on a Saturday, and the same evening the Saturday Club, of which he was a member, held its meeting at the house of a prominent citizen. I thought the affair one of great heartlessness, and the following week sent in my resignation.

Van Vliet had a fine head, with snow-white hair, and a face as red as the wattles of a turkey-cock. To wonderful gastronomic powers he added great *bonhomie* and a large fund of anecdotes picked up in his intercourse with the world and in his travels as a military officer. Shields and Beadle were model clergymen, zealous Presbyterians, eloquent preachers, and refined Christian gentlemen. The former was called early in life to a chair in the Theological

Seminary at Princeton. The latter died suddenly some years ago from the effects of overwork, and was deeply regretted by the church and by all who knew him.

During the meeting of the American Public Health Association, which embraces several thousand of the most respectable and influential citizens of the country— men representing all professions and all interests—held in Philadelphia, November, 1874, I read, by request, a paper on The Factors of Disease and Death after Injuries, Parturition, and Surgical Operations. The audience, although not large, was select, and was presided over by Mr. Morton McMichael, who kindly introduced me. The address was well received, except by a few physicians who thought it bore rather severely, if not unjustly, upon the usefulness of hospitals considered as civic institutions. It was afterwards published in the Transactions of the Association. On the last day of the meeting I called attention to the necessity of a National Sanitary Bureau, to be located at Washington, and offered the following resolutions to bring the subject fairly and forcibly before the notice of Congress and of the American people:

"*Whereas*, It is the solemn duty of every civilized government to provide means for the safety and happiness and preservation of the health and lives of its subjects:

"*And whereas*, A large number of the diseases incident to the human race are induced by causes inherent in our modes of living, and by a want of knowledge of the laws of hygiene: Therefore be it

"*Resolved*, That a committee, consisting of a member of this Association from each State and Territory of the Union, of which the president of this Association shall be chairman, be appointed to petition Congress at its next session to institute a Bureau of Health, to be located at Washington City, with a branch at the seat of each State and Territorial government.

"*Resolved*, That we hereby invite the earnest coöperation of the auxiliary branches of the Association, and of all kindred bodies in the Union, in carrying out the objects of the foregoing resolution.''

Dr. Josiah Curtis, of Washington, stated that such a bureau for collecting health statistics was in operation in Europe and had effected much good. He favored the resolution.

Dr. J. J. Woodward asked me whether this resolution proposed the formation of a body that would collect the statistics of the whole country, or whether it would be such a body as had been previously appointed and never accomplished the desired result. He was not opposed to the resolution, but merely wanted efficient action in the matter.

I then addressed the meeting as follows:

"I rise, Mr. President, to ask you a question which, in listening to the discussions here a few mornings ago, has instinctively come into my mind, and you will, I am sure, pardon me if I take the liberty of answering it myself. The question is simply this: What constitutes the highest type of civilization in a nation? You will agree with me at once that it is the attention which it bestows upon the preservation of the health and lives of its subjects—the guardianship which it exercises over the welfare of its people.

"As American citizens we boast, and very justly too, of our progress in commerce, agriculture, manufactures, literature, the arts and sciences, and of the general diffusion of knowledge among all classes of society; but what have we done as a nation for our sanitary condition, for those things which so vitally concern the public health, the dearest interest of every family in the land? The government has done nothing; it has not even recognized the necessity of a great Bureau of Health, so essential in a sanitary point of view. Our local boards of health, as they are denominated, are mere shadows, the creatures for the most part of municipal authorities, who farm out our health and our lives to the highest bidder at so much a head. Surely the first, the greatest duty of a nation is to protect the lives of its citizens, by teaching them how to live, how to guard against disease, and how to improve the race. The sanitary condition of a community is intimately associated with its moral and religious welfare. People cannot be good or happy if they are not healthy. 'Cleanliness is indeed next to godliness,' says John Wesley. Millions of our fellow-creatures die every year from preventable diseases. The treatment of the more common affections, or such as are of daily occurrence, has attained a high degree of perfection. In surgery many of the operative procedures are as perfect as it is, apparently, possible to render them. But in regard to what are known as the zymotic diseases, such as measles, scarlatina, whooping-cough, cholera, smallpox, yellow fever, and typhoid fever, which annually destroy many millions of lives, our knowledge is still exceedingly defective; and it is to this class of affections, especially to the causes which underlie their origin and propagation, that the attention of this Association should be mainly directed, and through it the attention of our General and State governments. Most of these diseases are, under proper sanitary regulations, in a great measure, if not wholly, preventable. Sensible men no longer ascribe the frightful outbreak of those epidemic disorders which occasionally ravage whole nations, to the wrath of an offended Deity; they know better; they know that they are due, for the most part, to man's ignorance or to man's criminal neglect. At this very moment, at Darwen, a manufacturing town in Lancaster County, England, upwards of fifteen hundred persons, at least one-sixteenth of the entire population, are groaning under an epidemic of typhoid fever, due, beyond all question, to bad sewerage and other preventable causes of sickness.

"Have we not a right to ask for government assistance

in this matter? We have a minister of war and a minister of the navy to keep the country in a condition ready to meet any foreign bloodhounds that may threaten our liberties and deprive us of our territory. Why then should there not be a minister of health to see to our sanitary affairs, to enable us the better to cope with the enemies that visit us in our own dwellings and in those of our neighbors? Have we not a right, as dutiful citizens, to claim this much from the government? If a man robs me of my goods, the law takes cognizance of the offence, and punishes the thief with fine and imprisonment; but when my neighbor poisons my well, my food, or the air I breathe, I have no recourse, unless the case is so plain that it cannot be overlooked. Every man desires to live as long as possible, and not only so, but as happily as possible; but, owing to our ignorance, millions upon millions annually perish prematurely, simply because they do not know how to live, and how to guard against the occurrence of disease. So long as we are without well-organized government aid, so long will our people from the lowest to the highest pay the penalty of preventable disease.

"I have brought forward these resolutions in the hope that they will meet the prompt and undivided approval of this meeting. Let the influential men and women of the country unite with us in this grand effort; and my word for it, the time is not distant when we shall have a Health Department at the capital of the nation, with competent and well-qualified subordinates."

After further remarks by Dr. Curtis, the resolutions on motion of Professor Hartshorne were referred to the Special Committee on Legislation.

Upon this movement the New York World of November 15th, 1874, passed some severe strictures in a lengthy editorial. It deprecated the establishment of such a bureau on the ground that it would soon fall into the hands of certain rings, who would make it the means of extorting money from the government instead of promoting the public interest. The special committee to whom the resolutions were referred have never taken any action upon the subject, and thus the matter remains where it was in its original form. It is the merest sophistry to argue against the value of such a department; the fact that it is liable to abuse, and that it might thus fall short of its aims and ends, is surely no valid objection to its establishment. If there is any one public bureau in this country that is not open to abuse, or in which the most shameful abuses are not constantly carried on, the people have not yet discovered it. As we become more civilized and enlightened the necessity for such a department will become more and more apparent, and I have therefore no doubt of its ultimate accomplishment. The American Public Health Association is a live body, which has already done vast good, and which is daily exciting fresh interest in the cause of sanitary reform.

On Sunday, October 4th, 1874, Mr. and Mrs. Erichsen, who were very kind to us during our visit to London in 1872, met us at dinner. Among the guests were Professor and Mrs. Joseph Pancoast, Professors Rogers and Da Costa, Dr. Richard J. Levis, Dr. and Mrs. F. F. Maury, Miss Emily Schaumburg, Mr. and Mrs. Orville Horwitz, and my two sons. The *menu* was an elaborate one, and everything passed off pleasantly. Three hours, spiced with agreeable conversation and followed by music, were spent at table. My wife talked much and well; and the Erichsens seemed to enjoy themselves.

A few evenings after this a public dinner was given at Augustine's, in the best style of that famous caterer, to Mr. Erichsen by the physicians of Philadelphia, about thirty participating. It was my privilege to preside on the occasion, and to introduce the guest of the evening, whom of course everybody present knew, if not person-

ally, at all events by his writings, which have given him
a world-wide reputation. The Art and Science of Surgery has passed through many editions both in England
and in this country; and during our late war it was
placed on the supply-table to the number of more than
five thousand copies. Mr. Erichsen was in his happiest
mood; and his speech, conceived in the best taste, was
received with rapturous applause. Similar compliments
were paid to him in Baltimore and New York, if not
also in Boston; and the great surgeon left our shores well
pleased with his visit.

On Saturday, December 12th, at my college clinic, I
operated upon a woman for strangulated femoral hernia,
cut a boy for stone in the bladder, amputated a leg for a
girl, and operated upon a child for harelip. In addition
to this work, I prescribed for many clinical patients and
visited a number of persons in different parts of the
city, three of them in consultation. In the evening I
attended a social gathering, returning at eleven o'clock.
This assuredly was a large day's work for a man near the
latter half of his seventieth year; and yet I bore it all
wonderfully well, being not so much fatigued as I often
was in my younger days with less labor upon my hands.

The death of a good and virtuous wife is the greatest
calamity that can befall a human being, a blow well calculated to stagger the stoutest heart, and to render one's
future life a complete blank. Death had been absent from
my family for nearly a third of a century, when, on Sunday evening the 27th of February, 1876, I was called upon
along with my children to mourn the departure of the
noble woman who for nearly forty-eight years had been
the sharer of my joys and sorrows, and between whom
and myself there had always existed the warmest and
purest attachment. She expired at half past eight o'clock
in the evening in my arms, and in the presence of her son

Haller, who had watched all day at her bedside, in assiduous and tender devotion to her wants. Samuel was absent at the time, but arrived soon after the sad event. My two daughters reached the house shortly after ten o'clock—a despatch having been sent to Louisa to come on without delay. Fortunately she was accompanied by Maria, who had gone home only six days previously, after having been with her dear mother for the last two months of her life, and was persuaded that she must be dangerously ill. Although my wife had suffered more than usual during the last week of her life, I felt no special anxiety respecting her condition until about eighteen hours before her death, when, for the first time, symptoms of a grave character set in. The neuralgic pains under which she had so long labored had been uncommonly severe the previous evening; but under the influence of her accustomed dose of chloral and of the hypodermic injection of a grain of morphia she soon fell into a comparatively comfortable sleep until about two o'clock in the morning, when she awoke and complained of severe pain in the right shoulder and epigastric region. Her mind began to wander, and her delirium soon assumed a most distressing form, manifesting itself in constant moans and incoherent expressions. At half past four o'clock I summoned my sons to her bedside; for I was now grievously alarmed, and afraid she might die at any moment. Another hypodermic injection of morphia was administered, which, with brandy and milk, had the effect of putting her into a tranquil sleep, which lasted until after eight o'clock in the morning. She then awoke, and, with the exception of occasional snatches of sleep, continued more or less delirious and incoherent until she expired. Several hours before her death she suffered, at intervals, from nausea and also from vomiting. Her chief complaint during the day and evening was pain referred to the right shoulder and to the pit of the stomach. She died without a groan, and evidently, as far as could be determined, without consciousness that her end was at hand. She had been told early in the day that Louisa had been telegraphed for, and in her delirium she several times spoke of her by name. I was with her all day, except from one to two o'clock, when I was compelled to visit a patient in consultation. Six days before her death she rode with me to the upper part of the city; and, although she was a good deal fatigued, she seemed to be none the worse for the effort. For the next few days, however, her neuralgia assumed an unusual degree of severity. On Friday evening she was so much better that she spent several hours in light reading, and was deeply interested in the bouquets sent to Samuel and Haller by some of their lady friends; it was the night of a leap-year ball which they both attended, returning at a late hour.

My dear wife had suffered more or less severely from neuralgia and dyspepsia for upwards of ten years. I had visited Europe twice on account of her health—first in 1868, and again in 1872—and on both occasions she was much benefited. During her last visit she was very ill at Oxford, and again for a short time at London. However, she was able on the 13th of June to attend the Exercises in the University, and was greatly pleased at seeing me receive the degree of Doctor of Civil Laws. On our return voyage she suffered much from seasickness, and was but once on deck.

These neuralgic pains, together with frequent attacks of dyspepsia, gradually undermined her health, and at length wore out the machinery of life. In reflecting upon her case, the surprise is not that she died, but that she held out so long. At her death she was nearly sixty-eight years and a half old. I attribute her vital tenacity to the wonderful elasticity of her system, and to her determination to live despite the sufferings which her ailments inflicted upon her. Something, no doubt, was

also due to my care of her; to the incessant vigilance with
which I regarded her case; and to the promptness with
which I met the indications of her symptoms.   If she had
not been the wife of a physician, her life, I am satisfied,
would have been much shorter and her suffering much
more severe.

I made the acquaintance of my wife in 1827, in the
month of April, while I was a student at the Jefferson Medical College, in the third year of my pupilage.   If we did
not fall in love at first sight, we soon became warmly attached to each other.   Our attachment culminated in a
few months in an engagement which was consummated
the following year, she being at the time in her twenty-
first year and I in my twenty-third.   We were both poor,
and our affection was therefore of a pure and unselfish
character.   My wife was pretty, highly cultured for one of
her age, and a fine musician, both as a vocalist and pianist,
with charming manners.   By the father's side her descent
was German; by the mother's, English.   She was born at
Kensington, near London, August 22d, 1807, during a visit
of her parents to England.   Both parents died when she
was quite young.   Her mother, whose maiden name was
Davis, and who was educated at the celebrated female
seminary at Bethlehem, Pennsylvania, was an elegant, refined, and highly accomplished woman, from whom her
daughter evidently inherited her musical talents, afterwards transmitted to her own children and grandchildren.
Her father's name was Frederick Weissell, a Prussian
gentleman.   As the time for our marriage drew nigh, my
wife's friends tried hard to break off the engagement, on
the ground that I was in ill health, and that she would
therefore, ere long, again become a widow.   Their efforts,
however, were unavailing.   The truth is that my health
was not materially impaired; I was only a little dyspeptic,
and somewhat overworked.   The fact that I have lived to
the age of nearly seventy-one years is a sufficient proof, at

all events, that I had a good constitution, and that I had
no organic disease at the time referred to. I have, in the
main, all my life enjoyed excellent health, which is so
much the more surprising, considering the great amount
of labor I have performed as a practitioner, as a writer, as
a teacher, and as an operating surgeon.

In reflecting upon my married life I have great reason
for thankfulness. It was an eminently happy life. Few
men have ever been so blessed in their matrimonial relations. The attachment formed in our young days gradually increased in intensity as we advanced in years, and
burned with a steady flame until my wife expired in my
arms, mingling thus her last breath with mine. I know of
nothing more touching than the sight of a young and loving
wife encouraging her husband in his efforts to earn a livelihood for his family, and watching his rising fame. It
reminds one of the nurseryman watering his plants and
watching the unfolding of their petals. Such was my
wife. She was contented with her lot, and sympathized
in all my movements, labors, and aspirations. I never
knew her to be guilty of one selfish act. Her ambition
always was to accommodate herself to circumstances. She
ever exercised a laudable economy. Unlike many of the
women around her, she never lived above her means or
her husband's income. She took great pride in making
her house attractive to her husband, her children, and her
friends. Her musical talents, her remarkable intelligence,
her fine conversational powers, and her genial disposition
drew around her a coterie of friends, always as welcome as
they were improved and gratified, and made her one of
the most attractive women in the social circle whom I
have ever known. She was especially fond of young
persons ; she delighted to converse with them, and to
give them good advice. Not a few of her more intimate
young friends were indebted to her for spiritual counsel
and guidance. Into the hands of a number of them she

placed Nelson on Infidelity, McIlvaine on the Evidences of Christianity, and similar works, with a view of confirming their faith in the truth and beauty of the Christian religion. Although she was fond of fashionable society, she never allowed herself to be influenced by its exactions, or to be drawn aside by its allurements. She had a winsome smile and a cordial shake of the hand for every one who approached her. Her laugh was infectious. During her residence in Louisville, it was a common thing for her and for her two neighbors, Mrs. Graves and Mrs. Preston, on a pleasant summer evening, to walk up and down on the pavement, in front of their respective houses, talking innocent gossip, interspersed with laughter that made the welkin ring. Her reading was varied and extensive; and she had the happy faculty, possessed by few persons, of getting at the marrow of a book with marvellous rapidity. During the latter years of her life her reading was confined, in great measure, to religious books, especially the Bible and Barnes's Notes on the New Testament, and to novels, of which one or more were almost constantly upon her table. She also read a good many newspapers, and she was possessed of an extensive knowledge of the events of the day. Her memory was excellent, and she could converse, generally with ease and fluency, upon almost any literary topic. She was particularly well versed in mythological lore, of which she had in early life been a zealous student. One of the great sources of her happiness, during the last three years of her life, when unable to read on account of a weakness of her eyes, was to amuse herself in the evening with the game of *solitaire*, taught her by her only sister, Mrs. Casey. Not less than an hour—sometimes even twice that time—was passed in this way for evenings together, especially during the long winter nights.

With my wife religion was not a mere sentiment; it was a positive reality. Reared in the Episcopal Church, the church of her forefathers by the mother's side, she was a scrupulous observer of its rites and ceremonies, and a devout believer in the truth of its doctrines. A Sunday missed from church was to her a Sunday lost. She accepted, without reservation, the teachings both of the Old and the New Testament as emanations from the Deity— as the writings of men directly inspired by God. Upon this subject she was intolerant of the slightest scepticism. Her familiarity with the Bible enabled her readily to quote almost any of its more important passages. She was a frequent reader of Bishop McIlvaine's Evidences of Christianity. The author, for whom she had a warm regard, was a personal friend, and a copy of the work was presented to her by him during his sojourn in our house at Louisville nearly twenty-five years ago. In the religion of the Episcopal Church she strove to educate her children.

I cannot finish this brief sketch of the character of my wife without bearing witness to her kind and charitable disposition, to her refined tastes, and to the delicacy of her language in her ordinary intercourse with her family and her domestics, or with what properly constitutes one's household. No unrefined expression ever passed her lips; nor would she tolerate such an expression in others. In a word, her walk and conversation were, under all circumstances, pure and delicate. An oath uttered in her presence was almost an unpardonable offence, causing a shudder to run through her frame. She had a great love for flowers—a love which she instilled into her children, and from which she herself derived great happiness. She was a good judge of a picture, and an admirer of art in its higher forms. She was a frequent visitor of our beautiful park, and accompanied me in many a ride, especially in summer and autumn, through the neighborhood of the city abounding in fine rural scenery and pleasant drives. It was only about eight months before her death that I bought for her special use in New York,

I—47

a cabriolet with low steps, that she might have no difficulty in getting into and out of it. It was a source of great enjoyment to her.

It only remains that I should speak of her as a wife and as a mother. In both of these relations her conduct was eminently exemplary. As a wife, she was warm-hearted, tender, loving, confiding, sympathizing, ever ready to perform kind offices, to anticipate wants, and to take an active interest in everything pertaining to my welfare. I know she loved me with an intense ardor. I need not add how fondly I was attached to her, and how constantly I strove to augment her happiness. Her very sufferings endeared her to me. Is this at all surprising when it is remembered that our married life extended over a period of nearly forty-eight years? I found in her a wise counsellor; and I seldom wrote an address, introductory discourse, or valedictory without submitting the manuscript to her inspection and adopting her criticisms. She had excellent taste and fine judgment. Early in our married life she copied a number of papers for me, principally notes on scientific treatises; but she never wrote any of my discourses or published works. She was an admirable letter-writer, composing rapidly and fluently, always clothing her sentiments in apposite and correct language.

As a mother she was in every respect quite as exemplary; warm-hearted, generous, indulgent, and yet exacting, with an eye constantly alive to the moral and religious training of her children. I do not think there ever was a more loving, fond, or doting mother; and the best proof of the truth of this opinion is that her children literally idolized her. Always unselfish, it seemed as if all her efforts were bent upon making them and their father happy. Her grandchildren—seven in number—were most fondly attached to her; and in her departure they have lost one of their dearest, tenderest, and most devoted friends.

This good woman—the crown and jewel of a wife—never

had an enemy. If she ever gave offence, it grew out of unavoidable circumstances. She harbored no enmity or ill feeling. Her generous nature did not admit of such an indulgence. She was emphatically the friend of human kind, and an avowed enemy to harshness and cruelty, whether inflicted upon man or the lower animals. She considered life a great boon, and was ever in favor of its largest enjoyment. If she did not engage in works which brought her before the public, it was simply because her delicate and sensitive nature shrank from the public gaze. Her private charities, although not numerous, were creditable to her heart and in accord with her means.

My wife, as already stated, died on the 27th of February, and was buried on Wednesday, March 1st, the funeral being strictly private. The pall-bearers were Dr. P. J. Horwitz, U. S. N., brother of my two sons-in-law, and formerly Chief of the Bureau of Medicine and Surgery at Washington; Mr. Henry C. Carey; Professor Joseph Pancoast; and the Rev. Mr. Edmund C. Bittinger, Chaplain U. S. Navy—all intimate and valued friends. The services were performed at the house by the Rev. C. George Currie. My two sons, two daughters with their husbands, my wife's sister, Mrs. Casey, Mrs. Pancoast, and Mrs. F. F. Maury, with our servants, and Rev. Dr. William Rudder, of St. Stephen's Church, were the only persons present. The exercises were brief, but solemn and impressive; the day was cold and cloudy. The body was tenderly laid away in the family vault at Woodlands Cemetery, West Philadelphia, in a lot since inclosed with curbing and embellished with roses, geraniums, and heliotropes. The lot is beautifully situated, and is all that could be desired as the resting-place of one so much loved and so much missed. She herself had often visited the cemetery, and expressed her satisfaction at the beauty of its arrangements, its interesting site on the west bank of the Schuylkill, the abundance of its floral decorations, and the songs of its numerous birds perched upon lofty trees, rendering the air musical with their melody. Here I expect ere long to repose myself by the side of the woman whom I so much loved, and whose loss has left me in a state of utter desolation at a period of life when I am so greatly in need of that domestic comfort which she knew so well how to administer, and of which I was for nearly half a century the happy recipient. Thus we all, sooner or later, come to realize the words of the poet:

> "The night hath a thousand eyes,
> The day but one;
> But the light of the whole world dies
> At set of sun.

> "And the mind has a thousand eyes,
> The heart but one;
> Yet the light of a whole life dies
> When love is done."

My dear wife's tomb bears the following simple inscription:

"A NOBLE, CHRISTIAN WOMAN."

Eight children were born to us—three daughters and five sons. Joseph, Frederick, and Hunter died in infancy. Julia, the eldest, was called away in her ninth year. She was a child of great intelligence, sprightliness, and promise, and her death caused her mother and myself much grief and suffering. Even after the lapse of nearly forty years, when I look back to that event, the first shadow that overcast our domestic life, I never fail to heave a deep sigh. To me this affliction came with double force. A great sufferer in her infancy, I nursed her every night to afford her mother rest, exhausted as she generally was by the labors of the day; and during full nine months the dear child lay in my arms during those weary hours. The immediate cause of her death was arachnitis, brought on, apparently, by a severe cold as she was returning from

school one day in February. A singular discovery was
made in the examination of the body after death. In the
upper lobe of the left lung, near its middle, lay coiled up a
piece of worsted about an inch in length, which she must
have accidentally inhaled in a fit of coughing some weeks,
perhaps months, before her last illness, as was proved by
the fact that the tissues in immediate contact with it were
slightly ulcerated and indurated. Had Julia been spared
to us, there is every reason to believe that she would have
made a brilliant, if not a great woman. Her love for reading and studying was remarkable; and she had a quick,
active, observing mind, apt in imbibing knowledge. She
never seemed to be so happy as when she was sitting by
herself in a corner of a room with a copy of the Arabian
Nights on her knees. In this manner she would often
spend hours together, apparently forgetful of self and
everything around her. Her fondness and capacity for
music were unusual, and were manifestly the result of
hereditary transmission on the mother's side. Long before she was three years old she sang with much expression a number of songs and played several pieces on the
piano. In form she was very graceful; in temper, sweet
and loving; in disposition, social; in her attachments,
warm and steadfast. Without being what may be called a
beauty, her features were attractive, and denotive of great
intelligence; her eyes and hair were black. Of the three
boys who died in infancy, all that I can say is that they
were handsome children. What would have become of
them had they lived is a mystery. Like matrimony,
the life of a child is a lottery, in which there are many
blanks and few prizes. Life at best is a struggle;
and there are few youths who reach the goal of their
ambition.

Of my surviving children it does not become me to
speak. Suffice it to say that my two sons are actively engaged in the practice of their respective professions, medi-

cine and law; and that my daughters, two affectionate and accomplished women, are happily married to cultured and refined gentlemen, distinguished members of the Baltimore bar.

I stated elsewhere that I have seldom lost a lecture from illness. Last December, however, in consequence of a severe cold, seriously affecting my larynx, I was prevented for one entire month from meeting my class. For nearly half of this time I was barely able to speak in a whisper. My strength, too, had given way; and, although I did not at any time consider myself decidedly ill, some of my friends, and especially my dear wife, felt uneasy about the result. When I resumed my lectures on the first day of the year 1876 I was still very feeble; and when my domestic affliction took place, on the 27th of February, my strength was still somewhat impaired. The terrible blow again exhausted me; and it was not until after several weeks of sea-bathing at Cape May, an exercise of which I have always been very fond, that my health was perfectly restored.

In the winter of 1874 the Philadelphia County Medical Society appointed a committee, consisting of thirteen of its members, with myself as its chairman, to devise plans for the organization of an International Medical Congress to convene in this city in 1876. After a number of meetings the different medical societies of Philadelphia were embraced in the scheme; and a joint committee of delegates was appointed, known as the Centennial Medical Commission, with power to perfect all the arrangements necessary for holding the Congress and pushing it to a successful issue. The labors of this committee were immense, involving numerous meetings, a heavy and extensive correspondence, an uncommon degree of executive ability, and a considerable outlay of money. As the Commission was found to be too bulky, its work was finally confided to a

Committee of Arrangements, who, in the end, did it ample justice, as was shown by the success of the Congress.

The Congress convened in this city at twelve o'clock noon, September 4th, 1876, in the Chapel of the University of Pennsylvania, kindly placed at its disposal by the Trustees and Faculty of that institution. It was opened with prayer by the Right Rev. William Bacon Stevens, Bishop of Pennsylvania, after having been called to order by myself as Chairman of the Centennial Medical Commission. The attendance of delegates and citizens was large, the room being well filled. A committee, consisting of thirteen—nine Americans and four foreigners—had been appointed two days previously by the Committee of Arrangements to nominate officers for the Congress. After my address of welcome they reported partially the results of their deliberations. I was selected to be the president without one dissenting voice—an unsolicited compliment. The names of thirteen vice-presidents were then announced, at the head of whom was Dr. Paul F. Eve, of Nashville, Tennessee. The list embraced a Japanese professor, Dr. H. Miyake, of the Medical College of Tokio, and a number of distinguished American and foreign delegates. Dr. Barnes, Surgeon-General U. S. A., and Dr. H. V. P. Beale, Chief of the Bureau of Medicine and Surgery, Washington City, were elected Honorary Vice-Presidents, but neither of them attended the meeting. Dr. I. Minis Hays, son of the veteran editor of the American Journal of the Medical Sciences, was appointed Secretary. The Assistant Secretaries were Dr. W. B. Atkinson, Dr. Richard J. Dunglison, Dr. Richard A. Cleemann, Dr. William W. Keen, and Dr. R. M. Bertolet. The session lasted an entire week. The addresses delivered on the progress of American Medicine during the last one hundred years were for the most part highly interesting; a great deal of work was done in the Sections, nine in number; the utmost harmony prevailed throughout: and the Congress was a success in all its details. Four hundred and forty-two delegates, of whom seventy-one were foreigners, were in attendance, representing the British Dominion, Australia, England, Ireland and Scotland, Belgium, Germany, Austria, Russia, Sweden, Norway, Finland, Greece, Cuba, Mexico, Japan, and China. To preside over such a body of men, many of them of high reputation as scientists, teachers, and writers, I esteemed a great honor, and so expressed myself on taking the chair, adding that I considered it not so much a tribute to myself personally as to the physicians of Philadelphia, through whose agency the meeting had taken place. The public dinner of the Congress took place at St. George's Hall on Friday evening, September 8th. I occupied the chair, with Professor Lister, of Edinburgh, on my right, and Governor Hartranft on my left. About one hundred and sixty gentlemen sat down. I must not forget to add that my address of welcome was well received and favorably noticed by the press—medical and lay. The Congress, the Transactions of which are to be published, under the editorship of Dr. John Ashhurst, Jr., at an early day, was undoubtedly the best meeting of a medical character ever held on this continent, whether we consider the talents, scientific attainments, and position of its members, or the amount and character of its work.

The 10th of February, 1877, witnessed the death of one of the greatest surgeons of the age, Sir William Fergusson, at his residence in London at the age of sixty-nine years. The newspapers state that his health had been for some time declining, and that the event had consequently not been unexpected. The immediate cause of his demise was exhaustion from renal disease, accompanied with dropsy. During my sojourn in London in 1868 and 1872 I saw Fergusson repeatedly, first at King's College Hospital, in his capacity of clinical surgeon; secondly, as President of the Royal College of Surgeons; and lastly as Chairman of the Surgical Section of the British Medical Association at its meeting at Birmingham, in August, 1872. In all these relations, as well as in private life, he bore himself with the demeanor of a well-bred gentleman, although his manner was at all times cold and formal. His physique was splendid: in height he was fully six feet, with broad shoulders, a large head, and well-formed features, the *tout ensemble* betokening a strong and highly-cultured intellect incased in a vigorous frame. He might be said to have been a prince of a man. He had somewhat of a Scotch accent, and was slow of speech, stately in his movements, and quite erect in his gait. As an operator he possessed great dexterity, and he was generally acknowledged to be without a rival in the British metropolis. He certainly was master of his knife; and yet I saw him do things which I had often seen done quite as well before, both at home and abroad. What more especially impressed me was his calm and deliberate manner. There was no display or parade about him. He went about his business like an ordinary laborer who was not in a hurry to finish his task. The movements of his hands were slow and measured, and it seemed as if nothing could disturb his equanimity. These are certainly high attributes in an operator. As a lecturer he was dull, monotonous, inanimate, and deficient in power of expression. No one who listened to him while he was explaining the history of a case could fail to be struck with the paucity of his language, or the inadequacy of his remarks. To me it seemed as if he took everything for granted; as if the pupil knew as much about the matter as the master. "This, gentlemen," he said on one occasion, "this, gentlemen, is a fatty tumor, seated in the man's neck; it was first noticed some six years ago, and had, as you noticed, strong attachments. The patient is a butcher by occupation, and he will, I think, do well." On another occasion he performed his favorite operation of staphylorraphy without

I.—48

uttering one word of explanation as to the manner of executing it. Such clinical teaching would hardly be tolerated on this side of the Atlantic. Here a man takes great pains to explain fully to his class the history of his cases, their diagnosis and treatment, and, if an operation is required, the reasons for, and the manner of, its performance, with an account of the subsequent management of the patient. In all these details, so important in a clinical point of view, Sir William struck me as being quite at fault. How he ranked as a didactic lecturer at King's College in his character as professor I do not know ; but, judging from what I saw of him at King's College Hospital, he must have been slow, ponderous, and uninteresting, and his pupils must have been glad to get away from him at the expiration of his hour. His forte was his knife—not the explanation of the structure of a cell or the development of protoplasm. As a writer I should ascribe to Fergusson more than ordinary merit ; his style is clear, and his English has been excelled by few men in our profession. He was a liberal contributor to the periodical press ; and the author of a work entitled Practical Surgery, which has passed through five editions, and which will always be consulted as reflecting the views and experience of one of the greatest surgeons of any age or country. In 1867 he published a series of Lectures on the Progress of Anatomy and Surgery during the Present Century, delivered a short time previously in his capacity as Professor of Anatomy and Surgery at the Royal College of Surgeons of England, and originally published in the London Lancet. These discourses are far from being what they profess to be. One looks through them in vain for an account of the progress of anatomy and surgery in the nineteenth century. The great objective point of the book is Sir William Fergusson—what Sir William has done in regard to the operations for harelip and cleft palate, excision of certain joints, lithotrity, and lithotomy.

All this is well enough; for it is certain that he did more to advance operative surgery in England than all his London confrères put together, and he had therefore a right to speak of himself; but he had no right to delude the Fellows of the Royal College of Surgeons into the belief that, in doing so, he was giving them an account of what had been done in anatomy and surgery during the present century in different parts of the world, or even in his own country.

Fergusson was by birth a Scotchman, having been born at Preston Pans, East Lothian, in 1808. He studied medicine under Dr. Knox, the celebrated anatomist, at a time when the latter was so unpleasantly mixed up with the Burk and Hare scandal, which eventually drove him into partial exile, from the effects of which he never recovered. His pupil, whose greatness was early foreshadowed, firmly convinced of his master's innocence, continued to the last to sustain and to befriend him. After taking his degree at Edinburgh, in 1828, Fergusson delivered private courses of lectures on Anatomy and Surgery, and in 1836 was appointed assistant surgeon to the Royal Infirmary. In 1840 he went to London as Professor of Surgery in King's College and as Surgeon to King's College Hospital. Here he rose rapidly into notice as a dexterous operator, and as consulting surgeon to the higher classes of the metropolis, including the nobility. In due time he was appointed Sergeant Surgeon to the Queen. In 1865 he was made a baronet; and in 1870 he was elected President of the Royal College of Surgeons of England. At Birmingham he acted as chairman of the Surgical Section, and presided, in the absence of the President, Mr. Baker, at the public dinner. The following year, when the Association met in London, he occupied the chair, filling it with his accustomed dignity. This, I believe, was the last honor he received from a profession which had so long appreciated his worth as a surgeon, but with which he never was popular as a man. His pupils, however, were much attached to him. and many regarded him as the Ajax of British surgery.

King's College Hospital is one of the largest and best conducted establishments of the kind in the British metropolis, and I was indebted to Sir William Fergusson for the opportunity of seeing everything of interest about it. Like most similar institutions in London, it is devoid of grounds, being situated in a rather thickly-settled district, within a short distance of the Hunterian Museum. It has a capacity of three hundred beds, is thoroughly ventilated, and kept in perfect order. The edifice was erected at great cost, and is so lofty as to afford an excellent view of London and its vicinity from the upper wards. In the hall, on the first floor, opposite the door of entrance, stands a marble statue of Thomas Bentley Todd, one of the former physicians of the hospital, and the author of what I have called Toddism, the founder, or at all events one of the chief supporters, of the doctrine of a change of type in disease, and of the feeding system in its treatment—a system which, I do not hesitate to affirm, has slain millions of human beings by the indiscriminate manner in which it has been employed. The stairways are the finest I have ever seen. The lecture-room, although small, is very convenient, the seats rising abruptly one above another, and being furnished with iron backs, so that the students as they stand up, as most of them do, have rests for their arms and elbows. During one of my last visits, late in August, the audience consisted only of thirty-five persons, mostly physicians, representatives from America, Germany, Italy, England, Ireland, and the British army in India—all apparently anxious to see and hear Fergusson.

CHAPTER XIV.

FEBRUARY 27th, 1877.—This has been a sad day with
me ; for it is the anniversary of the death of my beloved
wife, whose place in my heart can never be filled. She
was dear to me beyond measure, and I miss her more
and more as time advances. Without her, the house is
desolate. The year, despite my grief, has passed rapidly
away, thanks to my incessant occupations, which leave me
little time to indulge in gloomy thoughts, and which I
have always found to be the best antidotes for grief. My
health in the main has been good, and I have much to be
thankful for. My children are all happy ; and Dr. S. W.
Gross has been fortunate enough to marry one of the best
and most lovely of women. I now live solely for my children. I have done no visiting since this calamity came
upon me, and I have promptly declined all invitations of
a social character. In truth, I have no inclination to go
anywhere.

This morning I completed my thirty-seventh course of
lectures on Surgery, delivered to five hundred and ninety-
eight matriculated students. I did not miss one lecture
during the entire session ; and I am sure that I never acquitted myself better as a teacher. The class was uncommonly attentive, and so well behaved that it was unneces-

sary for me to utter one word of rebuke during the whole winter. The clinics were rich in instructive cases; and I performed several important operations, among others lithotomy and ligation of the external iliac artery, both followed by recovery.

The examination of the candidates begins on the evening of February 28th, and as this is always up-hill business I anticipate much labor and not a little vexation. Indeed, this is always the hardest and most trying work of the session. I am informed that there are upwards of two hundred of these young men to be tortured. Few of them are prepared as they should be; most of them are unripe from a want of sufficient study and training; and not a few of them are destitute of brains. It is lamentable to think how imperfect the whole system of medical education is in this country. Our students are driven from one lecture to another, hour after hour, like so many cattle; and the wonder is that, when they come up for their final examination at the close of the session, they have any knowledge at all of a fixed or definite character.

March 7th.—The examinations are over and I am heartily rejoiced at it, as I am well nigh worn out, mentally especially. The answers hardly afford a fair average. I found most of the candidates lamentably deficient on the principles of surgery, that part of my course upon which I always dwell with great force and emphasis during the first six weeks of the session. The fact is much of what the student is taught in the early part of the session is knocked out of him before the close. He gets a daily surfeit from the beginning to the end; and the consequence is that his knowledge is vague and imperfect in every branch of his studies. We meet this evening to vote upon the candidates.

March 8th.—Of the two hundred and three candidates voted upon last evening fourteen are suspended, but as they are all entitled to reëxamination we shall have another hard day of it. We met at two o'clock in the afternoon, and passed all but five! If we had been just to ourselves we should have rejected every one of them as utterly unfit for the doctorate; but it is difficult, if not impossible, to meet with seven men who always think alike upon any one subject; and upon this subject especially I have always found the greatest divergence of views among my colleagues in all the schools with which I have ever been connected.

March 10th.—The Commencement takes place at twelve o'clock to-day at the Academy of Music. I have made up my mind not to attend, feeling convinced that I would break down, under the influence of the music and the brilliant assembly, by being too forcibly reminded of one who seldom failed on such occasions to grace the audience. My wounds are too fresh to bear the shock. I have promised my children a visit; and I am off in the 12.10 train for Baltimore. Joyous hearts will, I am sure, await me at the depot, followed by the cordial greetings of my grandchildren and sons-in-law.

To-day, March 13th, my two daughters—Mrs. Benjamin F. and Mrs. Orville Horwitz—and I have made an appointment to run over to Washington to take a peep at the Senate Chamber and to lunch with our good old friend, Mrs. J. Scott Laughton, late Madame Berghmans *née* Macalester. We find nothing in the Senate of special interest. The galleries are crowded with visitors, and the reporters are in full force; but few of the Senators are in their seats, although it is now past twelve o'clock. A young man near us kindly points out the most conspicuous men upon the floor. Presently the gavel falls, the Senators rise to their feet, and the chaplain offers a short prayer. Morton is easily recognized by his crutches and by his bulldog-looking face; he is tall and sombre, and walks with difficulty. He evidently feels the effects of the wild oats sown in his youth. Blaine is walking about the chamber with his overcoat hanging partially off his shoulders, as much as to say, "Don't you see me? I am Senator Blaine, lately an expectant candidate for the Presidency, and now engaged in punishing the man who defeated my nomination at Cincinnati." He is a tall man, with a dark complexion, and at the distance at which I am seated has a distinguished bearing. Simon Cameron has just resigned his seat, and is at Harrisburg electioneering for his son, who is to be his successor. Conkling has the appearance of a dignified gentleman. He has light hair, eyes, and complexion, is busily engaged in writing, and now and then looks up to shake hands with a colleague. "That stout, tall, sluggish-looking man coming towards us," says our chaperone, "is Mr. Davis, of Illinois, lately an Associate Justice of the Supreme Court." I had a good look at Hamlin, Bayard, and a number of others; but as I surveyed the scene, and examined the heads and faces of the men below me, I said to myself, "There are as many great men outside the Senate Chamber as there are in it." After the Senate had been in session for about twenty minutes it took a recess for one hour, and adjourned immediately after reassembling, as there was no business of any importance to be transacted.

From the Senate Chamber we went to the room of the Supreme Court. All the judges, in their official robes, were in their seats. One of them, an old friend of mine, Associate Justice Strong, was engaged in reading an "opinion," as it is called—about as dry a business, it seemed to me, as could possibly occupy any man's time. A sojourn of five minutes sufficed to satisfy us that nothing was to be gained by remaining here, and so, casting one more look at the dignified gentlemen in black gowns, we left the room.

We now passed into the rotunda, one of the finest structures of the kind in the world, desecrated by some of the worst paintings that ever disgraced the brush of an artist. Why these pictures are permitted to retain their place in so conspicuous a part of this great building passes all comprehension. The Landing of Columbus is the merest daub.

The luncheon at Mrs. Laughton's was delightful, well served, and fortified with the best wines and the best humor. The house, although not large, is in a fashionable part of the city, and is beautifully furnished, the walls being adorned with the elegant pictures belonging to Mrs. Laughton's late father. At half past four o'clock we were at the Washington depot, and in one hour more were in Baltimore, the iron horse having run a distance of forty miles within that short time.

I called this morning, March 16th, upon my friend and early anatomical preceptor, Professor N. R. Smith, the eminent Baltimore surgeon. As I had been led to fear from various reports, I found him greatly changed in his appearance from the effects of long-continued suffering. He was pale and attenuated, and, what shocked me greatly, his mind afforded unmistakable evidence of decadence. He was uncommonly garrulous, talked incoherently, and frequently repeated himself, showing clearly that his memory, once so acute and ready, had given way. Dr. Smith is now nearly, if not quite, eighty years of age; he has led a very active life, and is one of the most distinguished surgeons that our country has produced. He was for more than forty years the main pillar of the University of Maryland, and for nearly the same length of time the head of the medical profession in Baltimore, by whom, as well as by the community at large, he has been much beloved. The title of "Emperor" bestowed upon him by his confrères is an evidence of the esteem in which he is held by them. As a mechanical surgeon he has justly occupied a high rank; as a surgical pathologist and practitioner he has many equals. He has written little of value. His book on the Surgical Anatomy of the Arteries

is his best production.   He has devised several ingenious
instruments, one in particular for simplifying lithotomy ;
and his anterior splint for the treatment of fractures of
the lower extremity has made his name widely known at
home and abroad.   Dr. Smith has long been a member of
the Maryland Club, is passionately fond of a game of
euchre, and has the reputation of being one of the best
anecdotists in the country.   In person he is nearly six feet
in height and gracefully formed.   To look at such a man,
worn out by disease and protracted suffering, a mere wreck
of what he once was, is a melancholy sight.   After listening to him for half an hour, which he spent almost wholly
in giving me a disconnected account of his case, I sorrow-
fully took my leave, feeling convinced that, although he
might last a few months longer, I should never again see
him alive.

Professor Smith, like most men who have attained to
eminence, began life poor.   His father, the celebrated
Nathan Smith, of New Haven, a man of mark in his
day, left no heritage to his children save an honored
name.   When in 1825 the son, who had already been a
professor at Burlington, Vermont, came to Philadelphia to
enter upon the duties of the anatomical chair in the Jefferson Medical College, then recently created, he was hardly
thirty years of age, and almost wholly without means.
During the two years of his connection with the college
the fees from the students were very slender, and as he
was a stranger in a city which could boast of many of the
best medical men in the country he had little or no practice.   It was therefore not surprising that, in the autumn
of 1827, he eagerly accepted the chair of Anatomy in the
University of Maryland, with the assurance that upon the
resignation of Professor Davidge, then old and infirm, he
should succeed to the chair of Surgery.   The change was
one of great advantage to him, and a few years sufficed
to place Dr. Smith in independent circumstances.   For

more than a third of a century he enjoyed an immense practice, and his earnings must have been great, although, from some cause or other, his estate is now not large. Dr. Smith was for three years Professor of Medicine in Transylvania University under a guaranty, if I mistake not, of three thousand dollars a session and the privilege of retaining his residence in Baltimore.

During my sojourn in Baltimore I was the guest of my son-in-law, Mr. B. F. Horwitz. On the evening of March 17th he was kind enough to invite some gentlemen to meet me at a game of euchre, of which he knew me to be somewhat fond, although I have never been a good player. Soon after we sat down at the table Mr. Martin Farquhar Tupper was announced, and every one of course extended to him a cordial greeting. Other persons dropped in as the evening advanced, and the conversation was for a while quite animated. Presently Mr. Tupper got upon the subject of stammering, saying that he had had an impediment in his speech from early childhood, and that it was only by the most steady and persistent efforts during the last forty years, assisted by constant prayer, that he succeeded in curing himself of it. "I have," said he, "in my Proverbial Philosophy, described this distressing affection;" and, asking for a copy of the book, he read aloud with great feeling what is probably the most eloquent account of it to be found in the language. Upon asking him whether he had entirely broken himself of this habit, his reply was, "I still stammer occasionally, but only in a very slight degree, hardly noticeable in ordinary conversation." Most of the Proverbial Philosophy was written before he was twenty-three years old. Mr. Tupper is a gentleman of medium height, with a good forehead and a benevolent-looking face, very gray, bald, and well on, I should judge, in the seventies. The fingers of his right hand are crooked from the effects of articular rheumatism, and in writing he holds his pen with difficulty. He has now been in the country for some months, engaged in giving readings, mainly from his own writings, chiefly from his Philosophy, in the principal cities of the Union. He is not a good reader, even of his own works; his voice is sharp, discordant, and not well modulated. He receives much attention; and as he is of an eminently social disposition, he seems to enjoy life like a philosopher, as he is. What particularly gratified me was the complimentary manner in which he spoke of our country, and the liberal views he takes of our institutions. He had no hesitation in saying that the Americans speak English better, as a nation, than any people in the world. This is Mr. Tupper's second visit to the United States, the first having been made about twenty years ago. The company remained till a late hour, and the evening was one of the most pleasant I have ever spent anywhere.

On April 14th, 1877, at my college clinic, I performed one of the greatest and most delicate operations of my life. The case was one of lymphoma of the left side of the neck, in a young man of twenty-one years, a resident of Kentucky. It was of nearly two and a half years' duration, and had latterly increased very much in bulk. It extended from the base of the jaw to the collar bone on the one hand, and from near the middle line in front to near the middle of the neck behind on the other, and was composed of numerous nodules, the largest of which was about the size of a goose's egg. The dissection, which occupied nearly one hour, exposed the sheath of the common carotid artery and internal jugular vein, with its accompanying nerves, the digastric and omohyoid muscles, the hypoglossal nerve, the parotid and submaxillary glands, and other important structures. The sterno-cleido-mastoid muscle was divided in the lower part of its course, as it overlay some of the enlarged glands. The only important artery that was divided was the facial; but more than twenty vessels were tied, as blood flowed from numerous points, although probably not more than six ounces were lost in the operation. The youth suffered no pain, as he was kept constantly under the influence of chloroform by Dr. Hearne. My other assistants were Dr. S. W. Gross, Dr. Barton, Dr. Lopez, and Dr. Johnston. Dr. Sayre, of New York, happened to be present, and declared it was the most delicate and beautiful operation he had ever witnessed. Although I am now nearly seventy-two years of age, my sight is excellent and my hand is as steady as ever.

I spent the 20th of April at Florence Heights with Mr. William D. Lewis, an old banker, and one of our most respectable citizens. Mr. Henry C. Carey accompanied me. It was the first dinner I have taken away from my own family since the death of my dear wife, nearly fourteen months ago. It was pleasant, as well as edifying, to hear— these two octogenarians, lifelong and devoted friends, converse, telling anecdotes, and relating occurrences which took place half a century or more ago. Among the anecdotes told by Mr. Lewis was one which he gave upon the authority of Henry Clay, as tending to show that, however pure a man's character may be in private life, the moment he engages in politics it is sure to be assailed and vilified. A very intelligent and respectable farmer was solicited to become a candidate for the office of sheriff. It was supposed that a man of so spotless a character would exercise great influence in promoting the election of the nominee for Congress in his district. After much persuasion he reluctantly assented, with the understanding, however, that he was on no account to be called upon to address his fellow-citizens. Things went on pretty well for some time, when some of his friends called upon him and alarmed him by telling him that his honesty was called in question. "My honesty? I defy any one to prove that. What do they say?" "They assert that you are guilty of hog-stealing; that on one occasion some of your neighbor's hogs had gone into one of your fields, and that instead

of returning them you kept them. Now your friends
deem it proper that you should repel this charge. Of course
we know it to be false, but your opponents must be satisfied that it is false; otherwise it will jeopard your election." He forthwith took the stump, but only got deeper
in the mire. Meeting Mr. Clay some time afterwards, he
said, "Well, they not only accused me of hog-stealing,
but, by G—, they proved it on me, despite all I could say
to the contrary." The moral of all this is that, if a
man desires to retain his self-respect, he had better be
careful how he meddles with politics.

Mr. Lewis has a pleasant country residence on the banks
of the Delaware, where he spends most of his time in reading and meditation. Early in life he passed several years
at St. Petersburg, studying the Russian language, and
translating a small volume of Russian poetry. He is a
vigorous talker, and enjoys a hearty joke or good anecdote
as much as ever.

At our annual Faculty meeting on May 2d, while at
supper, the conversation turned upon various subjects;
among others the singular manner in which a man sometimes obtains practice. Dr. Richard J. Levis, it was
stated, had just gone to California to perform an operation for the relief of carcinoma of the rectum, his patient
having heard that he had recently operated in two
similar cases, one of which, I know, died within a few
days after. Dr. Da Costa said the circumstance reminded
him of one that had occurred in his own practice. A
gentleman of London, a man of wealth, the subject of a
thoracic fistule consequent upon an attack of chronic
pleurisy, was informed by an Italian organ-grinder who
was one day playing before his window that he had,
some years before, suffered in Philadelphia from a similar disease, of which he had been cured by Dr. Da Costa.
He forthwith embarked for the United States, and in due
time found himself in that professor's office. He had been

under the care of different physicians in London without material benefit, and was determined to see what American skill might have in store for him.

At my clinic on May 5th I removed a polyp from an elderly man's nose, operated upon a case of double club-foot, and cut a child three years of age for stone in the bladder—all in less than one hour.

On May 12th, at the college clinic, I cut a child eighteen months old for stone in the bladder, and lost him at the end of eighteen hours from the joint effects of shock, loss of blood, and urinary infiltration. The little fellow was much emaciated from severe and protracted suffering, and was therefore not in good condition for an operation. I made my incisions, as usual, with great care; but, despite this, a large vessel, probably the artery of the bulb, was divided, and the flow of blood could not be stopped without plugging the wound with lint wet with Monsel's salt—a catheter having previously been inserted into the bladder. This had the desired effect, and there was no recurrence of hemorrhage. The child was pale and feeble, but rallied some time afterwards. During the night he became worse, and gradually sank from sheer exhaustion. Some urine had passed around the plug in the wound into the scrotum and perineum, thus adding to the trouble. The stone was seven-eighths of an inch in its long diameter, and one and a half inch in its shortest circumference—a large mass for so young a child.

Altogether I have now performed this operation sixty-nine times upon young children, with two deaths, including the present one, the first having been caused by pyæmia at the end of the twenty-eighth day. This record, until the last mishap, was, as far as I know, without a parallel. Including the failure, it is still a very uncommon record, and one with which any lithotomist might well be satisfied.

What is fame? My son, Dr. S. W. Gross, one of the

party on board the revenue cutter which took Mrs. Grant
and her friends down to New Castle on May 16th to meet
the steamer Indiana, which was to take her and the General to Europe, was gravely asked by ex-Senator Simon
Cameron if I was still alive! My son assured the learned
ex-senator that his father was not only not dead, but that
he was able to perform as good a day's work as ever.
This circumstance revives a curious recollection respecting
Dr. Thomas D. Mütter and Dr. John K. Mitchell, both
eminent men in their day. Mütter had been dead for
five or six years, when one day Professor Dunglison, then
dean of our Faculty, received a letter from a physician in
New Hampshire, making inquiries concerning his old
teacher's whereabouts. Mitchell had been dead nearly
equally long when a sick man came to the college clinic
bearing a letter addressed to the deceased professor, dated
Florence Heights, New Jersey, a few miles above Philadelphia, on the banks of the Delaware!

The weather on May 20th and during the preceding three
days has been extremely hot, the thermometer, in many
places in the shade, ranging from 93° to 97° Fahrenheit,
an occurrence without a parallel at this season within the
last fifty-three years. The effect both upon man and beast
has been marked. The foliage of most of our forest trees
is fully expanded, and the wheat and grass in the neighborhood of Philadelphia look uncommonly well. Wild
flowers exist in abundance.

June 3d.—At a quarter of twelve o'clock in the morning I leave for Chicago, to attend the twenty-eighth meeting of the American Medical Association, which will take
place in that city on June 5th. The day is beautiful, but
the track is dusty and the air hot. The road passes
through a delightful region of country, embracing Lancaster County, one of the most fertile spots in the world,
distinguished for its excellent farms and fields, which are
covered with rich grain and grass, while the fences and

barns are in the best possible order. Everything seems to be in its appropriate place. The scenery as far as Pittsburgh and some distance beyond is interesting, and often grand and imposing, especially at the Horseshoe beyond Altoona, on the Allegheny Mountains. In Eastern Ohio the country is more level, and on reaching Illinois it is flat and smooth, and so continues along the entire route to Chicago, exhibiting a prairie in a state of high cultivation. Farms on an extensive scale are seen as far as the eye can reach upon each side of the road, which runs in a bee-line over a smooth, level track, with very little motion of the car. The fields are luxuriant, and the soil is loose and fertile, admitting of easy cultivation. The land is well watered. What strikes one as peculiar is the absence of stock, or the paucity of horses, sheep, cattle, and swine. The houses are small and of frame, and there are few barns to be seen.

I reached Chicago at twenty minutes past seven o'clock on the evening of June 4th, and took lodgings at the Palmer House, a hotel of immense size, erected at a cost of more than three million dollars. It is beyond question one of the finest cities in the world. Its stores are specimens of architectural beauty, and are five, six, and seven stories high. The streets are from eighty to one hundred feet wide. Many of the private houses are elegant, and surrounded by spacious grounds ornamented with flowers and shrubbery. I am told that ninety million bushels of grain were shipped from this city last year, and that sixteen hundred thousand hogs were slaughtered. Aladdin has evidently been here with his lamp. The population exceeds four hundred thousand. Less than fifty years ago the site of the city was a wild prairie at the foot of a lake.

The meeting was organized at eleven o'clock in the morning on the 5th of June, Dr. Bowditch, of Boston, President, in the chair. Six hundred and eighty-five names were registered. The meeting was harmonious,

I—50

but no important papers were read.   In the surgical section, presided over by Professor Frank H. Hamilton, of New York, I read a brief article on the proximate cause of pain, which elicited a few remarks from Dr. Hodgen, of St. Louis, who was evidently unprepared to discuss the subject.   On motion to refer it to the Committee on Publication, one delegate cried out lustily, "No."   I could not learn who he was.   Five or six female physicians were admitted as members.   One of them, near the close of the session, went to the President, and expressed a desire to thank the Association for its liberality in admitting them to the meeting; but he wisely withheld his consent.

Although the American Medical Association has done much good, it has by no means accomplished even a moiety of what it had promised to do, or what had been expected of it.   In regard to its educational reforms, it has been an utter failure, and I think the same may be said in regard to its scientific labors.   While the Transactions contains some excellent papers which would be creditable to a similar body of men anywhere, it contains many others which are entirely destitute of merit, and are disreputable as literary productions.   The Prize Essays are, for the most part, of a mediocre character.   A few possess genuine value.   The social relations of the Association have been quite a success, and these are one of its most valuable features.   The annual meetings bring into contact men from all sections of the United States, who are thus afforded an opportunity of renewing old acquaintanceship and of making new friends.   An attempt was recently made to unite the American Medical Association with the Canada Medical Association, but it failed, because, as each body is migratory, the attendance would often be very difficult, if not impossible, for both parties. The subject has been finally disposed of by an agreement to send delegates, as heretofore, each to the other. The annual addresses in medicine, surgery, midwifery,

and hygiene are worse than useless, and are not what such
an Association should listen to, covering, as they do, merely
the advances made in these branches during the preceding
year—a task which any youth of tolerable respectability in
the profession could execute as well as any veteran. Eight
or nine years ago, when I suggested the reading of these
addresses, it never occurred to me that they would be
limited to such humble work; and at the recent meeting
at Chicago the Committee on Nominations, at my instance,
brought the matter prominently before the Association, and
proposed an amendment to the by-laws by which, instead
of making it incumbent upon the chairmen of the sections
to deliver these addresses, the task shall be confided to
separate officers with a choice of subjects; so that, should
this suggestion be carried into effect, we may hereafter
reasonably expect a more reputable literary diet list. Another defect which should be promptly remedied, and
concerning which I expressed my mind freely more than
twenty years ago, is the lack of an anniversary dinner on
the evening of the third day of the meeting. The admission fee to this should be five dollars, and the attendance
should of course be optional. Much benefit would result
from such an arrangement by bringing the members into
more intimate social relations, to be secured in no other
way.

I was made Chairman of the Committee on Nominations. There were four candidates for the office of President at this meeting. Dr. T. G. Richardson received, on
the first ballot, fifteen votes, or a majority of one of all
the votes cast. He was nominated by Dr. Marsey, of
Massachusetts. The other candidates were Byford, of
Chicago; Parvin, of Indianapolis; and White, of Buffalo
—three gynæcologists. I interested myself in the election of Richardson. I was anxious to show our Southern
brethren, inasmuch as he was a representative man, and
lived in a State which, after long-continued suffering,

had just been rehabilitated, that we were desirous of seeing them reunited with us in the Association. I felt that,
although I might incur some odium on account of my
efforts, the effect must be good—just as I felt in 1868, when
I used my best endeavors to promote the election to the
same position of Dr. Baldwin, of Montgomery, Alabama,
an eminent physician, popular in the South, and therefore
well fitted to conciliate Southern feeling and allay Southern prejudice. That his election had this effect has been
generally admitted. In regard to Dr. Richardson, it is
not to be forgotten that the Association, mainly at his
instance and amid great opposition, met at New Orleans
in 1873, and that he spent much time and money in entertaining its members, while all the important offices were
conferred upon non-residents, regardless of the hospitalities
just received.

There were three entertainments given by prominent
citizens of Chicago every evening; but, as I had not yet
gone into society or accepted any hospitalities since the
death of my dear wife, I did not attend any of them. It
was my good fortune at the meeting to greet many of my
private pupils, some of whom have justly attained distinction; and there were few, if any, of the members who
were not personally introduced to me. It was quite
amusing, sometimes annoying, to hear them ask how old
I was and tell me how well I bore my age.

Several weeks ago I received from Dr. Alfred Hosmer,
of Watertown, anniversary chairman, a letter cordially inviting me to be present at the annual dinner of the Massachusetts Medical Society at Music Hall, Boston, to be
given June 13th, at one o'clock. This was backed by
a letter from that excellent and clever physician, Dr.
D. Humphreys Storer, and by a personal entreaty of Dr.
Bowditch, President of the American Medical Association,
whom I met at Chicago last week. I regret that I am unable to go, as I am an honorary member of the society. It

would afford me much pleasure to meet my Massachusetts friends, for many of whom I entertain the highest respect as practitioners of medicine and surgery, pathologists, writers, scholars, and gentlemen. I see by the newspapers of June 16th that eight hundred and fifty persons sat down at table, honored by the presence of Governor Rice, President Eliot of Harvard University, Professor Austin Flint, Sr., and Professor John C. Dalton of New York, and of many of the oldest and most prominent members of the Massachusetts Medical Society.

It is the lot of most medical men to die poor. Now and then there is of course an exception. Sir William Fergusson, who died on the 10th of last February, left an estate valued at thirty thousand pounds. One hundred and fifty thousand dollars of our money is a small sum when we consider his large practice—much of it among the English and Scotch nobility—and the immense fees he must have received for many years, to say nothing of his income as a teacher of surgery in King's College. Liston, who enjoyed a world-wide reputation as a surgeon, and who was the early contemporary of Fergusson at Edinburgh, died worth scarcely a few thousand pounds. On the other hand, William Coulson, who died a short time ago in London, where he had practised all his life, principally as a lithotomist, left an estate of upwards of one million dollars. How he accumulated this immense fortune, the bulk of which he bequeathed to a nephew, it is difficult to conceive. As a man of ability and an operative surgeon he was far inferior to Fergusson or Liston. During my visit to London in 1868 I called upon Mr. Coulson, and found him in obscure apartments in what is known as the Jewry, near St. Paul's. There, he informed me, he had resided for many years, actively engaged in practice, largely, if not chiefly, in urinary diseases. Upon these disorders, early in life, he had published a treatise, which, passing through a number of editions, had doubtless been of great service in securing for him business as a specialist.

I reached Boston at seven o'clock on the morning of June 27th, and at eleven o'clock went with Mr. John Revere, my son's father-in-law, to attend the Commencement of Harvard University. The interest of the occasion was enhanced by the presence of President Hayes and several of the members of his Cabinet, prominent among whom was General Devens, the Attorney-General, a native of Massachusetts and a gentleman of much popularity with the citizens of Boston. Sanders Theatre, where the exercises took place, was filled to overflowing with a fashionable and intelligent audience. The graduating class, it was said, acquitted itself with unusual credit. The degree of D. C. L. was conferred upon President Hayes, and that of LL. D. upon Mr. Devens. The alumni dinner came off at three o'clock in the large banqueting room in Memorial Hall, which on this occasion seated nearly twelve hundred guests, and which vividly reminded me of the banqueting hall at Christ Church, Oxford. The walls are adorned with the portraits and busts of the great men whose services have rendered Harvard the first university of the land. The founder, John Harvey, who is represented as a tall, slender man, arrayed in a morning gown and slippers, appropriately occupies the centre. General Devens, President of the Alumni, presided, and made a capital opening speech, full of feeling and of good sense. Other addresses followed, and caused much enthusiasm. The remarks of President Hayes were brief, and were simply expressive of his appreciation of the honors bestowed upon him by the University and of the pleasure he had experienced at the warmth of his reception since his arrival in Massachusetts. Among the more prominent speakers were Governor Rice of Massachusetts, George Bancroft, the historian, Postmaster-General Key, President Eliot of Harvard University, Carl Schurz, and Professor

James Russell Lowell, recently appointed Minister to Spain. The list of graduates in the different departments was a lengthy one, that in medicine embracing sixty-two names, of whom nearly one-half were bachelors or masters of arts—a circumstance which speaks well for this institution. Since the appointment of Dr. Eliot as President, Harvard has signalized itself by the adoption of stringent regulations in regard to the admission of pupils; and the result is manifested in a much higher standard of education in all the branches taught in the several schools. The example thus set cannot fail to exert a salutary influence upon the colleges of our country.

The grounds of Harvard University, with its dozen or more large edifices, remind one forcibly of those at Oxford and Cambridge in England. One's only regret is that they are not more spacious. Many of the buildings are old, and most of them are destitute of architectural taste. Memorial Hall is a splendid edifice, erected at great cost, and worthy of the place. It is the Sheldonian Theatre of Harvard, with the addition of the banqueting hall of Christ Church, Oxford. In the large vestibule are numerous marble tablets, inscribed with the names of the sons of Harvard who fell in defence of their country during the late war. The magnificent elms in the college grounds form a striking feature in the landscape.

On June 28th I attended, at Sanders Theatre, the exercises of the Phi Beta Kappa Society, the principal of which consisted of an oration by Mr. Thomas F. Bayard, of Delaware, on the Relations of the American Citizen to his Government. This was followed by a poem on Hawthorne, by Edmund C. Stedman, of New York. Judging from the frequent applause bestowed upon Mr. Bayard's address, I am disposed to think that it was meritorious; and this, I believe, was the general opinion of the audience who, for nearly two hours, listened to it. It was certainly a scholarly production, and it had the merit of being well

delivered. Through the politeness of my good friend, Dr.
Henry H. Bowditch, of Boston, I had the honor of dining
with the Society, and was again brought into contact with
a number of distinguished men. The presiding officer was
Edward Everett Hale, a tall man, with a peculiar voice
and not very prepossessing manners, although he was facetious and entertaining. The principal speakers were President Eliot, Bayard, Stedman, and Lowell. The occasion
was a very pleasant one; but I was obliged to leave before
the dinner was over, as it was necessary that I should
reach the half past five o'clock train for Canton, the residence of my friend, Mr. Revere—a grandson of the famous Paul Revere—with whose charming family I spent
my nights during my stay in Massachusetts.

I had not seen Boston since 1859, a period of eighteen
years, during which many changes had of course taken
place. Boston Common has a wide reputation. Its old,
umbrageous elms impart to it a classical appearance, and
afford on a hot day protection from the sun alike to the
poorest citizen and to the millionaire. The public garden,
close by, is a beautiful specimen of landscape horticulture,
and is at this moment arrayed in all its glory, the June
roses being in full bloom. The newer portions of the city,
built upon land reclaimed from marshes once the bed of
the ocean, are distinguished for their fine avenues and their
elegant private dwellings. Everywhere cleanliness is apparent, and, what is remarkable, I saw no evidence of poverty in my extensive rides through the city. Neatness is a
predominating feature of Boston.

With President Hayes I was favorably impressed. He
has a fine head, with an agreeable, expressive face, and a
modest demeanor worthy of a man in his high position.
Although I did not at all approve of the manner in which
he got into office, I accepted the situation the more willingly because I had formed a high opinion of his honesty,
and felt that he would do all he could to restore peace and

happiness to the Southern States at an early day after his inauguration.

My visit to Boston would have been incomplete without seeing Dr. Jacob Bigelow—*clarum et venerabile nomen*—now in the ninety-second year of his age. For two years he has been blind and has not left his bed; and when I seized his hand, he said, "I cannot see you; but I can press your hand and bid you a cordial welcome." As he lay on his pillow his countenance, calm and serene, with a most benignant expression, denotive of conscious repose and of resignation to the divine will, reminded me of what I had read of some Roman philosopher. I never looked upon a countenance in which dignity and gentleness were so beautifully blended. His mind was clear, and his memory seemingly unclouded. He made many inquiries about the medical schools and medical men of Philadelphia, and expressed much satisfaction when I told him that Philadelphia still maintained her supremacy as the emporium of medical science on this continent. It was to me a source of no ordinary gratification to learn that he was free from bodily suffering; and that he enjoyed sound sleep and an excellent appetite with a good, wholesome digestion—blessings not usually associated in one so far advanced in life. During the twenty minutes spent at the bedside of this remarkable man—a man to whom our profession is so much indebted for many happy suggestions—it was pleasant to see his venerable wife, a small, delicate-looking lady, only five years younger than himself, sitting near by, listening with profound respect and attention to the words of kindness and of wisdom as they flowed from his lips.

In company with my friend, Dr. Bowditch, I called upon Dr. Edward Hammond Clarke, who for the last two years or more has been a great sufferer from a malignant disease, which has made serious inroads upon his constitution. He received us in his chamber, reclining upon a lounge, from which he seldom rises, as he is unable to sit up. I became acquainted with Dr. Clarke about eight or nine years ago, when he brought me a letter of introduction from a common friend in Boston, and took breakfast with me the following morning. A more genial gentleman I have rarely met—highly cultured, refined, and intelligent. I said to him, "You must have composed under great difficulty, if not severe suffering, your paper, in the American Journal of the Medical Sciences, on the Progress of Medicine in America during the last Century?" "I wrote the whole of it," was his reply, "upon this couch with the aid of my wife as an amanuensis. When I found my pain coming on I called for pen and paper and began to dictate. In about an hour, as my mind became absorbed in my subject, the pain gradually subsided, and in this way I usually worked several hours every day until the task was completed. Thus, you perceive," he added, "not only did writing serve to amuse me, but it acted as an anodyne." What renders the situation of Dr. Clarke particularly sad is the loss, a few months ago, of his wife, an excellent woman, much beloved. He has an only child, a daughter, who does all she can to comfort him in his affliction. He has written many admirable papers, chiefly medical; and is the author of a clever little book on Sex in Education, which has attracted much attention. Sick as he is, he is now engaged in writing a work—probably destined to be a posthumous publication—on Psychology, in which he will trench largely on spiritualism. The loss of such a man, possessed of so many excellent qualities of head and heart, will be a serious one to our profession.

Of Dr. Bowditch this is not the time or place fully to speak. He is still an active man, although like myself advanced in years. He is a son of Nathaniel Bowditch, the illustrious translator of La Place's Mécanique Céleste, and a physician of rare gifts, a pupil of the renowned Louis of Paris, and an accomplished diagnostician and practitioner. He is skilled in the treatment of thoracic diseases, of which he has for many years made a specialty. His writings on Empyema have made his name well known both at home and abroad. Another excellent professional brother whom it was my good fortune to meet during this visit is Dr. J. B. S. Jackson, now old, but still fresh and vigorous, one of the best men in the world, enjoying a wide and enviable reputation as a pathological anatomist, to the study of which he has devoted a lifetime. For many years he has occupied the chair of Morbid Anatomy in Harvard College, and has been instrumental in diffusing a taste for the study of this important science, while at the same time he has thrown substantial light upon the diagnosis and treatment of many diseases. Strange to say, Dr. Jackson has never, I am told, engaged in practice, a circumstance due probably to two causes— his sensitive nature and the fact that he is wealthy. He has written very little. With the vast amount of material on his hands he ought long ago to have produced a great work on pathological anatomy.

Mount Auburn Cemetery is said to present many attractions to visitors, and yet, I confess, it fell behind my anticipations. While the grounds are fine, as if nature had designed them for a cemetery, and are kept in good order with flower-beds in every direction, one looks in vain for elegant monuments. There are only a few that properly come under this designation. That of Nathaniel Bowditch, a bronze statue, of life size, a good likeness of the great mathematician, with a globe at his side, is by far the best of all. There is a small monument erected by the city of Boston to the memory of Morton, who was the first to administer ether successfully for the prevention of pain in surgical operations. In the chapel the statues of Winthrop, the first Governor of Massachusetts, of Otis, of John Adams, and of Story, are fine works of art. Among the distinguished dead buried here are Sumner, Choate, Agassiz, Everett, Longfellow, Margaret Fuller, and Charlotte Cushman.

In the crowd on Wednesday a small gentleman of very plain appearance, and earnestly engaged in conversation, was pointed out to me by a friend at my side with the remark, uttered in a whisper, "That small gentleman is Charles Francis Adams." I looked, perhaps stared a little, but saw nothing in the "small gentleman" worthy of special notice—certainly none of the characteristics of a great man, of a man of genius, or of a descendant of illustrious sires. The grandfather, John Adams, was a man of short stature, with a large head and a majestic intellect. John Quincy Adams, the father, was of medium height, with a fine head and a superior brain, but of a less powerful mind than his father; and the grandson, Charles Francis Adams, and his children, are gradually tapering down, intellectually speaking, to the common level, in accordance with a law of God that great talent and genius shall not long remain in the same family. The sons of Clay and Webster have been of little account. It was my good fortune to meet with John Quincy Adams in July, 1832, on the New Brunswick and New York steamer, on which we were passengers. He and Mrs. Adams were on their way from Washington City to Massachusetts; and I was on mine to New York, to visit the cholera hospitals. There were but few people on board, and Mr. Adams was, of course, the observed of all observers. I scanned the venerable man from head to toe, and was particularly struck with his large bald head and his fine features, so expressive of benevolence. He had all the lineaments and characteristics of an aristocratic gentleman. Few persons approached him; and he wisely gave the infected city a wide berth. The vessel on which he was a passenger carried him directly to the New England boat, as he was, like every one else, afraid of the cholera. Mrs. Adams impressed me as a quiet, dignified lady, nearly of the same age as her distinguished consort.

A telegram to-day, July 3d, announces the death of Dr. N. R. Smith, the great surgeon, as having occurred this morning at six o'clock, in the eighty-first year of his age. He was born in the town of Cornish, New Hampshire, in May, 1797 ; graduated in the literary and medical departments of Yale College, receiving the degree of Doctor of Medicine in 1823 ; lived for a time in a Virginia family in the capacity of a classical instructor ; and a few years ago, under the name of "Viator," published a small volume entitled Legends of the South, consisting of romantic stories of life in Virginia and Kentucky. A long time will elapse before Baltimore will have another Nathan Ryno Smith, a man of the same commanding talents, influence, practical skill, and professional acumen. A generation produces few examples of such useful and distinguished men. I must not omit to add that Dr. Smith, during the last five years of his life, was a firm believer in the immortality of the soul, a constant attendant upon church, and a devoted Christian, freely confessing his sins before God, and earnestly preparing himself for the enjoyment of what he believed to be a higher and better world beyond the grave. His funeral was largely attended by all classes of citizens, but more especially by the members of his own profession ; and flowers, the gift of loving friends, in great abundance covered his coffin. It was a source of deep regret to me that it was not in my power to be present on the sad occasion to do honor to a man to whom I was so warmly attached and whom I so greatly revered.

Cape May, July 8th.—This is my seventy-second birthday, which finds me in excellent health and in better spirits than I was a year ago. My children are very kind to me, and send me their congratulations and best wishes. Haller, the dear boy, with a heart always brimful of love for me, sent me yesterday from the city a basket of magnificent flowers, principally red and yellow roses, to gladden my heart and grace our table. Dear Maria gives me a beautiful paper-cutter and a small portfolio; and the children pretty little Swiss flower-glasses. My good little friend, Mrs. Marsily, presents me with a very pretty brush, the top of which is enamelled and ornamented with pansies. If my dear wife were not forever separated from me, I should be perfectly happy.

I left Cape May on the morning of August 27th after a sojourn of six weeks spent in rest and sea-bathing. Every Monday morning I made a visit to the city to look after my patients, and returned either the same afternoon or the next day. My health, in consequence of this mode of life, has been much improved. I have gained flesh and strength, and I am told by all my friends that I look uncommonly well. The Stockton, the most fashionable hotel of the place, has been crowded with visitors; but few of them were persons of note. Before there were railway facilities, many of the most distinguished citizens of Philadelphia and Baltimore went there to spend a part of the summer, and the society, it is said, was all that could be desired. The great objection to Cape May as a summer resort is the mosquito, which, whenever there is a land breeze, is most annoying; always hungry, and always bent upon blood. Ugly sores are often engendered by its bite. The bathing is excellent, as good as anywhere in the world, and better than at any other place along the New Jersey shore. Cape May presents some of the most lovely and gorgeous sunsets I have ever witnessed; and the sky, in clear weather, is as beautiful as any ever seen in Italy. I have always considered sea-bathing as a great luxury, highly conducive, as a rule, to the promotion of health. The fight with the surf is in itself an excellent exercise, and the action of the water upon the surface an exhilarating stimulant.

Our new hospital on Sansom Street, near the College, was opened on the evening of September 30th, 1877, in the presence of a large and select audience. An address by the president gave an account of the enterprise; and in another address Professor Joseph Pancoast spoke in graphic terms of the founder of the Jefferson Medical College, Dr. George McClellan, and portrayed the advantages of clinical instruction to the medical student. My colleagues had requested me to deliver the address; but as Professor Pancoast, although now retired from active teaching, had been many years longer in the school, I insisted that this honor was due to him, and I was glad when, after some hesitation, he finally gave his consent, for I knew he would perform the task with his accustomed ability. The hospital has a capacity for one hundred beds, and contains the noblest amphitheatre that I have seen. The need of such an institution had been long felt. The trustees are now engaged in erecting, in close proximity to the College, workshops for the students, which when completed, as they shortly will be, will afford ample accommodations for the study of practical chemistry, microscopy, experimental physiology, and minor and operative surgery. It was my privilege to hold the first clinic in the new amphitheatre, and to perform in it the first surgical operation in the presence of the medical class several weeks before the formal opening of the hospital.

END OF VOL. I.

Medicine & Society In America

An Arno Press/New York Times Collection

Alcott, William A. **The Physiology of Marriage.** 1866. New Introduction by Charles E. Rosenberg.

Beard, George M. **American Nervousness:** Its Causes and Consequences. 1881. New Introduction by Charles E. Rosenberg.

Beard, George M. **Sexual Neurasthenia.** 5th edition. 1898.

Beecher, Catharine E. **Letters to the People on Health and Happiness.** 1855.

Blackwell, Elizabeth. **Essays in Medical Sociology.** 1902. Two volumes in one.

Blanton, Wyndham B. **Medicine in Virginia in the Seventeenth Century.** 1930.

Bowditch, Henry I. **Public Hygiene in America.** 1877.

Bowditch, N[athaniel] I. **A History of the Massachusetts General Hospital:** To August 5, 1851. 2nd edition. 1872.

Brill, A. A. **Psychanalysis:** Its Theories and Practical Application. 1913.

Cabot, Richard C. **Social Work:** Essays on the Meeting-Ground of Doctor and Social Worker. 1919.

Cathell, D. W. **The Physician Himself and What He Should Add to His Scientific Acquirements.** 2nd edition. 1882. New Introduction by Charles E. Rosenberg.

The Cholera Bulletin. Conducted by an Association of Physicians. Vol. I: Nos. 1–24. 1832. All published. New Introduction by Charles E. Rosenberg.

Clarke, Edward H. **Sex in Education;** or, A Fair Chance for the Girls. 1873.

Committee on the Costs of Medical Care. **Medical Care for the American People:** The Final Report of The Committee on the Costs of Medical Care, No. 28. [1932].

Currie, William. **An Historical Account of the Climates and Diseases of the United States of America.** 1792.

Davenport, Charles Benedict. **Heredity in Relation to Eugenics.** 1911. New Introduction by Charles E. Rosenberg.

Davis, Michael M. **Paying Your Sickness Bills.** 1931.

Disease and Society in Provincial Massachusetts: Collected Accounts, 1736–1939. 1972.

Earle, Pliny. **The Curability of Insanity:** A Series of Studies. 1887.

Falk, I. S., C. Rufus Rorem, and Martha D. Ring. **The Costs of Medical Care:** A Summary of Investigations on The Economic Aspects of the Prevention and Care of Illness, No. 27. 1933.

Faust, Bernhard C. **Catechism of Health:** For the Use of Schools, and for Domestic Instruction. 1794.

Flexner, Abraham. **Medical Education in the United States an Canada:** A Report to The Carnegie Foundation for the Advancement of Teaching, Bulletin Number Four. 1910.

Gross, Samuel D. **Autobiography of Samuel D. Gross, M.D.,** with Sketches of His Contemporaries. Two volumes. 1887.

Hooker, Worthington. **Physician and Patient;** or, A Practical View of the Mutual Duties, Relations and Interests of the Medical Profession and the Community. 1849.

Howe, S. G. **On the Causes of Idiocy.** 1858.

Jackson, James. **A Memoir of James Jackson, Jr., M.D.** 1835.

Jennings, Samuel K. **The Married Lady's Companion, or Poor Man's Friend.** 2nd edition. 1808.

The Maternal Physician; a Treatise on the Nurture and Management of Infants, from the Birth until Two Years Old. 2nd edition. 1818. New Introduction by Charles E. Rosenberg.

Mathews, Joseph McDowell. **How to Succeed in the Practice of Medicine.** 1905.

McCready, Benjamin W. **On the Influences of Trades, Professions, and Occupations in the United States, in the Production of Disease.** 1943.

Mitchell, S. Weir. **Doctor and Patient.** 1888.

Nichols, T[homas] L. **Esoteric Anthropology: The Mysteries of Man.** [1853].

Origins of Public Health in America: Selected Essays, 1820–1855. 1972.

Osler, Sir William. **The Evolution of Modern Medicine.** 1922.

The Physician and Child-Rearing: Two Guides, 1809–1894. 1972.

Rosen, George. **The Specialization of Medicine:** with Particular Reference to Ophthalmology. 1944.

Royce, Samuel. **Deterioration and Race Education.** 1878.

Rush, Benjamin. **Medical Inquiries and Observations.** Four volumes in two. 4th edition. 1815.

Shattuck, Lemuel, Nathaniel P. Banks, Jr., and Jehiel Abbott. **Report of a General Plan for the Promotion of Public and Personal Health.** Massachusetts Sanitary Commission. 1850.

Smith, Stephen. **Doctor in Medicine** and Other Papers on Professional Subjects. 1872.

Still, Andrew T. **Autobiography of Andrew T. Still,** with a History of the Discovery and Development of the Science of Osteopathy. 1897.

Storer, Horatio Robinson. **The Causation, Course, and Treatment of Reflex Insanity in Women.** 1871.

Sydenstricker, Edgar. **Health and Environment.** 1933.

Thomson, Samuel. **A Narrative, of the Life and Medical Discoveries of Samuel Thomson.** 1822.

Ticknor, Caleb. **The Philosophy of Living;** or, The Way to Enjoy Life and Its Comforts. 1836.

U.S. Sanitary Commission. **The Sanitary Commission of the United States Army:** A Succinct Narrative of Its Works and Purposes. 1864.

White, William A. **The Principles of Mental Hygiene.** 1917.